THE WESTERN AUSTRALIAN JURIST
VOLUME 13

AGAINST TYRANNY

AUGUSTO ZIMMERMANN
(EDITOR-IN-CHIEF)

&

JOSHUA FORRESTER
(EDITOR)

CONNOR COURT PUBLISHING PTY LTD

Published in 2025 by Connor Court Publishing Pty Ltd.

Connorcourt Publishing Pty Ltd
PO Box 7257
Redland Bay QLD 4165
sales@connorcourt.com
www.connorcourt.com

ISBN: 9781923224711

The image on the cover has been generated by ChatGPT, no copyright is claimed with respect to it

Printed in Australia

THE
WESTERN AUSTRALIAN
JURIST

CONTENTS

THE EDITORS

Augusto Zimmermann LLB (Hons), LLM cum laude, PhD (Monash), DipEd, CIArb is a former Law Reform Commissioner with the Law Reform Commission of Western Australia (2012-2017) and a former Associate Dean (Research) and Postgraduate Research Director at Murdoch University's School of Law. He is also the Founder and President of the Western Australian Legal Theory Association (WALTA), a former Vice-President of the Australasian Society of Legal Philosophy (ASLP), an Elected Fellow at the International Academy for the Study of the Jurisprudence of the Family (IASJF), and Editor-in-Chief of the *Western Australian Jurist* law journal. A prolific writer and the author of numerous articles and academic books, Professor Zimmermann was awarded the 2012 Vice Chancellor's Award for Excellence in Research, and two School Dean's Research Awards, in 2010 and 2011. He served on numerous academic bodies at Murdoch University, including: the Research Degree and Scholarships Committee; the Vice Chancellor's Awards and Citations Committee; the Academic Council's Freedom of Speech in Policies and Procedures Advisory Group; and the Academic Staff Promotions Advisory Committee. In January 2015, he was invited by the Tasmanian Chief Justice to address the 'Opening of the Legal Year' in that State. Professor Zimmermann is generally recognised as a fierce advocate for freedom of speech and the Rule of Law, contributing with numerous articles on the subject, including for *The Legal Doctrines of the Rule of Law and the Legal State* (Springer, 2014), a book edited by the President of the American Bar Association (ABA) that explores the development of both the civil law and the common law conceptions of the Rule of Law. He is the author/co-author/editor/co-editor of numerous academic articles and books, including *The Spirit Behind the Voice: The Religious Dimension of the "Voice" Proposal* (Connor

Court Publishing, 2023); *Foundations of the Australian Legal System: History, Theory and Practice* (LexisNexis, 2023); *Wokeshevism: Critical Theories and the Tyrant Left* (Connor Court Publishing 2023); *Fundamental Rights in the Age of Covid-19* (Connor Court Publishing, 2021); *Christian Foundations of the Common Law* (3 Volumes, Connor Court Publishing, 2018); *No Offence Intended: Why 18C is Wrong* (Connor Court Publishing, 2016); *Global Perspectives on Subsidiarity* (Springer, 2014); and *Western Legal Theory: History, Concepts and Perspectives* (LexisNexis, 2013). Professor Zimmermann has been included, together with only twelve other Australian academics and policy experts, in 'Policy Experts' – the Heritage Foundation's directory for locating knowledgeable authorities and leading policy institutes actively involved in a broad range of public policy issues, both in the United States and worldwide.

Joshua Forrester graduated with First Class Honours in Politics and International Studies from Murdoch University in 1999. Joshua practised in commercial litigation and has taught a number of law units. In 2008, he was awarded a Vice-Chancellor's Commendation for Teaching at the University of Notre Dame Australia. Joshua is the lead author of *No Offence Intended: Why 18C is Wrong*, which is listed as one of *The Spectator*'s best books of 2016. A solely-authored chapter of his appears in *Freedom of Religion or Belief: Creating the Constitutional Space for Fundamental Freedoms*, published by Edward Elgar Publishing. His shorter words have appeared in *The Conversation, Policy*, and *Quadrant*. Joshua has appeared before the Parliamentary Joint Committee on Human Rights inquiry into s 18C of the *Racial Discrimination Act 1975* (Cth), and the Joint Standing Committee on Foreign Affairs, Defence and Trade Human Rights Sub-Committee inquiry into freedom of religion and belief.

Contributors

Luke Barbrick is an associate litigation attorney at Hewson & Van Hellemont, PC in Grand Rapids, Michigan. Luke was admitted to the Michigan Bar Association in 2024. He is also a member of the Byron Center Historical Society and the Hillsdale College President's Club. From 2023 to 2024, Luke worked as a Law Clerk for Michigan Supreme Court Justice, David Viviano, and as a research attorney at the Michigan Court of Appeals. In 2023, Luke graduated from the Michigan State University College of Law where he earned his Doctorate in Jurisprudence (JD) with a focus in litigation. As a law student, Luke served as Managing Editor at the Michigan State University International Law Review. In 2019, Luke graduated cum laude from Hillsdale College where he earned his Bachelor of Arts (BA) in Economics and Politics. As an undergraduate student, Luke served as a research assistant to Hillsdale President, Larry P Arnn, where he assisted in the completion of the official Winston Churchill biography. In 2018, Luke worked as the Healthcare and Education Intern for United States Senator Michael S Lee. Luke has authored articles on various academic and legal topics such as the life and legacy of Sir Winston Churchill, Critical Race Theory, British efforts to restore the Welsh language, China's suppression of ethnic minorities' legal rights, and the fundamental divide between Christianity and Socialism. Luke has been awarded two prestigious legal fellowships with the Lynde & Harry Bradly Foundation in Milwaukee, Wisconsin and the Great Lakes Justice Center in Lansing, Michigan.

Christopher Brohier LLB (Hons) is Barrister practising in South Australia. He was admitted to the Bar in 1981 and has practised as a barrister and member of the South Australian Bar Association since

July 1993. He was the Director of Public Policy for the Australian Christian Lobby, which is a grassroots movement of about 200,000+ Australians contending for Truth in the Public Square, until August 2024, when he became the lead Senate candidate for the Family First Party Australia. He co-founded the Human Rights Law Alliance, and has represented many litigants in religious freedom type cases. He was counsel in the abortion exclusion zone trials *Avery v Preston* and *Edwards v Clubb* and was junior counsel in the High Court in both these cases: *Clubb v Edwards and Preston v Avery* [2019] HCA 11. He was co-founder of the Wilberforce Foundation, a coalition of lawyers and legal academics, has appeared before many government committees and has published papers in legal journals. He now holds an appointment as Counsel Assisting the Human Rights Law Alliance.

Renato S M Costa is a Lecturer at TC Beirne School of Law, the University of Queensland, Brisbane. He is also the Staff Editor of the *University of Queensland Law Journal*. Renato has graduated with an LLB (honours equivalent) at the Universidade Católica de Pernambuco, in Brazil. He has a postgraduate specialisation in Public Law at the Universidade Anhanguera, also in Brazil. Renato holds an LLM and a PhD at the University of Queensland, Brisbane. He is a member of the Australian Association of Constitutional Law (AACL), International Society of Public Law (ICON-S), International Association of Constitutional Law (IACL), and the UQ Centre of Public, International and Comparative Law (CPICL). Renato has published widely in his areas of specialisation, including constitutional and comparative law.

Kevin Donnelly AM, since first warning about the dangers of political correctness during the early 90s, has established a reputation as one of Australia's leading conservative commentators and authors. As well as appearing on Sky News, Kevin writes regularly for Australia's print and electronic media, including *The Australian, The Daily Telegraph, Spectator Online, Quadrant* and the *Catholic Weekly*. Publications include *Why our schools are failing, The Culture of Freedom, Taming the Black Dog, How Political Correctness Is Destroying Australia, How Political Correctness Is Destroying Education, A Politically Correct Dictionary and Guide, Cancel Culture and the Left's Long March, Christianity Is Good For Us, Christianity Matters In These Trouble Times* and the *Dictionary Of Woke*. As well as championing the strengths and benefits of Western civilisation and a liberal education Kevin also champions the Australia's Judeo-Christian heritage and on-going traditions that underpin our political and legal systems and way of life. Kevin taught for 18 years in Victorian government and non-government secondary schools and has also been a member of state and national curriculum bodies, including, the Victorian Board of Studies and the federally funded Discovering Democracy Programme. In 2014 Kevin co-chaired the review of the Australian National Curriculum for the Commonwealth Government. In the 2016 Queen's Birthday Honours List Dr Donnelly was appointed as a Member of the Order of Australia for services to education. Kevin's webpage is kevindonnelly.com.au.

Gigi Foster (Professor, UNSW School of Economics; Senior Scholar, Brownstone Institute; BA Ethics, Politics and Economics, PhD Economics) works in diverse fields including education, social influence, time use, lab experiments, behavioural economics, and Australian policy, publishing in both specialised and cross-disciplinary outlets (eg, *Quantitative Economics, Journal of Economic Behavior and Organization, Journal of Population Economics, Journal of Economic Psychology, Human Relations*). Named 2019 Young Economist of the Year by the Economic Society of Australia, her innovative teaching, featuring strategic innovation and integration with research, was awarded a 2017 Australian Awards for University Teaching (AAUT)

Citation for Outstanding Contributions to Student Learning. Professor Foster has filled numerous roles of service to the profession and engages heavily on economic matters with the Australian community as one of Australia's leading economics communicators in the media and at live events. She co-founded the think tank Australians for Science and Freedom (scienceandfreedom.org) in 2023 and is an author most recently of *The Great Covid Panic* (Brownstone Institute, 2021, with Paul Frijters and Michael Baker) and *Do Lockdowns and Border Closures Serve the "Greater Good"?* (Connor Court 2022) with Sanjeev Sabhlok.

Susan Hoddinott graduated with an Honours degree in Science from the University of Western Australia in 1980. She subsequently worked as a Research Assistant at Prince Henry Hospital in NSW and as a Management Trainee in the steel industry before spending time in the United States and gaining experience in the IT field. She graduated with a Masters in Business Administration from the University of Western Australia in 1990. She spent the majority of her career working internationally as a consultant, troubleshooting complex systems for many Fortune 500 companies. Susan completed her law degree from Murdoch University in 2016 and was admitted to the WA Supreme Court roll in 2022.

M Oliver Heydorn BSc (biology), MA (philosophy), graduated *summa cum laude* with a PhD in Philosophy from the International Academy of Philosophy at the Catholic Pontifical University of Santiago, Chile. His dissertation, undertaken under the directorship of Dr Josef Seifert, was entitled: *Insight and Existence: The Role of A Priori Knowledge in the Cogito according to Dietrich von Hildebrand.* After having taught as an Assistant Professor of Philosophy at three different universities in three different countries, he became the founder and director of the Clifford Hugh Douglas Institute for the

Study and Promotion of Social Credit (www.socred.org). He is the author of four books on Douglas Social Credit theory: *Social Credit Economics*, *The Economics of Social Credit and Catholic Social Teaching*, *Social Credit Philosophy*, and *Lives of our Own: Social Credit, Catholicism, and a Distributist Social Order* and is the main architect behind the Douglas Social Credit animated series which is viewable on youtube.com.

Weronika Kudła – PhD in Law (Faculty of Law and Administration) and MA in Italian Studies (Institute of Romance Studies), both at the Jagiellonian University in Cracow (Poland). Currently she is a research assistant at the Faculty of Social Sciences of the Pontifical University of John Paul II in Cracow and member of the expert team of Religious Freedom Laboratory administered by the Pro Futuro Theologiae Foundation in Toruń. Participant of an Erasmus Program Studies at Tor Vergata University of Rome, the VIII Edition of Academy of Young Diplomats at the European Academy of Diplomacy in Warsaw and the Harvard University program 'Bioethics: The Law, Medicine, and Ethics of Reproductive Technologies and Genetics'. She is the author of the book *Hostility to Religion. Warnings from the Supreme Court of the United States* and several articles on human rights issues. Her research activity has been linked to human rights, intellectual property and media law.

Gabriël A Moens AM is Emeritus Professor of Law, The University of Queensland. He served as Pro Vice Chancellor, Dean and Professor of Law, Murdoch University; Head, Graduate School of Law, The University of Notre Dame Australia; Garrick Professor of Law, The University of Queensland; and Professor of Law, Curtin University. He was a Visiting Professor of Law at J Reuben Clark Law School, Brigham Young University, and at Loyola University, New Orleans. In 1999, Professor Moens received the Australian Award for University

Teaching in Law and Legal Studies. In 2003, the Prime Minister of Australia awarded him the Australian Centenary Medal for services to education. He was named the 'International Alumnus of the Year' by the Pritzker Law School of Northwestern University in 2019. In June 2019 he was appointed a Member of the Order of Australia (AM) for services to the law and higher education. Professor Moens is a Member of the International Academy of Comparative Law, Paris; a Fellow of the Australian Institute of Management (WA); a Fellow of the College of Law; a Fellow of the Australian Academy of Law; and a Fellow of the Australian Centre for International Commercial Arbitration (ACICA). He is the author/co-author/editor/co-editor of *Foundations of the Australian Legal System: History, Theory and Practice* (LexisNexis, 2023); *Emergency Powers, COVID-19 Restrictions & Mandatory Vaccination: A 'Rule of Law' Perspective* *Connor Court Publishing, 2022); *Enduring Ideas* (Connor Court Publishing, 2020); *The Himalaya Clause* (Connor Court Publishing, 2020); *Law of International Business in Australasia*, The Federation Press, 2nd ed, 2019; *The Constitution of the Commonwealth of Australia Annotated* (LexisNexis Butterworths, 9th ed, 2016); *Arbitration and Dispute Resolution in the Resources Sector: An Australian Perspective* (Springer, 2015); *Jurisprudence of Liberty* (LexisNexis, 2nd ed, 2011); *Commercial Law of the European Union* (Springer, 2010); and *International Trade and Business: Law, Policy and Ethics* (Routledge/Cavendish, 2nd ed, 2006). Gabriël also authors novels, short stories, and opinion pieces. His debut novel, *A Twisted Choice*, a thriller about the origins of the COVID-19 virus, was published by Boolarong Press in October 2020. Connor Court Publishing published his second novel, *The Coincidence*, in November 2021. His most recent short story, *The Country Prowler*, was published by Boolarong Press in June 2023 in *The Outback: Anthology of Short Stories* (Volume 8).

Bill Muehlenberg has a BA with Honours in Philosophy (Wheaton College, Chicago), a MA with highest honours in theology (Gordon-Conwell Theological Seminary, Boston), and has worked on a PhD in Theology in Melbourne. He is a spokesman for the Family Council of Victoria. He has worked in social policy research for various organisations, including the Institute of Public Affairs and the Australian Family Association. He has authored a number of books including *Modern Conservative Thought* and *The Challenge of Euthanasia.* He has also penned thousands of articles – many hundreds published – on a wide range of topics, including politics, economics, theology, ethics and social issues. He has lectured part-time in theology, philosophy and ethics, and runs the website Culture Watch (http://www.billmuehlenberg.com).

Monika Nagel CertEd (Vienna), B Psych. (Murdoch), PhD (Org Psych) is the author of the book *Fatal Cocktails*, a provocative and compelling exposition on the reasons of the ills in our world with a call for change. The book finishes with a bleak outlook for the world if people keep doing things as they do. Monika reminds the reader that rights can only be upheld with correlating responsibility. Her recent book about C-19 – *Our Moral Ills: The Origins of C-19, A silent attack on humanity* – is a blunt account of our grim reality when societies' morals have kept declining. Earlier, she wrote an article on fundamental rights and C-19 - *The Age of C-19: Protecting Rights Matters* - published in *The Western Australian Jurist* (Volume 11). Her PhD research was about the impact of organisational culture on an organisation's performance. Before undertaking her doctoral research, Monika was a successful educator in Austria and Australia, teaching maths, science and arts, and working at a school for children with learning disabilities. Her qualification in psychology has prompted her special interest and research in human behaviour at work, addiction, and human rights. For the last three years, she devoted a lot of her time into research on C-19 issues.

Steven Alan Samson BA, MA (Colorado), PhD (Oregon 1984) is an Independent Scholar based in Washington State. After forty-one years of teaching political science, history, and geography in Oregon, Indiana, Michigan, Florida, Texas, and Virginia, Dr. Samson retired as Professor of Government, Liberty University, where he served as the founding department chair of the Helms School of Government (2004-2007). He is a member of Truth and Transformation, the Philadelphia Society, and the Academy of Philosophy and Letters. He has served as a board member of *The Western Australian Jurist*, GeoPolitica, and University Professors for Academic Order. He was a Salvatori Fellow at the Heritage Foundation (1994), spoke at the University of South Carolina's Bicentennial Year Symposium (2001), and gave a lecture entitled 'Rival Traditions of Liberty' at the Academia Romana in Bucharest. He has contributed articles to a wide variety of publications, including *The Western Australia Jurist*, *The Market for Ideas*, the *Review of Social and Economic Issues*, *GeoPolitica*, *Townhall Finance*, the *Review of Politics*, *Humanitas*, *Modern Age*, *Contra Mundum*. His articles may be found online at the Liberty University Digital Commons, Research Gate, and Academia.edu.

INTRODUCTION

Against Tyranny

JOSHUA FORRESTER AND AUGUSTO ZIMMERMANN

The war against tyranny is an age-old conflict. As the lead author of this introduction, Joshua Forrester, has noted, we are all in a war between liberty and tyranny. This is a war that started long before any of us were born, and will go on long after we all die. And it is a war that liberty has no choice but to fight, because tyranny will always fight liberty. It is a war fought on a number of fronts, not only around the world but also within us all (more on this in a moment).[1]

Most of the articles in this volume address tyranny from various perspectives. Several address the tyrannical measures governments adopted during Covid-19, and the effect of woke ideology. In this regard, the topic of this volume of *The Western Australian Jurist* continues to explore the topics of previous volumes, namely *Fundamental Rights in Age of Covid-19*[2] and *Wokeshevism: Critical Theories and the Tyrant Left*.[3] There are also works of general interest, namely Renato Costa's 'Law and Reality: A Dialogue Between Herman Dooyeweerd and John Finnis', and Christopher Brohier's legal note about the significant decision of the Supreme Court of the United States in *Dobbs v Jackson Women's Health Organization*.

In addition to the observations about tyranny made by the articles in this volume, we would add seven of our own. The first is that

---

[1] Joshua Forrester, 'Rights and the Rectification of Names' (Speech, National Civic Council, 24 February 2021). See also Joshua Forrester, 'The Woke Empire, and Tyrannies Old and New' (Speech, Civilisationists, 27 March 2023).

[2] Augusto Zimmermann and Joshua Forrester (eds), *Fundamental Rights in the Age of Covid-19* (Connor Court, 2021).

[3] Augusto Zimmermann and Joshua Forrester (eds), '*Wokeshevism*': *Critical Theories and the Tyrant Left* (Connor Court, 2023) ('*Wokeshevism*').

tyranny has taken a variety of forms through the ages. Hence, in what follows we draw on what thinkers have said about tyrannies in their times. By better understanding the qualities of tyranny in previous times, we can better identify and understand them in our own.

Our second observation is that (as noted above) one of the fronts in the war against tyranny is the war within us all. As Alexandr Solzhenitsyn once said of the line between good and evil, the line between liberty and tyranny runs through every human heart.[4]

Indeed, the soul's struggle against tyranny is found in one the foundational works of Western thought: Plato's *Republic*. In this work, Plato (through Socrates) thought the soul was comprised of three parts: rational, spirited, and appetitive.[5] In a well-ordered soul, reason (allied with spirit) governs the appetites.[6] A tyrannic soul, by contrast, is enslaved to one or more appetites.[7] This appetite acts like a 'great winged drone' that 'insist[s] [that] all available resources be distributed' to it and to other appetites.[8] Plato calls this appetite a 'tyrant love' that 'dwells [in] and pilots all the elements of the soul'.[9] This love 'lives like a tyrant within him in all anarchy and lawlessness'.[10] The tyrannic soul is 'drawn to complete hostility to law, though it is named complete freedom…'.[11] Further, 'if it finds in the man any opinions or desires accounted good and still admitting of shame, it slays them and pushes them out of him until it purges him of moderation and fills him with madness brought in from abroad'.[12]

---

[4] Aleksandr Solzhenitsyn, *The Gulag Archipelago 1918-1956: An Experiment in Literary Investigation* (Harper & Row, 1975) vol 2, pt IV, 615.

[5] Plato, *The Republic*, tr Allan Bloom, in Allan Bloom, *The Republic of Plato* (Basic Books, 2nd ed, 1991) 114-121 [436a]-[441c], 253 [572c]-[573a] ('*Republic*').

[6] Ibid 121-122 [441d]-[442d], 272 [589a]-[589b].

[7] Ibid 253 [572e]-[573c].

[8] Ibid 253 [572e]-[573a].

[9] Ibid 254 [573d].

[10] Ibid 255 [575a].

[11] Ibid 253 [572e].

[12] Ibid 253 [573b].

Such a soul is 'filled with much slavery and illiberality, and … further, those parts of it that are decent [are] slaves while a small part, the most depraved and maddest, [is] master'.[13]

Plato concludes that tyrannic souls 'live their whole lives without ever being friends with anyone, always one man's master or another's slave. The tyrannic nature never has a taste of freedom or true friendship.'[14] Such a soul is faithless[15] and, ultimately, wretched.[16]

Our third observation is that, of course, tyrannies are found in states and societies as well as the self. Hence, Plato also observed in *Republic* that a 'greediness'[17] for freedom leads people to regard any law limiting their actions as enslavement.[18] Ironically, this lawlessness is a precondition for tyranny.[19] (That said, Plato also noted that excessive laws were a sign of dysfunctional polities (including tyrannies).)[20] Tyrannical states stir up war so there is the need for a leader.[21] People become poor from contributing to the war effort.[22] Those who dispute the state's actions are treated as enemies, even those who initially supported the state.[23] The courageous, the great-minded, the prudent, and the rich, are purged.[24] The tyrannical state is hateful to its citizens,[25] and welcomes foreigners and flatterers.[26]

---

[13] Ibid 258 [577d].

[14] Ibid 256 [576a].

[15] Ibid.

[16] Ibid 256-257 [576c]. See also ibid 260-261 [580a].

[17] Ibid 240 [562b]-[562c].

[18] Ibid 242 [563d]-[563e].

[19] Ibid 240-241 [562b]-[562c].

[20] Ibid103-104 [425b]-[426b].

[21] Ibid 246 [566e].

[22] Ibid 246 [567a].

[23] Ibid 246 [567a]-[567b].

[24] Ibid 246 [567b]-[567c].

[25] Ibid 246 [567a]-[567b], 247 [567d].

[26] Ibid 247 [567d], 247-248 [568c].

Consequently, the people in tyrannical states are slavish: poor, fearful, and without agency.[27] Like the tyrannical soul, the tyrannical state's existence is, ultimately, a wretched one.[28]

It should not surprise that Plato's observations about tyrannical states were in some ways echoed by his student, Aristotle. In *Politics*, Aristotle noted that tyrannies aim to ensure that its subjects '(a) have little spirit of their own, (b) have no trust in each other, and (c) have no means to carry out anything.'[29] How is this done? Tyrannies:

- 'Lop off the eminent and get rid of independent men of spirit'.[30] Why? Because, 'resistance is not planned by puny spirits against anyone'.[31] Further, '[t]he typical tyrant dislikes proud and free-spirited people. He regards himself as the only person entitled to those qualities; and anyone who shows a rival pride and a spirit of freedom destroys the supremacy and master-like character of the tyranny'.[32]

- 'Do everything to ensure that people do not get to know each other well, for such knowledge increases mutual confidence'.[33] As Aristotle observed:

> [N]o tyranny is ever brought low until a certain degree of mutual confidence is established; hence tyrants are hostile to respectable men, as being dangerous to their rule, not only because of their repugnance to being ruled as though by a master, but because they command confidence, both among themselves and others, and

---

[27] Ibid 258 [577c]-[578a].

[28] Ibid 258-259 [578a].

[29] Aristotle, *The Politics*, tr TA Sinclair (Penguin Books, 1992) 347 [1314a12].

[30] Ibid 344 [1313a34].

[31] Ibid 347 [1314a12].

[32] Ibid 346 [1314a5].

[33] Ibid 345 [1313a34].

abstain from making accusations against each other or anybody else.[34]

- Disallow gatherings in messes, clubs, education and the like as 'these are the breeding grounds of independence and confidence, two things which a tyrant must guard against'.[35]

- 'Do not allow schools or other places where men pursue learning together'.[36]

- Keep city dwellers always under observation.[37]

- Keep aware of everything said and done among the population.[38]

- Have spies among the population.[39]

- Have city dwellers constantly perform servile actions.[40]

- Stir up strife among the population, by setting 'friends against friends, people against notables and the rich against each other'.[41]

- Make the population poor,[42] because 'no one attempts what is quite beyond his powers, so nobody attempts to destroy even a tyranny if the power to do so is not there'.[43]

- Are very ready to make war, 'for this keeps [the] subjects occupied and in continued need of a leader'.[44]

- Favour foreigners over citizens. The tyrant, 'is ... inclined to cultivate the company of foreigners and eat with them rather

---

[34] Ibid 347 [1314a12].
[35] Ibid 344-345 [1313a34].
[36] Ibid 345 [1313a34].
[37] Ibid.
[38] Ibid.
[39] Ibid.
[40] Ibid.
[41] Ibid [1313b16].
[42] Ibid.
[43] Ibid 347 [1314a12].
[44] Ibid 346 [1313b16].

than with citizens of his own state; for the latter he sees as potential enemies, the former as not making rival claims'.[45]

In both Plato's and Aristotle's works can be seen the distrust – even fear – that tyrants display towards those they rule. Those with even a modicum of wit, spirit, or wealth are treated as threats either individually or when gathered in groups.

St Thomas Aquinas in turn echoed Aristotle's observations.[46] To Aquinas, tyrants despise the common good, seeking their own private interest.[47] How the tyrant oppresses their people depends on their dominant passion.[48] Hence '[t]he one who is enthralled by the passion of cupidity seizes the goods of his subjects', while the one 'dominated by the passion of anger ... sheds blood for nothing'.[49] Aquinas observed:

> Thus there can be no safety. Everything is uncertain when there is a departure from justice. Nobody will be able firmly to state: This thing is such and such, when it depends upon the will of another, not to say upon his caprice. Nor does the tyrant merely oppress his subjects in corporal things but he also hinders their spiritual good. Those who seek more to use, than to be of use to, their subjects prevent all progress, suspecting all excellence in their subjects to be prejudicial to their own evil domination. For tyrants hold the good in greater suspicion than the wicked, and to them the valour of others is always fraught with danger.[50]

---

[45] Ibid 346-347 [1314a5].

[46] Which, again, should not surprise given the influence of Aristotle's works on Aquinas.

[47] St Thomas Aquinas, *On Kingship*, tr Gerald B Phelan (Pontifical Institute of Medieval Studies, 1949) 15 [26].

[48] Ibid.

[49] Ibid.

[50] Ibid.

Hence:

> [T]yrants strive to prevent those of their subjects who have become virtuous from acquiring valour and high spirit in order that they may not want to cast off their iniquitous domination. They also see to it that there be no friendly relations among these so that they may not enjoy the benefits resulting from being on good terms with one another, for as long as one has no confidence in the other, no plot will be set up against the tyrant's domination. Wherefore they sow discords among the people, foster any that have arisen, and forbid anything which furthers society and co-operation among men ... They moreover strive to prevent their subjects from becoming powerful and rich since, suspecting these to be as wicked as themselves, they fear their power and wealth; for the subjects might become harmful to them even as they are accustomed to use power and wealth to harm others.[51]

...

> It thus results that when rulers, who ought to induce their subjects to virtue, are wickedly jealous of the virtue of their subjects and hinder it as much as they can, few virtuous men are found under the rule of tyrants.[52]

Aquinas concluded:

> It is no wonder, for a man governing without reason, according to the lust of his soul, in no way differs from the beast. ... Therefore men hide from tyrants as from cruel beasts and it seems that to be subject to a tyrant is the same thing as to lie prostrate beneath a raging beast.[53]

---

[51] Ibid 16 [27].

[52] Ibid 17 [28] [citations omitted].

[53] Ibid 18 [29].

To Aquinas, rulers must pursue the common good. If a ruler does this, then the 'rulership will be right and just, as is suitable to free men'.[54] If a ruler does not do this but instead pursues their private good then 'it will be an unjust and perverted rulership'.[55]

Taking up this theme, John Locke thought that:

Tyranny is the exercise of Power beyond Right, which no Body can have a Right to. And this is making use of the Power anyone has in his hands; not for the good of those, who are under it, but for his own private separate Advantage. When the Governour, however intituled, makes not the Law, but his Will, the rule; and his Commands and Actions are not directed to the preservation of the Properties of his People, but the satisfaction of his own Ambition, Revenge, Covetousness, or any other irregular Passion.[56]

To Locke, the difference between a king and a tyrant is '[t]hat one makes the Laws the Bounds of his Power, and the Good of the Publick, the end of his Government; the other makes all give way to his own Will and Appetite.'[57]

Locke thought that it was not just from monarchies that tyrannies could arise; other forms of government were vulnerable:

For where-ever the Power that is put in any hands for the Government of the People, and the Preservation of their Properties, is applied to other ends, and made use of to impoverish, harass, or subdue them to the Arbitrary and Irregular Commands of those that have it: there it presently

---

[54] Ibid 6 [10].

[55] Ibid.

[56] John Locke, *Two Treatises of Government*, ed Peter Laslett (Cambridge University Press, 1988) bk 2, 398-399, §199 ('*Two Treatises*') [emphasis, capitalisation and spelling as found in original].

[57] Ibid 400, §200 [capitalisation and spelling as found in original].

becomes *Tyranny*, whether those that thus use it are one or many.[58]

Locke noted the role that law has in checking tyranny, but also foreshadowed the ultimate recourse the right of rebellion to end it:

> *Where-ever Law ends, Tyranny begins*, if the Law be transgressed to another's harm. And whosoever in Authority exceeds the Power given him by the Law, and makes use of the Force he has under his Command, to compass that up on the Subject which the Law allows not, ceases in that to be a Magistrate, and acting without Authority, may be opposed, as any other Man, who by force invades the Right of another.[59]

We would pause here to note that tyranny is arguably a form of elite failure. The elite that fails may be a monarch, aristocrat class, or representatives of the people. It may also be the 'elite faculties' of the human mind: reason and spirit. In each case, there is a failure of due regulation. In each case, the result is the same: insecurity, poverty, misery, even depravity.

Given that the state and the self are vulnerable to tyranny, it is unsurprising that society is likewise vulnerable. Here, Alexis de Tocqueville and John Stuart Mill warn of the dangers of a 'tyranny of the majority'. This form of tyranny imposes its will by prevailing mores and attitudes. Its principal tool is ostracism. Its reach is pervasive. As de Tocqueville observed:

> Under the absolute government of one man, despotism, to reach the soul, crudely struck the body; and the soul, escaping from these blows, rose gloriously above it; but in democratic republics, tyranny does not proceed in this way; it leaves the body alone and goes right to the soul. The master no longer says: You will think like me or die; he says: You are free not to

---

[58] Ibid 400, §201 [emphasis, capitalisation and spelling as found in original].

[59] Ibid 400-401, §202 [emphasis and capitalisation and spelling as found in original].

think as I do; your life, your goods, everything remains with you; but from this day on you are a stranger among us. You will keep your privileges as a citizen, but they will become useless to you. If you aspire to be the choice of your fellow citizens, they will not choose you, and if you ask only for their esteem, they will still pretend to refuse it to you. You will remain among men, but you will lose your rights to humanity. When you approach your fellows, they will flee from you like an impure being. And those who believe in your innocence, even they will abandon you, for people would flee from them in turn. Go in peace; I spare your life, but I leave you a life worse than death.[60]

And in taking up the theme advanced by de Tocqueville,[61] Mill added:

Society can and does execute its own mandates: and if it issues wrong mandates instead of right, or any mandates at all in things with which it ought not to meddle, it practises a social tyranny more formidable than many kinds of political oppression, since, though not usually upheld by such extreme penalties, it leaves fewer means of escape, penetrating much more deeply into the details of life, and enslaving the soul itself. Protection, therefore, against the tyranny of the magistrate is not enough: there needs protection also against the tyranny of the prevailing opinion and feeling; against the tendency, of society to impose, by other means than civil penalties, its own ideas and practices as rules of conduct on those who dissent from them to fetter the development, and, if possible, prevent the formation, of any individual not in

---

[60] Alexis de Tocqueville, *Democracy in America*, ed Eduardo Nolla, tr James T Schleifer (Liberty Fund, 2010) vol I, pt II, 418-419.

[61] John Stuart Mill, 'On Liberty' in JM Robson (ed), *The Collected Works of John Stuart Mill* (University of Toronto Press, 1977) vol XVIII, 219.

harmony with its ways, and compel all characters to fashion themselves upon the model of its own.[62]

Of course, there is a risk in guarding against a tyranny of the majority: that the interests – and even the rights – of the majority are disregarded to protect those of a minority. Doing so may give rise to another, more traditional, form of tyranny: the tyranny of the minority.

Our fourth observation is that tyrannies very rarely call themselves tyrannies. Sometimes, a tyrant will be open about their tyranny. For example, according to Pope Pius II, Sigismondo Malatesta, who was lord of the Italian city of Rimini, enjoyed doing terrible things. Malatesta engaged in theft, fraud, treachery, blasphemy, sodomy, adultery, incest, rape, and murder.[63] 'His bloody hand inflicted terrible punishments on innocent and guilty alike. He oppressed the poor, plundered the rich, spared neither widows nor orphans. No one felt safe under his rule.'[64] He involved Rimini in war after war. When the people of Rimini begged Malatesta to retire 'and spare his country, which had so often been exposed to pillage on his account, he replied, "Go and be of good courage; never while I live shall you have peace."'[65]

However, tyrannies are rarely that frank. Usually, tyrannies wear pleasing disguises while going about their work. They often cloak their attacks on rights and freedoms with superficially benign if not laudable rhetoric. So, for example:

- In Nazi Germany, it was the safety and security of the German people.[66]

- In Soviet Russia, it was justice and equality for the proletariat.

---

[62] Ibid 220.

[63] Pope Pius II, 'A Picture of a Tyrant' in James Bruce Ross and Mary Martin McLaughlin, *The Portable Medieval Reader* (Penguin Books, 1977) 288-289.

[64] Ibid 288.

[65] Ibid 289.

[66] See Augusto Zimmermann and Gabriel Moens AM, *Emergency Powers, COVID-19 Restrictions & Mandatory Vaccinations: A Rule-of-Law Perspective* (Connor Court Publishing, 2022) 91-108.

The use of such rhetoric is a major reason why one must be aware of tyranny's qualities, so the beast can be discerned behind the mask.

Our fifth observation stems from one Hannah Arendt made about totalitarian regimes: namely their 'conspicuous disdain for the whole texture of reality'.[67] This disdain, in our view, extends to the treatment of language in tyrannies. As we have just noted, tyrannies may employ pleasing rhetoric. However, tyrannies warp language, and exploit any confusion that results from the mismatch between rhetoric and reality.

This warping of language is not new. Confucius wrote that the first thing he would do if he governed would be to 'rectify the names'. Why was this? Because, as he wrote:

> If terms be incorrect, then statements do not accord with facts; and when statements and facts do not accord, then business is not properly executed;

> When business is not properly executed, order and harmony do not flourish; when order and harmony do not flourish, then justice becomes arbitrary; and when justice becomes arbitrary, the people do not know how to move hand and foot.[68]

(By way of explanation, cutting off hands and feet was an ancient Chinese punishment. Basically, arbitrary punishments make people afraid to act.)

Hence, to Confucius, there was the occasional need to rectify names: if words have lost their meaning, if concepts have lost their rigour, then they must be fixed.

---

[67] Hannah Arendt, *The Origins of Totalitarianism* (Penguin, 2017) xi.

[68] Confucius, *The Analects: or the Conversations of Confucius with his Disciples and Certain Others*, tr William Edward Soothill, ed Lady Dorothea Hosie (Oxford University Press, 1937) quoted in Geoffrey MacCormack, 'Rectification of Names in Early Chinese Legal and Political Thought' (1986) 72(3) *Archives for Philosophy of Law and Social Philosophy* 378, 380.

It was not only the ancient Chinese who recognised the need for clear language. In *Republic*, Plato (through Socrates) observed that in order to explore the concept of justice, one had to see sharply,[69] that is, to be clear. Centuries later, one of the first things Thomas Hobbes did in *Leviathan* was define the terms he would use. Hobbes noted that: 'in the right definition of names, lies the first use of speech … and in wrong, or no definitions, lies the first abuse; from which proceeds all false and senseless tenets.'[70]

However, returning to China, the warping of language to facilitate tyranny is illustrated by the ancient Chinese saying 'Point Deer, Make Horse' or 'Calling a Deer a Horse'. This saying arose from the following story:

> Zhao Gao was contemplating treason but was afraid the other officials would not heed his commands, so he decided to test them first. He brought a deer and presented it to the Emperor but called it a horse. The Emperor laughed and said, 'Is the chancellor perhaps mistaken, calling a deer a horse?' Then the emperor questioned those around him. Some remained silent, while some, hoping to ingratiate themselves with Zhao Gao, said it was a horse, and others said it was a deer.[71]

So what happened to those who correctly called the deer a deer? Well…

> Zhao Gao secretly arranged for all those who said it was a deer to be brought before the law and had them executed instantly.[72]

Why did Zhao Gao do this? He did it because he craved power,

---

[69] *Republic* (n 5) 45 [368c].

[70] Thomas Hobbes, *Leviathan*, ed GCA Gaskin (Oxford University Press, 1996) 24.

[71] Sima Qian, *Records of the Grand Historian: Qin Dynasty*, tr Burton Watson (Columbia University Press, 1993) 70.

[72] Ibid.

and wanted to know who would follow him in a lie. But why would Zhao Gao want that? It is because lies debase those who participate in them, making them subservient to the person or regime who lies. As Theodore Dalrymple said of communist propaganda:

> When people are forced to remain silent when they are being told the most obvious lies, or even worse when they are forced to repeat the lies themselves, they lose once and for all their sense of probity. To assent to obvious lies is to co-operate with evil, and in some small way to become evil oneself. One's standing to resist anything is thus eroded, and even destroyed. A society of emasculated liars is easy to control. I think if you examine political correctness, it has the same effect and is intended to.[73]

Here, it is interesting to note that the second Trump Administration has begun to 'rectify the names' when it comes to sex and gender. Trump's executive order *Defending Women from Gender Ideology Extremism and Restoring Biological Truth to the Federal Government*[74] anchors the terms 'women', 'woman', 'girls', and 'girl' to the biological category of female; and 'men', 'man', 'boys' and 'boy' to the biological category of male.[75] The term 'sex' refers to 'an individual's immutable biological classification as either male or female'.[76] Further, '[t]hese sexes are not changeable and are grounded in fundamental and incontrovertible reality'.[77] The executive order challenges 'gender ideology' which purports to replace 'the biological

---

[73] Theodore Dalrymple made this comment in an interview for *FrontPageMagazine*. Unfortunately, the link to *FrontPageMagazine* no longer works. However, the interview can be found at 'Dalrymple interviewed by Jamie Glazov', *Theodore Dalrymple writes* (Web Page, 31 August 2005) <theodoredalrymple.wordpress.com/dalrymple-interviewed-by-jamie-glazov>.

[74] Exec Order No 14168, 90 FR 8615 (2025).

[75] Ibid.

[76] Ibid.

[77] Ibid.

category of sex with an ever-shifting concept of self-assessed gender identity, permitting the false claim that males can identify as and thus become women and vice versa, and requiring all institutions of society to regard this false claim as true'.[78]

Our sixth observation is that tyranny's methods are dynamic, and adapt to the times. Here, another of Trump's executive orders, *Restoring Freedom of Speech and Ending Federal Censorship*,[79] is illustrative. As this order notes:

> Under the guise of combatting 'misinformation,' 'disinform-ation,' and 'malinformation,' the Federal Government infringed on the constitutionally protected speech rights of American citizens across the United States in a manner that advanced the Government's preferred narrative about significant matters of public debate.[80]

The problem the executive order identifies has been described elsewhere as the 'Censorship Industrial Complex'.[81] Here, 'government actors, social media companies, universities, and NGOs' engage in 'large-scale coordinated efforts' to 'monitor citizens and rob them of their voices'.[82] Some of these efforts involve direct government action.[83] However, in addition:

> [T]he Censorship Industrial Complex operates through more subtle methods. These include visibility filtering, labelling, and manipulation of search engine results. Through deplatforming and flagging, social media censors have already silenced lawful opinions on topics of national and

---

[78] Ibid.

[79] Exec Order No 14149, 90 FR 8243 (2025).

[80] Ibid.

[81] See 'The Westminster Declaration', *westminsterdeclaration.org* (Web Page).

[82] Ibid.

[83] Ibid.

geopolitical importance. They have done so with the full support of 'disinformation experts' and 'fact-checkers' in the mainstream media, who have abandoned the journalistic values of debate and intellectual inquiry.

As the Twitter Files revealed, tech companies often perform censorial 'content moderation' in coordination with government agencies and civil society.[84]

A major issue with the Censorship Industrial Complex is the sheer, staggering scale of the enterprise. It extends well beyond the United States,[85] and its efforts embrace a 'whole of society' approach.[86]

But behind the Censorship Industrial Complex are familiar themes of tyranny: disregard of fundamental rights, distrust of the citizenry, and warping of language. Indeed, the use of 'disinformation' and 'misinformation' to describe the views of the state's own citizens is especially perverse. Traditionally, the terms 'disinformation' and 'misinformation' were used in an intelligence context, and dealt with information operations by state actors. Indeed, 'disinformation' meant 'misleading information supplied intentionally, as in counterespionage'.[87] It is derived from the Russian term '*dezinformatsiya*'.[88] A more elaborate definition notes that it is 'the dissemination of deliberately false information, esp. when supplied by a government or its agent to a foreign power or to the media, with the intention of influencing the policies or opinions of those who receive it'.[89] Applying these terms, with their sinister

---

[84] Ibid.

[85] Ibid.

[86] Jacob Siegel, 'Learn This Term: Whole of Society', *Tablet Magazine* (Web Article, 26 July 2024).

[87] *Macquarie Concise Dictionary* (5th ed, 2009) 'disinformation'.

[88] Ibid.

[89] *The Oxford English Dictionary* (2nd ed, 1989) 'disinformation' (def a).

connotations, to citizens expressing views suggests that strong measures are justified against those citizens as they are a threat. Once again, the beast lurks behind a mask.

However, while the second Trump Administration is taking action, Michael Shellenberger notes that '[u]nfortunately, the Censorship Industrial Complex remains almost entirely intact, and Europe, Australia, Britain, Brazil, and other nations in the West continue to seek new forms of censorship and information control'.[90]

This leads us to our seventh and last observation, and it ties in with our observations in *Wokeshevism*.[91] The speed, scale and strength of the second Trump administration's effort to combat woke tyranny here and on other fronts is impressive. However, it is unwise to think that these efforts mean that anti-woke forces have won. Here, it is worth recalling similar instances when it was thought that the far left had been beaten decisively. The Nixon landslide in 1972, the Reagan Revolution in the early 1980's, and the collapse of the Soviet Union in 1991, were all thought to herald the end of the far left. In every instance, the far left retreated, rallied, and returned.

We should not think that the war against woke tyranny, or tyranny generally, is over. It is not. Rather, the battle has been joined. There are multiple fronts, and it remains for all people of goodwill to do their part. Fight on.

---

[90] 'The Censorship Industrial Complex', 119th Congress (2025-2026), 12 February 2025 (Testimony of Michael Shellenberger).

[91] *Wokeshevism* (n 3).

1

The Obedient Rebel:
Should Christians Always
Obey Their Government?

LUKE D D BARBRICK*

ABSTRACT

Does the Bible command obedience to leaders or law? Who are the true rebels, officials who abuse their God-given powers or citizens who remain loyal to the law in the face of tyranny? These age-old questions have recently returned to the forefront of Western politics. Some Christians believe that Scripture calls for total submission in the face of government overreach. These believers wrongly equate the authority that their leaders temporarily hold with the actual leaders. Such believers unwittingly chain themselves to a dehumanizing yoke of mind-numbing compliance. In truth, scripture, history, and plain reason confirm that a citizen's primary allegiance is to the office of leadership, not the officeholder. When an official exceeds the lawful authority of his or her office, it is the duty of every citizen to peacefully rebel against the official in a spirit of obedience to their true sovereigns: The laws of nature and nature's God.

I. INTRODUCTION

In recent years, a divisive yet extremely important question has reemerged in many American churches, a question which our ancestors grappled with for centuries. The question is this: Are Christians called

---

* Research Attorney, Michigan Court of Appeals; Juris Doctor, Michigan State University College of Law (2023); Bachelor of Arts, Hillsdale College (2019).

by God to follow every command from their government? Over the last few years, I encountered many believers in my own community who vehemently insisted that Christians are called to submit to leadership, without question and regardless of the circumstances. Such Christians frequently rely on Romans 13 for their assertion.

> [1]Let every soul be subject to the governing authorities. For there is no authority except from God, and the authorities that exist are appointed by God. [2]Therefore whoever resists the authority resists the ordinance of God, and those who resist will bring judgment on themselves. [3]For rulers are not a terror to good works, but to evil. Do you want to be unafraid of the authority? Do what is good, and you will have praise from the same. [4]For he is God's minister to you for good. But if you do evil, be afraid; for he does not bear the sword in vain; for he is God's minister, an avenger to execute wrath on him who practices evil. [5]Therefore you must be subject, not only because of wrath but also for conscience' sake. [6]For because of this you also pay taxes, for they are God's ministers attending continually to this very thing. [7]Render therefore to all their due: taxes to whom taxes are due, customs to whom customs, fear to whom fear, honor to whom honor.[1]

Admittedly, this argument appears convincing if one interprets "authority" as something inherent to or synonymous with persons in power. However, this overly literal interpretation of Romans 13 raises serious issues for the passage in light of other Biblical texts. For example, in Acts 5, the Pharisees, the religious leaders of the day, commanded the apostles to cease their preaching of the Gospel to the people. Peter replied, 'We ought to obey God rather than men'.[2] Should the apostles have kept silent according to the Pharisees' wishes

---

[1] Romans 13:1-7 NKJV.

[2] Acts 5:27-29 NKJV.

and thus disobeyed Jesus' command to '[g]o into all the world and preach the gospel to every creature?'[3] Was Rahab wrong to hide the Hebrew spies in defiance of her king?[4] Were Shadrach, Meshach, and Abed-Nego wrong to defy the wishes of King Nebuchadnezzar, the greatest of all kings at the time, by refusing to worship his golden image?[5] Was Daniel wrong to disobey the edict of King Darius by refusing to worship him?[6] As the Word of God is infallible, the Word cannot contradict itself because the Word is God and God Himself is without flaw.[7] Therefore, we can only assume that the flaw lies within this interpretation of Romans 13.

At the heart of the submissionists' interpretation lies the aforementioned confusion of persons in power (leadership) with authority. If these concepts are one and the same, Romans 13 unequivocally commands Christians to blindly submit to their rulers, without hesitation and without question, as the passage makes it clear that Christians have no cause to rebel against authority. For the absolute submissionist Christian, rebellion against leadership constitutes a rebellion against God Himself. This interpretation holds serious moral and practical consequences for the Christian life. For example, it implicitly teaches that Christians should overlook the fact that they are citizens of a Constitutional Republic and, therefore, they have a greater allegiance to the laws of the land than to the rulers who remain bound by the same laws. A second problem with the submissionists' interpretation is that it focuses solely on the Christian's duty to the state and completely ignores the state's duty to the citizens, Christian and non-Christian alike. In other words, this interpretation fails to examine the purpose for which God established

---

[3] Mark 16:15 NKJV.

[4] Joshua 2 NKJV.

[5] Daniel 3 NKJV.

[6] Daniel 6 NKJV.

[7] John 1:1; 2 Samuel 22:31 NKJV.

governments and completely ignores the question of how Christians should respond when their government acts beyond its God-given, lawful purpose and authority.

II. GOD INSTITUTED GOVERNMENT FOR THE GOOD OF HIS PEOPLE

To properly understand our duty to leadership in our capacity as citizens of two kingdoms, a heavenly and an earthly, we need to understand why God established governments over us in the first place. The famous Protestant theologian, Martin Luther, stated that God instituted government to restrain the 'unchristian and wicked so that they are obliged to *keep the peace outwardly*' [emphasis ours].[8] Likewise, John Calvin observed, 'We see that some form of organization is necessary in all human society to foster the common peace and maintain accord'.[9] Romans 13 affirms both Calvin and Luther's arguments in verses three and four which describe a governing authority or ruler as God's 'minister…for good' and as 'an avenger to *execute* wrath on him who practices evil.'[10] John Locke, a student of Calvin's writings, also agreed with Luther and Calvin's assertions concerning the role of government in society. However, underlying the ruler's duty to uphold the social order and restrain the ungodly rests an equally important duty: To preserve the God-given rights of the people. In his *Second Treatise of Government*, which greatly influenced the American Founding, Locke observed,

> [A]ll men are naturally in … a state of perfect freedom to order their actions, and dispose of their possessions and persons, as they think fit, within the bounds of the law of nature, without asking leave or depending upon the will of any other man.

---

[8] Gary Amos and Robins Simon, *Never Before in History* (Discovery Institute, 2016) 8.
[9] Ibid 12.
[10] Romans 13:3-4 NKJV.

> A state also of equality … no one having more than another; there being nothing more evident, than that creatures of the same species and rank, promiscuously born to all the same advantages of nature, and the use of the same faculties, should also be equal one amongst another without subordination or subjection.[11]

Thus, for Locke, all human beings are equal in their humanity and in their right to be free. Initially, humanity was born into a state of perfect equality wherein no person possessed official power over their fellow men and women. All individuals are equal in their right to pursue their own well-being and happiness in life. Locke further asserted that this 'state of nature' had a 'law of nature to govern it'.[12] This law of nature or Natural Law informed, and still informs, every person, through both reason and conscience, that all human beings are "equal and independent," and thus no one should harm the 'life, health, liberty, or possessions' of another.[13] In other words, 'whatever you want men to do to you, do also [unto] to them'.[14]

Whenever anyone transcends the self-evident Golden Rule of Nature, 'the offender declares himself to live by another rule than that of reason and common equity, which is that measure God has set to the actions of men, for their mutual security'.[15] As this quotation suggests, not all people abide by the dictates of Natural Law. Consequently, early humanity found it extremely difficult to enjoy their God-given rights in a pure State of Nature, devoid of any political unity or protection. When all people are "kings" and devoid of governance and order, humanity's enjoyment of their property remains 'very unsafe, very

---

[11] John Locke, *Second Treatise of Government* (Simon & Brown, 2011) 8.

[12] Ibid 9.

[13] Ibid.

[14] 'Matthew 7:12' in RC Sproul, et al (eds), *The Reformation Study Bible: New King James Version* (Thomas Nelson Publishers, 1995) 1515, 1515.

[15] Locke (n 11).

unsecure'.[16] For Locke, 'The great and chief end … of men's uniting into commonwealths, and putting themselves under government' was and remains the 'preservation of their lives, liberties, and estates'.[17] Thus, governments were founded to protect the sacred liberties of the citizens against infringement from sinister designs and persons. Government is a necessary product of human imperfection and remains, as James Madison observed, the 'greatest of all reflections on human nature'.[18]

Regarding the type of government mankind ought to have, John Calvin observed, 'Since such diversity exists in the customs of men, such variety in their minds, such conflicts in their judgements and dispositions, no organization is sufficiently strong unless constituted with definite laws'.[19] Calvin's ideas influenced many prominent American Founders, such as John Adams, who advocated for 'a government of laws, not of men' which is how he described the government of the United States.[20] Thus, for both Adams and Calvin, the best type of government is not one wherein the rulers govern through pure, unbridled will, but through clear and precise laws. Knowing this, our Founders sought to establish a republican form of government, headed by a national Constitution which would serve as the 'supreme Law of the Land'.[21] To avoid a 'gradual concentration' of power into a single ruler, our Founders divided our nation's federal government into 'distinct and separate departments' and assigned specific powers of governance to each.[22]

---

[16] Ibid 67.

[17] Ibid 67.

[18] James Madison, 'Federalist 51' in Hillsdale College Politics Faculty (eds), *The U.S. Constitution: A Reader* (Hillsdale College Press, 2012) 287, 288.

[19] Amos & Simon (n 8) 12.

[20] Ibid 44.

[21] 'The Constitution of the United States of America' in Hillsdale College Politics Faculty (eds), *The U.S. Constitution: A Reader* (Hillsdale College Press, 2012) 47, 57.

[22] Madison (n 18) 288-89.

III. The Hierarchy of Christian Allegiance to Government

The US Constitution divides the power of the Federal government into three departments or branches: The Legislative (Congress), the Executive (the President), and the Judiciary (the courts). The authority entrusted to these branches is as follows: Congress makes the national laws, the President enforces the laws made by Congress, and the courts, including the United States Supreme Court, interpret the laws of Congress and the actions of the President in accordance with the Constitution and other superior laws.[23] Neither the President nor the courts can make their own laws, nor can Congress enforce or interpret the laws. Moreover, pursuant to the Tenth Amendment, 'The powers not delegated to the United States by the Constitution, nor prohibited by it to the States, are reserved to the States respectively, or to the people.'[24] Since the US Constitution's drafting, the states too have adopted political systems governed by a separation of powers and checks and balances amongst their legislatures, governors, and supreme courts.

Therefore, if we apply Romans 13:1, 'Let every soul be subject to the governing authorities' to the setting of our Constitutional Republic, our hierarchy of authority and our allegiance thereto remain as follows: Our foremost authorities are God and His Natural Law followed by the United States Constitution.[25] Below the Constitution, we submit to Congress in matters of federal lawmaking, to the President in matters of federal law enforcement, and to the Supreme Court and all inferior courts in legal conflicts that fall within their jurisdiction. Similarly, per the constitutions of the particular states to which we are citizens, we submit to the legislature in matters of state

---

[23] The Constitution of the United States of America (n 21) 47-56.

[24] Ibid 60.

[25] Romans 13:1 KJV.

lawmaking, to the governor in matters of state law enforcement, and to the state courts in matters of state judicial dispute. Any powers that do not fall under the constitutional authority of the federal or the state governments are reserved to local governing bodies. Therefore, in all official matters not governed by Federal or State law, we must submit to local authorities.

IV. WE SUBMIT TO AN OFFICE OF AUTHORITY, NOT THE OFFICE HOLDER

A common error of many citizens, Christian and otherwise, is that they mistake the persons holding power for the government and its authority. This view has contributed immensely to the submissionist interpretation of Romans 13. Yet, when one examines the history of America's Founding and the writings of earlier generations who inspired our Founding Fathers, we find a very different argument. In the *Vindiciae Contra Tyrannos* ('A Defense of Liberty Against Tyrants'), an anonymous Huguenot (French Calvinist) observed that 'no one was ever born with a crown on his head and a scepter in his hand'. Moreover, 'no man can be made a king by himself nor reign without people'.[26] Because 'the people choose and establish their kings, it follows that the whole body of the people is above the king'.[27] Accordingly, 'he who receives authority from another is less than he from whom he derives power'.[28] The people are the true sovereigns. The author compares a country to "a ship" wherein the king or ruler 'holds the place of the pilot.'[29] The people are the 'owners of the vessel, obeying the pilot while he is careful of the public good'.[30] In other words, authority is embedded within the office(s) of government per

---

[26] 'Defense of Liberty Against Tyrants' in Hillsdale College History Faculty (eds), *Western Heritage: A Reader* (Hillsdale College Press, 2010) 717, 719.

[27] Ibid 720.

[28] Ibid.

[29] Ibid.

[30] Ibid.

the consent of the people who establish and sustain the ruler. Authority is neither inherent nor synonymous to persons in power.

This understanding of authority and the ruler as distinct concepts was not unique to the adherents of John Calvin or the Protestant tradition. Three hundred years before the Reformation, the Catholic barons of England forced their king, John, to sign the *Magna Carta* (The Great Charter) which limited the power of the English monarchy. The *Magna Carta* proved a foundational cornerstone for the British Constitution and, most importantly, established the authority of the law as superior to that of the king.[31] One century after the *Magna Carta*, the leaders of England's northern neighbor, Scotland, wrote a letter to the Pope which became known as the *Declaration of Arbroath*.[32] In the letter, Scotland's leaders explained how the English King, Edward I, through many barbarous acts of coercion, invasion, and mass murder, had cruelly attempted to subjugate the people of Scotland to his rule.[33] Although Scotland had been liberated under the extraordinary military and political skill of her king, Robert the Bruce, the Scottish leaders warned,

> [Should Robert the Bruce] give up what he has begun, and agree to make us or our kingdom subject to the King of England or the English, we should exert ourselves at once to drive him out as our enemy and a subverter of his own rights and ours, and make some other man who was well able to defend us our King … It is in truth not for glory, nor riches, nor honours that we are fighting, but for freedom – for that alone, which no honest man gives up but with life itself.[34]

Thus, for the medieval Scots, a king holds power to one primary

---

[31] Amos and Simon (n 8) 5, 18.

[32] 'Medieval Britain: Full Text of the Declaration of Arbroath, 1320', *The History Files* (Web Article, 4 February 2005).

[33] Ibid.

[34] Ibid.

end: The protection of his people and the safeguarding of their freedom. Should the king fail in his duty, the people and nobles have the right and the duty to replace him with a more capable individual. The monarchy and the powers thereof are not inseparably bound to the person of the ruler. The freedom of the people remains an absolute truth and, therefore, cannot be surrendered under any circumstances. Freedom is the end, and the king and his office are mere means to that end.

If we combine all these historical views concerning the relationship between the king, the law, and the nation, the result is this: The nation (the people) is the sovereign of the prince who, through the people's consent, holds the reins of power for a limited time. A ruler can be replaced should he or she fail to protect the rights and liberties of the people. Moreover, the office of the leader is defined and limited by the law of the land which remains the greatest mechanism for the people to hold the ruler accountable. Therefore, leadership and authority, two terms so often confused, indicate two distinct concepts. A leader is just a person entrusted by God, through the consent of the people, with the authority and powers of a governing office, which remains limited by the temporal laws of the land and the natural law. Because authority is inherent to the governing office, citizens must submit to the office, not the office holder.

The Bible explicitly supports this historical distinction between the office and the officeholder. In Matthew 22, Jesus said, 'Render therefore to Caesar the things that are Caesar's, and to God the things that are God's'. Notice that Jesus does not name the reigning emperor by name but by the title of his office, "Caesar".[35] Moreover, Jesus does not command His followers to render absolute allegiance to Caesar but rather to give Caesar that which is his and God that which is His. As both Christians and citizens of an earthly kingdom, our allegiance

---

[35] Matthew 22:21 NKJV

is to the office of the ruler, not to the person who rules. Additionally, our allegiance to that office remains limited by our allegiance to God.

In his highly influential work, the *Lex Rex* (The Law and the King), Samuel Rutherford, an author of the famous Westminster Confessions, also describes the authority of kings and rulers as tied to their offices rather than to the persons holding power.[36] Rutherford reminds his readers that a king would have no power had he not first formed a "covenant" with the people. He describes this covenant as "natural, tacit, and implicit" in nature, 'tying the king, by the nature of his office'.[37] The powers inherent to the ruler's office permit him to do 'no more than that which upon right and law he may do'.[38] Referencing Romans 13:3-4, Rutherford further contends, 'God's word equally ties him [the ruler] to the place of a mere minister in doing good, as in executing wrath on evil-doers'.[39] As human beings, all rulers remain God's "servants," subject to His will, their positions and offices exist only to do His bidding, not their own.[40] Therefore, no ruler can 'draw the sword against the innocent, nor absolve the guilty' as such acts would be outside the realm of justice and, therefore, outside God's will.[41] When a ruler uses his office for evil, that ruler acts outside God's will and beyond the authority of his office.[42] In other words, God has equipped all rulers, via their offices and the consent of their subjects, with sufficient 'power … to do good, not evil'.[43] *There is no such thing as an absolute earthly ruler or king.*[44] Therefore, no ruler is permitted to act beyond the authority or purpose entrusted to him

---

[36] Amos and Simon (n 8) 23.

[37] Samuel Rutherford, *Lex, Rex: The Law and the King* (Canon Press, 2020) 149.

[38] Ibid 276.

[39] Ibid 279.

[40] Ibid.

[41] Ibid 278.

[42] Ibid 278-279.

[43] Ibid 288.

[44] Ibid 149.

or her by God by doing evil. Such a person is no longer a legitimate ruler, but a usurper.

Remarkably, this distinction between leadership and authority logically aligns with Romans 13. Verse three states, 'For rulers are not a terror to good works, but to evil'.[45] If the term "rulers" in this verse refers to the often-corrupt persons and desires of the office holders rather than to the offices in which they serve, then this verse essentially says that people in power are never a terror to good works. History, Scripture, and common sense reveal this assertion to be both naïve and blatantly false. If, however, the term "rulers" references the impersonal aspect of leadership, namely political authority in the form of a political office, then this verse makes perfect sense. The office of king or emperor is never, in and of itself, a terror to good works any more than a car is a terror to pedestrians or a gun is a terror to human life. The true terror lies in the heart of the person who drives recklessly, who pulls the trigger, and who abuses political authority for personal gain.

V. THE ORIGINAL GREEK ALSO DISTINGUISHES AUTHORITY AND LEADERSHIP

In its original Greek, Romans 13 distinguishes leadership from authority. The word used in the passage for authorities, 'ἐξουσίαις' ('exousiais'), which translates as 'to the authorities' (Greek Concordance: ἐξουσίαις) identifies to whom or what Christians owe their allegiance when it comes to earthly government.[46] In its simpler form, the Greek term for an authority, 'εξουσια' ('exousia'), translates as a 'power to act.'[47] Thus the original term used for authorities in

---

[45] Romans 13:3 NKJV.

[46] Romans 13:1. 'Greek Text Analysis', *Bible Hub* (online). 'Greek Concordance: ἐξουσίαις (exousiais) – 3 Occurrences', *Bible Hub* (online); *The Interlinear Hebrew-Greek-English Bible* (Hendrickson Publishers, 2012) Vol 1, 881.

[47] Strong's Greek: 1849. *εξουσια (exousia) – Power to Act, Authority*, *Bible Hub* (online).

the passage, 'ἐξουσίαις,' literally translates as *to the powers to act*. Note that the verse does not use the Greek term for rulers, 'ἄρχοντες' ('archontes') when defining authority.[48] Therefore, in the original Greek, Christians are not ultimately called to submit to governing persons but to the powers held by those persons.[49] The limits of the rulers' powers are defined by their purpose, to be 'a terror ... to evil'.[50] Rulers are persons empowered to one end alone: To be a force for good. When a ruler becomes a force for evil, he or she is no longer acting in accordance with his or her legitimate, God-given powers or within the boundaries of authority. With regard to this passage, the King James Version offers a translation very similar to the original Greek.

> [1]Let every soul be subject unto the higher powers. For there is no power but of God: the powers that be are ordained of God.[2] Whosoever therefore resisteth the power, resisteth the ordinance of God: and they that resist shall receive to themselves damnation.[3] For rulers are not a terror to good works, but to the evil. Wilt thou then not be afraid of the power? do that which is good, and thou shalt have praise of the same:[4] For he is the minister of God to thee for good. But if thou do that which is evil, be afraid; for he beareth not the sword in vain: for he is the minister of God, a revenger to execute wrath upon him that doeth evil.[5] Wherefore ye must needs be subject, not only for wrath, but also for conscience sake.[6] For for this cause pay ye tribute also: for they are God's ministers, attending continually upon this very thing.[7] Render therefore to all their dues: tribute to whom tribute is due; custom to whom custom; fear to whom fear; honour to whom honour.[51]

---

[48] Greek Concordance: ἄρχοντες (archontes) — 9 Occurrences, *Bible Hub* (online).
[49] Ibid.
[50] Romans 13:3 NKJV.
[51] Romans 13:3 KJV.

According to the King James Version and the Greek, the Bible commands Christians to submit to authority which is defined simply as power or 'higher powers'.[52] In both versions, authority remains something impersonal in nature. As proof of this, the Greek uses two distinct words for rulers and authority and thus treats them as distinct concepts. Authority is simply the power to act towards a specified end. As the source of that authority, God has clearly defined that end in His Word: To be 'a terror…to evil'.[53] Thus, our allegiance to rulers remains rooted in our allegiance to the 'higher powers' (authority) and our allegiance to the 'higher powers' remains rooted in our allegiance to God.[54]

VI. Historic Examples

If we understand leadership and authority as distinct concepts, the question then becomes whether and when Christians ought to peacefully rebel against either. If we understand authority as something impersonal, and not as something inherent to the person to whom it has been entrusted, Christians may not rebel against authority. That which is impersonal, including power, is never a "terror" to good works in and of itself.[55] Only persons, including rulers, prove to be such terrors. Situations may arise when Christians are called to take a stand for what they believe in. This simple truth has led to some of the most remarkable and profound historic events of the last 380 years.

A *The English Civil War*

In the middle of the 17th Century in England, there arose a bitter division regarding the authority of the King in relation to the authority of England's legislative branch of government, Parliament. The

---

[52] Ibid.

[53] Romans 13:3 NKJV.

[54] Romans 13:3 KJV.

[55] Romans 13:3 NKJV.

English King, Charles I, stated, 'Remember, I am your king, your lawful king … I have a trust committed to me by God, by old and lawful descent: I will not betray it to answer to an unlawful authority'.[56] Charles' argument, otherwise known as the Divine Right of Kings theory, stated that since all authority comes from God, people have no choice but to render absolute allegiance to their rulers lest they join in rebellion against God.[57] By contrast, the Parliamentarians contended that the king remained bound by the laws of England, such as the *Magna Carta*, and he could not rule by pure royal will.[58] Through his writings, Samuel Rutherford became one of the most eloquent spokesmen for the Parliamentarian view.[59] In his *Lex Rex*, Rutherford argued, 'If the king be made absolutely, it is contrary to Scripture and to the nature of his office'.[60] Like his Huguenot brethren, Rutherford fervently contended that the monarch remained bound by the powers and purpose of his office and by his "contract" with the people. Such a contract between a sovereign and his subjects provides a 'co-active power to the king and the people to compel each other'.[61] The king serves as a check on the excesses of the people while the people serve as a check on the excesses of the king. Unfortunately, Charles I refused to heed the voice of his people's representatives in Parliament. After a bloody civil war which claimed the lives of thousands, the king was tried and subsequently executed for treason.

B *The Glorious Revolution*

Rutherford's belief in the people's duty to hold the king accountable to his contract and to his lawful authority proved essential a few decades following Charles I's execution. In 1685, a new monarch,

---

[56] Amos and Simon (n 8) 26.

[57] Ibid.

[58] Ibid.

[59] Ibid.

[60] Rutherford (n 37) 149.

[61] Ibid.

James II, ascended to the throne. As a firm believer in the Divine Right of Kings, James proved an oppressive ruler to his subjects in both Britain and America. Weary of the king's abuses, Parliament invited the Dutch prince, William of Orange, to be England's new king. In a bloodless revolution, Parliament and William deposed James and, in 1689, William and his wife, Mary, were proclaimed King and Queen of England.[62] However, during the coronation, the leaders of Parliament read a list of rights, the English *Bill of Rights*, outlining the conditions and principles under which rulers would be allowed to occupy the throne.[63] After years of turmoil, the people and their representatives in Parliament successfully forced the English monarchy to acknowledge Parliament's lawful sovereignty as Britain's lawmaking body. The king had finally acknowledged the Crown's inferiority to the English Constitution and the Common Law. Not least of all, the events of the Glorious Revolution vindicated and established the right and duty of the people to remove a king who had lowered himself to the level of a tyrant, bent on subverting the God-given rights of his subjects.

C *The American Revolutionary War*

The principles discovered and validated by the Glorious Revolution found their greatest expression in 1776, when Thomas Jefferson and his fellow delegates drafted their unanimous American Declaration of Independence. In this remarkable document, the members of the Continental Congress said it was a 'self-evident' truth that 'all men are created equal, that they are endowed by their Creator with certain unalienable Rights' including 'Life, Liberty, and the pursuit of Happiness.' For the protection of these rights, 'Governments are instituted among Men, deriving their just powers from the consent

---

[62] Amos and Simon (n 8) 35-37.

[63] *English Bill of Rights 1689* (2008), *Avalon Project*, Yale Law School Lillian Goldman Law Library.

of the governed'.[64] Drawing on the ideas of Rutherford, Locke, the Huguenots, and the medieval barons of Scotland and England, the Founders recognized the relationship between the government and the people as contractual and not as a mere exertion of the ruler's will or pleasure.

When a government becomes 'destructive' of the people's sacred rights, it becomes 'the Right of the People to alter or abolish' their old government and 'to institute new [g]overnment'. Jefferson and his fellow drafters warned that 'Governments long established should not be changed for light or transient causes'. Nevertheless, 'when a long train of abuses and usurpations, pursuing invariably the same Object evinces a design to reduce them under absolute Despotism, it is their right, it is their duty, to throw off such Government and to provide new Guards for their future security'.[65] Thus, the people should dissolve their government only when that government's abuses have grown so intolerable that freedom's last line of defense becomes a total and irrevocable separation of the subjects from the sovereign. When such abuses occur, the people have not merely a right, but a duty to rebel. When all else fails, the people are the last line of defense of their God-given, 'unalienable' rights.[66]

According to the Declaration, the Americans did not throw off the heavy yoke of British rule lightly or without just cause. The English *Bill of Rights*, which the king was lawfully bound to uphold, stated that a primary function of Parliament entailed the 'vindicating and asserting' of the people's 'ancient rights and liberties.'[67] Against this principle of representative government, the British monarch, George III, had 'dissolved the Representative Houses' of the colonies 'for

---

[64] 'The Declaration of Independence', in Hillsdale College Politics Faculty (eds), *The U.S. Constitution: A Reader* (Hillsdale College Press, 2012) 5, 5.

[65] Ibid 5-6.

[66] Ibid 5.

[67] English *Bill of Rights 1689* (n 63).

opposing his invasions on the rights of the people'.[68] To add insult to injury, the king and his government had repeatedly 'imposed taxes' on the colonists without allowing them representation in Parliament and, therefore, without the colonists' "consent". When the colonial leaders attempted to petition the king for redress of these grievous acts, their 'repeated [p]etitions' were answered 'only by repeated injury.'[69] According to the English Bill of Rights, '[I]t is the right of the subjects to petition the king and all commitments and prosecutions for such petitioning are illegal'.[70] In other words, George III had wrongfully and illegally punished the Americans for exercising their lawful right to petition their government. The king had broken the supreme law of the land.

The Declaration goes on to list many other abuses on the part of the king, all of which constituted a violation of the principles stated within the British Constitution and those of Natural Law. Together, these acts proved to the colonial leaders an obvious design on the part of George III's government to establish an 'absolute Tyranny' over the colonies.[71] George III, like James II and Charles I, had degraded himself to the level of a 'Prince whose character is thus marked by every act which may define a Tyrant' and, therefore, was 'unfit to be the ruler of a free people'.[72] For these reasons, the American Founders declared that 'these United Colonies are, and of Right ought to be Free and Independent States; that they are Absolved from all Allegiance to the British Crown'.[73]

In summary, the Americans, like their British forebearers, were not acting out of a spirit of disobedience to the king's authority, but

---

[68] The Declaration of Independence (n 64) 6.

[69] Ibid 7-8.

[70] English *Bill of Rights 1689* (n 63).

[71] The Declaration of Independence (n 64) 6.

[72] Ibid 8.

[73] Ibid.

out of obedience to the higher authorities that reigned over both them and the king. These authorities included God, Natural Law, the British Constitution, and the common law of England. George III was the true rebel. If the Americans submitted or remained silent to the king's usurpations, they would stand guilty as accomplices to the king's lawlessness. Ultimately, the English Civil War, the Glorious Revolution, and the American Revolution had this in common: They were initiated and fought, not to overthrow authority, but to maintain it by taking a stand against those leaders who persistently acted beyond their lawful, God-given powers.

VII. The Consequences of Equating Leadership with Authority

Ultimately, the submissionist interpretation of Romans 13 constitutes a 21st century reincarnation of the long discredited Divine Right of Kings mindset. Simply put, this viewpoint asserts that all authority comes from God and, therefore, Christians are not permitted to challenge leaders in any way lest they also rebel against God. Again, this view naively assumes that leadership and authority are one and the same. To their credit, some modern adherents of this view have acknowledged the need for limits to their dangerously broad rule of absolute submission. Unfortunately, such individuals often fail to explain at what point Christian submission to leadership should cease. Instead, they avoid such questions by arguing that we should focus our time and efforts on preparing for the so-called big battles and not on relatively minor issues such as the government requiring Christians to wear masks during worship or limiting church attendance. They classify such intrusions as mere inconveniences, beneath our notice. Such Christians would do well to heed the voice of Pastor Martin Niemoller who lived in Germany during the reign of Hitler's National Socialist (Nazi) party.

First, they came for the socialists and I did not speak out – because I was not a socialist. Then they came for the trade unionists and I did not speak out – because I was not a trade unionist. Then they came for the Jews and I did not speak out – because I was not a Jew. Then they came for me – and there was no one left to speak for me.[74]

With every small victory achieved, tyranny and usurpation grow in power. If we ignore our responsibilities as both Christians and citizens and turn a blind eye to lawless government oppression, when the time comes to fight the so-called decisive battle, our churches will be so weak and compromised that there will be little to anything left worth defending. Think well on this. If a government can regulate the number of people who receive the Word every Sabbath and whether or not they should wear masks while receiving the Word, what is to prevent them from eventually mandating how or whether the Word itself is preached? Nevertheless, if we hold with a Divine Right of Kings interpretation of Romans 13, such intrusions into the churches will prove the unintended, yet inevitable consequence. People often forget that the most sinister and successful type of tyranny is not one born out of foreign conquest, but that which arises internally from the people's gradual surrender of freedom for a fantasy of security. God forbid that such a regime should take hold in this country or that our nation of laws should descend into a nation of men.

VIII. THE CONSEQUENCES OF SEPARATING LEADERSHIP FROM AUTHORITY

Unsurprisingly, if we understand leadership and authority as distinct concepts, our interpretation of Romans 13 will differ radically as will the consequences for the Christian. Again, Christians are called to

---

[74] Martin Niemoller: 'First They Came for the Socialists…', *United States Holocaust Memorial Museum* (Web Article, 30 March 2012).

submit to leadership when the leaders act within the boundaries of their powers or authority. If we understand authority in an impersonal light rather than as something magically tied to the life and will of the person, authority can also include powers entrusted to constitutions and laws, whether federal, state, or local. Our allegiance to such impersonal forms of leadership, since they too come from God, should be at least as great as our allegiance to persons in power. However, in a nation of laws like ours, we have a greater allegiance to the laws of the land than to the persons empowered and sustained by God through those laws. For example, should a state executive leader, such as a governor, attempt to make law via endless executive orders contrary to that state's constitution, that governor stands in violation of state law and authority. Unless and until that governor has retracted his or her overreach of power or until the matter has been resolved by the legislative or judicial branches, the citizens of that state, including Christians, cannot remain silent in the face of such abuse. In disputes over laws or lawmaking between the executive and the legislative branches, the citizens have a duty to submit to the legislature (the lawmakers), not to the governor, unless some law expressly authorizes executive action or until the matter is resolved by the judiciary against the legislature. To do otherwise would constitute a violation of law and authority.

This does not mean that Christians should blindly accept constitutions and laws as absolute or flawless. For instance, should the US Constitution, the Supreme Law of the Land, become corrupted by sinister political interests and persons, citizens must turn to the one type of law which remains incorruptible and universally applicable to all humanity, namely the Natural Law. To understand the concept of Natural Law, it is necessary to briefly return to the ideas of Martin Luther and John Calvin. For Luther and Calvin, the Christian life ventures into two, distinct realms: The natural and the spiritual. The former deals with a person's life and citizenship in civil society while the latter deals with a person's spiritual life.[75] The former realm is governed by the Laws of Nature or Natural Law which includes the physical laws governing the universe and the moral laws governing the conscience.[76] Sir Edward Coke, an English Puritan whose works greatly influenced Thomas Jefferson, stated, 'The law of nature is that which God at the time of creation of the nature of man infused into his heart, for his preservation and direction; and this is lex aeterna [the eternal law]'.[77] Coke further asserted that Natural Law was 'infused into the heart of the creature at the time of his creation' and, therefore, takes precedence over all manmade laws and remains open to people of all faiths and creeds.[78] The Apostle Paul confirmed Coke's sentiments when he said, '[F]or when Gentiles, who do not have the law, by nature do the things in the law…show the work of the law written in their hearts, their conscience also bearing witness'.[79] Consequently, one does not need to be a Christian or a Jew to know that it is wrong to steal, to murder, or to defy one's parents.

Drawing on the ideas of Coke and Locke, Thomas Jefferson asserted in the Declaration that 'all men are created equal.'[80] This truth is 'self-evident' because it remains embedded in the 'Laws of Nature and Nature's God' which He has made known to all.[81] The most effective laws and constitutions are those established on such self-evident truths. Because the King and Parliament had refused to protect the rights of their American subjects, the British Constitution had been rendered ineffective as safeguards of freedom. The Americans had no choice but to appeal to a higher, eternal authority (Natural Law) in order to justify their resistance to British oppression. Likewise,

---

[75] Amos and Simon (n 8) 7.

[76] Ibid 8.

[77] Ibid 129-30.

[78] Ibid.

[79] Romans 2:14-15 NKJV.

[80] The Declaration of Independence (n 64) 5.

[81] Ibid.

should the US Constitution ever be altered or amended to include an immoral provision, we must submit to Natural Law as dictated by our consciences. For example, should Congress amend the Constitution to require the euthanization of all elderly citizens above a certain age, we cannot submit in good conscience because such a provision would violate the self-evident truth that all men and women are 'endowed by their Creator with certain unalienable Rights', including the right to 'Life, Liberty, and the pursuit of Happiness'.[82] As God informs all people of His eternal and omnipresent Natural Law, we ultimately need not rely on any official law or document to inform us that such a provision is wrong. Such things are written on our minds and hearts. Yes, we must honor the Constitution as the Supreme Law of the Land and all inferior laws passed thereunder but only when they accord with the 'self-evident' truths of Natural Law.[83] Our submission to the Constitution, like our submission to rulers, must be rooted in submission to a Higher Authority.

IX. THE DUTIES OF CHRISTIANS AS CITIZENS OF A CONSTITUTIONAL REPUBLIC

The distinction of leadership and authority places great responsibilities on Christians within a republic like ours wherein the US Constitution and all lesser laws reign supreme. First, as citizens within such a political setting, Christians are called to select leaders who will uphold the authorities that their Maker has placed over them, including the Constitution and all other laws of the land. Additionally, they must select leaders who will make and enforce laws for the general good of all. This requires no small amount of political research and, in some situations, activism on the part of the individual Christian. Note that this duty does not entail the Christianization of society, the establishment of a state church, or the dictation of official policy to the

---

[82] Ibid.

[83] Ibid.

State on the part of the Church. On the contrary, such attempts would constitute a violation of the First Amendment and would run afoul of the lessons of Scripture and history.[84] As Martin Luther observed,

> This is what commonly happens: The temporal lords want to rule the church, and conversely, the theologians want to play the lord in the town hall…. [T]his is ruling very badly…. Noblemen and young lords want to rule conscience and issue commands in the church. And someday, when the theologians get back on their feet, they will again take the sword from the temporal authorities.[85]

For the integrity of both institutions, the Church and the State must be kept separate and independent. However, this does not mean that the Church cannot make unofficial recommendations to the State and vice versa, nor does it mean that individual Christians cannot be involved in the affairs of the State as activists or as elected officials. On the contrary, history shows that the State generally benefits from Christian involvement as does society as a whole.

Second, Christians must know what their ultimate authority is. This requires a basic understanding of the Constitution and the separation of powers stated therein. While this may suggest the need for Christians to become experts in constitutional law, this assumption is false. Given the relatively simple framework of our Constitution's separation of powers and checks and balances, the average citizen does not need a law degree to understand the basic functionalities and boundaries of the governing branches. It does not take a legal expert to recognize that a president or governor making their own laws fundamentally violates the US Constitution and most, if not all, state constitutions. It does not require a brilliant legal mind to recognize that an infringement into a church's affairs constitutes a violation

---

[84] The Constitution of the United States of America (n 21) 56.

[85] Amos and Simon (n 8) 8.

of the First Amendment. Granted, not all constitutional disputes and violations are so straightforward. In more complex situations, Christians should follow in the footsteps of their fellow citizens and seek counsel from reputable lawyers and constitutional scholars.

Finally, and perhaps most importantly, as citizens of a Constitutional Republic, Christians have a duty to hold government accountable to its contract. Knowing how and when to perform this duty can be challenging and dangerous at times. Fortunately, our own history provides an ideal blueprint for us to follow. When challenging a government abuse, our first step should always entail seeking solutions through the law. This may entail petitioning the government to rescind its unlawful actions, requesting our elected representatives to stand up for their constituents' interests, or both. If all lawful attempts fail, the people must look to means outside the temporal laws, though never outside Natural Law. Such attempts must be handled with great care and prudence. For example, if the government forces its citizens to pay an illegal tax, the first stage of rebellion should be a peaceful course of action, such as refusing to pay the tax, while simultaneously negotiating with government officials towards some reconciliation. In the end, the proper severity of the people's response to their leaders depends on the severity and level of lawlessness within their leaders' actions.

In many ways, this hypothetical follows the pattern of our nation's Founding. George III continually allowed laws and taxes to be passed without the consent of the people and abused the Americans for standing up for their lawful rights. Moreover, the king denied his American subjects their right to representation in government, both at home and abroad. Nevertheless, the Americans initially sought relatively peaceful solutions to the Crown's abuses. True, when one examines certain events of the time, such as the Boston Massacre, it becomes clear that not all Americans sought peaceful solutions in their disputes with Britain. Regardless, for nearly a decade, many thousands of Americans nobly endured the harshness of British rule and pursued reconciliation with the mother country via petitions and means within the law. In the end, it was the king's troops, not the Americans, who initiated the bloodshed when redcoats attempted to seize colonial arms at Concord. Even after the first blood had been shed, it took a whole year before the American leaders voted to separate from Britain.

As our Founders stated in the Declaration, people are not permitted to rebel against their government whenever it does something the majority disagrees with. Doing so would only end in anarchy, the very thing that government has been commissioned by God through the people and the law to counter. Such an overreaction to unpopular government action would violate the boundaries of authority. For example, when the government issues a tax within the proper constitutional and legal channels, the rulers have acted within their lawful authority and, therefore, we have no choice but to pay the tax for the time being. When the time comes, we can always elect new leadership more sensitive to our sentiments and needs. But whenever a government acts outside the law, whether it be Natural Law, the Constitution, or any lower law, we must remain loyal to the law by holding government accountable. Still, we must always keep in mind that any kind of resistance to leadership, even passive disobedience, is a very grave undertaking. We resist leadership only when leadership acts outside authority, whether accidentally or intentionally, in the hopes that our leaders will see the error of their ways and restore peace and order for the common good. Thus, resistance to leadership should always arise from compassion and never from personal vengeance.

X.   SUMMARY AND CONCLUSION

In summary, the kind of power the absolute submissionist believers seek to grant their rulers is power that no mortal ruler could ever hope to wield. On a practical level, it is impossible for a single mind, no matter how enlightened or knowledgeable, to comprehend, let alone govern, the vast resources and complexities of society in a truly efficient manner. The growing complexity of modern society renders such governance progressively unrealistic. On a moral level, such Christians forget that all human leaders are just that, human. Like us, they are imperfect by nature. It has been said that '[a]ll power tends to corrupt; absolute power corrupts absolutely.'[86] Even the noblest Christian rulers are not immune from this unpleasant reality. Absolute power corrupts even the kindest of hearts and the best of intentions. Most concerning of all, the kind of power that the submissionists seek to grant their rulers is a type that God Himself has not entrusted them with. Even rulers who claim to hold absolute power remain limited by God's Law, which, in His wisdom and grace, He wrote on the minds and hearts of all Adam's sons and daughters, Christian and non-Christian.

Without Natural Law, humanity would have no sense of right or wrong upon which to forge societies or offices of authority. Without Natural Law, humanity could write neither constitutions nor laws to hold persons in power accountable to their purpose of being a force for good rather than evil. Beyond such limits, a ruler has no authority. As Samuel Rutherford rightly observed, there is no such thing as a legitimate absolute ruler or tyrant. There is only one King worthy to wield absolute power, Jesus Christ, the Man who never knew sin. Therefore, it is to Him alone that we render absolute allegiance. Whenever any earthly ruler demands such submission from us, as Christians, our allegiance to our Savior demands that we submit to His rule, not to man's.

In conclusion then, there are only two ways to interpret Romans 13:1-7. If authority and leadership are the same, the wording of the passage gives us no choice but to render absolute submission to our leaders, given that we must submit without question to all persons in power under such an interpretation. Consequently, all impersonal

---

[86] Ben Moreell, 'Power Corrupts', *Acton Institute* (Web Article, 20 July 2021).

rulers, including laws and constitutions, are meaningless; the people have no rights beyond the will of their rulers; verses like Acts 5:29 are ultimately false; and our nation's entire Founding rests upon lies.[87]

The only alternative interpretation rests on the assertion that authority and leadership are distinct concepts. Within such an interpretation, the notion of an absolute leader is a human myth and our rightful submission to leadership remains limited, not absolute. If this view of Romans 13 is correct, we submit to leadership only when our leaders act within the lawful confines and powers of their offices. Whenever a ruler steps outside the authority that God has entrusted to him or her, we can neither submit nor remain silent lest we join in their petty rebellion against authority and against God. In the Constitutional Republic of the United States, our allegiance to authority is as follows: First we submit to God and His Natural Law; second, to the US Constitution and state constitutions; third, to the laws of the land (federal, state, and local); and fourth, to all ruling persons.

Whenever any ruler violates this God-given hierarchy of authority either by violating or corrupting the US Constitution or any other temporal law or by violating Natural Law, peaceful resistance on the part of the citizens, including Christians, becomes an unfortunate but necessary duty. The question is not whether Christians have a right to peacefully resist leadership, but when. The answer is both simple and profound. Christian rebellion against leadership becomes permissible only when it becomes necessary. Rebellion only becomes necessary when rulers usurp power beyond their lawful limits as established by God via higher authorities. In the end, all justified rebellions against leadership remain rooted in allegiance to God, the one true Absolute Ruler. Without authority, there are no rulers and without God, there is no authority.

---

[87] The Declaration of Independence (n 64) 5.

This article is not intended to encourage presently disgruntled citizens to take up arms against their leaders. One way or another, such an undertaking would inevitably lead to tragedy for all concerned. Rather, it is an attempt to instruct my readers on a more historically and biblically accurate understanding of the fundamental relationship between leadership and authority. Like it or not, this distinction remains deeply embedded in America's founding principles; in its laws and institutions; in its rich Judeo-Christian heritage; and in our immortal legacy as citizens of this great nation.

2

Law and Reality: A Dialogue Between Herman Dooyeweerd and John Finnis

RENATO S M COSTA*

ABSTRACT

Herman Dooyeweerd and John Finnis are two legal philosophers from distinct Christian traditions. Chiefly due to the differences between their theological viewpoints, their theories have not been compared much. In this article, I propose an exchange between the two philosophers' legal theories. I believe there are similarities in their general conceptions of law and how they reason about the interplay between law and reality. Each has developed an all-encompassing philosophical system that has the idea of law as a cornerstone. When dialogue between their theories is achieved, at least at the theoretical level, it is possible to see how they share similar foundations in developing their own idea of law. In this article, I propose such dialogue and demonstrate what these theoretical grounds are. There are more similarities in Dooyeweerd's and Finnis's theories than first meets the eyes.

I. INTRODUCTION

Herman Dooyeweerd and John Finnis are two law theorists from distinct Christian traditions. Mainly due to their divergencies in

* Lecturer in Law, TC Beirne School of Law, The University of Queensland. The author wishes to thank Professors Alan Cameron, Chris Gousmett, and Nicholas Aroney for commenting on earlier drafts of this paper.

terms of theological convictions, their philosophies have not been subject to many comparisons. The time has come for this scenario to change. In this article, I propose an exchange between these two grand philosophers. Such an attempt sets aside the often-mentioned disparities regarding the theology that underlies their theories. It also does not take sides on their views about the direct influence of God or the 'divine law' in their theories. Instead, the article shows how their philosophies of law intersect in more ways than first meets the eyes.

The intent of this article is to facilitate our comprehension of law and legal systems generally. The comparison here promoted does not reflect an attempt of clustering different theories together. Identifying the similarities between Dooyeweerd's and Finnis's theories is nothing more than promoting cooperation to facilitate the legal theorist's understanding of law. That is the reason for limiting the scope of this study.

Any comparison between philosophies needs a standpoint. The place where I stand in relation to both philosophers is that of a legal theorist. It is thus from such a theoretical standpoint that I identify the intersections between Dooyeweerd's and Finnis's jurisprudence. This is a theoretical exercise purposefully limited in scope.

Both philosophers have a complete philosophical system. They have woven their law theories in a broader theoretical framework that considers epistemological, ethical, and metaphysical formulations. They both search for truth and pursue knowledge. And, in doing so, they both analyse the meaning and purpose of law. Such comprehensive philosophies enable us to endeavour a comparison – albeit a preliminary one – that considers the similarities in their legal theories.

Dooyeweerd's and Finnis's philosophies share the understanding that reality is not fully appreciated or investigated by the theoretical sciences. There is an all-encompassing, totalising dimension to human experiences that fall outside of the specific study of the theorist of a particular science. Theoretical knowledge focuses only on one of the multiple dimensions of life. Theoretical analysis of, say, the law, therefore, deals with only a small portion of the many aspects of reality. As such, the sciences tend to be reductionist. 'Reductionist' not necessarily in the pejorative sense but as a statement about the reductive understanding of the broader, more comprehensive aspectual reality. In asserting a multi-modal framework of human life and experience, both philosophers urge descriptive theorists to analyse all kinds of phenomena – including the legal ones – externally, that is, by using a viewpoint outside of the internal standpoint of their own theoretical sciences.

Dooyeweerd and Finnis assert that their external viewpoints can untangle the many aspects of reality or the domains according to which speculative reasoning is expressed. For Dooyeweerd, the appropriate viewpoint is the 'supratheoretical' attitude of social philosophy. For Finnis, it is the viewpoint of practical reasonableness. The intriguing similarities in their legal philosophies that flow from there reveal how both achieved a non-reductionist concept of the law. Dooyeweerd and Finnis have formulated their respective, all-inclusive legal philosophies without the reductionist 'isms' typical of the theoretical sciences. There are many correlative tenets in their theories concerning the concept of law.

When we achieve a dialogue between Dooyeweerd and Finnis, it becomes easy to see how different Christian traditions share similar grounds in their view about law. Further, and more importantly, it becomes plausible to associate different law claims in cooperation and coherence, making of it an even stronger argument against a non-reductionist understanding of law. In this article, I propose such a dialogue.

In Part II, I introduce Dooyeweerd's philosophy and explain his modality-based theory of reality. The jural aspect informs the meaning and purpose of law according to Dooyeweerd's philosophy. In Part III, I endeavour to present Finnis's theory of law. Drawing from Thomas Aquinas, Finnis understands law as an instantiation of practical reasonableness that pervades what he calls the four domains of reality. These domains correlate with Dooyeweerd's order of the modal aspects. Thus, in Part IV, I compare the two philosophies of law in these intersection points. Finally, in Part V, I briefly discuss the theological presuppositions of each philosopher and indicate some more areas of potential convergence in their jurisprudence.

II. Dooyeweerd's Concept of Law

Dooyeweerd developed a law and state theory that presupposed God's sovereignty over all spheres of life. His theory is known as the 'Philosophy of the Cosmonomic Idea', which philosophically systematised a worldview commonly named 'sphere sovereignty'.[1]

In general terms, sphere sovereignty is a social theory that places the State in equal position to all other civil associations.[2] The straightforward implication of such a theory is that the State, one of the many spheres of life, is sovereign in a defined territory, and its head has authority over the people of that same territory, but only to a certain extent. The State is limited to act only in particular matters. It has specific attributions and limits, which should prevent it from encroaching on other spheres.[3]

When it comes to Dooyeweerd's cosmonomic philosophy, one finds that each sphere has an individual structure. This justifies the impossibility of one sphere indistinctly mingling with another. Dooyeweerd affirms that each thing or phenomena has a specific

---

[1] Renato Saeger Magalhães Costa, 'A Sphere Sovereignty Theory of the State: Looking Back and Looking Forward' (2019) 3(1) (August) *International and Public Affairs* 13.

[2] Abraham Kuyper, 'Sphere Sovereignty', Speech at the inauguration of the Free University, Amsterdam, 8 March 1880.

3 Abraham Kuyper, *Lectures on Calvinism* [1931] (Cosimo Classics, 2009).

internal structure dictated by what he calls the modal aspects.[4] Entities have a particular structure determined by their own set of rules, unique for each of them. For Dooyeweerd, different modal aspects constitute the rules of each of these individuality-structures. Thus, no individuality-structure will have the same typical modal grouping.[5] To maintain a structural coherence, each entity has a particular 'set of laws' in its intrinsic nature, and these laws are distinct from the laws of another individuality-structure.

Each entity has two functions defined by two modal aspects. On the one hand, there is the formative or foundational function, which is the fundamental modality without which the sphere would not exist. On the other, the leading or qualifying function that guides how each sphere must perform.[6] A particular individuality-structure, therefore, will be uniquely defined by its foundational and leading functions.[7]

Dooyeweerd's is a theory that depends upon a more profound understanding of reality. The reality, according to Dooyeweerd, is construed by multiple modalities. Each modal aspect that forms the internal laws of an individuality-structure represents a particular aspect of human life.[8] That is why Dooyeweerd calls it the 'laws-spheres' or 'cosmonomic'; it pertains to the universal laws of reality.[9] It is through law-spheres, the cosmonomic way, that reality functions.

---

[4] Herman Dooyeweerd, *A New Critique of Theoretical Thought* (tr David Freeman and H De Jongste) (Paideia Press, 1984) vol III ('*NC*').

[5] Herman Dooyeweerd, *Encyclopedia of the Science of Law*, tr Robert D Knudsen, ed Alan M Cameron (Paideia Press, 2012) 27 ('*Encyclopedia*').

[6] Dooyeweerd, *NC* (n 4) 58-63.

[7] Dooyeweerd, *Encyclopedia* (n 5) 209.

[8] Herman Dooyeweerd, *Roots of Western Culture*, tr John Kraay, eds Mark Vander and Bernard Zylstra, DFM Strauss) (Paideia Press, 2012) 49 ('*Roots*').

[9] 'From the start, I have introduced the Dutch term *wetsidee (idea legis)* for the transcendental ground-Idea or basic Idea of philosophy. The best English term corresponding to it seems to be "Cosmonomic Idea", since the word "law" used without further specification would evoke a special juridical sense which, of course, cannot be meant here.': Dooyeweerd, *NC* (n 4) 93-94.

Dooyeweerd lists 15 modal aspects: Quantitative, Spatial, Kinematic, Physical, Biotic/Organic, Sensitive/Psychic, Analytical, Formative, Lingual, Social, Economic, Aesthetic, Juridical, Ethical/ Attitudinal, Pistic/Faith.[10] And they have a particular temporal order of succession. There is an interrelationship of foundational and anticipatory dependency between them. For Dooyeweerd, the later aspects depend on the former, and the former anticipate characteristics of the latter.

Therefore, in Dooyeweerd's terms, it is possible to identify not only the social structures but also events and non-human beings through engaging with and relating these modalities. Take a tree, for example. It functions as a subject in the quantitative modal aspect (for we refer to it as one, countable tree), the spatial modality (because of its height, density, volume), the kinematic aspect (ie the branches move and the tree grows), the physical aspect (the tree as an 'energy-mass'),[11] and the biotic modal aspect (it produces oxygen, it is alive, etc). It does not go beyond the fifth modal aspect, for a tree, as a subject, does not have feelings (sensitive) or conceptualises and categorises things (analytical), creates (formative) or expresses anything (lingual).

However, trees can have an economic value. Or be an object of the jural modality in, for example, a neighbours' dispute over the tree's fruits. This is because trees, as any other individuality-structure, will function in the modal aspects as objects as well as subjects. Non-human entities do not function as subjects in all the modal aspects of reality. Humans, however, can function in what are called the 'normative' aspects as subjects. From the analytical aspect onwards, non-humans will only function as objects.

In sum, Dooyeweerd sees an aspectual coherence in the relationship between, and operation of, the modal aspects in the temporal order.

---

[10] After him, some other scholars have built upon this list to either expand or reduce it – but this discussion goes beyond the intent of the present article.

[11] Dooyeweerd, *Encyclopedia* (n 5) 23.

MODAL ASPECT	GROUPS OF ASPECTS
Quantitative	Determinative or Non-Normative Aspects
Spatial	
Kinematic	
Physical	
Biotic / Organic	
Sensitive / Psychic	
Analytical / Logical	Normative Aspects
Formative	
Lingual	
Social	
Economic	
Aesthetic	
Juridical	
Ethical	
Pistic / Faith	

The different modalities are the interdependent aspects of reality that form our concrete (either as subjects or objects) experiences.

To talk about modalities, in Dooyeweerd's philosophy, then, is to refer to the irreducible aspects of the practical reality that make up everything that one can experience. However, one does not always perceive these aspects as neatly and fragmentedly as Dooyeweerd has described. As he advises, 'one is familiar with these aspects only indirectly in everyday life, where we experience them by way of the individual totalities of concrete things, events, social relations etc.'[12] Things and social structures are conceived immediately, in their unity 'in which of these aspects are presented as an unbroken coherence' without any separated analysis.[13] This is why Dooyeweerd distinguishes reality into two main forms of experiences ('two types of structure within our temporal reality').[14] There is, first, the naïve or ordinary experience. Through the naïve experience, one experiences reality in its totality. It is the day-by-day approach to life. The second, the theoretical or scientific experience, is the experience where phenomena and subjects are dealt with analytically. It occurs when the observer analyses things in more detail. Using a helpful simile, Dooyeweerd says the reality is like a beam of light that refracts into the rainbow's hue when it passes through a prism.[15] At first glance, in an ordinary experience, one sees things and social structures in totality as concrete beings or events (like the beam of light). However, with more trained eyes, and if one is interested in looking further into the composition of the thing ('theoretical experience'), it will be possible to identify, in the case of a beam of light, the wealth of colours and the diversity of lights in that unity. Thus, 'it is only in the scientific, theoretical attitude of knowing whereby the aspects of

---

[12] Herman Dooyeweerd, *In the Twilight of Western Thought*, ed. James KA Smith (Paideia Press, 2012) 44 ('*Twilight*').

[13] Dooyeweerd, *Encyclopedia* (n 5) 23.

[14] Dooyeweerd, *Twilight* (n 12) 44.

[15] Ibid 8, 41.

reality are individually analyzed and distinguished from each other that the possibility of the separate special sciences arises'.[16] That brings us to the juridical (or jural) modal aspect.

In his or her scientific capacity, the jurist views full reality from the standpoint of the jural aspect of reality. He or she studies how reality functions, both subjectively and objectively, from within the jural aspect. The reason is simple: in scientific investigation, an appeal to the ordinary experience of reality, in order to defend a particular theoretical view, has no apparent meaning.[17] When facing the paradigms of the sciences, the observer shifts his or her lenses from naïve to theoretical hence 'appealing to a coherence of reality which they have already broken up into its aspects'.[18] But there is a caveat:

> As scientists, they must keep in mind that the reality which has been theoretically analyzed in this fashion is no longer the reality which presents itself to them in ordinary experiencing, but is, on the contrary, a theoretical view of reality. This view, if it is truly to be a view of reality, cannot limit itself to theoretical insight into a particular aspect; it must always be a view of reality within the structure of the mutual interrelationships of its aspects.[19]

What does Dooyeweerd mean when he says that the theoretical attitude compels one to consider only one aspect of reality, but that the true comprehensive view of reality demands from that same observer a consideration about the mutual interrelationship of the many modal aspects? First, if Dooyeweerd's 15 modal aspects are ordered in a cohesive ontic interlacement of retrocipation and anticipation,[20] and if they are irreducible to each other, then to affirm the existence of the

---

[16] Dooyeweerd, *Encyclopedia* (n 5) 23.

[17] Ibid

[18] Ibid 24.

[19] Ibid

[20] Ibid 103.

juridical aspect is to say it must relate in some form of dependency to the previous modal aspects of reality. Previous modalities cannot be reduced to the jural aspect, and neither can the latter be wholly dispersed in the former. For Dooyeweerd, the later modal aspects in the order (say, the social modality) is intertwined with the previous ones (say, lingual, physical, and quantitative aspects) in a relationship of foundational dependency (the later modality is facilitated by the former), and with the next ones (say, faith) in a relationship of anticipatory dependency (the potential to facilitate the meaning of later modalities).[21] Perhaps put more clearly: the jural modal aspect connects with other modalities that come before it (quantitative, spatial, kinematic, physical, biotic, sensitive, analytical, formative, lingual, social, economic, aesthetic) because those modalities anticipate the jural aspect.

Scientific descriptions tend to consider the primacy of the individual aspect that concerns the specific area of investigation. Scientists pick one of the modalities as paramount over the others and use it as a standpoint according to which the other modal aspects will be assessed. The tendency, then, is to absolutize one modality over the other. However, to equate the theoretical abstraction of one single modality with 'true reality' would be to dissolve the boundaries of ordinary experience and transgress the special sciences themselves.[22] Hence the mistake of, for example, saying that 'everything is language'. This is an example of a reductionist account of the reality that Dooyeweerd rejects. Indeed, it is the absolutization of a modality over all other modal aspects that Dooyeweerd interprets as an incoherent view of reality.

Instead of isolating one modal aspect from the rest of the temporal order or giving an absolute prevalence of one modality over the other (reducing one to another), the theorist must not ignore the pervading relationship between their object of study and the modalities that

---

[21] Ibid 103-104.

[22] Ibid 25.

anticipate and retrocipate them. Thus, a descriptive theorist in law must consider the conception of law not exclusively in itself, from the standpoint of the jural aspect only. The legal sciences (the study that gives primacy to the jural modality)[23] should cohesively relate the jural aspect to the other modal aspects of reality.[24] To reduce the other modal aspects to the jural one is to dissolve the multi-modal reality.

Those who intend to define the law ought to consider it in relation to the multiplicity of the modalities that anticipate and retrocipate the jural aspect. A genuine science of law must account for the jural aspect in its connections to all the other modal aspects. A concept of law that disregards all the modal aspects of reality will fail to express what the law really is. Indeed, there is no purely *jural reality*, only a jural *aspect* of reality:[25]

> The science of law ought not to allow itself to be satisfied with such purely practical criteria if it is to continue making the claim of being scientific. The basic concept of law ought to be conceived in such a fashion that it indeed gives a theoretical account of the relationship and mutual coherence of the legal with the nonjural aspects of reality, and for this purpose, … a philosophical ground-idea is a prerequisite.[26]

The second reason why Dooyeweerd says that the full comprehension of reality demands an evaluation of all modal aspects relates to his rejection of deriving *ought* from *is*. Although he is not explicit about this in these terms, his legal theory entails a necessary dependence of reality on a normative experience. Dooyeweerd says that it is philosophy's role to grasp the aspects 'in their deeper

---

[23] The exchangeable use of *legal sciences*, *law* and *jural aspect* is not to say they are the same thing. However, it is to assert that they are intrinsically related. See: Dooyeweerd, *Encyclopedia* (n 5) 197.

[24] Ibid 104-105.

[25] Ibid 205.

[26] Ibid 89.

unity and in their mutual coherence'.[27] The science of law and the definition of law cannot be considered a theoretical science without grasping beyond the jural aspect of reality; without attaining certain philosophical presuppositions (embedded in the analysis of the non-jural modal aspects of reality).[28] This is the role of true philosophy.[29] It provides a viewpoint 'on the basis of which we can conceive the aspects in their deeper root-unity'.[30] True philosophy needs a starting point of view above the aspects that have been theoretically set apart.[31] For Dooyeweerd, theoretical analysis and synthesis are impossible without such a viewpoint.[32]

Dooyeweerd finds that current concepts of law are inadequate because of their theorist's viewpoint (which he calls the 'Archimedean point'). Dooyeweerd chooses his Archimedean Point from the 'supratheoretical' experience, within the ground-motive of the Creation-Fall-Redemption in Jesus Christ.[33] This, in his perspective, shields him from antinomies and allows for an external standpoint that can analyze and synthesize the theoretical experience without reductionisms.

---

[27] Ibid 33. This conclusion is part of Dooyeweerd's answer to the 'first transcendental basic problem of any conceivable philosophic system': at 26-34. The 'second basic problem' is what Dooyeweerd calls the Archimedean Point: the viewpoint that makes theoretical synthesis initially possible: at 34-37.

[28] Dooyeweerd, *Encyclopedia* (n 5) 85.

[29] Dooyeweerd, *NC* (n 4) vol I, 542.

[30] Dooyeweerd, *Encyclopedia* (n 5) 90.

[31] Ibid 35.

[32] Ibid 90.

[33] 'Supratheoretical' is the *a priori* attitude that surpasses the temporal experience and allows for a big-picture appreciation of reality. The 'ground-motives' are the four types of worldviews that Dooyeweerd identifies in his philosophy as driving forces in history and theoretical thought. The only 'ground-motive' in his account that does not fall into contradiction is the Christian ground-motive anchored in the biblical narrative of the Creation of the world by God, the Fall of humankind into sin, and the Redemption that Jesus Christ provided through his death on the cross. (Dooyeweerd, *Twilight* (n 12) 3-19, 30-32; Dooyeweerd, *Roots* (n 8) 9-15, 28-39; Dooyeweerd, *Encyclopedia* (n 5) 47-48, 58-61).

For Dooyeweerd, legal theory is filled with immanent viewpoints that ultimately produce reductionist theoretical accounts of reality. The fact that their chosen viewpoint stands within, and not outside of, the (cosmonomic) modal reality – such as his – prevents legal theorists from grasping the fullness of our practical reality:

> If the choice of the Archimedean point is now immanent to theoretical thought, then the basic denominator of the aspects must be sought within a theoretical synthesis. And because theoretical synthesis itself is always of a specific character – depending on the aspect towards which it directs theoretical thought with its logical concept-forming – a particular synthetically conceived aspect will be elevated to be the basic denominator for all the rest.[34]

Jurists tend to adopt reductionist viewpoints in their definitions of law. This is the problem with Kelsen and Savigny.[35] For Kelsen, it was the logic modal aspect. For Savigny, the social modality. It is the adoption of these reductionist views that create the 'isms' in the special sciences more generally and in legal theory more specifically.[36]

One may ask: What is the benefit that Dooyeweerd's viewpoint brings to the science of law? And, notably, what is his definition of law? Dooyeweerd's law concept emanates from his understanding of the jural aspect of reality in coherence with its analogical modalities. 'In particular', as Alan Cameron says, 'it is the analogies within the jural aspect pointing back to earlier aspects founded in the cosmic order of time ("retrocipations") that provide the datum for ... the full concept of law'.[37] For Dooyeweerd, the jural modality pertains to the

---

[34] Dooyeweerd (n 5) 90.

[35] Ibid 91.

[36] Dooyeweerd, *NC* (n 4) vol I, 46; Dooyeweerd, *Encyclopedia* (n 5) 36, 90.

[37] Alan Cameron, 'Between Norm and Fact: The Jurisprudence of Herman Dooyeweerd' (Unpublished work, Australian National University, *Annual Conference of the Australian Society of Legal Philosophy*, 2000) 11 ('Norm and Fact').

notion of 'retribution'.[38] It consists, broadly speaking, of a 'juridical meaning of legal justice'.[39] It relates to the classical formulation of *suum cuique tribuere*.[40] In his conception of law, one that observes the jural aspect in coherence with the other analogical modalities, the jural modal aspect consists of balancing and harmonising legal interests.[41] The jural modality is:

> an irreducible mode of balancing and harmonising individual and social interests. This mode implies a standard of proportionality regulating the legal interpretation of social facts and their factual social consequences in order to maintain the juridical balance by a just reaction, viz. the so-called legal consequences of the fact related to a juridical ground.[42]

Dooyeweerd's definition of the jural aspect implies the analogical dependency of other aspects. Jonathan Chaplin's opinion is that, when referring to 'balancing', for example, Dooyeweerd is appealing to the economic aspect.[43] For Cameron, in using 'harmonizing', Dooyeweerd refers to the aesthetic aspect of reality in an analogical sense.[44] The same happens with any other modal aspect that anticipates the jural modality. Notwithstanding, it is advised that 'whilst an account of the

---

[38] Dooyeweerd, *NC* (n 4) vol I, 129-130. Later, Dooyeweerd recognises that the term *retribution* is not ideal for summarising the nuclear moment of the juridical aspect. But he does not propose and alternative: Herman Dooyeweerd, 'Die Philosophie der Gesetzidee und ihre Bedeutung für die Rechts-und Sozialphilosophie', *Archiv für Rechts- und Sozialphilosophie* (1967) 1–30, 465–513, *apud* Jonathan Chaplin, *Herman Dooyeweerd: Christian Philosopher of State and Civil Society* (Notre Dame University Press, 2011) 192.

[39] Alan Cameron, 'Dooyeweerd on Law and Morality: Legal Ethics – A Test Case' (1998) 28(1) *Victoria University of Wellington Law Review* 266 ('Law and Morality').

[40] In English, 'To give each their due': Dooyeweerd, *NC* (n 4) vol II, 132.

[41] Ibid 134.

[42] Ibid 129.

[43] Jonathan Chaplin, *Herman Dooyeweerd: Christian Philosopher of State and Civil Society* (Notre Dame University Press, 2011)189.

[44] Cameron, 'Law and Morality' (n 39) 267.

jural aspect necessarily appeals to its constituent analogical elements, its core meaning is not reducible to any one of them or even to all of them together'.[45]

For Dooyeweerd, there is a necessary relationship between the concept of law (as the kernel of the jural aspect) and the list of modalities of reality.[46] Notably, the definition of law ought to consider the meaning of the jural modal aspect and its integration with the other modalities. Law can be defined, therefore, as the 'heteronomous-normative ordering of community'.[47]

III. Finnis's Concept of Law

Finnis is a Roman Catholic scholar whose studies encompass, but are not limited to, the relationship between law and morality. His legal philosophy follows the Thomistic-Aristotelian tradition. Much of the current dissemination of the classic natural law theory of law, and the re-emergence of the debate between law and morality is owed to Finnis.

Law, for Finnis, is a consequence of human nature. The proper understanding of the law, or the nature of law, cannot be detached from the broader understanding of human nature because 'law has the nature it has because human persons have the nature they have'.[48] He is not Augustinian in the sense that laws result from the fallibility of individuals and exist to mitigate human corruption.[49] Instead, he is

---

[45] Cameron, 'Norm and Fact' (n 36) 15.

[46] Ibid 12 n 61.

[47] Herman Dooyeweerd, 'Calvinism and Natural Law' [1925]), in Herman Dooye-weerd, tr John Witte Jr and Alan M Cameron, ed DFM Strauss, *Essays in Legal, Social and Political Philosophy* (Paideia Press, 2012) 21 ('Calvinism').

[48] John Finnis, 'The Nature of Law' in John Tasioulas (ed), *The Cambridge Companion to the Philosophy of Law* (Cambridge University Press, 2020) 57 ('Nature of Law').

[49] Although Finnis assesses that 'Natural law theories all understand law as a remedy against the great evils of, on the one side anarchy (lawlessness), and on the other side tyranny. And one of tyranny's characteristic forms is the co-optation of law as a mask for fundamentally lawless decisions cloaked in the forms of law and legality.': John Finnis, 'Natural Law Theories', *Stanford Encyclopedia of Philosophy* (Stanford University, 2015) ('Theories').

aligned with Thomas Aquinas's teachings that law exists and takes shape as a form of communal coordination.

For Aquinas, authority is necessary for the coordination of individuals and groups towards their common purpose.[50] Finnis explains that authority is one of two ways (unanimity being the other) to make 'a choice between alternatives of co-ordinating action to the common purpose or common good of any group'.[51] Authority provides sufficient reasons for a person to believe and act towards something.[52] Authority is required for the realisation of the common good of the people in a particular state.[53] Aquinas affirmed that 'everything that man is naturally inclined to, reason naturally understands as good and so as to be pursued by action'.[54] This means that the instantiation of the common good is related to the exercise of (legal) authority.[55] For Finnis, laws are authoritative (at least if they promote or secure justice),[56] and their justice depends on how the rulers balance the benefits and burdens within a community.[57]

Law, in Finnis teleology, is an aspect of the pursuit of the common good.[58] It 'is a modality of authority, available in specifically political

---

[50] John Finnis, *Aquinas: Moral, Political, and Legal Theory* (Oxford University Press, 1998) 35-37. ('*Aquinas*').

[51] John Finnis, *Natural Law and Natural Rights* (Oxford University Press, 2nd ed, 2005), 232 ('*NLNR*').

[52] Ibid 233.

[53] Ibid 246.

[54] '*Omnia illa ad quae homo habet naturalem inclinationem, ratio naturaliter appre-hendit ut bona, et per consequens ut opere prosequenda, et contraria eorum ut mala et vitanda*': Thomas Aquinas, tr Fathers of the English Dominican Province, *Summa Theologica*, (1485) I-II, q 94 ('*Summa Theologica*'); John Finnis, *Reason in Action: Collective Essays* (Oxford University Press, 2011) vol 1, 145). Aquinas seems to follow the Aristotelian tag 'the good is what all things desire': Finnis (n 50) 70-71. See also: Finnis, *Aquinas* (n 50) 255.

[55] For an analysis of this claim, see chapter 6 of Jonathan Crowe, *Natural Law and the Nature of Law* (Cambridge University Press, 2019).

[56] Finnis, *NLNR* (n 51) 260.

[57] Ibid 263.

[58] Ibid.

communities'.[59] It lays down a common standard of action, 'not merely for the avoidance of evils but also in the pursuit of goods.'[60] As Finnis concludes, laws relate the reasons for action and the actions themselves.[61] So, if they are authoritative and just, laws will authoritatively tend towards, or direct to, the common good of a particular community.

In his definition, Aquinas says that laws are a set of promulgated principles of practical reason that inform what actions ought to be pursued towards a perfect community's common good.[62] More precisely, law is 'an ordinance of reason for the common good, made by him who has care of the community, and promulgated'.[63] In other words, Aquinas says that the law consists of the 'practical propositions conceived in the reason of the ruler(s) and communicated to the reason of the ruled so that the latter will treat those propositions, at least presumptively, as reasons for action'.[64] Law, therefore, consists of principles of reason 'that direct us to understand and pursue, coherently, the flourishing of all human persons and communities with reasonable prioritizing and essential respect for persons in each basic aspect of their flourishing – each basic human good'.[65] Only through an exercise of evaluation and understanding of the basic goods one could achieve practical reasonableness, which is foundational to what law is. Law and legal systems, Finnis says, would be better understood if regarded as a set of 'principles, norms and institutions adopted by a people extended in time and in

---

[59] John Finnis, 'Natural Law Theory: Its Past and Present' (2012) 57 *The American Journal of Jurisprudence* 81, 100 ('Past and Present').

[60] John Finnis, *Reason in Action: Collective Essays* (Oxford University Press, 2011) ('*Reason*').

[61] Ibid 105.

[62] Thomas Aquinas, *Summa Theologica* I-II, q 90-108.

[63] Ibid I-II, q 90.4.

[64] Finnis, 'Theories' (n 49).

[65] Finnis, 'Nature of Law' (n 48) 51-52.

48   THE WESTERN AUSTRALIAN JURIST

territorial bounds, in more or less adequate fulfilment of its moral responsibility to do so'.[66]

It is common that, when having their ordinary experiences, individuals do not analyse events through the lenses of a theorist. Individuals do not perceive all phenomena as law-phenomena. People tend to see the world in totalities, as whole things and events. What Dooyeweerd calls the naïve experience resembles this so-called 'awareness'[67] that Finnis says individuals have in assimilating reality *as it is*. Germain Grisez, who has had a significant influence on Finnis's philosophy,[68] attributes to Aquinas the perception that there is a certain order of preference in individuals' understanding of the world.[69] This order is perceived in two distinct ways: by theoretical or speculative[70] knowledge (which is the reasoning about what already *is* – ie *scientia*) and practical knowledge (which consists of the reasoning about what *ought to be*).[71] The first is a description of reality according to what is known. The second is the result of the mind questioning the practical reality and directing action towards adding to and instantiating the intelligibility of the good known through theoretical knowledge.[72] In

---

[66] John Finnis, 'What is the Philosophy of Law?' (2014) 59(2) *The American Journal of Jurisprudence* 133, 142 ('What is?').

[67] Finnis, *Reason* (n 60) 32.

[68] Finnis, *NLNR* (n 51) vii.

[69] Germain Grisez, 'First Principle of Practical Reason: A Commentary on the Summa Theologiae, 1-2, Question 94, Article 2' (1965) *Natural Law Forum* 107, 168, 170.

[70] 'using the term "speculative" here, not to make the Aristotelian distinction between the *theoretike ̄* and the *praktike ̄*, but to distinguish knowledge as sought for its own sake from knowledge as sought only instrumentally, i.e. as useful in the pursuit of some other objective…': Finnis, *NLNR* (n 51) 39.

[71] According to the Thomistic tradition of natural law, the first principle of practical reason(ableness) is that *good is to be done and pursued, and evil is to be avoided*. This principle does not limit what the 'good' is, but establishes that all action is directed towards an end. The epistemic axiom that comes out of this principle is that the *ought* is never derivable from *is*. It means that the nature of a thing is found first in the study of its objects or purposes: Finnis, *Reason* (n 60) 32-33, 146-148.

[72] John Finnis, Germain Grisez and Joseph Boyle, 'Practical Principles, Moral Truth & Ultimate Ends' (1987) 32 *The American Journal of Jurisprudence* 99, 115-117; Grisez (n 69) 175-176, 179.

sum, practical reason directs how an individual will interpret their reality-experience by having a prescriptive attitude. Practical reason is the mind prescribing what ought to be done in a particular scenario.[73] While speculative knowledge provides understanding according to what already *is*, practical reason goes beyond, prescribing what *ought to be*, according to a thing's purposes.

Finnis builds on Grisez's explanation to say that human reason is still one and complete. There is 'only one human intellectual potency or faculty, and that the differences between speculative and practical reason are differences between intellectual operations with differing objectives.'[74] For him, 'there are paradigm cases of purely speculative and purely practical intellectual activity but most actual reasoning is *both* speculative *and* practical'.[75]

It is interesting to realise that Dooyeweerd and Finnis share a similar starting line in their legal theories. When it comes to the description of law, they agree that the observer (in this case, the jurist) must consider his or her conceptions in light of a more extensive reality than that of his or her particular theoretical domain.[76] Theorists must understand their sciences within the broader, interdisciplinary reality of the world.

In Finnis's theory, the concept of law is predicated upon under-

---

[73] Grisez (n 69) 179.

[74] John Finnis, 'Natural Law and the Is – Ought Question: An Invitation to Professor Veatch' (1981) 26 *Catholic Lawyer* 266, 272. It is valid to bear in mind that, for Finnis and Aquinas, 'speculative', 'theoretical' and 'practical' are all analogous terms.

[75] Ibid 272.

[76] 'this is not to say that there is a 'wall of separation' between the 'is' of our speculative (including informal, common sense) knowledge of human nature, and the 'ought' of the practical norms. On the contrary, 'ad determinationem cognitionis [principiorum rationis practicae] sensu et memoria indigemus' [we need sense(s) and memory to settle knowledge of the principles of practical reason]: *Sent.* II d.24, q.2, a.3 sol.; and thus these first practical principles, like the first principles of speculative reason, can be said to be 'induced' from experiences, an experience which will include not only the stirrings of desire and aversion, but also an awareness of possibilities, likelihoods, *ut in pluribus* [typical] outcomes, and so forth.': Finnis, *Reason* (n 60) 178.

standing law's potentialities (capacities) and comprehending it in light of its objectives, in accordance with human ends. Finnis says: 'no theorist can give a theoretical description and analysis of social facts without also participating in the work of evaluation, of understanding what is really good for human persons, and what is really required by practical reasonableness'.[77] Practical reason is, therefore, Finnis's viewpoint.[78] From the perspective of practical and reasonable thinking, a more thorough understanding of reality (or, say, the law) is achieved.[79] Like Dooyeweerd's 'Archimedean viewpoint', legal philosophy, for Finnis, if it is 'fully practically-reasonable',[80] will include all the attention to facts and realities necessary to the understanding of the law that a purely descriptive, theoretical or speculative philosophy might include.[81]

Finnis says that 'a sound natural law theory' ought to distinguish between the orders of sciences with which both speculative and practical reasoning are concerned.[82] These orders (or domains) of reality are irreducible to and distinct from each other. But this is not a strict separation:

---

[77] Finnis, *NLNR* (n 51) 3.

[78] 'Accounts of laws and legal systems from a purely descriptive viewpoint lack generality or theoretical character. Any aspiration to provide a descriptive general account, or theory, will be dependent, for its accomplishment, on adopting some participant's viewpoint as the criterion for selection and formation of concepts with which to give the account, or state the theory. The only participant's viewpoint that it is philosophically justifiable to adopt is the reasonable (and thus morally sound) participant's. That was the argument of chapter I of *Natural Law and Natural Rights*...': John Finnis, 'Law as Fact and as Reason for Action: A Response to Robert Alexy on Law's "Ideal Dimension"' (2014) 59 (1) *The American Journal of Jurisprudence* 85, 95 ('Response').

[79] Finnis, *NLNR* (n 51) 11-15.

[80] 'Practical philosophy is a disciplined and critical reflection on the goods that can be realized in human action and the requirements of practical reasonableness.': Finnis, *NLNR* (n 51) 12.

[81] Finnis, 'Response' (n 78) 94.

[82] Finnis, *Reason* (n 60) 217.

Almost every form of reductionist deformation in social (say, political) theory, and many destructive misunderstandings in almost every aspect of, say, legal theory, can be traced to oversight of the complexities and ambiguities created by the irreducible distinctions between these four orders—whose irreducibility to one another is disguised by the fact that each includes at least aspects of all the others.[83]

Finnis, like Dooyeweerd, urges descriptive theorists to define law as an all-encompassing, comprehensive concept. For both, jurists must consider other domains of reality when formulating a concept of law.[84] They must stand outside of the mere theoretical sphere in order to accomplish a wide-ranging definition of law. The legal theorist must communicate with other aspects of reality to avoid reductionist pitfalls in his or her conception of law.[85] Indeed, legal theory is irreducible to other sciences, although it includes the same aspects of the other sciences.

According to Finnis, there are four 'patterns of explanatory description', or, more simply put, 'domains of reality'.[86] They are also called 'orders' because they constitute a set of 'unifying relationships' that suggest a 'concreteness' to the complexity of human affairs.[87] They are 'irreducibly distinct though all found in the life and nature of human persons and their groups'.[88] Aquinas previously identified these domains.[89] Aquinas separated the propositions of moral philosophy from the natural sciences' propositions, the principles and norms of

---

[83] Ibid 218.

[84] Ibid 217.

[85] Ibid 218. It is useful to see how Finnis also uses the word 'aspects' in his account of the domains of sciences. It does not have the same specific connotation as the word's use by Dooyeweerd, but it highlights the resemblance between this feature in their theories.

[86] Finnis, 'Nature of Law' (n 48) 39-40.

[87] Finnis, *NLNR* (n 51) 136.

[88] Finnis, *Aquinas* (n 50) 39.

[89] Ibid 21.

logic, and the realm where individuals technically manipulate matters according to their will.[90] Following such an account, the four domains of reality consist of nature, logic, artefacts (or technical), and existence (moral or rational):[91]

> (1) Sciences of matters and relationships {ordo} unaffected by our thinking, i.e. of the 'order of nature {rerum naturalium}' studied by the 'natural philosophy' which includes 'natural science' {[scientia] naturalis}, mathematics, and metaphysics; (2) the sciences of the order we can bring into our own thinking, i.e. logic in its widest sense; (3) the sciences of the order we can bring into our deliberating, choosing, and voluntary actions, i.e. the moral, economic, and political sciences compendiously called *philosophia moralis*; (4) the sciences of the multitude of practical arts, the technologies or techniques which, by bringing order into matter of any kind external to our thinking and willing, yield 'things constituted by human reason.[92]

Each domain has a primary aspect that differentiates it and prevents it from being reduced to another. For example, in the domain of nature, the attribute relates to the biological, climatic, physical, or similar state of affairs and principles. The second domain, that of logic, is characterised by humans' reflective capacity to operate their thoughts and establish an internal coherence when bringing about their understanding of things. This is the kind of domain that is studied by epistemology, methodology, logic, and similar disciplines. In the artefacts' domain, the main features relate to the technical making of a thing or the subjection of something to human powers. Finally, in the existential or *philosophia moralis* domain, the critical feature lies with human intelligent deliberation and creation according to practical reason.[93]

---

[90] Finnis, *Reason* (n 60) 200.

[91] Finnis, 'Nature of Law' (n 48) 39.

[92] Finnis, *Aquinas* (n 50) 21.

[93] Finnis, *NLNR* (n 51) 136-138, 380.

'Law', Finnis says, 'belongs within each of the four domains'.[94] If it is to be in accord with the viewpoint of practical reason, his concept of law ought to integrate the four domains of reality. This is the only way to avoid describing or explaining law reductively.[95] Indeed, as Finnis says, 'almost every form of reductionist deformation in … legal theory, can be traced to ambiguities created by the irreducible distinctions between these four orders':[96]

> Insofar as philosophers of law strive to avoid 'reductivism' – the restriction of strategies of inquiry and reflection to inappropriate models – they more or less explicitly acknowledge that laws and legal systems, like their human makers and subjects, somehow belong to all the four 'orders' with which (as Aquinas argued) human reason is concerned – roughly, nature, logic, morality, and culture (Finnis, *Aquinas: Moral, Political and Legal Theory*). Using the conventional symbols of an ordinary language, and supplementing them with new conventions and techniques, legal rules articulate conceptions of the natural order (which reason does not make but only considers), of logical consistency and implication, and above all of rightness and wrongness in official and unofficial deliberation and action.[97]

Laws are technical and, in this sense, artefactual. However, 'few morally significant choices can be carried out without employing some culturally formed technique; and no technique can be put to human use without some morally significant choice'.[98] So, a description of law that applied Finnis's philosophy must affirm the law to be a set

---

[94] Finnis, 'Nature of Law' (n 48) 39.

[95] Ibid 40.

[96] Finnis, *Reason* (n 60) 218.

[97] John Finnis, *Philosophy of Law* (Oxford: Oxford University Press, 2011) vol IV, 166 ('*Philosophy*').

[98] Finnis, *Reason* (n 60) 218.

of promulgated propositions (domain of logic) that form part of an integrated system that exists – in the sense of it being 'efficacious' as a currently acknowledged and applicable system – (domain of nature), created to operate as an instrument or a technique (domain of artefacts) and that is positively and reasonably inclined towards the common good as a human flourishing end and need (domain of the *philosophia moralis*).[99]

IV. THE INTERSECTION BETWEEN DOOYEWEERD'S AND FINNIS'S JURISPRUDENCE

Is there a correlation between Dooyeweerd's modalities and Finnis's four domains of reality? The above has shown that, for both philosophers, a genuine understanding of law cannot be dissociated from a more comprehensive analysis of reality. In Dooyeweerd's terms, this demands a conception of law that observes the non-normative and normative modalities. For Finnis, it means that law must pervade the four domains of reality. Both philosophers, therefore, say that a true philosophy of law will not isolate or absolutize the legal aspect but will consider law comprehensively, that is, in all of the aspects or domains of reality.

Finnis's nature domain, which relates to the existence of laws and legal systems, is relatable to some of the non-normative aspects of Dooyeweerd's theory. Firstly, the law (or the legal system) is a set of quantitatively numbered propositions (like Dooyeweerd's quantitative aspect). They have the characteristic of continuous expansion through simultaneity and continuity (which is central to Dooyeweerd's spatial aspect).[100] For Dooyeweerd, the spatial aspect also renders possible the idea of territorial jurisdiction.[101] Laws are also kinematic. They are dynamic in their possibility of change and variation. Furthermore,

---

[99] The definition is a compound of Finnis's explanation of law in each of these four domains: Finnis, 'Nature of Law' (n 48) 39-57.

[100] Dooyeweerd, *NC* (n 4), vol II, 85-86.

[101] Cameron, 'Norm and Fact' (n 37) 11.

DOOYEWEERD'S MODAL ASPECTS		FINNIS'S DOMAINS OF REALITY
Quantitative	Determinative Aspects	Natural Domain
Spatial		
Kinematic		
Physical		
Biotic / Organic		
Sensitive/Psychic		
Analytical	Normative Aspects	Logical Domain
Formative		Artefactual Domain
Lingual		
Social		Existential Domain
Economic		
Aesthetic		
Juridical		
Ethical		
Pistic / Faith		

there is a physical side to the law. And it is not only because they can be written, codified, signed, etc. Laws have 'energy-effect'.[102] They have a field of interaction and causality which is essential to the physical aspect of reality.[103] Additionally, laws are integrated into a system, somewhat roughly organic, that is alive (biotic aspect) and can be willed, perceived, engaged and interacted with (sensitive aspect).[104]

---

[102] Ibid 12.

[103] Dooyeweerd, *NC* (n 4) vol II, 99-100.

[104] Cameron, 'Norm and Fact' (n 37) 12 n 61.

As a single group or domain, all of these aspects anticipate some features of the jural aspect and contain characteristics of what law is. They concern matters and relations unaffected by human thinking and thus subsume to the nature domain as per Aquinas and Finnis.[105]

Moreover, Finnis's logic domain is virtually a perfect fit with Dooyeweerd's analytical aspect. In fact, Dooyeweerd often calls it the 'logical' aspect.[106] In Dooyeweerd's terms, the analytical aspect of reality has the same explanation as Finnis's logic domain. For Dooyeweerd, the kernel of the analytical aspect is the act of distinction, clarification, categorisation or cogitation.[107] It expresses how individuals think about the world. The logic domain, in Finnis, pertains to the 'unity of order which we can bring into our understanding … the order which is studied reflectively'.[108] The logic domain asserts the law's internal coherence, avoiding legal contradiction.

For Finnis, the artefactual domain corresponds to the operational-isation of things that humans use as instruments. The formative and lingual aspects of reality can be directly placed within the domain of artefacts. The formative aspect concerns the 'free formative control' that individuals exercise over a thing.[109] It introduces the idea of achievement and innovation to practical reality. Further, the lingual aspect instantiates the externalisation of a human's intended meaning through expression and interpretation.[110] It concretises symbolism and signs into a coherent language that can be used as an instrument for communication and information.[111] Laws and legal systems are instruments of social life developed according to specific legal language and technique.

---

[105] Finnis, *Aquinas* (n 50) 21; *NLNR* (n 51) 136-137.

[106] Dooyeweerd, *NC* (n 4) vol II, 118-125.

[107] Ibid, Vol I, 39 [footnote 2]; vol II, 118-125.

[108] Finnis, *NRNL* (n 51) 136-137.

[109] Dooyeweerd, *NC* (n 4) vol II, 192-217, 238.

[110] Ibid vol II, 222-224.

[111] Ibid

In relation to the last domain, the remainder of Dooyeweerd's normative aspects seems to converge with Finnis's idea of the existential domain. This domain, for Finnis, relates to social collaboration, co-ordination, co-operation, or commitment instantiated by human deliberation and choosing.[112] The social aspect, in Dooyeweerd, expresses the intelligible interactions between individuals. It finds its central meaning in human association, coordination, or intercourse.[113] The social aspect could be expressed in the law's coordination of life according to the particularities of each community. Further, the economic aspect in Dooyeweerd relates to humanity's zeal in sustainably establishing limits to increasingly scarce resources.[114] The law plays an important role in instrumentalising human frugality and placing boundaries to individuals' expenses. Finally, the law ought to be harmonious and instrumental in contemplating the whole of human life (which is the kernel of the aesthetic aspect).[115] In Finnis's terms, the existential domain 'is the unity… we bring into our own actions and dispositions by intelligently deliberating and choosing… Part of our unity in human community, then is the unity of common action'.[116]

Both philosophers would agree to a concept of law that considered the logic of the legal propositions as an analytical and organised system of precepts, principles, and norms (logic domain or analytical aspect). Insofar as law is existent and applicable to different facts and events of nature and societies, they both would agree that it relates to the domain of nature or that it functions in the determinative aspects of reality. Furthermore, law has historical and communal tenets, and it possesses a language proper of its sphere, which reveals its technicality (and this pertains to the artefactual domain or the formative and

---

[112] Finnis, *Aquinas* (n 50) 21; (50) 138.

[113] Dooyeweerd, *NC* (n 4) vol II, 140-141 n 1.

[114] Ibid vol II, 66-67, 122-7.

[115] Ibid vol II, 128, 139.

[116] Finnis, *NLNR* (n 51) 137-138.

lingual modalities). Finally, laws are social commitments, dictates, or ordinances that direct communities to their just, sustainable common good (which belongs to the realm of the remainder of the normative modalities, or the existential domain).

V. An Addendum: Theology, Philosophy, and Law

A final remark seems necessary. As I have already stated, the article's main scope is to find similarities in Dooyeweerd's and Finnis's philosophies of law. This effort by no means represents an attempt of blending their philosophies into a unified law theory. The present article serves no purpose if it dissociates the philosopher from his own philosophy. As acknowledged before, Dooyeweerd and Finnis belong to different traditions within Christianity. Their theologies are distinct, and the repercussions that follow from that fact are too great to be analysed here. That is why this is a short addendum.

There is one major divergence between Dooyeweerd and Finnis that one cannot ignore. While Dooyeweerd is open and clear about the 'ontic a priori' elements of his philosophy, Finnis is not. This is a significant point for Dooyeweerd and a criticism he would have of any theorist who failed to acknowledge his or her normative presuppositions.

Dooyeweerd is a Calvinist. He is one of the chief representatives of the Dutch Calvinist movement (or commonly referred to as neo-Calvinism).[117] There are many aspects of Dooyeweerd's theory that contradict Catholic teachings. Notably, Dooyeweerd repeatedly rebukes the 'ground-motive' of the Thomistic-Aristotelian thought.[118] According to Dooyeweerd, the nature-grace dualism typical of Thomism is a failed attempt to assimilate Aristotelian and Stoic philosophies into a Christian framework.[119] The grace-nature dualism

---

[117] Dooyeweerd sets the challenge of separating Calvinist natural law from the classical theories for himself. See: Dooyeweerd, 'Calvinism' (n 47) 3-6.

[118] Dooyeweerd, *NC* (n 4) vol I, 66-67; (n 8) 111-147; (n 12) 61-63.

[119] Dooyeweerd, *Twilight* (n 12) 32; *Encyclopedia* (n 5) 61.

does not correspond, Dooyeweerd argues, to the biblical truth of a Sovereign God and the strict separation between the Creator and the creature.[120] As his argument develops, Dooyeweerd says that Scholasticism ultimately fails to explain the Fall's radical effects on human nature.[121]

The starting point in Dooyeweerd's theory of law is his religious beliefs in the 'Creation-Fall-Redemption ground motive'. For Dooyeweerd, the 'Origin' of his philosophy is God.[122] And all philosophies that do not acknowledge God as the Beginning of their theories are idolatrous in Dooyeweerd's terms.[123] For him, all that there is 'is' because God has commanded it to be. This ontic reality, for Dooyeweerd, has a determinative character in his idea of law and in the ordering of the modal aspects of reality. Law has this ontic a priori characteristic of being interwoven in the Creation-reality.

Further, Dooyeweerd disagrees with the foundations of Aquinas's natural law. Notably, he opposes the definition of *lex naturalis* as participation of human will (reason) in the *lex eterna* (eternal, moral laws of God).[124] According to Dooyeweerd, Scholasticism leads to the realisation that human reason has such a status that it can share in God's ordinances. This, Dooyeweerd argues, renders God ultimately subjected to His laws.[125]

Despite Dooyeweerd's open criticism towards Scholasticism,[126] some of his arguments are contrasted by Finnis's interpretation of Aquinas. An example is that Dooyeweerd's argument against

---

[120] Dooyeweerd, *Twilight* (n 12) 96; 'Calvinism' (n 47) 15-16.

[121] Dooyeweerd, *Twilight* (n 12) 97; *Encyclopedia* (n 5) 62.

[122] Dooyeweerd, *Twilight* (n 12) 23.

[123] Ibid 24.

[124] Dooyeweerd, 'Calvinism' (n 47) 15.

[125] Ibid 13-15

[126] Dooyeweerd has written three volumes analytically criticising scholasticism. See: Herman Dooyeweerd, *Reformation and Scholasticism in Philosophy*, ed DFM Strauss) (Paideia Press, 2012) vol A5, A5/2, and A7.

Thomism's ignorance of the relationship between positive and natural law[127] is weakened by Finnis's tempered exegesis of Aquinas's *dictum* 'unjust laws are not laws'.[128] According to Finnis, laws are both sheer facts (*positiva iura*) and dictates of reason for action (*rationis ordinatio*). This comes from his interpretation of Aquinas's understanding of human laws as either a process of conclusion (direct entailment) from natural law, or from *determinatio*, which is the positivisation of reasonable choices according to broader dictates of practical reason. Law, for Dooyeweerd, is authoritative, and it has direct communication to the positive laws as promulgated by the political authority.[129] Finnis's description of Aquinas's legal theory (often called the 'weak natural law theory') is not far from that statement. Specifically, it considers the relevance of political authority as well as the idea of human positive laws as conclusions or determinations from the *lex naturalis*.[130] Therefore, at least in a sense, Dooyeweerd might be closer to the Thomism than he would have conceded.

Although Dooyeweerd claims his theory is outside the legal positivist and the classic natural law theories of law, he is, in some respects, close to Finnis's interpretation of Aquinas.[131] This should be enough to render the current analysis a positive step towards establishing a dialogue between the two traditions. As Chaplin has said, 'when viewed against the background of the variety of historical schools of legal philosophy, there is no doubt that the affinities

---

[127] Dooyeweerd, 'Calvinism' (n 47) 20.

[128] John Finnis, 'The Truth in Legal Positivism' in Robert P George (ed) *The Autonomy of Law* (Oxford University Press, 1996); John Finnis, 'On the Incoherence of Legal Positivism' (2000) 75(5) *Notre Dame Law Review* 1597; Finnis, *Aquinas* (n 60) 209; Finnis, 'Nature of Law' (n 48) 54; Finnis, 'Past and Present' (n 59) 94-95; Finnis, 'What is?' (n 66) 137-141.

[129] Dooyeweerd, 'Calvinism' (n 47) 20.

[130] See footnote n 126, above.

[131] At least in the sense that they both affirm that legal and moral principles relate to each other and are expressed (even if to a certain degree) in the positivity of the law.

between [Dooyeweerd's] theory of law and natural law theory are far more significant than the differences between them'.[132]

To the same extent, there is no doubt that Finnis' jurisprudence is influenced by his Catholicism. However, and to a certain degree, as we have proposed a re-reading of Dooyeweerd, one should acknowledge the links between Finnis's exegesis of Aquinas's philosophy and Dooyeweerd's philosophy.

In a sense, Finnis's philosophy is religious-free.[133] In the Preface of his *Natural Law and Natural Rights* (*'NLNR'*), he expressly says that the natural law theory of law developed in his book is independent of any external authority or religious commitment.[134] Indeed, Finnis only brings the idea of God to his legal theory in the last chapter of *NLNR* (the same happens in his *Aquinas*) as a sort of explanatory addendum regarding what he understands as human life's ultimate end.[135] Only then, Finnis affirms God's sovereignty and the existence and applicability of His eternal ordinances (eternal law) to human endeavours.[136]

Such an attempt is unthinkable in Dooyeweerdian terms. However, this is how Finnis articulates his account of the self-evident goods to be comprehended by both theists and non-theists alike. He diverts from the ontological question about the basis for his natural law theory, except when resting it on the idea of practical reasonableness and rationality. And this is where some accuse him of misrepresenting or misinterpreting Thomist legal theory.[137]

Finnis, Grisez, and Boyle say that one's choices are unable to

---

[132] Chaplin, *Dooyeweerd* (n 43) 320.

[133] A claim that *per se* would be the object of Dooyeweerd's criticism.

[134] Finnis, *NLNR* (n 51) vi.

[135] Ibid ch 13.

[136] Ibid 390.

[137] Famously: Russell Hittinger, *A Critique of the New Natural Law Theory* (University of Notre Dame Press, 1988).

instantiate divine goodness. God is far superior to human willpower and reason-capacities. For them, 'God is not the ultimate *reason* for acting'.[138] Because humans can only actualise their own (humane) possibilities, individual actions cannot instantiate divine goodness unless one is willing to admit that God's goodness can be achieved by human action, which they are not.[139] As the argument goes, 'the heart of human persons, considered precisely according to their human nature, are not made for God'; thus, 'there can be no *natural* desire for what is *not the natural* end of human persons'.[140] In specific soteriological terms, this can be read as an expression of God's sovereign grace in salvation due to the inexistence of human participation in the salvation-act.[141] Neo-Calvinists, like Dooyeweerd, would say that it is by grace alone, through faith alone, that an individual can become a child of God.[142] Here, Finnis, Grisez and Boyle adopt a somewhat similar reasoning: 'Christian faith requires no such natural desire, for, according to it, that intimate vision of God is attained, not through human nature, but by a sharing in the divine nature, received as a gift by "water and the Spirit" (Jn 3:5) or by "adoption" (Rom 8:14-17, 23).'[143] There is no human-led way to God except through the Sovereign's own will and intervention, with the caveat that God's will remains uncorruptedly imprinted in humans hearts even after the Fall:

> This Christian view that human persons can *be given* a share
> in the divine nature is perfectly consistent with the … reason

---

[138] Finnis, Grisez and Boyle (n 72) 133.

[139] Ibid 133-134.

[140] Ibid 134.

[141] Westminster Assembly, *The Westminster Confession of Faith*, III, v. ('*WCF*').

[142] Hence two of the Reformation slogans (the 'Five Solas'): *Sola Fide* and *Sola Gratia*. See, also: *The Canons of the Synod of Dordt*, I.v-vii, ix-x, II.iii, III-IV.iii-iv, x, xiv; *WCF*, III.v-vi, VII.iii, IX.iv-v, X.i-ii, XII, XVI.vii; *The Belgic Confession of Faith* arts 2, 14.

[143] Finnis, Grisez and Boyle (n 72) 134.

why divine goodness cannot be the ultimate reason for one's actions: that human action cannot lead to the instantiation of divine goodness. For there is a difference between being given something as a gift and achieving it through one's action ...[144]

If Reformed Christians say the ultimate end of human beings is to glorify God,[145] the person who achieves it is because of a gift of God's gracious agency. Those who received this saving grace from God can regard Him as the source of the basic goods' goodness towards which their regenerated natural self is directed. This is a conclusion one could derive from the above quote from Finnis, Grisez and Boyle.[146] In this sense, Finnis's proposal of the basic goods being pre-moral (meaning that the 'good' is not a 'good' as opposed to a 'bad', but the objective of a pursuit) further brings Dooyeweerd's theological convictions closer, or more in tune with, the classical natural law theory of law. Humans cannot assimilate the divine goodness by reason or will alone, but they can nonetheless act towards an end that is objectively non-moral (or even 'idolatrous', if using Dooyeweerd's terms).

The theological implications of Dooyeweerd's and Finnis's theories are numerous.[147] However, further discussions about them are

---

[144] Ibid.

[145] Westminster Assembly, *The Westminster Shorter Catechism*, q.1 a.1.

[146] 'While each of the principles of practical knowledge directs that some good be done, all of them in common direct that good be done, and this common aspect of their directiveness corresponds to the will's natural openness to goodness. For this reason, if one believes that unqualified goodness—goodness itself—is found in God, one will regard him as the source of the goodness of all the basic goods.': Finnis, Grisez, Boyle (n 72) 135.

[147] And so can be the similarities. For example, the distinction between political natural law and primary natural law (Dooyeweerd, 'Calvinism' (n 47) 34-35), which can be interpreted in a relationship with Aquinas's idea of human law's being made either from deductions (conclusions from natural law) or from a process of *determinatio* (Finnis, *Philosophy* (n 97) 266-267). Further, for both Finnis and Dooyeweerd legal systems are founded in the context of a political community (Dooyeweerd, *Encyclopedia* (n 5) 145; Finnis, *Philosophy* (n 97) vol IV, 428). And the list could go on.

outside the scope of this article. Dooyeweerd and Finnis may disagree theologically. Their theories may be rooted in distinct views about God, the church, and postlapsarian human nature. They may diverge in their presuppositions and ontic a priori explanations of law. But the theoretical commonality between their understanding of the concept of law within the four domains of reality remains.

VI. Conclusion

This has been a first attempt to correlate Dooyeweerd's and Finnis's law theories in these terms. However, this is by no means an exhaustive account of how their legal philosophies might agree or disagree. The general conclusion is simple: Despite the many differences in their traditions and philosophies, Dooyeweerd and Finnis share similar grounds in their concepts of law.

This article has demonstrated how both demand of the legal theorist, in his or her theoretical consideration, to perceive law as a phenomenon that transcends the mere theoretical-legal point of view. There must be a broader analysis of law, one that goes beyond the theoretical or speculative experience. Law is an all-encompassing, comprehensive concept. For Dooyeweerd, an elementary concept of law depends on the jural aspect's relationship with the other modalities that compose reality. For Finnis, a definition of law must be comprehensive enough to explain the law in the context of the four domains of reality.

The parallel between the two should now be clear. The modal aspects in Dooyeweerd's theory correlate with Finnis's four domains of reality. A comprehensive view of the law considers the analytical aspect or logic domain (ie it has propositions that are logically established in a cohesive system) and instantiates the determinative modalities, or nature domain (ie it exists, is alive, and is applied in a particular territory). Further, it ought to consider the technical domain related to the formative and lingual aspects (ie that there is a historical foundation and justification to it, and that it has proper language and operation), and, finally, contain the other normative aspects, or the existential domain (ie it produces social intercourse, directing individuals in a community towards a good).

This work has been mainly concerned with starting a dialogue between Dooyeweerd and Finnis. If this exchange proves relevant, it can lead to further interactions. It also admits refinements. For now, the conclusion remains that a genuine concept of law ought to contemplate other areas of knowledge or sciences. Legal theorists will fall short of the genuine understanding of the law if they ignore the interconnection between law and the modal aspects or domains of reality. A definition of law cannot be formulated in merely jural terms without being reductionistic. The true concept of law permeates the four domains of reality.

3

Our Present Fight Against Tyranny

KEVIN DONNELLY AM*

ABSTRACT

The right to what the American Declaration of Independence describes as "life, liberty and the pursuit of happiness" is a precious, fragile gift that should never be taken for granted. Proven by recent global events, including draconian and inflexible responses to the Covid-19 pandemic, the increasing impact of scientism and technology and the debilitating rise of cultural-left ideology on university campuses, such freedoms face an existential threat. A threat that challenges and undermines long held freedoms and, unless addressed, that will lead to a dystopian world like George Orwell's 1984 where liberty and free expression are crushed by totalitarian mind control and group think.

I. First Considerations

One of America's founding fathers Thomas Jefferson is often attributed with the expression 'the price of freedom is eternal vigilance'. Recent global events, including responses to the Covid-19 pandemic by governments and health officials, the increasing influence of scientism and the technological state and the rise of politically correct Woke ideology on university campuses prove Jefferson's warning is even more relevant now than what it was all those years ago. We now live in a time when the cherished and long fought for liberties and freedoms unique to Western, liberal democracies like Australia face

---

* Senior Fellow, PM Glynn Institute, Australian Catholic University.

an existential threat. An ever increasing and powerful threat, unless challenged, that will lead to a totalitarian, oppressive and soulless future much like the dystopian world so vividly portrayed in George Orwell's *1984*.

A *Covid-19 and liberty and freedom denied*

As argued by Lord Jonathan Sumption, an ex-justice of the United Kingdom's Supreme Court, such was, and continues to be, the unjust and oppressive nature of government responses to the Covid-19 pandemic, including the United Kingdom and Australia, '[w]e are now entering a Hobbesian world, the enormity of which has not dawned on our people'.[1] Sumption argues, unlike previous epidemics such as the Spanish flu (1918-1921), the Asiatic (1957) and the Hong Kong flu (1968), where governments took no special steps to stop transmission, responses to Covid-19 involved unwarranted and draconian government interventions on a grand scale. Such interventions included forcing citizens into lockdowns,[2] imposing border restrictions and denying freedom of movement, denying free speech, the right to peaceful assembly and forcing citizens to be injected with experimental drugs whose efficacy and safety had yet to be proven.[3]

The responses to the pandemic orchestrated by the Victorian government led by Premier Daniel Andrews illustrate how totalitarian such measures were and how quicky essential freedoms and liberties are denied.[4] Melbourne had one of the longest total period of lockdown

---

[1] Lord Jonathan Sumption, 'A State of Fear Covid-19 and the Lockdowns' (Speech, Robert Menzies Institute, *2022*) 27.

[2] Sumption describes lockdowns as 'a sustained attack on our humanity' – Ibid 20.

[3] For an account of how government responses cancelled essential liberties and freedoms as well as the legal principles underlying Westminster forms of government, see. Augusto Zimmermann and Joshua Forrester (eds), *Fundamental Rights in the Age of COVID-19* (Connor Court Publishing, 2020). This is the printed version of Volume 11 of *The Western Australian Jurist*.

[4] See the video 'Battleground Melbourne' for an account of the draconian and oppressive measures forced on citizens, available at <https://www.youtube.com/watch?v=-TrG97Qt31w>.

of any city in the world where police used capsicum spray and rubber bullets against peaceful demonstrators, teachers, firefighters and nurses lost employment for refusing to be inoculated and family and friends denied the right to see sick and dying relatives. Instead of abiding by the rules and conventions underpinning the state's Westminster inspired parliamentary system, Premier Andrews acted as an autocratic, one-man government ignoring the need for checks and balances and for cabinet and parliamentary oversight.

Much like George Orwell's Big Brother in *1984* and previous dictators including Adolf Hitler and Joseph Stalin, Andrews also used a range of techniques to consolidate his power and to weaken any opposition. One of the principal strategies to control and manipulate citizens is to engender fear against a powerful and unforgiving enemy.[5] In the same way The Party used Big Brother to incite irrational fear against the enemy Emmanuel Goldstein, Andrews portrayed Covid-19 as a terrifying, deadly and unstoppable beast preying on the weak and vulnerable. Andrews in his daily media appearances, with the help of a compliant media and ineffectual Liberal Party opposition, also presented himself as a supportive and caring authority figure whose sole purpose was to safeguard an at-risk, vulnerable population.

As noted by Sumption, such was the success of Andrew's strategies in dealing with the pandemic as a well as the commonwealth government's policy of closing borders and instilling a prevailing sense of fear, a poll carried out by the Lowry Institute found 84% of Australians felt governments had handled the pandemic very well or fairly well. Both levels of government were so effective in denying rights based by cultivating fear, the ex-Prime Minister Tony Abbott observes:

> [T]he most vexing thing about these Covid-19 pandemic times
> is the aversion to almost any risk. The daily drum beat of

---

[5] See Mattias Desmet, *The Psychology of Totalitarianism* (Chelsea Green Publishing, 2022).

infections and deaths, the constant stress on obeying the rules, has gone beyond accommodating people's fears to the point of playing on them.[6]

When detailing the destructive impact of what he terms 'coercive state intervention' that arose during the pandemic, Sumption quotes Alexis de Tocqueville who, when warning about the democracy's potential for despotism, wrote:

> The will of man is not shattered, but softened, bent, and guided: men are seldom forced by it to act, but they are constantly restrained from acting: such a power does not destroy, but it prevents existence; it does not tyrannize, but it compresses, enervates, extinguishes, and stupefies a people, till each nation is reduced to be nothing better than a flock of timid and industrious animals, of which the government is the shepherd.[7]

Such were the draconian and irrational rules imposed in Australia during the height of the Covid-19 pandemic that drivers alone in cars wore masks, people on empty beaches and sitting on park benches were warned to move on and passengers while flying allowed to remain maskless if holding a drink container. The fact the overwhelming majority of Australians remained passive at a time when essential freedoms and liberties were lost also proves how prescient Alexis de Tocqueville was.

B *Scientism and the technological society*

When explaining the rise of what he terms a new form of totalitarianism equally as dangerous as communism and fascism the Italian academic and cultural critic Augusto Del Noce refers to scientism

---

[6] Tony Abbott. 'Cancel Culture in the time of Covid-19', in Kevin Donnelly (ed), *Cancel Culture And The Left's Long March* (Wilkinson Publishing, 2021) 95-105.

[7] Alexis de Tocqueville. *Democracy in America,* Chapter VI – What Sort of Despotism Democratic Nations Have To Fear' (Web Article, 23 February 2023).

and the technological society.[8] Unlike science that has its strengths and benefits Del Noce warns of a totalitarian form of science that sees itself as preeminent and beyond criticism. A situation where:

> Science is regarded as the 'only' true form of knowledge. According to this view, every other type of knowledge – metaphysical or religious – expresses only 'subjective reactions', which are able, or will be able, to explain by extending science into the human sphere through psychological and sociological research.[9]

The Australian academic James Anthony Gibbons, after citing various authors including Michael Oakeshott, Jürgen Habermas and Alasdair Macintyre, draws the same conclusion about the dangers of a restricted and narrow definition of science when he warns, '[a]ll legitimate knowledge is equated with scientific knowledge, other claims to knowledge are dismissed'.[10]

In addition to rejecting religion and any sense of a higher moral order, scientism also denies the validity of a spiritual and transcendent sense of human nature and the world in which we live. Science is seen as preeminent and faith, the need to nourish the soul and to respect the God given nature of what it means to be human is either ignored or considered without foundation. Such is the all-consuming power of scientism that whether a particular procedure or action is acceptable or not simply depends on its utility and whether those individuals involved are happy to comply and, regardless of the consequences, to accept the outcome.

What was once seen as immoral and against natural law is now

---

[8] In addition to scientism and the technological society Del Noce, when detailing what he describes as the new form of totalitarianism, also refers to eroticism and the theology of secularization.

[9] Augusto Del Noce, *The Crisis Of Modernity* (McGIll-Queen's University Press, 2014) 89.

[10] James Anthony Gibbons, *On Reflection* (*Flinders University Institute of International Education Research*, 2004) 83.

considered beyond criticism as there is no objective or absolute criteria by which to judge what is right and what is wrong. By eliminating religious concepts such as good and evil and the necessity to abide by God given inalienable rights such as liberty, justice, freedom and the inherent dignity of the person, tyranny prevails.

Such is the pervasive influence of scientism that state sanctioned suicide is common across so-called civilised countries including Australia, Belgium, Germany, the Netherlands and Canada, abortions are common-place where the sanctity of life no longer prevails and it is considered acceptable to use aborted foetal tissue for vaccines and medical research.

Del Noce argues equally as dangerous as scientism is a new form of totalitarianism represented by the rise of 'the technological society'.[11] In the same way Del Noce differentiates between science and scientism, he also differentiates between technical progress and activity and the technological society. While the first is beneficial, the second is seen as totalitarian in nature leading to a situation where progress is measured in terms of its utility and the extent to which it promotes individual fulfillment and wellness. Carlo Lancellotti, when detailing what characterises a technocratic society writes, 'the technological society is no longer unified by any shared idea of the good, and the only possible common "moral" goal is the expansion of individual well-being'.[12]

One of the defining features of the technological society is that it promotes an absolutist, secular vision of society, one where religion is no longer present:

> Generally speaking, the new totalitarianism does not persecute religion directly. It progressively empties it out by denying its cognitive significance, by declaring meaningless the

---

[11] Del Noce (n 9) 89.

[12] Carlo Lancellotti, 'Augusto Del Noce On The "New Totalitarianism' 2017) 44 (Summer) *Communio* 323, 326.

very questions that faith is supposed to answer and pushing it to the private sphere of feelings. Thus, religion becomes a therapeutic, vitalizing practice, what Del Noce describes (quoting Simone Weil) as a 'drug'.[13]

Given the freedoms and liberties we take for granted and the Westminster inspired parliamentary system and British common law are underpinned and enriched by Christianity then scientism and the technological society represent significant threats.

Gain-of-function research and numerous governments' responses to the Covid-19 pandemic represent an example of the dangers associated with scientism and a technological view of the world. Gain-of-function research involves weaponizing viruses in order to study them more closely and, hopefully, find remedies once people are infected, and is supported by a number of scientists. As detailed by David Zweig, a journalist with *The Free Press,* there are also scientists who oppose gain-of-function research on the basis it is too dangerous as any benefits are far outweighed by the risks. Scientists questioning the safety and efficacy of gain-of-function research include Dr Laura Kahn, Kevin M Esvelt, Marc Lipsitch and Richard Ebright.[14] David Zweig quotes reports from the US Energy Department,[15] the FBI[16] and a number of scientists[17] concluding Covid-19 that escaped from a laboratory in Wuhan China is the result of gain-of-function research.

Illustrated by the emergence of Covid-19 and the subsequent global pandemic, scientism represents a clear and present danger, not only

---

[13] Ibid 325.

[14] David Zweig, 'Is Gain-of-Function Research a 'Risk Worth taking'? Or 'Insanity?', *The Free Press* (Web Article, 7 March 2023).

[15] 'Lab Leak Most Likely Origin of Covid-19 Pandemic, Energy Department Now Says', *The Wall Street Journal* (Web Article, 6 February 2023).

[16] Ibid.

[17] 'Covid-19 lab leak theory cannot be ruled out, leading scientists say', *Reuters*(Web Article, 14 May 2021).

to citizens' health, but also to the freedoms, rights and liberties that underpin and are vital for the survival of a civilised society. Governments around the world, with rare exceptions, responded to the pandemic by denying freedom of movement by forcing people to stay indoors, imposing travel restrictions and closing borders. As previously mentioned, in Victoria, Premier Daniel Andrews acted as a one-man government where freedom of assembly and freedom of speech were denied and where police used violence and intimidation to enforce inflexible and unnecessary regulations. Even worse was the decision to force citizens to be injected with unproven and untested vaccines by making it a condition of employment and socialising in restaurants and public spaces to be vaccinated.

C *The rise of neo-Marxist inspired mind control and group think and its impact on the academy*

> But the peculiar evil of silencing the expression of an opinion is, that it is robbing the human race; posterity as well as the existing generation; those who dissent from the opinion, still more than those who hold it. If the opinion is right, they are deprived of the opportunity of exchanging error for truth: if wrong, they lose, what is almost as great a benefit, the clearer perception and livelier impression of truth, produced by its collision with error.[18]

Tyranny comes in many forms, ranging from the most violent and terrifying to less violent and less obvious forms involving indoctrination, mind control and group think. Totalitarian regimes, illustrated by the Russian and Chinese communist revolutions and the rise of fascism in Nazi Germany, employ starvation, violence, imprisonment and death to overthrow the status quo and enforce

---

[18] John Stuart Mill, *On Liberty* (1859) ch 2.

domination and control. As argued by Roger Kimball,[19] Giles Auty[20] and Augusto Del Noce,[21] while not as violent and destructive as communism and fascism, neo-Marxist inspired, cultural-left ideology also represents a threat to hard fought for liberties and freedoms. Of special concern is the way academic freedom has been undermined and compromised by an unrelenting Woke ideology dedicated to cancelling any opinions and arguments considered unacceptable.

One of the bulwarks against tyranny and one of the defining features of a liberal democracy is freedom of conscience and freedom of expression. Such is the importance of such freedoms the American Constitution's First Amendment, as well as freedom of religion, 'protects freedom of speech, the press, assembly, and the right to petition the Government for a redress of grievances'.[22] The *Universal Declaration of Human Rights* also acknowledges freedom of conscience and freedom of expression when it argues in Article 19:

> Everyone has the right to freedom of opinion and expression; this right includes freedom to hold opinions without interference and to seek, receive and impart information and ideas through any media and regardless of frontiers.[23]

While Australia does not have a similar declaration of human rights to protect freedom of conscience and freedom of expression such rights, unless qualified by specific acts of legislation, are protected under a common law system inherited from the United Kingdom. As noted by the Australian Human Rights Commission:

> Australia is unusual among common law countries in not having a Constitutional Charter or Bill of Rights. However,

---

[19] Roger Kimball, *The Long March* (Encounter Books, 2000).

[20] Giles Auty, *Culture At Crisis Point* (Connor Court Publishing, 2013).

[21] Del Noce (n 9). See Chapter titled 'Authority and Power'.

[22] *The United States Constitution* amend I.

[23] *The Universal Declaration of Human Rights* art 19.

common law courts have power to provide significant protection of human rights principles including the rule of law, except where legislation specifically overrides this power.[24]

Academic freedom is especially vital as the search for wisdom and truth relies on the ability to engage in research, debate and discussion based on objectivity, tolerance and a willingness to be proven either right or wrong. Arguments defending the ability to think freely and openly can be traced back to early Greek philosophers including Aristotle, Socrates and Plato.

As noted by the George Orwell, one of the most powerful strategies employed by totalitarian regimes is to coerce citizens and enforce domination by controlling how they think and how they express themselves. Orwell makes the point 'But if thought corrupts language, language can also corrupt thought'.[25] Debasing language by resorting to slogans and clichés, disguising one's intent by clouding arguments in emotive language and hyperbole and presenting arguments as beyond dispute are all strategies directed at enforcing compliance. In the novel *1984*, as well as fear and physical violence enforced by the Thought Police, the Party and Big Brother employ doublethink. Orwell describes this as 'the power of holding two contradictory beliefs in one's mind simultaneously, and accepting both of them'. Examples include the slogan 'War is Peace, Freedom is Slavery, Ignorance is Strength'.[26] Such is Orwell's fear about the power of totalitarian regimes in controlling how people think he states we now live in a world:

If the Leader says of such and such an event, 'It never happened'

---

[24] Australian Human Rights Commission, 'Common Law Rights, Human Rights Scrutiny and The Rule of Law' (Web Article, 3 August 2023).

[25] George Orwell, 'Politics and the English Language' [1946] (Web Article).

[26] A more recent example of doublethink is the Victorian state government forcing citizens to be isolated at home during Covid-19 while arguing 'Staying apart, keeps us together'.

– well, it never happened. If he says that two and two are five – well, two and two are five. This prospect frightens me much more than bombs – and after our experiences of the last few years that is not a frivolous statement.[27]

Big Brother also dominates and controls by ensuring any citizens guilty of questioning or doubting the Party are guilty of thoughtcrime. Any hint, conscious or unconscious, of deviating from official orthodoxy is immediately condemned and punished. One chilling example in *1984* is when a young boy hears his asleep father mumbling the phrase 'down with Big Brother' and reports the crime to the Thought Police. Such is the power of conditioning and mind control the father accepts his guilt and sees nothing wrong in being betrayed by his son.

As argued by Roger Scruton, while *1984* is a fictional world drawing on Orwell's knowledge of communism and fascism, there is much about what is happening in contemporary Western societies since the rise of cultural-Marxism that proves the adage truth is often stranger than fiction. No-where is this Orwellian dystopia more evident than in the West's universities – universities once committed to a liberal education based on the search for beauty, wisdom and truth but now infected with a rainbow alliance or radical theories including critical theory, deconstructionism, postmodernism, and gender, sexuality, critical race and postcolonial theories. After noting the need to defend Enlightenment values including rationality and reason as a bulwark against intellectual tyranny represented by political correctness (rebadged as being Woke), Scruton writes:

In effect, Orwell's political fables contain an accurate and penetrating prophecy of the political correctness that has since invaded intellectual life in Britain and America. The humourless and relentless policing of language, so as to

---

[27] George Orwell. 'Looking back on the Spanish War' (Web Article).

prevent heretical thought from arising, the violence done to traditional categories and natural ways of describing things, the obliteration of memory and assiduous policing of the past – all these things so disturbingly described in Nineteen Eighty-Four, are now routinely to be observed on university campuses on both sides of the Atlantic …[28]

Another British academic Frank Furedi also stresses the dangers of cultural-left language and mind control when he makes the point such is the fear and uneasiness about being guilty of thoughtcrime people are silenced. Furedi writes:

On campuses and in the workplace, self-censorship is rife. The 'you can't say that' sentiment encourages individuals, who fear their views might provoke a hostile reaction, to remain silent. That applies to the office just as much as the seminar room. Cancel culture's greatest success lies in language control.[29]

Evidence the cultural-left now dominates universities and intellectual discourse across the English-speaking world is easy to find. Instead of open and free enquiry any academic who fails to conform to the prevailing cultural-left ideology in areas like race, ethnicity, gender, sexuality and climate change is victimised and cancelled. A notable past example is the Australian historian Geoffrey Blainey who, after raising doubts about the rate of Asian immigration in a speech given to a Rotary meeting in the Victorian town of Warrnambool in March 1984, was censured by fellow academics at the University of Melbourne. Such was the force of the campaign to vilify Blainey he found it impossible to continue lecturing and eventually left the university. Keith Windschuttle makes the point Blainey was not condemning Asian immigration as such, but rather

---

[28] Roger Scruton, *Conservatism* (Profile Books, 2017) 122.
[29] Frank Furedi, 'The Free-Speech Crisis is not a Right-Wing Myth' (Web Article, 12 March 2023).

the rate of immigration at a time of increasing economic dislocation. Windschuttle describes Blainey's treatment as a violation of academic freedom 'clearly the worst in Australian history'.[30]

Another Australian example of an academic being cancelled for committing thought crime is Peter Ridd who lost his position at James Cook University after questioning the dire narrative about the death of the Great Barrier Reef due to climate change. After being charged for serious misconduct for questioning the prevailing orthodoxy, Ridd was eventually removed on the charge of breaching a confidentiality agreement with the university. Ridd's case was reported as follows:

> The High Court of Australia's verdict in favour of James Cook University's right to sack one of its employees, a professor of physics, for questioning the science of climate change is an endorsement of the culture of censorship suffocating Australian life and further confirms that the nation's universities are in crisis.[31]

A third example of cultural-left victimisation involves the British academic Kathleen Stock who argues gender and sexuality, instead of being a social construct and a matter of self-identification, is primarily biologically determined. As a result of being vilified and attacked for failing to conform to the prevailing ideology regarding transgenderism, Stock concluded her only option was to resign. Stock argues:

> There's a small group of people who are absolutely opposed to the sorts of things I say and instead of getting involved in arguing with me, using reason, evidence, the traditional university methods, they tell their students in lectures that I

---

[30] Keith Windschuttle, 'Stuart Macintyre and the Blainey Affair', *Quadrant Online* (Web Article, 24 November 2021).

[31] Morgan Begg, 'Ruling Against Ridd Shines Light on Cancel Culture', *The Australian* (Web Article, 14 October 2021).

pose a harm to trans students, or they go on to Twitter and say that I'm a bigot.[32]

While not involving threatening academic tenure, another form of silencing free speech is 'no platforming'[33] – a situation where students either ban or demonstrate against academics and public figures asked to speak on campus guilty of what the American journalist Bari Weiss describes as "Wrongthink".[34] Examples of those threatened with no-platforming include Ayaan Hirsi Ali, Germaine Greer and Australia's Bettina Arndt. In opposition to the argument no-platforming is only used to protect the vulnerable against views calculated to offend the Australian journalist Claire Lehmann argues, 'While the stated aim of this approach is to reduce harm, the end result is enforced ignorance. No-platforming does not change people's hearts and minds, it intimidates people into silence. It is an anti-Enlightenment movement'.[35]

In addition to academics judged as heretical being pressured to resign and others being no-platformed, equally as concerning is the way cultural-left academics deny academic freedom by restricting what is taught. Academics at Sydney University rejected funding to establish a Centre for Western Civilisation funded by the Ramsay Centre on the basis such a centre would promote a 'conservative, culturally essentialist, and Eurocentric vision'.[36] A second Australian example involves the University of Western Australia rejecting government funding to establish a climate change research centre headed by the Danish academic Bjorn Lomborg. Critics argued Lomborg failed to

---

[32] Excerpt from an interview on the *BBC Women's Hour*, 3 November 2021.

[33] Jeremy Sammut, 'Off With The Campus Gag: Give All opinions a Voice,' *Centre for Independent Studies* (Web Article, 8 August 2023).

[34] Bari Weiss, 'Resignation Letter' (Web Article, 8 August 2023).

[35] Claire Lehmann, 'Germaine Greer and the scourge of no-platforming', *ABC The Drum* (Web Article, 25 October 2015).

[36] 'Staff Against The Ramsay Centre – Open Letter' (Web Article, 7 August 2023).

properly recognise the calamitous nature of man-made global warming and the need for immediate action.[37]

A good illustration of how cultural-left ideology enforces group think is is the global move to de-colonise the university curriculum. Academics at the University of Sheffield's Department of Animal and Plant Sciences define decolonisation as:

[A]bout confronting how European imperialism, colonialism and racism have shaped our modern world. It is a framework that helps to tackle racial injustice – but more than that, it seeks to interrogate and tear down the structures that embed racism in our society.[38]

The academics argue, instead of the scientific method associated with the Enlightenment being privileged, it must be condemned as 'a fundamental contributor to European imperialism and a major beneficiary of its injustices'.[39] Instead of being beneficial or inherently worthwhile UK science is also condemned as 'inherently white' with the authors suggesting 'decolonisation presents an alternative vision for science'.[40] As noted by the University of Sydney academic Omid Tofighian, decolonizing the curriculum is a global movement impacting on universities in the UK, South Africa, Australia and America. In suggesting why Australian universities should be involved, Tofighian argues:

We need to improve the discussion about the role of whiteness, coloniality (two interrelated concepts) and intersectional discrimination in the curriculum. An intersectional approach is critical because it recognises different forms of domination

---

[37] Leigh Dayton, 'Australian University Pulls Plug on Climate Skeptics' Centre', *Science* (Web Article, 12 May 2015).

[38] 'Decolonising the Curriculum: A Guide for Biosciences', *University of Sheffield*, Department of Animal and *Plant Sciences* (Web Article, July 2020).

[39] Ibid 1.1.

[40] Ibid 1.1.

and marginalisation – such as racism, sexism, classism, historical injustice and prejudice based on religion – as inextricably linked.[41]

Such is the pervasive influence of decolonisation a report into free speech and British universities concludes '70 per cent of UK universities are undertaking some form of decolonisation – either by official university policies/statements or academics within the university advocating for it'.[42] Based on an analysis of Australian universities, including inclusive language guides and the implementation of the recommendations arising out of the 2019 review of free speech, the IPA report concludes:

In 2023, almost all Australian universities are hostile to freedom of speech on campus:

- 38 of Australia's 42 universities (90%) are rated 'red' for having policies that are hostile to free speech on campus, an increase from 33 in 2018 and 31 in 2017.

- Four of Australia's universities (10%) are rated 'amber' for policies that threaten free speech on campus, a decrease from 8 in 2018 and 10 in 2017.

- Zero universities are rated 'green' for supporting free speech on campus, a decrease of one institution, The University of New England, in 2018.[43]

As noted by Roger Scruton, whereas universities once allowed academics to pursue their research free of interference and hostility we now face a situation where any who fail to conform are guilty of

---

[41] Omid Tofighian, 'To Tackle Extremism in Schools We Must Challenge the White Curriculum', *The Conversation* (Web Article, 5 October 2015).

[42] Richard Norrie, 'Free Speech and Decolonisation in British Universities,' *Civitas* (Web Article, October 2022).

[43] Briana McKee, 'Free Speech on Campus Audit 2023', *Institute of Public Affairs* (Web Article, 10 August 2023).

'racism, sexism, homophobia, transphobia, Islamophobia, etc'.[44] The retreat from rationality, reason and free and open debate has reached the stage where Jennifer Oriel writes:

> The highest purpose of the university, to cultivate the flourishing of high culture and bequeath its bounty to future generations, is all but lost. Academics who benefitted from classical education watched universities transformed from sites of higher learning into revolutionary colleges during the late 1960s. Politics replaced the pursuit of truth, beauty and harmony as the raison d'etre of higher education. Today, the university is a hollow man stripped of purpose and devoid of substance.[45]

II. WHEN TOLERANCE IS DEFINED AS INTOLERANCE

As detailed in this chapter, Western, liberal democracies across the globe are facing a rising tide of tyranny illustrated by responses to the Covid-19 pandemic, the impact of scientism and the technological society plus the imposition of cultural-left mind control and group think. Of particular concern is the way academic freedom has been, and continues to be, threatened as without such freedom there is no counter-weight to group think and tyranny prevails. The question arises as to why such freedoms are under threat and why rationality, reason and common sense no longer apply?

One explanation centres on Antonio Gramsci's concept of cultural hegemony. As suggested by TJ Jackson Lears,[46] while Gramsci offers no specific definition, what the Italian Marxist refers to is the way ruling elites are able to enforce domination and control by conditioning

---

[44] Ibid.

[45] Jennifer Oriel, 'Universities', in Kevin Donnelly (ed), *Cancel Culture and the Left's Long March* (Wilkinson Press, 2021) 51.

[46] TJ Jackson Lears, 'The Concept of Cultural Hegemony: Problems and Possibilities' (1985) 90(3) *The American Historical Review* 567-593.

subordinate groups to accept as legitimate, in fact, what is a situation where they are disadvantaged and oppressed. As noted by Lears, the closest definition Gramsci does provide is when he refers to:

> The 'spontaneous' consent given by the great masses of the population to the general direction imposed by social life by the dominant fundamental group; this consent is 'historically' caused by the prestige (and consequent confidence) which the dominant group enjoys because of its position and function in the world of production.[47]

The reason why the Marxist revolution never eventuated in the West is because workers are conditioned to believe private ownership, working for a wage and profit making are beneficial and worthwhile. Louis Althusser's concept of the ideological state apparatus ('ISA') also helps explain the rise of cultural-Marxism and the campaign to take control of universities and silence disagreement and dissent. Althusser differentiates between two forms of capitalist control when he writes:

> What distinguishes the ISAs from the (Repressive) State Apparatus is the following basic difference: the Repressive State Apparatus functions 'by violence', whereas the Ideological State Apparatuses function 'by ideology'.[48]

Instead of a violent, physical revolution where workers and activists take to the streets and storm the barricades, Althusser argued the cultural-left should infiltrate and take over key institutions, including family, church, political and trade union organisations, the media and schools and universities. By destroying capitalist control and imposing a revolutionary ideology the expectation is the socialist utopia will eventuate and equality and freedom will prevail.

---

[47] Antonio Gramsci, *Selections form the Prison Notebooks* (International Publishers, 1980) 12.

[48] Louis Althusser, 'Ideology and Ideological State Apparatuses' (Web Article).

Since the establishment of the Frankfurt School in Germany during the early 1920s universities especially have been targeted and fallen victim to cultural-left ideology.[49] Arising from the belief universities have no inherent value or benefit as they operate as key institutions to enforce capitalist hegemony and false consciousness, the argument is academic freedom is simply a smokescreen disguising an institution complicit in oppressing and denying the 'other'. The movement to decolonise the curriculum and purge academic studies of whiteness and Eurocentric supremacism represents one of the more recent ideologies directed at cancelling academic autonomy and freedom.

Such is the radical intent on overthrowing capitalism that the Marxist academic Herbert Marcuse, in his essay 'Repressive Tolerance',[50] argues academic freedom must not be tolerated. Marcuse argues 'what is proclaimed and practiced as tolerance today, is in many of its most effective manifestations serving the cause of oppression' and '[t]olerance is extended to policies, conditions, and modes of behavior which should not be tolerated because they are impeding, if not destroying, the chances of creating an existence without fear and misery'.[51]

Published in 1965, Marcuse's denial of free speech and open enquiry provided an intellectual justification and rationale for the rising tide of student activism that swept across Western universities during the 1960's cultural revolution. In Paris students from the Sorbonne University took the streets and radicals including the German academic Rudi Dutschke called for socialist inspired direct action. This was a time, as noted by Allan Bloom, when '[t]he American university in the sixties was experiencing the same dismantling of rational inquiry as had

---

[49] Wanda Skowronska, 'Christianity Under Attack', in Kevin Donnelly (ed), *Cancel Culture and the Left's Long March* (Wilkinson Press, 2021) 132-147.
[50] Herbert Marcuse, 'Repressive Tolerance' (Web Article).
[51] Ibid.

the German universities in the thirties'.[52] The irony being, at the same time radical students argued in favour of free speech and the right to be heard, any academics who failed to conform were attacked and silenced.

Associated with the rise of intolerance and that helps explain why academic freedom has been undermined is the concept of critical theory. Originating in the Frankfurt School, critical theory critiques and undermines the status quo based on the belief Western capitalist societies are inherently corrupt and must be overthrown. Wanda Skowronska argues:

> Critical theory did not aim to tear down the economic base of western society as, with the force of history, it was inevitably going to collapse anyway. It aimed rather at tearing down the cultural superstructure which supposedly reflected the powerful controllers of the economic system and this would enable the collapse of western civilisation.[53]

Linked with critical theory is a radical alliance of theories, including postmodernism, deconstructionism and gender, sexuality, race and post-colonial theories intent on subverting the academy's commitment to rationality, reason and the search for objectivity and truth. Any who disagree and fail to conform are either ignored, silenced or vilified and attacked. As argued by Camille Paglia:

> [U]niversities and mainstream media are currently patrolled by well-meaning but ruthless thought police, as dogmatic in their view as agents of the Spanish Inquisition. We are plunged, once again, into an ethical chaos where intolerance masquerades as tolerance and where individual liberty is crushed by the tyranny of the group.[54]

---

[52] Allan Bloom, *The Closing of the American Mind* (Touchstone, 1988) 313.

[53] Wanda Skowronska, '1960's Psychologists: Beguiling Ideologues and Smiling Assassins', in Thomas Gourlay and Daniel Matthys (eds), *1968 Culture and Counterculture: A Catholic Critique* (Wipf and Stock Publishers, 2020).

[54] Camille Paglia, *Free Women Free Men: Sex, Gender, Feminism* (Pantheon Books, 2017) viii.

III. Concluding Comments

There's no doubt tyranny comes in various guises, ranging from overt violence and terror to restricting freedom of speech and enforcing language control and group think. There is also no doubt long fought for liberties and freedoms are under attack across the Western world as totalitarian governments and cultural-left activists enforce conformity, intolerance and dogmatism. At the same time, as history suggests, the thirst for rationality, reason and the freedom to seek wisdom, beauty and truth is difficult to extinguish. Such is human nature that even in the darkest hours there are those lighting small fires dedicated to safeguarding a patrimony committed to an open and free society.

4

What Invites Tyranny?
A Post-Covid Reflection on the Individual and Social Contributors to Social Enslavement

GIGI FOSTER*

ABSTRACT

Covid-era policy-making has caused enormous damage to Australia's health, wealth, and wellbeing. While we wait for this to be acknowledged by those in authority and by the broader society, we can find direction for our anger and sadness in recognising what within our control can be changed to make such abuse less likely in future moments of crisis. In this article, I explore the weaknesses of our personal psychologies, our local social spaces, and our broader communities that make us vulnerable to would-be tyrants at the state level. I remain optimistic that our personal collaborative, principled actions can build a society that is stronger, healthier, and better protected from abuse in the coming decades.

1. Introduction

Since March 2020, Australia and most Western countries have witnessed the most grievous mass violations of individual liberty on domestic soil seen in generations. These violations were explicit and long-lasting, yet they were not resisted by our allegedly democratic governments founded in part to secure and defend individual liberty. In fact, it was those governments themselves and the machinery of state

* Professor, UNSW School of Economics, Sydney, NSW. I extend my gratitude to Professor Augusto Zimmermann for the invitation to contribute to this Special Issue, and to Michael Baker for providing research assistance. All errors are my own.

they commanded that directly perpetrated the violations. How could this have happened? This is the most pressing question of the modern era, to which social and legal scholars writing today are ethically bound to provide answers, for the sake of our children's future freedom and the restoration of post-Enlightenment Western civilisation.

Much has been made of the failures of our governance systems during Covid times not only to preserve our basic human rights but to deliver positive health outcomes. The failures were catastrophic and occurred in almost every dimension of life that governments touched during this period. What dampened the damage, if only minimally due to the sheer power of the state and the lack of organisation of dissident voices, was the resistance of individual people and communities who recognised the travesty in their midst and found ways to protect and preserve local health, freedom, and morality in spite of what was happening around them. Sadly, such resistance was rare, especially in Australia.

In this paper I will first review the damage done by governments-turned-tyrants in this period and the weak resistance mounted against the policies that caused this damage, and then I will turn the looking glass onto the population that in most cases so willingly acquiesced to Covid-era violations. What individual and community attributes fed into the development of the government Hydra of the Covid era? Which social and psychological trends of modern life served to catalyse the destruction? An attitude of victimhood about what we were subjected to during Covid is not going to protect society the next time a similar perceived threat opens the door to would-be dictators. Instead I ask what latent vulnerabilities we as individuals and members of our local communities must recognise within ourselves and our groups that we might take action towards healing, thereby reducing the likelihood of finding ourselves in the grip of future tyrants. What ingredients of our minds and our communities, innocuous as they may seem in normal times, are fuel to tyrants in a crisis?

II. A Short History of the Destruction

It is difficult to overestimate the damage that has been done to Australian society by the suite of government policies enacted since March 2020 allegedly to fight the respiratory illness known as Covid. In our book, *The Great Covid Panic: What happened, why, and what to do next*, published in September 2021 by Brownstone Institute, my co-authors and I write in detail about the proximate economic, psychological, and political factors that led our society and most of the rest of the West to arrive at a situation in which Western governments made eye-wateringly destructive decisions daily for years and with seeming impunity.[1] We also offer in that book a sketch of the type and scale of the global destruction caused by Covid policies.

In August 2020, after waiting for months for any Australian government to justify its draconian policies of lockdowns, school closures, border closures, and many other freedom restrictions, I appeared by invitation of David Limbrick MP at the State of Victoria's Public Accounts and Estimates Committee ('PAEC') to give evidence about the state government's response to the Covid phenomenon.[2] I used my allocated time to sketch in broad strokes the damage that lockdowns and border closures were causing, and the dangers of allowing broad society-level policies such as these to be dictated by those who were counting only a small slice of the human costs of the policies. Subsequent to my appearance at the PAEC, I submitted to the committee a proof-of-concept cost-benefit analysis in which I enumerated the many different categories of costs of lockdowns, and roughly estimated the magnitude of four of them, which was enough to demonstrate that the total size of the costs of the lockdowns being thrust upon Australians almost surely significantly exceeded their plausible benefits. In my analysis, those benefits were estimated from real data taken from the counterfactual no-lockdown setting of Sweden, rather

---

[1] Paul Frijters, Gigi Foster and Michael Baker, *The Great Covid Panic: What Happened, Why, and What to do Next* (Brownstone Institute, 2021).

[2] Footage available at: <https://www.youtube.com/watch?v=mpyYwQFtF-U>.

than from models or computer simulations of reality. As I mentioned explicitly in my PAEC testimony, the sole assumption contained in my rough cost-benefit analysis of lockdowns that had no support in the literature was that lockdowns would have any direct positive gross effect (not net of costs) on the quantity or quality of human lives.

Sadly, the mainstream narrative had by that time taken full hold of the minds of not only bureaucrats but Australians at large, with those who questioned the wisdom of the policies being publicly attacked as advocating for people to die[3] and protestors arguing against lockdowns being summarily labelled in mainstream media reports as "conspiracy theorists".[4]

As the months went by after my PAEC testimony, the deafening silence continued from governments imposing these unproven and unprecedented whole-of-society policies. No justification was offered on holistic grounds, with the only arguments used against the odd objection or complaint being exclusively focussed on narrow objectives like "slowing the spread" or "protecting people from Covid". Even on those comically limited measures that were arguably inappropriate even as measures of success in the fight against Covid,[5]

---

[3] This specific accusation was levelled against me when I appeared on the television program 'ABC Q&A' in July 2020 (Paul Johnson, 'Heated Q+A discussion sees economist Gigi Foster deny she is 'advocating for people to die'', *news.com.au* (Web Article, 28 July 2020). Other epithets applied to me in various electronic forums during the Covid era included "granny-killer", "neoliberal Trumpkinaut death cult warrior", and "piece of human excrement".

[4] NCA Newswire, 'Australian coronavirus conspiracy theorists plan protests to declare 'national sovereignty', *news.com.au* (Web Article, 4 August 2020).

[5] One could make the argument that in light of the negligible danger of even the original strain of Covid to healthy young people, a reasonable strategy for promoting the health of a whole society facing Covid would be to do nothing at the state level to attempt to prevent its spread amongst the young and healthy, and thereby to encourage the prompt acquisition of immunity amongst those in that group who chose to take the risk of exposure. High levels of immunity in the young and healthy would then assist in protecting the more vulnerable groups in society, such as people in aged-care homes. Such a strategy runs counter to the implication carried in the narrative supporting lockdowns that stopping or slowing the spread of the virus was obviously a wise objective.

no convincing evidence about the efficacy of lockdown policies was offered.

In 2021, once my co-authors and I had found in Jeffrey Tucker a publisher for *The Great Covid Panic*,[6] I began fleshing out my proof-of-concept cost-benefit analysis with the excellent assistance of Sanjeev Sabhlok, a former economist at the Victorian Treasury and author of *The Great Hysteria and the Broken State*, the earliest book I know of that argued vehemently against Australian governments' Covid policies.[7] In late 2022, our updated and expanded cost-benefit analysis of Australia's Covid lockdowns was published in book form by Connor Court.[8]

In this book, Sanjeev and I use the newly developed currency called the wellbeing year, or WELLBY, to estimate separately both the costs and the benefits of Australia's Covid-era lockdowns and border closures. As with my initial proof-of-concept analysis presented to the Victorian PAEC two years prior, in our work we draw on real data from low-restriction countries, rather than simple susceptible-infected-recovered ('SIR') or other theoretical models or computer simulations, to estimate the benefits of lockdowns. We attempt to count all categories of foreseeable costs, including those paid immediately and those that will have to be paid in future, and consider impacts on every group in Australian society. We also mention, but do not attempt to quantify, losses in intangible dimensions such as trust and motivation. We find that the total cost of Australian Covid lockdowns in the years 2020 and 2021 amounted to at least 68 times the value of the benefits that they could possibly have delivered. We

---

[6] We sent Mr Tucker a copy of our draft book manuscript in May 2021, when Brownstone Institute (brownstone.org), which he would soon found, was still a twinkle in his eye. In September 2021, *The Great Covid Panic* became the first title published by Brownstone.

[7] Sanjeev Sabhlok, *The Great Hysteria and the Broken State* (self-published, 2020).

[8] Gigi Foster with Sanjeev Sabhlok, *Do Lockdowns and Border Closures Serve the 'Greater Good'? A cost-benefit analysis of Australia's reaction to COVID-19* (Connor Court, 2022).

conclude, to paraphrase Douglas Allen, that lockdowns may go down as Australia's worst-ever peacetime policy failure. Lockdown policies such as Australia's would have been implemented in no society where those in authority were coolly prioritising the holistic welfare of the population with whose care they had been entrusted.

Other researchers too have found that lockdowns carried massive costs not incorporated into the decision to impose them, and thus that lockdowns would not pass a cost-benefit test (or, it must be said, the traditional Aussie 'pub test'). Examples of such work are Yanovskiy and Socol who conclude that 'lockdowns may claim 20 times more life years than they save';[9] Ari Joffe who concludes that 'lockdowns are far more harmful to public health (at least 5–10 times so in terms of wellbeing years) than COVID-19 can be';[10] and Douglas Allen, who concludes that '[u]sing a mid-point estimate for costs and benefits, the reasonable estimate for Canada is a cost/benefit ratio of 141'.[11] In his dollar-based cost-benefit analysis of Australia's Covid lockdowns, Martin T Lally estimates a '[c]ost per Quality Adjusted Life Year saved by locking down of at least 11 times the generally employed figure of $100,000 for health interventions in Australia,' also correctly pointing out that the information required to determine this was available in March 2020.[12] Even the mainstream-establishment National Bureau of Economic Research in the United States published a working paper in September 2022 that ignored any long-term costs of lockdowns but still found that, counter to

---

[9] Moshe Yanovskiy and Yehoshua Socol, 'Are Lockdowns Effective in Managing Pandemics?' (2022) 19(15) *International Journal of Environmental Research and Public Health* 9295.

[10] Ari R Joffe, 'COVID-19: Rethinking the Lockdown Groupthink' (2021) 9 *Frontiers in Public Health* 625778.

[11] Douglas W Allen, 'Covid-19 Lockdown Cost/Benefits: A Critical Assessment of the Literature' (2022) 29(1) *International Journal of the Economics of Business* 1.

[12] Martin T Lally, 'A Cost–Benefit Analysis of COVID-19 Lockdowns in Australia' (2022) 40 *Monash Bioethics Review* 62.

the claim of saving lives on the basis of which they were sold to the peoples of the world, lockdowns (referred to in the paper as 'shelter-in-place', or 'SIP', policies) did not deliver even in this dimension: 'We do not observe differences in excess deaths before and after the implementation of SIP policies'.[13] In sum, an international consensus has emerged amongst independent researchers using a variety of approaches that the costs of lockdowns of the sort imposed on populations around the world in starting in 2020 offer too meagre a harvest of benefits and/or are too costly ever to have been defensible by someone purporting to act in the public interest. On this basis, they should never have been implemented.

To my knowledge, at time of writing in September 2023, no defence of government-mandated Covid lockdowns has been offered on the grounds of total welfare, health, wealth, or wellbeing by anyone in any government or by any independent analyst anywhere in the world. What we see instead, issued from researchers and institutions that used to command scientific credibility, are analyses that perpetuate the mistake of evaluating these whole-of-society policies based only on a tiny slice of their costs. One example close to home is the blindered analysis by Philip Clarke and Andrew Leigh published in *BMJ Global*,[14] in which they analyse the effect of Australian lockdowns only on short-term excess deaths. The authors find that no excess deaths were caused by lockdowns in the short run, on the basis of which they imply in the text of their paper that lockdowns were not so bad after all (contra their critics, such as the authors of the Great Barrington Declaration),[15] and in fact that we should consider using

---

[13] Virat Agrawal, Jonathan H Cantor, Neeraj Sood and Christopher M Whaley, 'The Impact of the COVID-19 Pandemic and Policy Responses on Excess Mortality' (Working Paper 28930, National Bureau of Economic Research, 2021 (revised 2022)).

[14] Philip Clarke and Andrew Leigh, 'Understanding the Impact of Lockdowns on Short-Term Excess Mortality in Australia' (2022) 7 *BMJ Global Health* e009032.

[15] 'The Great Barrington Declaration', <https://gbdeclaration.org/> (Web Page).

them regularly during the winter months.[16] Another leading recent example is a study released in August 2023 by the Royal Society in the UK that concludes that non-pharmaceutical interventions ('NPIs'), by which is meant policies like lockdowns and mask mandates, decreased the spread of Covid.[17] The modest effect found for these interventions on this narrow measure of success is interpreted by the report's writers and journalists reporting on the work to imply that these draconian measures were "effective".

The sleight of hand is tragic and unmistakeable: 'effectiveness' has been redefined to make the Covid policy mistakes vanish, in the process sweeping under the rug the litany of dimensions of life in which NPIs were most certainly not "effective", but rather acutely destructive. Through such casual and callow means, our collective understanding of the meaning of the word 'effective' becomes yet another casualty of the cascading charade of Covid-era blunders made by people in authority. Such studies are worse than useless in guiding societies back towards a sane approach to policy selection and evaluation after the maniacal era of Covid lockdowns.

Lockdowns and border closures were not the only hindrances of personal freedom imposed by states-turned-tyrants during Covid times. People around the world were subjected to social and economic coercion during the mass-scale roll-out in 2021 of injections that they were told, by lying, ignorant, and/or cowardly drug company representatives, politicians, bureaucrats, and doctors, would prevent

---

[16] On seeing this paper, Sanjeev Sabhlok and I composed a formal response to it which was ultimately published in the same journal: Gigi Foster and Sanjeev Sabhlok, 'Response to 'Understanding the Impact of Lockdowns on Short-Term Excess Mortality in Australia' by Philip Clarke and Andrew Leigh" (2023) 8 *BMJ Global Health* e012741. The original authors then published a response to our response in the same journal that displayed continuing deafness to the argument that their entire exercise was useless for policymaking, contra their claims, due to the narrowness of the outcomes examined.

[17] The Royal Society, 'COVID-19: Examining the effectiveness of non-pharmaceutical interventions – Executive summary' (2023).

infection or prevent transmission of the virus. Opting not to take these injections was a perilous personal decision, frequently resulting in social shunning and job loss. Families and work communities were fractured as the central modern medical concepts of personal medical autonomy and free and informed consent were summarily ignored or conveniently redefined. As time has elapsed and the real dangers of these rushed-to-market injections have been increasingly brought to light by independent researchers, the public's enthusiasm for further injections has waned. Trust in our public health system has been lost, according to independent observers.[18] Family solidarity and trust in our national institutions are pillars of our society and economy. Declines in these measures are yet another type of cost paid by the Australian people for the mistakes of our leaders during Covid times.

Perhaps worst of all from the perspective of the legal profession, those Australian institutions specifically tasked with upholding human rights – such as the Australian Human Rights Commission – did nothing to forestall or protest the most obvious and substantial cancellation of rights in the modern Western era. Multiple legal cases brought by people harmed by lockdowns failed or went unheard, in many cases signifying that our judges too have been captured by the false narratives sold to us in this period. It would be fair to ask at this moment what the words 'freedom' and 'human rights' mean anymore to those whose sworn duty is to defend Australians' access to them.

It is easy to point fingers of blame towards people in authority between 2020 and 2023 who in ways small and large aided and abetted the implementation of the catastrophic Covid policies to which Australia has borne witness. I hope and expect that as the years pass, our collective capacity to focus on the events of this time will improve, and we will see at least some small degree of justice done publicly for the tyrannical criminal actions of this time. While we wait for that day,

---

[18] See, eg, Kara Thomas, 'Restoring Trust in Public Health', *The Spectator Australia* (Web Article, 11 April 2023).

let me suggest that we use our time and efforts in understanding the ways in which our plight in the Covid era was facilitated by factors that lie more within our control than does the criminal and corrupt behaviour of particular individuals in authority.

III. Fuel to Tyrants 1: Individual Weaknesses

The modern age is replete with technological advances beyond the wildest dreams of our ancestors that, deployed with wisdom, can support myriad dimensions of human living. From advanced food production techniques to clickable online encyclopedias to automated house-cleaning, the architecture that underpins the modern way of life for most people in a country like Australia leads to easy living by the standards of anyone's honest historical reckoning.

The dark side of this good fortune is that in an environment of such ease and abundance, in which most of us rely on technological crutches every day in performing our core activities in and outside the home, humans' nature leads us to develop unhealthy habits of mind and body unless we consciously resist. Physical exercise is far less embedded into most people's necessary daily activities than it was 100 years ago, and can be almost totally absent from our daily lives unless we actively insert it in the form of a disciplined exercise routine. The problems we must solve at home, in our communities and in our jobs are more likely to be high-level and complex, involving little mortal risk to our persons or loved ones and instead requiring us to engage with nuanced arguments, political hierarchies, organisational norms and psychological subtleties. This breeds a creeping mental model of the world that includes few elements of risk, since so little risk is regularly encountered. More than that, our daily battles can seem on reflection to be a far cry in significance or meaning from the battles fought by our ancestors. The very material abundance we see around us in developed countries like Australia invites us to view our own existence and potential to improve the world as feeble, or even pointless: if so much has been achieved and we are now living in a Golden Age, or so goes the unfortunate reasoning, what more is there to do that one such as I could possibly hope to accomplish?

On top of these problems, the core features of some modern technologies are inherently suppressive of human thriving. Social media platforms like TikTok and X (the platform formerly known as Twitter) are leading examples. The hours spent expressing one's disembodied opinions or desires on a digital platform are hours not spent flexing the social, emotional, and intellectual muscles required to engage in person with other human beings in real time. The large bureaucracy seen in most successful organisations today is a modern technology (in a broad sense of the term) whose primary purpose is not to help people, or even to help the organisation in which it is situated, but to find ways of surviving and growing regardless of the human casualties. The endless forms, checklists, protocols, procedures, regulations, and other monitoring mechanisms that characterise the output of a modern large bureaucracy are often defended as being necessary to organise the activities of a large group, but also carry the unseen costs of strangling human innovation, crowding out intrinsic motivation, and deterring interpersonal trust.

Many of us have been lulled into a false sense that with all of our technology and all of our magnificent organisational structures to "protect" us, our lives are reliably risk-free. In developed countries like Australia, our children only rarely now die from childhood diseases that plagued humans for eons; our men only rarely die violently; our women only rarely die in childbirth. Only rare and horrific injuries or illnesses are expected to be seriously dangerous, and even those are thought to happen only to other people we see on the news. The embarrassing inevitability of death itself is hidden away from the rest of society in aged care homes. We can easily be seduced into believing that our world is one in which all we see around us is helpful, all activities we engage in or hire from others are 100 per cent safe, and effort on our behalf is needed to keep everything running only if we decide we feel like it.

Possessed of such utopian beliefs, implicitly trusting our state-run systems of protection, and unused anymore to encountering and coping in a proportional manner with real risks to the health or safety of ourselves and our loved ones, is it any wonder that so many in Australia were so easily frightened by the spectre of a new respiratory disease upon their exposure to sufficient videos, screaming headlines, and state-sponsored alarms?

Although today's relatively peaceful material abundance may be fairly seen as an awesome indicator of human achievement, what living in such an abundant setting does to people's habits of mind must be recognised in order for us to continue to advance. We must interrupt the lullaby being sung to us like the Siren's call by modern society, force ourselves to take real risks and be prepared to fail, and remind ourselves continually of the inherent fallibility of the state, which is run by mere people after all. Without forcing courage to develop in ourselves via our own personal, everyday choices about how to live our lives, we will not develop courage in such rich times. Without forcing ourselves to track the decisions of state actors and evaluate them against our own moral and scientific standards, we allow ourselves to develop the habit of not questioning what those in authority tell us. Without real courage and a critical attitude towards authority, we will be ripe for exploitation the next time some bogeyman that a would-be tyrant can exploit starts flashing in the headlines.

IV. Fuel to Tyrants 2:
Social Psychological Weaknesses

A broader view of the vulnerabilities of our people can be achieved by recognising that individuals are not defined merely by their internal psychological make-up, expectations, and atomistic decisions, but by how they are influenced by, relate to, and are seen by others.Sadly in this dimension as well, modern society abounds with damaging messages.

Damaging what is perhaps the most fundamental relationship of a stable society, that between a man and a woman, are messages about the dangers of one of these groups to members of the other. Women in modern Australia can be forgiven for viewing any given man with fearful scepticism, anxiously alert to any evidence of the bad behaviour that would confirm what stories about "the patriarchy" that oppresses women[19] and men's innate "toxic masculinity"[20] have led them to believe about men for years. Men could be forgiven for seeing their interactions with women as being predicated upon their performance of a continuous self-derogating eggshell-dance, with those unwilling to descend to this level of obsequiousness at risk of giving up in frustration or even detaching from interacting with women at all (cf the recent growth and increased extremity of the "incel" movement).[21] As a result, far from seeing intimate, supportive relationships with one another as a major player in the achievement of their own personal happiness and the health and peace of their society, we see men and women still needing one another yet feeling vaguely unsatisfied with one another. This is indicated by statistics like the steady increase in age at first marriage,[22] increasing rates of children being born out of wedlock and decreased fertility rates.[23] The declining divorce rate since 1970 is one of few positive signs in regard to the health of Australian families today.

---

[19] See, eg, Charlotte Higgins, 'The Age of Patriarchy: How an Unfashionable Idea Became a Rallying Cry for Feminism Today', *The Guardian* (Web Article, 22 June 2018).

[20] <https://en.wikipedia.org/wiki/Toxic_masculinity>.

[21] <https://en.wikipedia.org/wiki/Incel>.

[22] Lixia Qu and Jennifer Baxter, 'Marriages in Australia: Facts and Figures 2023' *Australian Institute of Family Studies* (Web Article, March 2023).

[23] Ibid.

Similar divisive fractures have been enlarging in our society between other groups that have historically collaborated in building the Australia of today. The most prominent of these is the fracture between socially recognised races. Damaging messaging in this area includes the invention of the term "invasion"[24] to replace other terms historically used to describe the initial arrival of Europeans into Australia; the increased emphasis on including performative "welcome to country" messages at large gatherings; and the most recent such messaging, in the form of the campaign for voting "yes" in the referendum for an Indigenous Voice to Parliament.[25] These phenomena underscore and elevate the differences between, rather than the similarities and common interests of, Indigenous and non-Indigenous Australians. By no means have relations always been smooth between these groups, but that is true of any human groups in any society throughout history, including different Indigenous tribes before the arrival in Australia of Europeans. The presence of extreme differences in commanded force at the first meetings between groups long ago is the fault of no person or group, and neither is it the fault of all non-Indigenous people today that the quality of life of Indigenous Australians significantly lags that of non-Indigenous Australians. All of us are lucky enough, generations beyond those initial meetings, to be united in a single country, with resources richer than our ancestors could possibly have imagined. The shame is not that some historical insult was visited upon one group of people by another, but rather that we put our modern resources into performative virtue-signalling exercises, face-saving, and power grabs rather than fervently continuing to experiment with practical steps for raising the living standards and outcomes of Australians as a whole, including and especially the presently disadvantaged.

---

[24] See, eg, Hilary Whiteman, 'Every year, 'Invasion Day' forces Australia to confront some painful truths', *CNN* (Web Article, 27 January 2023).

[25] <https://voice.gov.au/>.

We are bombarded with messages in modern Australia about how our fellow man is a threat to us. He may give us a dread respiratory disease (particularly if "unvaccinated"); he is likely to rape us[26] and may even kill us.[27] If he is on the 'other' side of the political spectrum, he is either "loony"[28] or a "conspiracy theorist",[29] and in either case, dangerous. The stories of sin that our fellow man, or we, may commit against ourselves and others range from driving our car (and thereby causing the Earth to warm and so killing millions of people in the future)[30] to breathing (and therefore risking the life of anyone in our immediate vicinity) to questioning the possibility or safety of sex selection, or even merely misgendering someone (and thereby causing mental health damage or even violence).[31]

In such an environment, we are weakened because we see enemies all around us, many of whom are not really our enemies. In reality, our real enemies have been hiding in plain sight in positions of power. "Divide and rule" is a central rule of thumb in political strategy for good reason: division is a powerful tool against being uprisen against. When we acquiesce to the divisive ideologies of our time, accepting the implicit narrative that the only people around whom we can feel safe are those whom we have personally vetted, we in effect lay down the red carpet to would-be power-abusers.

---

[26] This is a conclusion easily reached by female university students seeing alarming reports of on-campus sexual violence, whose accuracy has been called into dispute by male rights advocates – eg, Bettina Arndt, 'Are University Campus Sexual Assault Statistics Inflated?', *The Spectator Australia* (Web Article, 13 September 2023).

[27] Jasmine Kazlauskas, "More Than You Think': Truth About Australia's Secret Serial Killers', *news.com.au* (Web Article, 30 August 2022)

[28] See, eg, News Corporation Australia, "Loony Left' Want to 'Shut Down Coal"', *skynews.com.au* (Web Article, 3 February 2020).

[29] See, eg, Stuart A Thompson, 'As Covid-19 Cases Tick Higher, Conspiracy Theorists Stoke New Fears', *The New York Times* (Web Article, 11 September 2023).

[30] See, eg, Alex Blair, 'Radical climate activists pushing to 'inconvenience SUV owners' by deflating 4x4 tyres in major cities', *news.com.au* (Web Article, 30 May 2023).

[31] See, eg, Madison Lutz, 'Misgendering is an 'Act of Violence,' University Argues', *Campus Reform* (Web Article, 30 May 2023).

V. Fuel to Tyrants 3: Weaknesses in Communities

The fabric of traditional, real-world communities had been weakening in the West long before the Covid era. Scholars in sociology, economics and anthropology have remarked upon downward trends since the 1970s in indicators like church-going,[32] participation in community activities like sports and block parties,[33] looking out for one's neighbours, and feelings of community safety, trust, and identity.[34]

Families facing a decline in community strength have two options, apart from trying to find a better option elsewhere: either to accept living in a less rich, less secure, and less socially supportive real world, or to find alternative sources of social input and security. The first option leads to a more stressful everyday existence, which weakens the family over time. The second option can manifest through the family itself attempting to fill the gap in security and social support, which once again places additional stress on the family, although it may have both positive consequences (eg, stronger parent-child, sibling, and spousal relationships) and negative ones (eg, 'helicopter parenting' as an attempt to patch that weakened community safety net, as implied by Mary Eberstadt's writings and interviews on the topic). Another way that families may fill the gap in social support and security when their real-world communities weaken is to look for a different community, whether online or at a different level of aggregation – such as the state – in the real world.

Replacing real-world communities with online communities again

---

[32] Kathy Jacka and Ruth Powell, 'Changes in Church Attendance in Australia', *NCLS Research* (Web Article, October 2021).

[33] 'Aussies are losing their competitive spirit for sport', *Roy Morgan* (Web Article, 20 March 2017); Australian Sports Commission, 'Addressing the decline in sport participation in secondary schools: Findings from the Youth Participation Research Project' (Web Article, November 2017).

[34] 'Social isolation and loneliness', *Australian Institute of Health and Welfare* (Web Article, 7 September 2023).

weakens families, as they are then vulnerable to the many dysfunctions of the online socio-informational world. Replacing a reliance on local communities with a reliance on the state makes families vulnerable to poor service, neglect, or even abuse by that state, which itself is far removed from the family's actual situation and needs and hence is more likely to provide generic solutions that are not customised to the requirements of the family. For example, a functioning local community – say a couple of residential suburban or city blocks – in 1960 might collectively look after a local elderly grandfather living alone on one of the blocks in a way that today's state would struggle to do, given the lack of local information available to the state about that particular person's situation. Another example is seen in the low number of adoptions approved per year by state systems in Australia, as compared with the larger numbers of adoptions routinely managed by communities before the state inserted itself into such affairs, claiming to represent the best interests of children.[35]

Replacing informal with more formal networks and insurance systems has been shown by economists and others to be part of the standard coming-of-age developmental trajectory of modern societies.[36] The formalisation of insurance structures offers clear benefits for societies: for example, formal insurance markets can assist by more widely pooling risk and thereby offering a more consistent and reliable service than a typical informal insurance system operating at the level of a local community. However, such anonymous structures carry an unseen cost as well. Informal community-based insurance mechanisms demand, for their continued successful operation, a continuous demonstration of interpersonal integrity by participants,

[35] 'Adoptions Australia 2021-22', *Australian Institute of Health and Welfare* (Web Article, 28 April 2023); Institute of Family Studies, *Adoption Law in Australia* (Australian Family Briefings No 1, 1992); 'Adoption legislation in Australia', *Institute of Open Adoption Studies* (Web Article).

[36] See, eg, Rafael La Porta and Andrei Shleifer, 'The Unofficial Economy and Economic Development' [2008] (Fall) *Brookings Papers on Economic Activity* 275.

a requirement that is reinforced by the community. Formal systems, by contrast, are removed from community-supported integrity monitoring mechanisms. It is possible to move too far in the direction of formalisation, particularly when the accountability of formal providers (like insurance companies) is weak, to a point at which the formal market (for insurance or indeed for other goods or services) no longer brings needed consistency and reliability but rather shoehorns people with heterogeneous needs into mass-scale template solutions for the sake of profit.

During the Covid era, the slow disintegration of communities that had been occurring for decades accelerated, rapidly in some cases. Locked in their homes and hooked on their screen feeds of daily death and case counts from doomsday-proclaiming politicians and bureaucrats, families found themselves dependent for their livelihoods, their sense of security, and even their sense of reality on a state that had left its core business by the wayside in the fanatical pursuit of more power and more technocratic "solutions" to support its control. Religious and other community leaders in the main also succumbed to the mind-numbing lockdowns and other dogmatic state diktats, acquiescing with little fight when told by the state to close houses of worship, sports events, and so on. With such outlets unavailable, families were denied access to most of the sole remaining modern structures working to give people security, social connection and motivation in their local areas, and in the unprecedentedly stressful times of lockdown nothing was available to fill that gap apart from online communities and the state.

In such a depleted state, is it any wonder that Australian communities all but rolled over when the state turned tyrant during Covid times? If we wish to forestall a recurrence of the Covid tragedy, we must pour our efforts in the coming years into rebuilding real communities – geographical, interest-based, faith-based, and otherwise – as a bulwark against a future tyrant's usurpation and subsequent abuse of the role that communities have played in meeting core human needs.

VI. Conclusion

The three-year-long era of fanatical Covid policy-making destroyed a significant fraction of Australia's wealth and health as those stocks stood in early 2020. We will be repairing the damage done to our country during this era for at least the next generation. Our healing, restoration and rebuilding efforts must be devoted not only towards the individuals who have been directly harmed and their families, but also towards the overwhelming majority of Australians who went along with the madness. To see in stark relief the human destruction that they have explicitly or implicitly condoned and even participated in directly, in the sober light now dawning as the reckless Covid crowd recedes, will be a major psychological shock. We must be able to offer a path forward that does not deny their humanity and yet honestly acknowledges the weaknesses in our society, our communities, and our individual psychologies that allowed the madness to take hold.

We have a huge uphill battle ahead, not only with the elites in charge during the Covid era who destroyed so much human health and wealth, but with ourselves and our social nature. We owe it to our children to invest in personal and community strategies that can help us and all of Australia to avoid becoming sitting ducks for the next would-be cadre of tyrants.

5

CH Douglas on Tyranny:
Its Nature, Origin and Remedies

M OLIVER HEYDORN*

ABSTRACT

Major CH Douglas was the founder of the original Social Credit movement. Social Credit theory has much to contribute to a deep and accurate understanding of the vexing financial, economic, cultural, environmental, and political problems with which we are confronted. In both his philosophical and technical writings, Douglas identified the single greatest threat to the well-being of society in the modern world: the tyranny of plutocratic oligarchy. He analysed its nature and origins and then proceeded to outline the correct orienting principles and the appropriate mechanisms by means of which this threat could be effectively neutralised. The final aim of the Douglas Social Credit movement was to restore society to a state of optimal and harmonious functioning.

[A]s far as it is possible to sum the matter up, the general problem seems to be involved in a decision as to whether the individual should be sacrificed to the group or whether the fruits of group activity should be always at the disposal of the individual. – CH Douglas (1924)[1]

---

1 CH Douglas, *Social Credit* (Gordon Press, rev ed, 1973) 27-8. Douglas was convinced that it is only by taking the second path, ie, by elevating the individual above the group, that we can lay the foundation for a satisfactory and sustainable future. The first path described, where the individual is to be sacrificed to the group, is the path of tyranny.

* Dr. M. Oliver Heydorn graduated *summa cum laude* from the International Academy of Philosophy at the Pontifical University of Santiago, Chile. He is the founder and director of the Clifford Hugh Douglas Institute for the Study and Promotion of Social Credit (socred.org).

I. Introduction

CH Douglas (1879-1952) was a British engineer and the founder of an international campaign that was inspired by his many articles, books, and speeches. This campaign became known as 'The Social Credit Movement'. Throughout the inter-war years, 'Social Credit' was a household phrase in many parts of the British Empire. There were even Social Credit governments that had held power for many decades in the Canadian provinces of Alberta and British Columbia and 30 Social Credit MP's in the federal Canadian parliament as a direct result of the 1962 election. While Douglas, his ideas, and his movement, are chiefly associated with economics and the urgent need for a particularly radical type of monetary reform, he was also a profound and original thinker in his approach to key philosophical, political, and historical questions. The overall thrust of his thought was chiefly concerned with the functionality of the financial, economic, and political systems, and of the social order in general, and with what he saw as the due requirements for that functionality: the decentralisation of power to the lowest degrees feasible and the protection and promotion of true human liberty.

Before we proceed any further, two clarifications are in order. The first is that in spite of the presence of the word 'social' in 'Social Credit', Douglas' economic vision was not only not socialist, but was actually anti-socialist. He was against Big Government, high taxation, excessive regulation, a command economy, and so forth. The idea that 'Social Credit' must be some form of 'socialism' is a common misconception that has plagued the Social Credit movement for many decades. The second clarification has to do with the fact that – for some inexplicable reason – the Chinese Communist Party has decided, in much more recent times, to name their totalitarian surveillance, reward and punishment programme 'social credit'. Needless to say, Douglas Social Credit has nothing at all in common with the CCP's social control system. If anything, it would rightly be described as something which stands in complete opposition to the Chinese system. Douglas Social Credit is as *anti-totalitarian* as it is *anti-socialist*:

> The set of ideas which became the movement known as Social Credit began with an examination of the problem of the relationship of the individual to the group, and the financial proposals which emerged were consciously, and in all their developments, designed to free the individual from group domination.[2]

II. The Basics of Douglas' Social Philosophy

One of CH Douglas' central insights in the field of social philosophy (an insight that was by no means unique to him) was that whenever humans associate together in groups there is some advantage or benefit that comes into existence 'on the back' of the association as a supervenient quality. Indeed, it is precisely for the sake of obtaining this advantage – which he termed 'the increment of association' – that people associate with others in the first place. This increment takes the form of a particular kind of power, in this case, a social power. Accordingly, Douglas also referred to it as an association's 'social credit', ie, the association's capacity to achieve various ends and, derivatively, the well-grounded belief in the same. The 'increment of association' as it applies to society in general, or to societies of a certain kind, is thus the most basic of meanings that might be ascribed to the term 'social credit' within the context of Douglas' body of thought. Far from referring to a system of centralised surveillance and control, the original 'social credit' describes a concrete phenomenon: *the power of human beings, working in association, to achieve intended results.*

Now, the fundamental idea behind the increment of association (or the 'social credit') is that the whole is greater than the sum of its parts;

---

[2] CH Douglas, *The Development of World Dominion* (Tidal Publications, 1969) 1.

ie, there are certain objectives which people can achieve more easily or better when they work together in co-operation as opposed to when they are working on their own. Four average men, for example, by associating with each other can move a 200 kg table more easily than what one stronger-than-average man would be able to manage. There are, in addition, other objectives that cannot be reached at all on one's own, but only in association with others. Reproduction would be, perhaps, the simplest exemplification of this latter category. In both cases, the *plus ultra*, the profit, that accrues to association is unearned; ie, it is inherent to the nature of association itself and is not something for which any one person or group can take exclusive or proprietary credit.

Reality is so constructed by its Designer that when we bring two or more elements into a positive association with each other we can gain something 'more' as a superabundant gift of the association.[3] By bringing a lever and a fulcrum into association, for example, it takes less force to lift a weight. There is a mechanical advantage that comes into being on the basis of the association. By bringing people into various forms of social association, we likewise gain some benefit in terms of the ease, quality, efficiency, or the possibility/probability, etc, of achieving some collectively-valued end.

There is, however, an important caveat: not all human associations are automatically of equal worth. Merely bringing people together is not a sufficient condition for the unearned increment, the 'social credit', to supervene, in its maximal expression, on the association, nor does it ensure that that power will be deployed in the most satisfactory manner, nor does it guarantee that the fruits derived from the application of the unearned increment will be equitably distributed. We can therefore distinguish between high-quality or healthy associations and low-quality or unhealthy associations. The difference between

---

[3] I am obviously employing the term 'association' here in a broader sense than when it is used specifically in relation to human groups or society.

them depends on how effectively and efficiently the true purpose of the association, ie, the particular increment the association is aiming for, is maximised or rather optimised, and how fairly that unearned increment is then distributed amongst the individual members of an association.

When it comes to the question of distributing the fruits or benefits of an association (ie, the increments), different patterns of distribution can emerge and some of them will prove to be less satisfactory than others. The same is true of what might be termed the decrements of association, since associating also imposes a cost on the individuals who participate in the association:

> It appears to be a fundamental instinct of conscious life, well developed even in the animal kingdom, that certain advantages can be gained by the association of individuals into a group, which cannot be attained in other ways. It is equally true that in a primitive state of existence the advantages of the group carry with them definite disadvantages to the individual. It is true that many hands make light work, but it is not less true that he travels the fastest who travels alone. The developments of modern industrial society, founded upon the division of labour and co-ordinated by the financial system, have at one and the same time increased this unearned increment of association, and still further subordinated the individual to the group.[4]

What we are actually talking about when we speak about 'fairness' or 'justice' in a realistic sense is the pattern of distribution of benefits and burdens within the context of association that will maximise the general satisfaction with the operation of the association, while assuring that at least a basic minimal degree of satisfaction can be guaranteed

---

4 CH Douglas, *The Monopoly of Credit* (Bloomfield Books, 4th ed, 1979) 11.

to those occupying the lowest rung amongst the membership.[5] This requires ensuring that everyone's interests are taken into account as part and parcel of the association's due functionality:

> [A] nation or other corporate body exists to further the interests of individuals; or, to put it in a more technical form, there is an increment of association derived from the co-operation of individuals, which should be distributed amongst the individuals, if the object of their co-operation is to be achieved successfully.[6]

Because individuals associate into groups for the sake of maximising or optimising their individual benefit, as well as that of others (because helping others to flourish should ricochet in various ways so as to further enhance one's own well-being), and for the sake of simultaneously minimising the decrements of association, 'fairness', or the successful distribution of the unearned increment of association in favour of each individual to the greatest extent feasible, is a prime mark of functionality.

Healthy associations are those which fulfill well, ie, in ways that are effective, efficient and fair, the true purposes for which the associations were established in the first place. Put simply, they work well; they are highly functional. A healthy economy, for example, is one which fulfills its purpose well by delivering the goods and services that individuals need to survive and flourish, with the least amount of labour and resource consumption. In a healthy association, the aggregate benefit is maximised, while burdens are minimised and the general pattern of distribution might be described as equitable (not necessarily equal). This equitable distribution is both a condition for and a constitutive component of an association that is successful in fulfilling its purpose. That groups exist only to serve the concrete

---

[5] This way of understanding fairness or justice may be reminiscent of John Rawls' famous 'theory of justice' that was popularised in his book of the same name.

[6] CH Douglas, *Warning Democracy* (Stanley Nott, 3rd ed, 1935) 92.

individuals who compose them and to serve them well is the *leitmotiv* of the healthy association according to Douglas' social philosophy: 'institutions exist only legitimately to serve individuals, ...'[7]

Unhealthy associations, by contrast, are those which significantly fail, to one extent or another, to fulfill their true purposes in ways that are effective, efficient, and fair. They don't maximise or optimise the unearned increment of association, ie, the objective for which the association was first established, and they don't embody a pattern of distribution of those benefits and burdens which might rightly qualify as 'fair' or 'equitable'.

Now, there are undoubtedly a number of factors that might be responsible for causing an association to deviate from its due course and to degenerate into an unsuccessful or unhealthy association. Incompetence, lack of social concern (apathy), mismanagement, bad luck, unforeseen circumstances, cultural changes, etc, etc, might all play a part in the downfall of an association. I want to focus, however, on one particular factor that stalks every association, at least in the form of a potential threat. It is the phenomenon known as parasitism.

III. The Nature and Origin of Tyranny

If we think of the unearned increment of association as an amorphous whole, the bounty that it represents constitutes a grave temptation to those more unscrupulous and powerful members of an association who

---

[7] CH Douglas, *The Big Idea* (Veritas Publishing Company, 1983) 69. On Douglas' view, it is for the sake of the individual that all groups, institutions, laws, and regulations, etc, exist. Cf CH Douglas, *Economic Democracy*, (Bloomfield Publishers, 5th ed, 1974) 29-30: 'Systems were made for men, and not men for systems, and the interest of man which is self-development, is above all systems, whether theological, political or economic. Accepting this statement as a basis of constructive effort, it seems clear that all forms, whether of government, industry or society must exist contingently to the furtherance of the principles contained in it. If a State system can be shown to be inimical to them – it must go; if social customs hamper their continuous expansion – they must be modified; if unbridled industrialism checks their growth, then industrialism must be reined in. That is to say, we must build up from the individual, not down from the State.'

are in a position to alter the design and operation of that association in order to suit themselves. Such individuals or groups might wish to capture more than their due share of the unearned increment of association as per the norms of equitable distribution, but this goal can only be achieved at the expense of the common good or the public interest. In other words, elites can become corrupted and wish 'to feast' on the unearned increment of association as much as possible to the neglect of their due responsibilities to the association.

Whenever, or to the extent that, a parasitic class is successful in this anti-social aim, it necessarily gives rise to an unhealthy association which does not fulfill well, ie, in ways that are effective, efficient, and fair, the true purpose for which it was first established. For, in order to achieve their ends of maximising the unearned increment of association while minimising the decrements of association *for themselves* (and quite apart, therefore, from what the fulfillment of the true purpose of the association objectively requires), the parasitic class must, in one way or another, artificially limit and then misdirect the activities of an association. The artificial limiting gives them leverage over the common members because it is a limitation that can be alleviated but will only be alleviated on the condition and to the extent that some tribute is paid to the elites in exchange. And, in this way, the association becomes, in some significant manner, restricted and crippled because it is serving a different purpose apart from and in defiance of its true purpose. There is, in consequence, a failure to maximise (or optimise) the unearned increment of association where the general welfare is concerned to the extent that this fulfillment is physically or objectively possible, coupled with the imposition of inequitable distributions of benefits and burdens that harm the regular members of an association for the advantage of the parasitic class. If the 'harvesting' is taken too far, there is a risk, of course, that it could even kill the host.

Such associations may be described as having an 'anti-democratic' rather than 'democratic' structure. That is, it is taken for granted in the basic operation of the association that the bulk of individuals exist for the purpose of serving the group and, by extension and in reality, the parasitic interests who dominate the group. When this 'anti-democratic', dysfunctional structure is then forcibly imposed by one means or another, we arrive at tyranny. The parasitic class (which hitherto might have operated exclusively by trickery or persuasion) becomes an oligarchy (that operates mainly by force).[8]

In the broadest sense of the term, then, a *tyranny* would describe any social arrangement which allows an oligarchic elite to self-servingly employ some form of *coercive power*, whether private or public or both, to establish, maintain, or expand a pattern of distributing the unearned increment of association that will benefit that elite at the expense of the authentic common good. The goal is to seize as much of the unearned increment of association for one's own group as is possible, ie, insofar as doing so remains compatible with a tolerably functioning association. The use of coercive power to achieve that goal is experienced by those who are not part of the oligarchic elite as abrasive, arbitrary, constraining, burdening, violating, etc, ie, as the imposition of rules, conditions, etc, that are not compatible either with the full functioning of the association or with the common individual's well-being. In sum, the attempt to seize the unearned increment of association on the part of the elites presupposes an illegitimate and unjustified (non-functional) limitation on the freedom of the general membership of an association, a limitation which they naturally resent. Since the objectives of the elites operating a tyranny and those of the common members of the association are in such a stark conflict, tyrannies are fundamentally unstable and this necessitates all sorts of wiles and stratagems on the part of the oligarchs to maintain the tyranny and to increase its hold over the people if at all possible.

---

[8] There can, of course, be varying degrees of oligarchic tyranny.

The possibility and indeed the reality of tyranny in human association means that we are always faced with an inevitable choice as members of an association, or of society in general. We have to decide whether we will work and fight for the association to embody a policy of freedom for all of its members (only limited by the functional necessities of the association) alongside a maximisation of its due benefits for each individual, or whether we will acquiesce to a policy of domination, of tyranny, which will unduly limit our freedoms and deprive us to some significant extent of our due share in the unearned increment of association:

> There are only two Great Policies in the world to-day – Domination and Freedom. Any policy which aims at the establishment of a complete sovereignty, whether it be of a Kaiser, a League, a State, a Trust, or a Trade Union, is a policy of Domination, irrespective of the fine words with which it may be accompanied; and any policy which makes it easier for the individual to benefit by association, without being constrained beyond the inherent necessities of the function involved in the association, is a policy of Freedom.[9]

---

[9] CH Douglas, *These Present Discontents and The Labour Party and Social Credit* (Cecil Palmer, 1922) 5. See also M Oliver Heydorn, *Social Credit Philosophy* (IAP Press, 2016) 66-7: [Please confirm that the quote below is from Social Credit Philosophy. The part I've highlighted in green appears to be a comment on Douglas, not a quote from Douglas.]

It may be opportune to clarify the notion of 'functional necessity.' From the Social Credit point of view, the only limitations on individual freedom that can be justified by the inherent nature of things are those regulations that are shown to be required in practice in order to produce the complete and effective subordination of the group to the individual.

The individual freedom which Social Credit advocates is not libertarian freedom, however; i.e., there is never a right to interfere with or disregard those regulations which are necessary, on account of the nature of reality, to maximise the benefits of group association for *each* individual to the greatest extent possible. While it is true that what might count as appropriate regulations will likely differ depending on time and place, that these should always be kept to the minimum that is needed, and that they should be summarily discarded once they are no longer required, there are indeed restrictions, which, being grounded in what Douglas referred to as 'the Canon' i.e.,

This talk of a 'complete sovereignty' and a 'policy of domination' bring us to the subject of monopoly and monopolistic control. As far as the use of coercive power is concerned, the pursuit and eventual establishment of monopolies is a key tool in the arsenal of the oligarchic interests, so much so that the policy of domination just referenced may also be called 'the policy of monopoly'. Whenever a monopoly exists, can be established, or else captured on behalf of oligarchic interests, this provides a tremendous amount of leverage with which the participation of individuals can be effectively enjoined and more or less one-sided conditions imposed for the benefit of the oligarchy. Monopoly as a policy is something that is thus pursued in every area of significance in order to maximise the harvest that can be attained *via* the oligarchic usurpation of the unearned increment of association.

However, since there are, even with the benefits that can be afforded by monopolistic control, definite limits as to how much a parasitic class can take for itself from the pool of unearned increments without risking the demise of 'the goose that lays the golden egg' (in this case, the host association), there is also an inherent tendency on the part of that same class to seek ways of extending the jurisdiction of their monopoly power so as to encompass more and more people as well as resources. By this means, even greater benefits can be secured for the oligarchy. Thus we observe in history that city-states coalesce into kingdoms, kingdoms into countries, and countries into empires. Some of this coalescing might be organic, but on a Douglasite reading

---

the natural law, reveal themselves as authoritative if the true purpose of association as envisaged by the democratic model of association is to be adequately fulfilled.

The correct set of regulations is not, therefore, a matter of mere preference or arbitrary choice; it must be discovered and then obeyed in practice. It is certainly possible that disagreements amongst people of good faith may arise concerning what the correct regulations actually happen to be, but this fact should not cause us to abandon the will either to implement or maintain whatever shows itself to be a correct regulatory principle. Any disputes of this type should be settled by free inquiry and debate and, if necessary, trial and error.

of history a lot of it would be the result of deliberate policy with an anti-social, ie, tyrannical, motive in view. The logical endpoint of this deliberate movement towards centralisation would be the establishment of a world super-state, a one-world order with a one-world government. This would be the monopoly of monopolies, the mother of all monopolies, a comprehensive centralised monopoly on a global scale.

As Douglas remarks in 'The Monopolistic Idea' (a speech that he gave in Melbourne, Australia, during his 1934 world tour), the idea of 'world-monopoly' is not new. It is something that has served as the overarching objective for many groups of people throughout history: 'Practically all the world's historical empires, beginning with the Roman Empire, although there were others before that, were attempts at world power.'[10] Douglas goes on to point out that these attempts were primarily military in nature; ie, the typical means that were employed in an attempt to achieve world power involved the use of the armed forces of the state to physically impose an oligarchic policy on other states and peoples.

What *is* new in the last few centuries, however, (though the role of the Money Power as a determining force in world history goes back several millennia) is the increasing use of financial mechanisms and financial power, ie, the financial software on which we run our economies and the strategic deployment of the various advantages that are derived from its operation, to serve as the method *par excellence* for enthroning a plutocratic oligarchy at the top of the social pyramid and for extending their hegemony throughout the world. In Douglas' view, the tyrannical threat of our time might be identified as 'the financial world state, the financial hegemony of the world by a selected group of central banks, crowned by the Bank of International Settlements.'[11] What is often termed 'the New World Order' is, above all, a financial

---

[10] CH Douglas, *The Monopolistic Idea* (The Institute of Economic Democracy, 1979) 1.
[11] Ibid 1.

world order. It is the attempt to transform the existing monopoly of credit, which is the prerogative of the banking system, into a monopoly on all things that money can buy or otherwise influence. The power to create and issue money and to profit enormously thereby becomes political by necessity because it enables the financiers to impose policy in all other areas of society in order to forward their own objectives: wealth, privilege, and, above all, more and more power:

> Further, it is to be remembered that the financial system is a centralising system; it can only have one logical end, and that is a world dictatorship. There seems to be little doubt that the temporary headquarters of this potential world dictatorship have been moved from country to country several times during the past five or six centuries. At one time it was in Italy and specifically in Genoa, then in the Low Countries and Lombardy, from whence came the Jewish Lombards who gave their name to Lombard Street. During the eighteenth and nineteenth centuries it has unquestionably been in London, but there is every indication that a change of headquarters to New York is contemplated.[12]

IV. Douglas's Analysis of the Financial System

In order to *begin* to understand the tremendous policy-making power that is resident in the banking system given its power of money-making and issuing and how this power can be used to extend and to consolidate the 'empire of finance', we will have to proceed to an examination of Douglas' analysis of the fundamental flaws which characterise the current financial system.

We might begin with the observation that the existing banking system incorporates three features in its standard operations that are ethically and functionally problematic: 1) usury, 2) fraud, and 3) the 'creation' of money *ex nihilo*.

---

[12] Douglas (n 1) 160.

By 'usury' I do not mean the mere charging of interest on loans, but rather the practice of economic rent-taking in the lending of money. Whenever someone lends money at arbitrarily high rates that significantly exceed the corresponding costs or risks and that are imposed independently of the success or otherwise of the borrowers, the lender is making an unjustified profit at the expense of those others. Rather than sharing in the profit of a borrower (in the case of a profitable business, let's say) on some equitable basis, the banks make huge profits by implicitly claiming the ownership of the money that they lend out and by charging rent for it. The vast bulk of the money supply in every Western country (95%+) is rented from the private banks in this way. By this means, the banks use money to 'make money' without contributing something of equivalent value to society in terms of the flow of goods and services.[13]

Usury thus enriches and empowers one section of the community at the illegitimate expense of the others. It may be described as a racket, the true dimensions of which might be gauged by considering that, in principle, an organ of the state could provide a nation's money supply in its entirety at a mere fraction of the present cost in interest payments. Currently, only notes and coins (which are 5% or less of the money supply) are available as state money. This currency is typically issued at face value (the difference between the cost of production and the face value constituting a profit or seigniorage for the state). Instead of expanding the issue of currency to cover expenditures, governments at all levels borrow a good part of the money that they spend from the private banking system and pay interest on that money, interest charges which must then be covered by the public in their taxes. This means that the public are being taxed for private gain on account of public expenditures when that money could be supplied at cost as a

---

[13] We should pay the banks for their services, but not pay them rent as if the money were a scarce commodity, the price of which can vary depending on interest rate changes.

public service or utility and the burden of taxation correspondingly eased.

But the story doesn't end there. The lending of money is also fraudulent insofar as the banks do not lend money in the strictest of senses or what we might term '1ˢᵗ class money' in the form of legal tender, ie, currency or state money in the form of bills and coins, that has been deposited with them (as people are generally led to believe). Rather they lend their own 'promises-to-pay', ie, bank credit. Nor does the story end there. These 'promises to pay' are actually created *ex nihilo via* accounting operations. When making a loan, for example, the bank expands both sides of its balance sheet such that the newly created bank credit is treated as the corresponding liability of a newly created debt (which is held as the bank's asset). Since the volume of bank credit greatly exceeds the supply of state money or currency, there is an additional element of fraud in that these 'promises-to-pay' are not fully backed up by currency. In the case of a bank run that has been induced by a financial crisis or even an irrational panic, they may not be fully convertible into currency upon demand. These 'promises-to-pay' thus rest on a very shaky basis and may prove to be invalid.

Douglas once summed up the matter this way:

> As the situation stands at present, the banker is in an unique position. He is probably the only known instance of the possibility of lending something without parting with anything, and making a profit on the transaction, obtaining in the first instance his commodity free.[14]

Having explained some of the key problems with the banking system from the point of view of healthy associations, there are a few caveats that must be added immediately.

Firstly, we must be clear that Douglas is not an advocate for the

---

[14] CH Douglas, *The Breakdown of the Employment System* (The Institute of Economic Democracy, 1979) 6.

nationalisation of the private banks. He is not against private banking, nor is he against the private banks existing on a for-profit basis. Indeed, we should have more private banks about in order to guarantee competition, not fewer. What he insists on, however, is that the private banks should profit by assisting the community in the achievement of its legitimate, independent interests to the fullest measure, ie, by facilitating a common economic policy in the public interest, not by exploiting the community (by holding the community at ransom *via* a financial system that keeps credit artificially scarce, as we shall soon see).

Secondly, and quite interestingly enough, Douglas is not chiefly preoccupied with the problem of usury or even with the fraud inherent in the bank creation and lending of (in the absence of full reserves) 'promises-to-pay' as the bulk of our money supply. Certainly, he does recognise that banking, as it is currently operated, is 'the most colossal lucrative fraud that has ever been perpetrated on society.'[15] He also recognises that the usury and associated financial mechanisms are significant because they are amongst the chief means by which the financial elite usurp the unearned increment of economic association and centralise wealth, power, and privilege into their own hands at the expense of the common good. These matters are not non-issues by any means. However, there is a deeper, more technical problem that is at the core of the Douglas' diagnosis of our financial ills. Eliminating usury would not solve or even address this more technical issue. Even so, the two problems are intimately related insofar as the technical issue actually creates a situation which delivers even more opportunities to the banks, indeed their best opportunities, for renting out 'promises-to-pay' (as we shall soon see). In other words, the defect in question greatly enhances the degree to which the private banking system can lay hold of the unearned increment of economic association. For this reason, if one could, *ex hypothesi*, eliminate usury, this would

---

[15] CH Douglas, 'Money: An Historical Survey' (1936) 2 *The Fig Tree* 139, 146.

simultaneously remove one of the chief incentives that the financiers currently have for not fixing the technical problem along the lines that Douglas suggests.

On Douglas' understanding, the technical problem with the existing financial system can be encapsulated as follows: *it is an unbalanced debt-money system*. It is a debt-system in the sense that all money (or nearly all money) is created and/or injected into the economy alongside a corresponding debt (or debt-equivalent). This, in itself, would not be a problem if it were not for the second aspect: the fact that the system is also inherently unbalanced. It is an unbalanced in the sense that the rate at which costs and hence prices are being built up in the course of multi-stage modern production under the existing financial system necessarily exceeds the rate at which consumer incomes are simultaneously being distributed by the same productive processes. The imbalance in question thus takes the form of an *underlying* deficiency of consumer buying power *vis-à-vis* the corresponding flow of costs and prices from all sources. At a macroeconomic level, this underlying deficiency may or may not express itself as a *de facto* deficiency in the global flow of income relative to the global or total flow of *consumer* prices. In other words, the flow of total prices (of capital and consumer production) always exceeds the flow of total incomes, but the flow of prices attached to consumer goods and services may or may not exceed the total flow of incomes at any given moment.

So we have a situation in which money is being created and destroyed all the time by the banking system. It is created when loans are made (or when a bank purchases securities or other assets) and is destroyed when the loans are paid down (or the bank purchases are sold to the public). At the same time, costs and prices are being generated (as money is spent on production) and liquidated (as money received as revenue by businesses is used to cancel costs and prices). The problem is that these two basic accountancy cycles of the economy are out of sync with each other. Costs/prices are being built up as money is created and destroyed at a faster rate than these claims can be finally liquidated by the flow of consumer income that is simultaneously being distributed. That is, for every cycle that a certain volume of money completes from creation to cancellation, so much, call it 'A+B', is being generated simultaneously in costs and prices, but only so much, a lesser amount, call it 'A' is being finally liquidated in consumer purchases. The 'B' component represents a portion of unliquidated costs/prices that can only be liquidated by a separate, additional cycle of money creation/destruction. This 'B' element corresponds, in the main, to the various costs associated with real capital (machines, equipment, software, etc). Because of standard accountancy conventions, 'B' costs have to be covered at least twice, once to cover their manufacture/production and another time to cover their depreciation and maintenance. The consumer is not automatically given enough income to cover even one of those payments. It is this 'double-costing' of real capital that is the main cause behind the price-income gap.

Naturally, the imbalance has to be overcome in some way in order for the economy to achieve equilibrium and to remain in operation. Since the existing system is a debt-money system, the only way to supply the economy with the additional consumer buying power that is needed to balance the flow of incomes and the flow of consumer costs/prices so that goods and services can be distributed in full and costs can be met is to get someone, ie, governments, businesses, or consumers, to borrow the needed money into existence from the banking system. This results, over time, in the building up of a mountain of public, corporate, and consumer debts that is unrepayable, ie, irredeemable, in the aggregate. Thus we see that one imbalance (that between prices and incomes) leads to another imbalance (the excess of debt). The deleterious effects of those two imbalances are too numerous to survey within the space of this article in their full horror. Some of the key manifestations include: the instability of the business cycle, constant inflation (mostly cost-push, but also demand-pull), the misdirection of economic resources, economic inefficiency, waste, and sabotage alongside forced economic growth, recurring financial crises, heavy and often increasing taxation, wage and debt-slavery, servility, forced migration, cultural dislocation, unnecessary stresses and strains, social conflict, environmental degradation, and international economic conflict leading to war, etc, etc.

V. The Nature of Financial Tyranny

So why are these imbalances tolerated? The answer can be found when we consider the consequences that directly result from the existence of the first imbalance (ie, the price-income gap) in conjunction with how the existing system attempts, in the main, to compensate for it (ie, *via* increased indebtedness), namely: the usurpation of the unearned increment of economic association by the private banking system and the centralisation of economic wealth, privilege, and power in fewer and fewer hands. Relying on the banking system to fill the price-income gap with additional debt-money puts the banking system and its owners in a commanding position. Since they possess a *de facto* monopoly on the creation of bank credit they can impose self-serving conditions on the issuance of that additional credit upon which the rest of the economy depends in order to make ends meet. This compensatory credit tends to be associated with long-term and, in the aggregate, unrepayable debt on which compound interest is levied. The ultimate result is that wealth, power, and privilege accrue to them in a *disproportionate* manner and the unearned increment of economic association is, to a corresponding degree, captured in their favour and at the expense of the common good.

This is the essence of the *financial tyranny* which Douglas saw as embedded in our existing financial and economic arrangements. But since sufficient money gives its holders the power to buy anything that can be bought (or that has a price) and since a monopoly on money-creation potentially affords its holders the ability to monopolise everything else that is sellable, the financial tyranny must, by degrees, transform itself into a more formal political tyranny. That is, the inner logic of the existing financial system in combination with the intentional use of the great power that is derived from its operation results in the imposition of, or at least the heavy 'encouragement' of, governmental, corporate, personal, social, and cultural policies that further the narrow interests of High Finance: the final monopolisation of power in all of its forms. As Douglas once put it: 'The great monopoly which gives the power to monopolise other things is what we call the monopoly of credit.'[16]

To employ an analogy from Tolkien's famous novel *The Lord of the Rings*, the power of money creation and the benefits it delivers constitute 'the one ring to rule them all' as it gives its possessors the power to buy (if they can be bought and they can be) or at least heavily influence (through direct funding, donations, sponsorships, advertising, etc) all the other centres (or rings) of power in the society: the educational establishment, the media (news and entertainment), the military, the health system, the government (both politicians and bureaucracies), the legal system, the churches, and so forth. As the money power expands its control in 101 different ways and by 101 different means that cannot be properly explored here, the nature and use of that power tends to become ever more despotic and tyrannical. We live, first and foremost, under the rule, the governance, of finance:

> [I]t appears to be proved beyond argument that Lord Action, in his much misquoted dictum that all power tends to corrupt, and absolute power corrupts absolutely, was enunciating a natural law so that the more powerful a Government is, the more certainly it will deteriorate.[17]

---

[16] CH Douglas, *The Monopolistic Idea* (The Institute of Economic Democracy, 1979) 5.
[17] Douglas (n 2) 71.

So the recipe for tyranny in the modern world can be ultimately reduced to the following equation: an unbalanced debt-money system + the banks' monopoly on credit-creation = financial tyranny, which ultimately must equal a political tyranny. As the basis for a further analogy, consider the 'increment of association' that is generated between a lever and a fulcrum. The monopoly on money-creation in the form of bank credit that is possessed by the banking system might be likened to the lever, a lever which, in this case, rests on the artificial scarcity of consumer buying power relative to prices that is built into the system. This artificial scarcity thus plays the role of the fulcrum. Monopoly plus artificial scarcity equates to despotic power in the service of increasing tyranny. As power is centralised more and more, the freedom, prosperity, and independence of the bulk of the population must necessarily decrease. Quoting once again from Douglas' speech, 'The Monopolistic Idea':

> This credit and this power of issuing money have become, through the process I have explained to you, a monopoly, and that monopoly remains.

> It is quite obvious that such monopoly achieves enormous power by restricting its output, as you might say. If everybody has enough money money becomes less important in proportion to the amount of money you have. If you do not know from where your next meal is coming, and you cannot get your next meal without money, money looms before you as the one essential of your life; but if you have a reasonable income it does not loom quite so large; you are not quite as much worried as to whether something costs you 6d. or 7d.

> Therefore, it is in the very nature of monopolies of all kinds – and I say this after great consideration and as being a very important thing to consider – that they shall restrict their output, so that you shall desire it, to make it have a scarcity value.

I do not believe it is conceivable, or in the nature of monopolies, for a monopoly to supply the world to the extent either that the world is capable of producing a commodity, or is really desiring it.

That is one of the strongest objections to monopolies. You will notice in the world at the present time that restrictions of all kinds are increasing – restrictions on the growth of wheat, possibly restrictions on the shipment of wool, I do not know, but there are restrictions of this, that and the other kind, restrictions on entering this country or that country, restrictions on taking this thing into one country or taking something out of another country. All of these restrictions are part and parcel of this policy of growing monopolies of various kinds.[18]

The reality of the financially-grounded attempt at world power which characterises the 'monopolistic idea' in our times was openly admitted and independently confirmed by no less a personage than Georgetown Professor Carrol Quigley (Bill Clinton's mentor) in his magnum opus *Tragedy and Hope*:

[T]he powers of financial capitalism had another far-reaching aim, nothing less than to create a world system of financial control in private hands able to dominate the political system of each country and the economy of the world as a whole. This system was to be controlled in a feudalist fashion by the central banks of the world acting in concert, by secret agreements arrived at in frequent private meetings and conferences. The apex of the system was to be the Bank for International Settlements in Basle, Switzerland, a private bank owned and controlled by the world's central banks which were themselves private corporations. Each central bank, in the hands of men like Montagu Norman of the Bank of England,

---

[18] Douglas (n 16) 10-11.

Benjamin Strong of the New York of the New York Federal Reserve Bank, Charles Rist of the bank of France, and Hjalmar Schacht of the Reichsbank, sought to dominate its government by its ability to control Treasury loans, to manipulate foreign exchanges, to influence the level of economic activity in the country, and to influence cooperative politicians by subsequent economic rewards in the business world. ...

The growth of financial capitalism made possible a centralization of world economic control and a use of this power for the direct benefit of financiers and the indirect injury of all other economic groups.[19]

VI. The Douglas Social Credit Remedy for Tyranny

Thankfully, Douglas not only analysed the problem of tyranny in the modern world in terms of its nature and origins, but also offered solutions. We can distinguish between his general remedy, which is applicable to every association, and his specific remedy, which was designed to neutralise the financial and economic tyranny and, by extension, the emerging political tyranny that currently grows out of the former.

Since tyranny in any association involves a significant deviation from the correct principles of association, the general remedy for tyranny is to identify which of these principles is being violated and then to bring the association back into alignment with the blueprint for a healthy, functional, and flourishing association.

According to Douglas, 'The general principles which govern association for the common good are as capable of exact statement as

19 Carroll Quigley, *Tragedy and Hope: A History of our World in our Time* (GSG & Associates, 2004) 324, 337. Apart from teaching at Georgetown from 1941 to 1976, Quigley taught at Princeton and Harvard and gave lectures at the Brookings Institute, the US Naval Weapons Laboratory, the Foreign Service Institute, and the Naval College in Norfolk, Virginia.

the principles of bridge building, and departure from them is just as disastrous.'[20] So what are the correct principles of associations?

There are three of them: 1) the policy of the association must be democratic (this constitutes the right end), 2) the administration of the association must be hierarchical (this constitutes the right means), and 3) the sanctions over the association must be decentralised (this constitutes the right integration of the ends and the means).

When we say that the policy of an association must be democratic what we mean is that the only policy which we might expect all individual members to agree on and fully support is that the true purpose of the association should be optimally fulfilled. This is because the true purpose of an association coincides with the *raison d'être* of an association or the reason why people decided to enter into association in the first place. It is thus the only policy which could truly be designated as a *common* policy:

> [A] genuine democracy of policy is the fundamental basis of association, and that no association which disagrees with this idea can continue.[21]

When we say that administration must be hierarchical we mean that a pyramidal, top-down structure allows for a clearly recognised and respected division of duties, for rapid decision-making, and for the effective dissemination of these decisions from the apex to the lower levels. This makes it as easy as possible to effectively and efficiently carry out any given policy-directive on behalf of an association:

> In regard to administration, I do not propose to say very much beyond the fact that it is and must be essentially hierarchical and therefore it is a technical matter in which the expert

---

[20] CH Douglas, *The Tragedy of Human Effort* (The Institute of Economic Democracy, 1978) 3.

[21] CH Douglas, *Dictatorship by Taxation* (The Institute of Economic Democracy, 1978) 11.

must be supreme and ultimately autocratic. The idea that administration can be democratic ... is not one which will bear the test of five minutes' experience. It may be consultative, but in the last resort some single person must decide.[22]

But let it be re-emphasised, since the problem of tyranny remains the central topic in this article, that hierarchies exist in Douglas Social Credit theory in order to serve; they are not there to dominate. Hierarchy exists to facilitate a democratic or common policy, not a self-serving policy:

That you must have policy democratic and execution hierarchical is one of our fundamental conceptions in Social Credit; ...[23]

When we say that sanctions must be decentralised we mean that the common members of an association must have an effective means by which they can steer an association's activities back on track, back into line with the association's true purpose, should it ever deviate. The type of control needed is a negative control, ie, the power to reprimand or replace administrators in the hierarchy who cannot or will not carry out the common policy effectively, efficiently, and fairly, the power to atrophy functions that do not serve their best interests, and even the ability to opt out of the association altogether if necessary, with no other penalty but the loss of the association's benefits:

---

[22] Douglas (n 20) 5. Cf: CH Douglas, *Economic Democracy*, (Bloomfield Books, 5th ed, 1974) 37: [A] centralized or pyramid form of control ... is in certain conditions, the ideal organization for the attainment of one specific and material end. The only effective force by which any objective can be attained is in the last analysis the human will, and if an organization of this character can keep the will of all its component members focussed on the objective to be attained, the collective power available is clearly greater than can be provided by any other form of association.

[23] CH Douglas, *The Policy of a Philosophy* (The Institute of Economic Democracy, 1977) 8. Cf CH Douglas, *Economic Democracy* (Bloomfield Books, 3rd ed, 1974) 39: 'it is vital to devise methods by which technical co-ordination can be combined with individual freedom. To crystallize the matter into a paragraph; in respect of any undertaking, centralization is the way to do it, but is neither the correct method of deciding what to do nor the question of who is to do it.'

Since the analysis of existing conditions which we have undertaken shows that any centralised administrative organisation is certain to be captured by some interest antagonistic to the individual, it seems evident that it is in the direction of decentralization of control that we must look for such alteration in the social structure as would be self-protective against capture for interested purposes.[24]

The power to contract out was to serve as the final safeguard against tyranny:

[A]ssociation for the attainment of an objective inevitably becomes a tyranny (*i.e.*, an attack on individual initiative) unless it can be broken at any time, without incurring any penalty other than the loss of association itself.[25]

In the case of a tyrannical association, the group, and more particularly the oligarchy that controls the group, is elevated over and above the common individual to one extent or another. This happens because the first and the third of the correct principles of association are not being respected and/or effectively embodied. That is, instead of serving its true purpose optimally in a single-minded fashion, resources have been diverted through various mechanisms (some of which we examined before specifically in reference to financial/

---

[24] Douglas (n 22) 91-2. It seems that the lack of adequate decentralised sanctions is one of the single greatest flaws in present social arrangements: 'at the present time, there is no question that it is in the domain of sanctions that the human race is in-volved in its great difficulties.': Douglas (n 20) 6. Cf also CH Douglas, *The Control and Distribution of Production* (Cecil Palmer, 1922) 51: 'It has frequently and rightly been emphasised that the essence of any real progress towards a better condition of society resides in the acquisition of control of its functions by those who are affected by its structure; and it is well if somewhat vaguely recognised by the worker of all classes that this control is at present not resident in, but is external to, society itself, and that in consequence men and women, instead of rising to an ever superior control of circumstance, remain the slaves of a system they did not make and have not so far been able to alter in its fundamentals.'

[25] CH Douglas, *The Control and Distribution of Production* (Cecil Palmer, 1922) 101.

economic tyranny: monopoly in combination with artificial scarcity, etc) to enfranchise a parasitic class at the expense of the authentic common good. Policy ceases to be fully functional and democratic. At the same time, the common members have been sufficiently sidelined by the power structure that they are in no easily effective position to restrain and ultimately neutralise the oligarchy. They lack effective sanctions.

So how do we respond to such a situation, ie, a situation in which an oligarchy is tyrannising society? Douglas says that the only way to neutralise this threat is, quite appropriately enough, by *associating* in favour of the common good. That is, Social Crediters (those who have a concern for the well-being of an association or of a society generally) must work together so that, through education and appropriate action, an association is consistently moved in the direction of full functionality, while the threats to that functionality are constantly unmasked. This is the only way to effectively neutralise tyranny:

> What is important is that we should become conscious of our sovereignty – that we should associate consciously, understanding the purpose of our association, and refusing to accept results which are alien to the purpose of our association.[26]

This task may not be as difficult as it may first seem, provided that we keep one basic truth before the minds of the public: the Social Credit policy is, above all, a policy of unity, not of division. Indeed, a truncated synonym for the fully functional association could be the simple word: freedom, ie, not just freedom of choice, or the freedom not to be unjustifiably interfered with, but also freedom *from* want, from fear, from insecurity, and freedom *for* flourishing. Freedom, in this, most ample of senses, is the greatest unifying force possible that might be put before the public:

---

[26] Douglas (n 20) 16.

> There is no possible definition of a policy which is all-embracing in its acceptance other than the word 'Freedom'. People only unite in wanting what they want.[27]

Furthermore, while everyone wants freedom for himself, he must come to realise that it is only by ensuring the freedom of his neighbours that his own freedom can become secure. Once it is understood that seeking the full functionality of an association must, by necessity, promote the best interests of each individual, it also becomes obvious that 'It is most probably true that there can be no divergence between true Public Interest and any true private interest; ...'.[28] Instead of polarising different sections of the community and pitting them against each other, insisting that every association should be formed on the basis of the correct principles and that it must function accordingly brings resolution by harmonising interests. In other words, freedom and the fruits of freedom necessarily presuppose a respect for and due application of the truth concerning the nature of human association for the common good:

> To Social Crediters it is a fairly common-place saying that what we are trying to do with the money system is to make it reflect facts, but what we are also trying to do is to make the relationship between individuals and their institutions reflect facts. To borrow from the Dean of Canterbury's vocabulary, what Social Crediters have in mind is 'to know the truth in order that the truth shall make you free,' ...[29]

On the basis of this unity grounded, as it is, on a recognition of the mandatory nature of freedom as a condition of and a constitutive component for a fully functioning association, it becomes possible for

---

[27] Douglas (n 25) 37. Cf: Douglas (n 22) 102: 'The pyramidal structure of Society gives environment the maximum control over individuality. The correct objective of any change is to give individuality maximum control over environment.'

[28] Douglas (n 1) 55.

[29] CH Douglas, *The Approach to Reality* (KRP Publications Ltd, 1936) 6.

a conscious Social Credit movement to defeat tyranny by embodying in a very concrete manner in its own operation 'the necessity for exalting the individual over the group.'[30] This serves as a living testament, as a sign-post, calling all associations back to their roots. The group or the association is merely a means; the well-being of each concrete individual is the proper end:

> The first proposition which requires to be brought out into the cold light of the day, and to be kept there remorselessly, at the present time in particular, is that nations are, at bottom, merely associations for the good of those composing them. Please note that I say 'at bottom'.[31]

More specifically, Douglas' solution to this problem of financial tyranny (and of the political tyranny to which it inevitably gives rise) was to break the banks' monopoly on credit-creation by using the money creation powers of the state to fill the price-income gap with sufficient debt-free consumer credits. This would make the financial system balanced in a sustainable way (because there would be no piling up of unrepayable debts). An unbalanced debt-money system would be replaced by a balanced system incorporating both debt-money and debt-free credit in properly calculated proportions. Since the private banks would no longer be called on to fill the recurring price-income gap with additional debt-money, all of the interest and other charges that are currently levied on that compensatory debt would be eliminated, as would their leverage over the financial and

---

[30] Douglas (n 6) 74.

[31] Douglas (n 6) 3. That the 'common good' is to be understood distributively and not collectively, that it is the good of each individual which needs to be promoted to the greatest degree feasible and not the well-being of the whole at the expense of some individual or group of individuals, follows quite logically from the ontological priority which the individual holds over the group. On this understanding, the true purpose of any association is to forward as effectively, as efficiently, and as equitably as possible, the well-being of each one of its individual members in line with the particular types of benefits with which the association deals. Any association can be evaluated in terms of how adequately it satisfies individual requirements.

economic policy of other sectors in the society. This would help massively in putting an end to the usurpation of the unearned increment of economic association by financial elites and to the centralisation of wealth, power, and privilege in fewer and fewer hands.

The volume of 'debt-free' credit needed to bridge the recurring price-income gap would be issued to or on behalf of consumers by the National Credit Authority, which would be an organ of the state that would function independently of the government of the day. The direct payment would take the form of a National Dividend, ie, a periodic, say monthly, payment that each citizen would receive independently of employment status. This would be justified pragmatically by the fact that the economy needs that extra money in the hands of consumers in order for it to function in equilibrium, in order for costs to be met in full, and for the full range of goods and services to be distributed. It would be justified ethically by the fact that each citizen is rightly regarded as a shareholder in his economy, as an heir to the cultural heritage (which, by means of its embodiment in real capital, is responsible for the gap). The indirect payment would be (in its usual formulation at any rate) a payment of debt-free credit issued to retailers in exchange for the latter reducing their prices (thus increasing the purchasing power of consumer incomes) in accordance with the economy's overall consumption/production ratio. This Compensated Price Discount is based on the observation that the true cost of production is consumption and therefore no production should be offered on sale at prices that exceed the financial costs associated with the consumption that was needed to bring that production into being. Hence, if the average C/P ratio were ¾, then prices would be reduced by ¼ and retailers would be reimbursed the ¼ reduction *via* an infusion of debt-free credit from the National Credit Authority.

By breaking the monopoly credit with a carefully calculated flow of compensatory consumer credits that are issued debt-free we are not merely stopping the flow of the usurious tribute that is paid on the debt-money that is currently issued to fill the gap, we are using the money creation and issuing power of the state to enfranchise the individual by making his life easier: goods and services become more affordable by means of the discount, while the dividend distributes, in an unconditional manner, a basic share in the power of money to everyone in the society. When an individual is thus enfranchised he is in a much stronger position to chart his own course independently of the course that would be set for him if obtaining his 'meal tickets' were overly dependent (as it is now) on co-operating with the agenda of financial interests:

> If it is true, as seems probable, that effective resistance to an imposed group policy is nearly impossible so long as the group has control of the credit of the individuals composing it, it is beside the point to pay serious attention to such a factor. The only line of action which can be effective in the emergency with which the world is confronted must be one which can paralyse or break up the group control of credit to which the majority of individuals in every country have become helpless slaves; ...[32]

Indeed, the National Dividend plays a very special role as a bulwark against tyranny. If every citizen is guaranteed a share in his country's communal profit as an inherent right whenever it is profitable (with prices exceeding incomes), then each citizen will enjoy a minimum employment-independent source of income that he can fall back on regardless of circumstances. This lessens the leverage which either the government of the day or private employers can use to impose policies on people against their will. It provides a measure of security, independence, and freedom for each individual as part of the basic operating system of the society. It is the most practical method for achieving 'the emancipation of the individual from the domination of the group, ...'.[33]

---

[32] Douglas (n 1) 163.
[33] Douglas (n 6) 74.

The opposite of financial and economic tyranny thus shows itself to be financial and economic freedom, real freedom, concrete freedom, for every individual. That freedom should be the fundamental aim of economic association:

> It is suggested that the primary requisite is to obtain in the readjustment of the economic and political structure such control of initiative that by its exercise every individual can avail himself of the benefits of science and mechanism; that by their aid he is placed in such a position of advantage, that in common with his fellows he can choose, with increasing freedom and complete independence, whether he will or will not assist in any project which may be placed before him.[34]

In other words, the remedy for tyranny is to recognise that power needs to be distributed, not concentrated, and it needs to be distributed in a very practical way that has teeth: '*power to make decisions is freedom for the individual, ...*'[35] And money is one of the most basic forms of power:

> Salvation is not to be found in greater and still greater agglomerations of power ... It is, and can only be found, in bringing into actuality the existing cleavage between the individual desire to pursue an individual end and the group pressure to reduce the individual to an amorphous mass – a biological entropy.[36]

In many, if not in most cases, the failure of other associations, non-economic associations to embody the proper democratic structure and to achieve proper functioning is due to the fact they are subject, in turn, to an economic and financial system which is fundamentally despotic in nature. The opposite holds true, ie, restoring the financial

---

[34] Douglas (n 22) 28.
[35] CH Douglas, *Credit Power and Democracy* (The Social Credit Press, 1933) 6.
[36] CH Douglas, *The Brief for the Prosecution* (KRP Publications Ltd, 1945) 63.

system and economic association to full functionality would have a beneficial effect on all other associations within society, making it significantly easier for them to overcome the various challenges and barriers which prevent them from attaining to a state of full functionality.

Fixing the financial system would thus be very stabilising, whereas persisting with the current dysfunction is inherently destabilising:

> [A]s soon as Society ceases to serve the interests of the individual, then the individual will break up Society ... those persons who wish to preserve Society can do no worse service to their cause, than to depict their idol as an unchangeable organisation whose claims are to be regarded as superior to those of the human spirit.[37]

VII. Concluding Remarks

By way of conclusion, it behoves me to now address the most common objection to Douglas' alternative vision, ie, that it is somehow 'utopian', ie, unrealistic or otherwise unattainable. The standard response of Social Crediters would be that it is not utopian in the sense that we are not aiming at a mathematically perfect world, but rather we are aiming at a healthy world, ie, highly functional financial and economic system to replace the existing dysfunctional and unhealthy system. Clearly, the current system benefits an oligarchy and that oligarchy will resist any changes to the system that would lessen their power, privilege, and position, etc. At the same time, there is no appeasing that oligarchy. We either resist them by promoting functionality and health or we abdicate our responsibilities and permit them to run civilisation into the ground. The path to a better today always remains open to us; Douglas is merely showing us the way forward:

---

[37] Douglas (n 1) 73.

[S]o far from the realisation of some machine-made Utopia which would embrace us all, I think what we all as individuals desire is a state of affairs which would enable us to use the benefits conferred upon us by science and education for the furtherance of our own individual ideals and desires, which must be just as different, in the nature of things, as our personalities are different, and must become increasingly different as our personalities become further individualised.

The Social Credit proposals at any rate start from this point of view, and in one sense they may be considered as a complete inversion of either State Socialism, Fascism, or Sovietism. So far from desiring to impose some abstract ideal called the 'common will' upon the individual, their proposals have for their objective the employment of the common heritage … for the furtherance of the individual objective, whatever that may be, and without defining it.[38]

---

[38] Douglas (n 6) 24-5.

6

Rex Non Potest Peccare an Rex Est Super Legem:

A Study on Property Rights in Western Australia with Particular Attention to Land Tax

SUSAN HODDINOTT[*]

ABSTRACT

Can the King do no wrong? Is the King above the law? This paper looks at the historical ideal of Government versus what is the situation within Western Australia. The paper looks at the statutes which have been created and their incompatibility with indefeasibility of title and historical Imperial law.

I. INTRODUCTION

The latin maxim *Rex non potest peccare* is translated to mean 'the King can do no wrong' or 'the King cannot sin'. The idea comes from the notion of the "divine right of Kings". As God's anointed representative on earth, decisions of the King were not open to question. Even if an error caused loss, deprived a subject of liberty or life, or was based upon malicious intent, the King was not responsible for his mistakes and could not be called to account for them personally.[1] If an evil act is done, though emanating from the

---

[1] Fred Peterson, 'Rights and Immunities of a Sovereign Ruler' (1919) 88 *North Carolina Central Law Journal* 28; Herbert Broom, *A Selection of Legal Maxims Classified and Illustrated* (Sweet & Maxwell Ltd, 10th ed, 1939).

[*] LLB Murdoch University, BSc (Hons) University of Western Australia, MBA University of Western Australia.

King, it is imputed to his ministers, for whose acts the King is in no way responsible.[2] With the introduction of parliamentary democracies, the Crown is no longer a *divine monarch* but a collection of public servants, including ministers, capable of both negligence and tortious omission.[3]

A related maxim, *Rex Est Super Legem,* is translated to "the King is above the law". This has been tested several times within English history resulting in revolutions and it is generally accepted that the King is not above the law. Despite this, statutes and legislation have been introduced in Western Australia which are contrary to both Imperial law and established common law. It would appear that the State of Western Australia is, indeed, above the law.

II. Historical Antecedents

A *Warlords and the Existence of the Modern State*

In earlier times, agrarian communities were under constant threat from those who would take what they had produced by force and threats of force. The provision of "protection" was essential to provide security, order and protection of property rights to facilitate trade and economic development.

Konrad and Skaperdas note that alleged providers of protection, typically compete with violence instead of price.[4] Historically, the provision of "protection" is often considered the defining attribute of the State.[5] However, officers of the State such as political rulers, police and soldiers, can extract more than the robbers and bandits they are supposed to guard against.[6] Arguably, a self-governing State could

---

[2] *R v Canadian Broadcasting Corporation* [1980] *Canadian Legal Information Institute* 68.

[3] Lloyd Durhaime, *Durhaime's Law Dictionary* (Lloyd Durhaime, 2000).

[4] Kai A Konrad and Stergios Skaperdas, 'The Market for Protection and the Origin of the State' (2012) 50(2) *Economic Theory* 417.

[5] Ibid.

[6] Ibid.

survive in the absence of predators, and the welfare of the "protected" would be highest under such a market structure.[7] In the presence of competing predators no long-run equilibrium was found in which a self-governing State would be viable.[8] Being small in the presence of larger predators results in too much expenditure per person on both external and internal security.[9]

Hierarchy and predatory behaviour towards subjects is the most stable form of internal organisation; and competition for the rents thus created is the dominant market structure.[10] In contrast to other economic markets, the more competition there is for protection, the worse it is – competing lords and their entourages extract what would have been taken in their absence by simple bandits.[11] This helps in understanding the wide prevalence of autocracy,[12] instead of self-governance, in the provision of protection and more generally in the organisation of governance.[13] If we want protection, therefore, it would seem that we are doomed to a single large State as our least worst option. It remains to be seen at what point the State, and by extension the State of Western Australia, is failing to provide protection when it is the source of attacks upon property rights.

B *Roman Law*

Under Roman Law there was an absolute ownership of land by a private citizen (*absolutum et directum dominium*), subject only to the exception of State necessity (*dominium eminens or* 'eminent

---

[7] Ibid.

[8] Ibid.

[9] Ibid.

[10] Ibid.

[11] Ibid.

[12] Autocracy is a system of Government in which absolute power over a state is concentrated in the hands of one person.

[13] Konrad and Skaperdas (n 5) 5.

domain').[14] There is a lack of agreement as to the extent to which the Roman Empire used its power of eminent domain over private landholders.[15] What we know, however, is that there is little direct evidence in Rome of the use of eminent domain and a strong emphasis on inviolable private property.[16]

With respect to the colonies of Rome, including Britain, the system of land law was different from land owned by Roman citizens.[17] The colonies were classified as conquered territory whose inhabitants were Roman subjects with status as '*dediticii*', that is, the status of capitulants without legal rights. The land of the conquered provinces was considered the property of the Roman Empire or '*ager publicus*' and was held under charter, or revocable grant, and not *in dominium*.[18]

The provinces paid to the Emperor a *tributum soli* (land tax) and a *tributum capitis* (head poll tax based on personal property). Legal land ownership of the Imperial '*ager publicus*' was in the Emperor.[19] For these provinces, gaining Roman citizenship was of immense benefit in terms of ownership of property because it brought the new citizen under the Roman law of property, meaning that they could now be held to own wholly, and in perpetuity, land which formerly may have belonged to the tribe or a tribal chief.[20]

---

[14] Standing Committee on Public Administration and Finance, Parliament of Western Australia, *Report in Relation to the Impact of State Government Actions and Processes on the Use and Enjoyment of Freehold and Leasehold Land in Western Australia* (2004).

[15] Errol E Meidinger, 'The "Public Uses" of Eminent Domain: History and Policy' (1980) 11(1) *Environmental Law* 1, 7-8.

[16] Ibid.

[17] Standing Committee (n 15).

[18] Ibid.

[19] Will Durant, *The Story of Civilization: Part III, Caesar and Christ, A History of Roman Civilization and of Christianity from their beginnings to AD 325* (Simon and Schuster, 1944); John Cook, *Law and Life of Rome* (Cornell University Press, 1967).

[20] Colin Wells, *The Roman Empire* (Harvard University Press, 1984); Jim Powell, 'Ancient Roman Contributions to Private Property Rights', *Liberty Story*, 14 April 2004, 1.

Currently, Western Australian citizens appear to have far less property rights than a conquered Roman slave. These land rights are way short of those afforded to a Roman citizen. Not only may property be taken for alleged 'public purpose',[21] property may also be taken for unsecured debts, fines and the acts or omissions of third parties via the *Proceeds of Crime Act 2002* (Cth),[22] *Criminal Property Confiscation Act 2000* (WA),[23] *Water Services Act 2012* (WA)[24] and even by councils holding property owners responsible for tenant infringements, such as for garden maintenance via legislation such as the *Bush Fires Act 1954* (WA). The ownership of property is being used as security for what should be, at most, unsecured debts of third parties.

C *The English Feudal Land System, Magna Carta 1297 (Imp) and the Tenures Abolition Act 1600 (Imp)*

The English feudal land system was developed from the 11th century by the Normans. This is the basis for current real property law systems in the United Kingdom, Australia, the United States, Canada and New Zealand.

Prior to the Norman Conquest, land ownership in England depended primarily on possession. There were no courts or police force ready to recognize or enforce 'legal rights'.[25]

In 1066, William the Conqueror claimed ownership all of the land in England by right of conquest and only granted subjects an interest in portions of the Crown estate.[26] Land grants were given by the King to his Norman officers or to those of the English who

---

[21] *Land Administration Act 1997* (WA) pts 9, 10.

[22] *Proceeds of Crime Act 2002* (Cth) ss 7(b), 7(c) and Part 2-2, with onus of proof reversed in s 54(c).

[23] *Criminal Property Confiscation Act 2000* (WA) s 4(c).

[24] *Water Services Act 2012* (WA) s 124(b).

[25] Standing Committee (n 15).

[26] Ibid.

were ready to recognize him as King.[27] Nobody owned land but the King. The expressions *dominion directum* and *dominion utile* describe the ownership of the King and Lords; the former as landlord, the latter as tenant.[28] All allodial holdings were abolished.[29] The Lords as landholders became tenants-in-chief and were required to provide fixed quotas of cavalry. A tenant-in-chief who failed in his duties forfeited his lands to the Crown.[30] In those countries that have inherited this tenurial system, all land belongs to the Crown. Subjects only own an estate, or rights, in the land.[31]

1 *Magna Carta*

Approximately four hundred years after the Norman conquest, King John was overtaxing the barons based upon the alleged value of their properties, to fund foreign wars. This led to a revolution culminating in the *Magna Carta*. Since its creation, the *Magna Carta* has stood for the principle that no man is above the law, not even a king. When the King is in violation of the provisions of that 'Great Charter', the barons have the authority to seize the King's properties by military force – or "distrain" him – until he complies.[32]

The barons' threat of military force against the King made *Magna Carta* a symbol of the supremacy of the law over the will of the King. Any act by the King or one of his agents that violated the terms of the Charter was void, and, in the language of Edward I's 1297 Confirmation of the Charters, 'should be undone and holden for naught'.[33] However,

---

[27] Ibid.

[28] Ibid.

[29] Richard Pipes, *Property and Freedom* (Alfred A Knopf, 1999) 126.

[30] Richard Pipes, *Property and Freedom* (Alfred A Knopf, 1999) 126; Peter Butt, *Land Law* (Lawbook Co, 4th ed, 2001) 58-59.

[31] Lloyd Duhaime, *History of Real Estate Law: The Old English Landholding System* (Duhaime & Company, 1996).

[32] 'Magna Carta: Muse and Mentor Exhibition', *Library of U.S. Congress* (Web Page, 6 November 2014).

[33] Ibid.

any protections we might have expected from the *Magna Carta* have now been unequivocally rejected. As authoritatively stated by McHugh J in the Australian High Court case of *Essenberg v The Queen*,

> [T]he *Magna Carta* and the *Bill of Rights* 1688 are not documents binding on Australian legislatures in the way that the *Constitution* is binding on those legislatures … Any legislature acting within the powers allotted to it by the *Constitution* is entitled to legislate in total disregard of the *Magna Carta* and the *Bill of Rights* … They are not constitutional documents in the sense that the *Australian Constitution* and the *United States Constitution* are … They are political ideals which most citizens would hope that Parliaments would follow but if Parliaments do not follow them, the remedy is the ballot box because we do not have a Bill of Rights in this country.[34]

2 *English Civil War and the Tenures Abolition Act 1600*

Another 400 years on from the Magna Carta, and the King, Charles I, was using non-parliamentary means and various impositions, particularly upon land owners, to fund an extravagant navy and wars. This led to the English Civil War and the beheading of the King. Upon restoration of the monarchy under Charles II, the *Tenures Abolition Act 1600* 12 Car 2 was enacted which again outlawed the taxing of property, again supposedly, in perpetuity.

Approximately another 400 years to the present time and the taxing of property is again in full swing and goes largely unquestioned. The power to tax property is the power to expropriate through taxation. The strategy of gradual but never-ending increases in property taxes, justified by regular re-valuations, eventually prices everyone out of their properties. It was for this reason that taxes of this nature were outlawed, in perpetuity, by laws such as the *Magna Carta 1275*, specifically its clause 32, and the *Tenures Abolition Act 1660* (Imp),

---

[34] *Essenberg v The Queen* [2000] HCA.

which further imposes a penalty of double the amount for any attempt to impose such a tax in the courts via s 39.

These important laws, which form the foundation of our constitutional democracy, should be in force in Western Australia.[35] However, their significance and importance has been ignored and overridden by subsequent State legislation and statutes. In Australia, prior to the *Australia Acts* of 1986, the Judicial Committee of the Privy Council (on appeal) could still exercise a power of judicial review of legislative acts on various grounds of repugnancy to Imperial Acts.[36] We no longer have this protection.

D *The Application of English Land Law in Australia*

Since 1770, when possession of Australia was taken by Britain, all land was vested in the British Crown and all land titles issued in Australia since that date are derived from Crown grants. These were "fee simple" grants which alienated the land from the Crown and gave complete ownership rights to the grant holders, save for allodial title which reserved the rights to the minerals under the ground to the Crown.[37] In some Australian states, grantees were required to pay an

---

[35] 'United Kingdom Statutes in Force in Western Australia', *Law Reform Commission of Western Australia*, Project No 75 (1994).

[36] Richard Darrell Lumb, *Australian Constitutionalism* (Butterworths, 1983) 42.

[37] Fee Simple land is held without benefit to the Crown and alienated from the Crown. Subsequent ownership occurs via contract from the previous owner. Fee Simple permits an owner to do with his property as he might wish. It is the highest form of land ownership available. The *Property Law Act 1958* (Qld) s 21 and *Property Law Act 1958* (Vic) s 18A, clearly state that fee simple is without licence and without fine. In s 20 the Queensland act further stipulates that a person who owns a parcel of land in fee simple is assured that they hold that land without benefit for the Crown. Once the Crown agrees to create the title, that title is registered, written into the register, given a Lot number, Volume and Folio number, there is no benefit for the Crown other than the reservation of minerals etc. below the ground. Although there is no similar section written into the WA Act, under s 117 of the *Australian Constitution*, subjects are not to be subject to any disability or discrimination which would not be equally applicable if the subject of the Queen were resident in another State. A fee simple confers an absolute right, both of alienation *inter vivos* and of devise by will.

annual sum of money to the Crown in exchange for the land grants (which amounted to five per cent of the value of the land by 1825).[38] From 1813, debt recovery laws in the Australian colonies treated real and personal property almost alike.[39] This may be contrasted with the English technical distinction between real property (land and interests in land) and personal property (all property, or chattels, other than land and incorporeal hereditaments).[40] The allocation of Crown Land to settlers in Western Australia in 1829 was initially proportional to the amount of capital introduced. These grants were subject to forfeiture to the Crown if the land had not been improved within ten years of the grant.[41]

E *The Association of Property Ownership with Voting Rights*

In Britain, the right to vote was originally not seen as a 'basic right' but rather as a right affixed to the ownership of property.[42] The *Knights of the Shire Act 1432* 10 Hen 6 was the first parliamentary legislation to establish who was enfranchised to vote. Only the owners of real property, who paid taxes to the Crown of at least 40 shillings per year, were given the right to vote. This remained the status quo for another 400 years and in 1780, the number of enfranchised voters amounted to only 3 per cent of the United Kingdom's population.[43]

---

[38] Peter Butt, *Land Law* (Lawbook Co, 4th ed, 2001) 58-59; Standing Committee on Public Administration and Finance, Parliament of Western Australia, (Report 2004) 'Report in Relation to the Impact of State Government Actions and Processes on the Use and Enjoyment of Freehold and Leasehold Land in Western Australia', 755.

[39] Adrian J Bradbrook, Susan V MacCallum, Anthony P Moore, Scott Grattam and Lyndon Griggs, *Australian Real Property Law* (Thomson Lawbook Co, 3rd ed, 2002) 5.

[40] Ibid.

[41] 'Special Article: Early History of Land Tenure', *Australian Bureau of Statistics* (Web article online, 3 February 2004).

[42] Ryan Goss, 'Voting Rights and Australian Local Democracy' (2017) 40(3) *UNSW Law Journal* 1008; Bob Watt, *UK Election Law: A Critical Examination* (Glass House Press, 2006) 34.

[43] John Rabon, 'The History of Voting Rights in the United Kingdom', *Anglotopia* (Web Article, 23 November 2020).

The *Reform Act 1832* (UK) expanded voting rights to men above the age of 21 who were freeholders of property. A further *Reform Act*, in 1867, enfranchised householders, expanding the category of eligible voters to include the working classes.[44] In the 19th Century, the Women's Suffrage movement got started and kept political pressure on Parliament, through both non-violent and violent means, until the passage of the *Representation of the People Act 1918* (UK). It still required women to own property, but it did do away with the property requirements for men, giving the right to vote for all men regardless of race or class.[45]

The *Representation of the People Act 1928* (UK) did away with the property requirements for women, finally opening the door to all persons 21 years of age or older.[46] This was followed by the *Representation of the People Act 1969* (UK), which extended the right to vote to all persons aged 18 to 20.[47] Despite these hard fought gains, in 2016, almost half of eligible voters in Britain chose not to vote.[48]

The earliest British settlers of colonial America imported many of the laws and customs of England. One of those laws stipulated that only 'free holding' men, or those who owned property and paid taxes, could vote. Only 6 per cent of the American population were eligible to vote to elect the first US President, George Washington, in 1789.[49] In 1856, the vote in the US was expanded to include all white men.[50] In 1868, black men got the vote and, finally, in 1920 women got the right to vote.[51] In 1972, during the Vietnam war, the voting age was lowered to 18 to ensure those old enough to fight could also vote.

---

[44] Ibid.

[45] Ibid.

[46] Ibid.

[47] Ibid.

[48] Ibid.

[49] Grace Panetta and Olivia Reaney, 'How Voting Rights In America Have Changed Over Time', *Business Insider India* (Web Article 31 October 2018).

[50] Ibid.

[51] Ibid.

Similar to colonial America, Australia as a British colony inherited much of the English law. The first parliamentary elections were held in New South Wales in 1843.[52] It was limited to men with freehold valued at £200 or paying rent of at least £20 per year.[53] This was reduced to £100 free-hold or £10 annual rent in 1850.[54] The requirement to own or rent property was eliminated in 1856 in South Australia and in 1893 in Western Australia.[55] Voting was still restricted to men over 21 years of age.56 Women over 21 years obtained the vote in 1894 in South Australia and in 1899 in Western Australia.[57] Aboriginal men and women could vote at federal elections and referendums from 1949 provided they had served in the Australian Defence Forces. This was extended to all Aboriginal people in 1962. In 1973, the qualifying age for enrolment, voting and candidature for all federal elections was lowered from 21 years to 18.[58] In 1984, enrolment and voting for Aboriginal people became compulsory[59] and franchise qualification changed to Australian Citizenship. British subjects on the roll immediately before January 26, 1984 retained enrolment rights.[60]

It has been suggested that the removal of the property requirement and the lowering of the voting age has led to a steady dumbing down of the voter pool.[61] Arguments to reinstate the connection between voting and property ownership include that: ownership of property demonstrates the ability to contribute to society, but the

---

[52] 'History Of The Voting Franchise In Australia (1995-2021)', *Australian Electoral Commission Publications* (Web Page).

[53] Ibid.

[54] Ibid.

[55] Ibid.

[56] Ibid.

[57] Ibid.

[58] Ibid.

[59] Ibid.

[60] Ibid.

[61] 'Only Property Owners Should Vote', *Debate Politics* (Web Page, 25 September 2013).

main thing is you have *skin in the game;*[62] that people on welfare and kids have nothing to lose and everything to gain by voting for give away programs which benefit them and will vote in their own self-interest instead of considering what is best for the country;[63] and that illiterate and impoverished people have become a valuable, political voting block and political asset for exploitation by paid political activists.[64]

Arguments against restoring the voting and property ownership link include: that there are lots of intelligent, dynamic people who do not own real estate, for various personal reasons such as being young, or highly mobile, or they live in places where rental properties dominate the local landscape;[65] that not everyone who owns property is highly intelligent or motivated and may live in the homes they grew up in, having inherited the places from their parents; that many people cannot afford to buy property in an economy that provides lots of low-wage jobs with little job security, or they are burdened by medical bills or student debt, or they have disabilities that make it tough to work;[66] that it would be equivalent to only literate people being voters, similar to requiring English literacy to vote;[67] that everyone pays property tax even if indirectly so voting to raise property tax will result in it being passed on in the next rental agreement;[68] that setting a bar for voters is regarded as a form of voter suppression; that governments derive their powers from the consent of the governed and landowners and non-landowners are

---

[62] Ibid.

[63] Ibid.

[64] Mike Varga et al, 'Why Doesn't The USA Go Back to Only Allowing Property Owners to Vote?', *Quora* (Web Page, 15 March 2021).

[65] Ibid.

[66] Ibid.

[67] Ibid.

[68] Ibid.

both governed, therefore, both should have the right to vote.[69] Our democracy is based on the notion that everybody has a vote,[70] and instead of democracy, that would be proposing oligarchy.[71]

The outcry, understandably, focuses on voter suppression. The idea that Government was originally about protecting property has been lost. It is assumed renters will be excluded, which historically they were not.

Be that as it may, one might question whether the removal of the requirement of property ownership for enfranchisement has actually led to the rise in crony socialism[72] and the increasing attacks on property rights. Recent examples would be calls for caps on rents and recent changes to the *Residential Tenancies Act 1987* (WA) to allow pets and modifications by tenants to an owner's property.[73]

F *Constitutional Beginnings and the Legitimate Functions of Government*

Our *Australian Constitution* is influenced by the *United States Constitution*. The framers of the *US Constitution* were very aware of the legitimate functions of government in a free society. By defining the legitimate functions of government, the boundaries between the individual and the state were also defined.[74] The powers

---

[69] Ibid.

[70] Ibid.

[71] Ibid.

[72] Crony capitalism is when special interests lobby for subsidies and other concessions at the taxpayers or the economies expense. Within this context the term "crony socialism" may also be applied such as when concessions are given to classes of individuals in order to buy votes. For a discussion of the negative effects see Peter Enderwick, 'What's Bad About Crony Capitalism?' (2005) 4 *Asian Business Management* 117.

[73] 'WA Tenancy Law Modernisation to Strike a Balance Between Tenants and Landlords', Government of Western Australia, (Web Page, 26 May 2023).

[74] James A Dorn, 'The Scope of Government in a Free Society' (2012) 32(3) *Cato Journal* 629.

of government were thereby limited to the protection of persons and property enhancing both personal and economic liberties and limiting the power of a potentially overreaching government.[75]

The chief architect of the *US Constitution*, James Madison, sort to limit the powers of government and protect individual rights rather than to create an engine for economic growth. Economic development was seen as an expansion of the range of choices open to individuals.[76] Madison held that the legitimate and primary function of a just government is to protect property of every sort, including the rights of individuals.[77] He thought that there is no separation between good government, personal liberty, private property, and justice.[78] Madison stated 'it is sufficiently obvious, that persons and property are the two great subjects on which Governments are to act; and that the rights of persons and the rights of property are the objects for the protection of which Government was instituted'.[79]

In this sense, the American constitutional republic was to have limited powers under the rule of law, rather than being an intrusive state aimed at redistributing income and wealth.[80] Justice requires that government and law, which operate through power/coercion, be limited to the prevention of injustice – that is, to the defence of one's person and property, viewed as natural rights that exist prior to government.[81] For the Framers of the *US Constitution*, the checks and balances that operated between the three branches of government were a necessary means to prevent any single branch of the government from governing capriciously.

The high costs of regulation, the heavy excess burden of high

---

[75] Ibid.

[76] Ibid.

[77] Madison 1792, cited in Dorn (n 75).

[78] Ibid.

[79] Madison 1829, cited in Dorn (n 75).

[80] Ibid.

[81] Ibid.

marginal tax rates, the waste inherent in rent-seeking, and the damage to our moral fibre from the rise of the welfare state have eroded property rights, personal responsibility, and freedom. The promotion of 'social justice' via redistribution under-prices risk, impedes the market process and misallocates resources.[82]The growth of government crowds out private entrepreneurs, turning market liberalism into market socialism eroding the ethos of liberty and responsibility.[83] Of course, the purpose of a just government is precisely to prevent injustice by protecting property and securing liberty.[84]

Perfect rights are consistent with the principle of freedom and with justice because they are impartial and safeguard property.[85] Imperfect rights favour special interest groups at the expense of the general welfare, refer to distributive not commutative justice, and violate property rights.[86] However, modern liberals (so-called 'progressives') see the role of government to "do good" (with other people's money) rather than to "do no harm." Instead of asking whether the rules are just, they ask whether the outcomes are fair. This change from a focus on justice as a protection of property to justice as the redistribution of property to satisfy special interests, with numerous laws enacted that redistribute income and wealth via the tax and transfer system, has undermined the constitutional model of protection of property rights and freedom.[87]

For Thomas Jefferson, the 'sum of good government' is precisely to 'restrain men from injuring one another,' to 'leave them free to regulate their own pursuits of industry and improvement,' and to 'not take from the mouth of labour the bread it has earned.'[88] In 1837, John

---

[82] Ibid.

[83] Ibid.

[84] Ibid.

[85] Ibid.

[86] Ibid.

[87] Ibid.

[88] Ibid.

O'Sullivan, editor of the *United States Magazine and Democratic Review* wrote: 'The best government is that which governs least and should be confined to the administration of justice, for the protection of the natural equal rights of the citizen, and the preservation of the social order'.[89] This is the fundamental principle of the philosophy of democracy, to furnish a system of the administration of justice, and then to leave all the business and interests of society to themselves, to free competition and association.

Unfortunately, the "perfect" fundamental rights to be secured by the Constitution have been supplanted by the "imperfect" welfare rights that conflict with freedom and private property. The idea that liberty comes first and democracy second, and that limited government and equal rights under the law of the Constitution generate a harmonious social and economic order, has been lost.[90] Most politicians now seek to expand, not reduce, the size of government – and use every crisis to do so.[91] If a government program fails, there will be a demand for more, not less, spending.[92] The idea that policymakers, with the help of economists, can design a complex system like the market, fine-tune the economy, and use discretionary monetary and fiscal policy to achieve a real GDP growth target is a "fatal conceit".[93]

In countries under the English Crown in the 16th through the 18th centuries, law took the form of an external limitation on (or a diminution of) royal power.[94] This has been supplanted with the idea that the State is the active producer of markets and that the prevalent

---

[89] Ibid.

[90] Ibid.

[91] Ibid.

[92] Ibid.

[93] Ibid.

[94] David Schneiderman, 'Constitutional Property Rights and Elision of the Transnational: Foucauldian Misgivings' (2015) 24(1) *Social & Legal Studies* 65.

role of law and the State is the construction and maintenance of markets which includes responding to crises of its own making.[95] Of course, there may be an argument that certain natural monopolies, such as utilities, are more appropriately held in the hands of a non-profit Government, thereby protecting the people from exploitation. Neo-conservative misunderstanding and misapplication of this concept has led to both a sell off of these assets into private hands or exploitation by the Government itself.

G *The Henry George Fallacy*

In the 19th century, in stark contrast to this ideology of protecting property, Henry George, an influential American political economist, proposed that a land value tax, could cover all government expenditure.[96] Its premise was socialising land rents through taxation.[97] Its justification was the idea that land value increases are due to societal changes rather than individual efforts. George was a Fabian Socialist and student of Marx, thus explaining the attack against private property rights and ownership.

Many authors highlight the importance of private property

---

[95] Ibid.

[96] Henry George, *Progress and Poverty: An Inquiry into the Cause of Industrial Depressions and of Increase of Want with Increase in Wealth* (Schalkenbach Foundation, 1879) vol VI; also later promoted by others as the Henry George Theorem, for example see Richard Arnott and Joseph Stiglitz, 'Aggregate Land Rents, Expenditure on Public Goods and Optimal City Size' (1979) 93(4) *The Quarterly Journal of Economics* 471; Fred E Foldvary, 'The Marginalists Who Confronted Land' (2008) 67(1) *American Journal of Economics and Sociology* 89. It is still frequently touted by Socialists as a cure all for raising tax revenue.

[97] Michael McDermott, *Wicked Valuations, Chapter 1: Framing the thesis of this book* (Imprint Routledge, 1st ed, 2018).

ownership in the economic[98] and social[99] development of countries. Based upon this extensive literature, any argument that a land value tax is without significant consequence to productive output is without merit. However, the idea of replacing other taxes and raising all taxes via property taxes derives from Henry George's teachings and

---

[98]   Jens Ladefoged Mortensen and Leonard Seabrooke, 'Housing as Social Right or Means to Wealth? The Politics of Property Booms in Australia and Denmark' (2008) 6 *Comparative European Politics* 305; John Humphreys, 'Real Property Rights' (2012) *IPA Review* 40; Małgorzata Barbara Havel, 'Delineation of Property Rights as Institutional Foundations for Urban Land Markets in Transition' (2014) 38 *Land Use Policy* 615; Steven Devaney, Pat McAllisterb and Anupam Nanda, 'Determinants of Transaction Activity in Commercial Real Estate Markets: Evidence from European and Asia-Pacifc Countries' (2017) 34(4) *Journal of Property research* 251; Robert J Hill and Iqbal A Syed, 'Hedonic Price–Rent Ratios, User Cost, and Departures from Equilibrium in the Housing Market' (2016) 56 *Regional Science and Urban Economics* 60.

[99] Rollin F Tusalem, 'Determinants of Coup d'État Events 1970–90: The Role of Property Rights Protection' (2010) 31(3) *International Political Science Review* 346; Robert Home, 'Culturally Unsuited to Property Rights?: Colonial Land Laws and African Societies' (2013) 40(3) *Journal of Law and Society* 403; Shanthi Robertson and Dallas Rogers, 'Education, Real Estate, Immigration: Brokerage Assemblages and Asian Mobilities' (2017) 43(14) *Journal of Ethnic and Migration Studies* 2393; Amelia Thorpe, 'Hegel's Hipsters: Claiming Ownership in the Contemporary City' (2018) 27(1) *Social & Legal Studies* 25; Neil T Coffee, Tony Lockwood, Graeme Hugo, Catherine Paquet, Natasha J Howard and Mark Daniel, 'Relative Residential Property Value as a Socioeconomic Status Indicator for Health Research' (2013) 12 *International Journal of Health Geographics* 22; Eilleen Webb, 'Housing an Ageing Australia: The ideal of Security of Tenure and the Undermining Effect of Elder Abuse (2018) 18 *Macquarie Law Journal* 57; Margaret Moore, 'Legitimate Expectations and Land' (2017) 4(2) *Moral Philosophy and Politics* 229; Pal Czegledi, 'Why Are Civil Liberties More Important Then Executive Constraints in Economic Development? A Property Rights Approach (2014) 36(1) *Society and Economy* 37; Sarah Keenan, 'Property as Governance: Time, Space and Belonging in Australia's Northern Territory Intervention' (2013) 76(3) *The Modern Law Review* 464; Malcolm Voyce, 'Property and the Governance of the Family Farm in Rural Australia' (2007) 43(2) *Macquarie University Journal of Sociology* 131; Daniel Melser and Robert J. Hill, 'Residential Real Estate, Risk, Return and Diversification: Some Empirical Evidence' (2019) 59 *Journal Real Estate Finan Econ* 111; Bronwyn Bate, 'Rental Security and the Property Manager in a Tenant's Search for a Private Rental Property' (2020) 35(4) *Housing Studies* 4, 589; Gary D. Libecap, 'The Tragedy of the Commons: Property Rights and Markets as Solutions to Resource and Environmental Problems' (2009) 53 *The Australian Journal of Agricultural and Resource Economics* 129.

is frequently raised within the Australian context. The idea that this would not affect tenant rents and cripple the housing market is naïve. In a situation where rental vacancies are low, the situation is exacerbated by these additional charges which must be passed on to tenants. The provision of rental property is also discouraged where owners must meet these constantly increasing and unpredictable additional levies.

The legal right to own, occupy and use land provides a cornerstone of the system of private property in western culture.[100] More than 80% of all housing in Australia is owned or controlled by private individuals.[101] The government provides between 12 to 14% of all housing in the form of rental assistance and public housing, including refuge accommodation and caravan facilities.[102]

Henry George wrote in a different era that was typified by an entirely different situation. At that time, large aristocratic landholdings were the norm rather than many small ones, which is the current Australian situation. For example, in the 2017-8 tax year,[103] there were 2,207,905 property investors in Australia or around 20% of Australian households holding an investment property.[104] The ownership was distributed as follows:

- 1 investment property – 71% (1.57million)
- 2 investment properties – 19% (418,000)
- 3 investment properties – 6% (129,784)
- 4 investment properties – 2% (47,469)
- 5 investment properties – 1% (19,861)
- 6 or more investment properties – less than 1% (20,756)[105]

---

[100] Michael Peters, 'The Right to Housing', (Conference Paper, Legal Studies Students Conference, May 1998).

[101] Ibid.

[102] Ibid.

[103] Australian Taxation Office figures cited in below 105.

[104] Kate Forbes, 'How Many Australians Own an Investment Property?', *Property Investment*, (Web Article, 20 October 2020).

[105] Ibid.

The fact that 90% of investors only own one or two investment properties has been the status quo for many years.[106] Of the 2,207,905 property investors who filed a rental schedule, rental income is typically low or negative.

Table 1: Private property rental losses (ATO data):

No of Property Interests	Overall net rent loss	Overall net rent neutral/profit
2018	59.97%	40.03%
1 interest	60.02%	39.98%
2 interests	60.77%	39.23%
3 interests	58.80%	41.20%
4 interests	57.51%	42.49%
5 interests	56.89%	43.11%
6 or more interests	55.95%	44.05%

As per above, around 40% of owners are cash flow neutral or cash flow positive and roughly 60% were in a net rental loss situation (negatively geared). The owners experiencing a positive or negative position may vary from year to year based upon their particular circumstances and the quality of tenants. This is consistent with the large costs of maintenance for publicly provided housing which, in Western Australia, runs in deficit with a total cost of services of $1,099,615,000 to achieve rents of $282,598,000.[107] In the same period there were 38,000 state housing homes.[108] This represents a cost to the taxpayer of $21,500 per year, per property.

With a long social housing wait list, almost 1,927 social houses

---

[106] Ibid.

[107] Note that a proportion of the rents paid also comes from the Commonwealth Government in the form of Centrelink rental assistance.

[108] 'Department of Communities Annual Report 2021-22', *Department of Communities* (Web Page, 2022).

across the WA state are empty and in need of repairs.[109] This is the highest number of vacant social houses since 2019.[110] Major refurbishments are required because of the condition in which the properties have been left.[111] A lot of public housing is decrepit and needs to be demolished or repaired.[112] A substantial proportion of housing stock is approaching end of life.[113] Without substantial ongoing investment, operating costs will continue to increase.[114] Recent announcements indicate that the Government's solution is to throw more money at the problem.[115] This includes AU$ 169.8 million to renovate 500 homes.[116] That is a staggering AU$ 339,000 per home! In addition, another $12.8 million will be used to carry out building assessments on more than 10,000 ageing public and regional government homes.[117] It is claimed these projects will provide a pipeline of work for the building industry.[118] However, the building industry is already under pressure due to subsidies for building work by the Commonwealth Government. Some WA state government tenders are already failing to attract contractors.[119]

Prior to the additional issues from the Covid response, maintenance costs were also high as indicated by the Table 2 figures.

---

[109] Jacqueline Lynch and Patti Brook, 'Number of Vacant Social Homes in WA Rises by 25 Per Cent as Housing Crisis Continues', *ABC Radio Perth* (Web Article, 12 August 2022).

[110] Ibid.

[111] Ibid.

[112] Tabarak Al Jrood and Keane Bourke, 'WA government to allocate an extra $875 million to social housing in 2021-22 state budget' *ABC News* (Web Page, 5 September 2021).

[113] 'Foundations for a Stronger Tomorrow – State Infrastructure Strategy', *Government of Western Australia* (Web Page, 2022).

[114] Ibid.

[115] Al Jrood (n 113).

[116] Ibid.

[117] Ibid.

[118] Ibid.

[119] Lynch and Brook (n 110).

Table 2: WA maintenance budget and actual spend[120]

	2017/18		2018/19	
	Budget	Actual	Budget	Actual
Public Housing	$162,247,788	$164,892,000	$162,186,261	$149,640,001
Government Regional Officer Housing	$20,200,123	$22,114,874	$19,237,283	$22,612,458
Aboriginal Housing Services	$24,772,272	$16,200,000	$23,145,147	$24,600,000
Community Housing	$916,754	$6,064,000	$2,430,172	$2,951,000
Key Workers Housing and NonGovernment Organisation	$381,574	$597,000	$515,565	$597,564
Total	$208,518,511	$209,867,874	$207,514,428	$200,401,023

The table above indicates an average actual spend of AU$ 179,075,834 on maintenance for Public Housing, Aboriginal Housing Services and Community Housing, over the 3-year period between 2017 and 2019. It is assumed that private owners are immune from these high maintenance costs and are able to afford to pay additional taxes as well as these costs. The provision of rental property fulfils an important societal function and is largely a philanthropic endeavour. Tenants may lose jobs, succumb to family violence, may need counselling for hoarding issues and experience other difficulties which become

---

[120] Peter Collier, Submission Number 3437 to Parliament of Western Australia Legislative Council Tabled Papers Response to Questions Without Notice, *Department of Housing – Maintenance budget and actual spend for 2017-18, 2018-19 and 2019-20* (26 November 2019).

difficulties passed on to private owners. These private owners may be self-funded retirees excluded from any unemployment or pension payments due to 'means test' exclusions based upon the capital value of their properties, rather than any obtainable income. Owners who have employment, business or other income to offset their losses are likely to be time-poor with Government compliance obligations exacerbating the situation. Requirements to fulfil Government imposts force owners to treat the provision of rental housing as a business to cover these costs and therefore are forced to evict tenants falling upon hard times. Low vacancy rates and higher rents may not necessarily help owners as they may result in more rent defaults and difficulties in evicting tenants who have no where else to go.

There is no doubt that land tax is an effective tax for Governments because it is based upon an illiquid asset. It creates secured debt where there should be none and these taxes, therefore, are much easier to collect. Furthermore, the argument that land value increases are due to societal changes rather than individual efforts is highly questionable. Most infrastructure has already been undertaken when development occurs.[121] Redirecting money paid into property taxes into maintenance and improvement of properties is most likely to improve the values of both the properties and the local area, especially if these same properties are currently run down as the result of damage by tenants and attempts to meet these taxes.

H *Historical Interaction of WA Land Tax Laws with Commonwealth Jurisdiction*

Under s 114 of the *Australian Constitution*, a state shall not impose any tax on property of any kind belonging to the Commonwealth. The Commonwealth means the common people's wealth and includes the

---

[121] 'State Planning Policy 3.6-Infrastructure Contributions', *Department of Planning, Lands and Heritage*, Government of Western Australia (2022), cl 6 and specifically cl 6.1(c), 3.

land. The Commonwealth already taxes property as Commonwealth property in the form of both Income and Capital Gains Tax.[122] That alienated fee simple land is under Commonwealth jurisdiction is confirmed by case law as stated in *Commonwealth v New South Wales*:[123]

> It is obviously right, therefore, to say that under s85(i) the Commonwealth holds the land for an estate of fee simple in possession, that having no reference to any tenure under the State. The title transferred by s85 is taken from the State, adversely to State law and by a law superior, and by that superior law is vested in the Commonwealth; and, as that superior law is the sole source of title, it follows that nothing henceforth can depend on State registration laws or State laws of any kind.

The *Land Tax Assessment Act 2002* (WA) ('LTAA') clearly has as its purpose the imposition of a state tax upon property which is rightfully Commonwealth. The correct Commonwealth seal still appears on original grant legal title documents. Consistent with this federal jurisdiction, the Commonwealth introduced a nominal land tax in 1910, the *Land Tax Act 1910* (Cth). There were numerous amendments to this Act and its associated *Land Tax Assessment Act 1910* (Cth), until 30 June 1952 when it was abolished by the *Land Tax Abolition Act 1953-1956* (Cth) and subsequently by the *Land Tax Abolition Act 1956* (Cth). It was abolished at Commonwealth level as it unduly targeted urban property and cost more to collect than it raised.[124] Recognition of the unfairness of a tax on the "capital base"

---

[122] See *Income Tax Assessment Act 1997* (Cth) and the *New Business Tax System (Capital Gains Tax) Act 1999* (Cth). There is no correction in the supposed capital gain for the decline in real value of the currency over the time the asset is held. The decline in real value will be especially high in times of "quantitative easing" (money printing).

[123] *Commonwealth v New South Wales* [1923] HCA 34 (1923) 33 CLR 1.

[124] Stewart Smith, 'Land Tax: An Update' (Briefing Paper No 5/05, NSW Parliamentary Library Service, 2005).

of someone's "major income producing asset" led to the *Land Tax Abolition Act 1956* (Cth) and to the exclusion of farms in the *Land Tax Act 1976* (WA). Arguably, rental properties should be no different as it is also likely to be a tax on the "capital base" of someone's "major income producing asset". No similar taxes are levied on other assets of any type.[125]

Under s 109 of the *Australian Constitution*, when a law of an Australian state is inconsistent with a law of the Commonwealth, the latter shall prevail, and the former shall, to the extent of the inconsistency, be invalid. States cannot usurp the *Australian Constitution*. Despite this, the states, including Western Australia, have claimed land tax as their prerogative, initially in place of council rates.[126] There is an assumption that there should not be double taxation on the same objects.[127] Any such assumption has been well and truly abandoned when it comes to property and we now have both council and water rates, as well as Metropolitan Regional Improvement Tax ('MRIT'), stamp duty and land tax.[128] This is in addition to property taxes such as Capital Gains Tax and taxes upon income at the Commonwealth level. In the ownership of property we therefore have not just double, but septuple taxation!

Land is transferred in Australia in fee simple and not "fee simple conditional". Transfers are not conditional upon the payment of a

---

[125] Ibid.

[126] Western Australia introduced land tax in 1907, Tasmania and Victoria in 1910 and Queensland in 1915. Prior to 1884, the colonies gained revenue primarily through the sale of Crown Land, although there existed in some colonies taxes based on the annual assessed value of the land, representing a tax on imputed income gained from the land, see above 127.

[127] Chloe Burnett, 'A Part IVA that goes the Other Way? The Rule against Double Taxation' (2012) 27(3) *Australian Tax Forum* 467.

[128] In 1906, the NSW Premier, J H Carruthers, abolished land tax altogether as part of his major reform of local government. The aim was to provide local councils with an independent revenue source, land tax, for which they no longer had to compete with the State. Where the local government levied rates of at least 1 penny in the pound, the State was not to impose additional land tax.

yearly rent charge, fee or license to anyone, including the Western Australian Government. Privity of contract between previous and subsequent owners is notoriously ignored. Land owners never entered into an agreement with the Crown, or the State Government, and therefore should not involuntarily incur debts against these properties. As stated in *Halsbury's Laws of England*, '[t]he condition is invalid also if it is unlawful, and, since an estate in fee simple is in its nature inalienable, a condition in restraint of alienation is repugnant and therefore void).[129]

The doctrine of separation of powers has a long history and states that the Legislature (Parliament) makes the laws; the Executive (Government) administers the laws; and the Judiciary (Courts) interprets the laws.[130] The importance of separating the powers of the State is essential to a check on the abuse of executive power and the ultimate goal of limited and accountable government.[131] John Locke, the celebrated English philosopher, writing in 1690 emphasised that the same person should not have the power to make laws and to execute them. Likewise, Sir William Blackstone concentrated on the separation of judicial power and the importance of the common law to protect fundamental rights to life, liberty and property.[132]

---

[129] Hardinge Giffard, 1st Earl of Halsbury and Quintin Hogg, Baron Hailsham of St. Marylebone, (eds), *Halsbury's Laws of England: Being A Complete Statement of the Whole Law of England* (Butterworths, Vol. 24, 1973) 164-173.

[130] Charles-Louis de Secóndat, Baron de Montesquieu, T. Nugent tr, *L'Espirit des Lois (The Spirit of the Laws)* (Hafner Publishing Company New York, 1966); Garry Willis (ed), *The Federalist Papers: Alexander Hamilton, James Madison and John Jay* (Penguin Random House, 1982); Maurice John Crawley Vile, *Constitutionalism and the Separation of Powers* (Clarendon Press, 1967); Gregory S Mahler, *Comparative Politics: An Institutional and CrossCultural Approach* (Prentice Hall, 1995); Haig Patapan, 'Separation of Powers in Australia' (1999) 34(3) *Australian Journal of Political Science* 391.

[131] John Locke, *Two Treatises of Government, A Critical Edition with an Introduction and Apparatus Criticus by Peter Laslett* (Cambridge University Press, 1963).

[132] Thomas M Cooley (ed), *Commentaries on the Laws of England: in Four Books by William Blackstone* (Callaghan and Company, 3rd ed).

Under the *Australian Constitution*, we are meant to have a certain separation of powers. The courts are meant to protect us from the excess of government. The common law is said to incorporate fundamental moral principles, against which the legality of governmental decisions, and even Acts of Parliament, may be tested.[133] Courts are therefore meant to protect fundamental rights, and to test the moral credentials of what purports to be law but may, on inspection, prove to be an infringement of the rule of law.[134]

However, Australia only has a partial separation of these three powers at the Commonwealth level.[135] To make it worse, we do not seem to have a real separation of powers at the WA State level.[136] State-based legislation is not tested against established common law for validity by either the Upper House, the Department of Attorney-General or by the courts themselves. Instead, the courts claim themselves to solely be the administrators of these statutes. The courts, therefore, just act as an arm of Government.

We are witnessing an era of legal positivism, much like Nazi Germany. The doctrine of separation of powers is interpreted to only be that the legislature cannot interfere with, or change, judicial decisions. At the WA State level, unlike at the Commonwealth level, there is no constitutionally entrenched separation of power.[137] To

---

[133] Thomas Poole, 'Dogmatic Liberalism? TRS Allan and the Common Law Constitution' (2002) 65 *The Modern Law Review* 463, 463.

[134] Trevor RS Allan, 'In Defence of the Common Law Constitution: Unwritten Rights as Fundamental Law' (2009) 22 *Canadian Journal of Law and Justice* 187, 190.

[135] Richard Darrell Lumb, *Australian Constitutionalism* (Butterworths, 1983) 24; Richard Darrell Lumb, *The Constitutions of the Australian States* (University of Queensland Press, 5th ed, 1991) 132-137; Patrick Harding Lane, *An Introduction to the Australian Constitutions*, (The Law Book Company, 6th ed, 1994) 220.

[136] John Ralph Alvey, *The Separation of Powers in Australia: Issues for the States*, Master of Business (Research) in Public Policy Thesis, Faculty of Business, Queensland University of Technology, 2005.

[137] Richard Darrell Lumb, *The Constitutions of the Australian States* (5th ed, University of Queensland Press, 1991) 132-137.

establish the separation of powers doctrine at the State level, the Australian States need to entrench a more rigid and clear separation of powers in their State constitutions to overcome the flexible nature of their State constitutions.[138]

Generally, the parliaments of the respective Australian states have plenary power to make laws for 'the peace, order and good government' of the community, subject however to express and implied limitations from the *Australian Constitution*, which leaves to the government of these states the freedom to legislate on the terms chosen by themselves.[139] As a result, no inquiry by the courts has been admitted as to whether, as a matter of fact or law, any particular statute is, or is not, a prudent exercise of the power under the principles of constitutional government, or is calculated to attain its particular end or object.[140] As McHugh J stated in *Essenberg* (2000):

> We are ruled by law and law is the law of Parliament; it is called legal positivism. It is the law laid down. This Court makes decisions and, unless they are constitutional decisions, the Parliament can overrule them and often does. We lay down a law, Parliament can change it.[141]

McHugh J, in *Essenberg*, then provides the following example of the extent of plenary state power: 'Parliament … can, in effect, do what it likes. As it is said, some authorities could legislate to have every blue-eyed baby killed if it wanted to'.[142] After all, as Dawson J had communicated in *Kable*,

---

[138] Suri Ratnapala, *Australian Constitutional Law: Foundations and Theory* (Oxford University Press, 2002).

[139] *Union Steamship Co of Australia Pty Ltd v King* (1988) 166 CLR 1, 9-10; 82 ALR 43; 62 ALJR 645; See also *McCawley v R* (1920) 28 CLR 106; [1920] AC 691, 712 (Lord Birkenhead); *Ibralebbe v R* [1964] AC 900, 923; [1964] 1 All ER 251; [1964] 2 WLR 76.

[140] *Riel v The Queen* (1885) 10 App Cas 673, 678; *Bone v Mothershaw* [2002] QCA 120, [4] (McPherson JA).

[141] *Essenberg v The Queen* [2000] HCATrans 385, [4].

[142] Ibid.

[Legislation is] binding upon them and cannot be questioned by reference to principles of a more fundamental kind. Indeed, it is a principle of the common law itself that a court may not question the validity of a statute but, once having construed it, must give effect to it according to its tenor. Expanding on the judgement in *Union Steamship*, he stated that the words "for the peace, order and good government did not confer on the courts jurisdiction to strike down legislation on the ground that in their opinion, it does not promote or secure the peace, order and good government, and that the exercise of legislative power is not susceptible to judicial review on that score. [143]

There is not a single common law principle that cannot be overwritten by legislation, such is the supremacy of Parliament. No attention needs to be paid to it by legislators, even with previous legislation, if there is an inconsistency, the latter acts to repeal the former. The only real question is whether the particular Parliament possesses the appropriate legislative power under the *Australian Constitution* in order to pass any such a law. As already mentioned above, *Essenberg*, *Kable* and *Union Steamship* all confirm they have this power to abrogate even the most basic of our rights and freedoms.

State courts are not subject to the separation of powers doctrine, because such separation only applies when they are exercising federal jurisdiction, not state jurisdiction. However, people still assume they are protected by the *Australian Constitution*, and established common law, regardless of whether they are dealing with a state or federal court and would be outraged to discover that this is not the case.

If we do not have separation of powers at state level, then we do not have it at all. We assume that we have the protection of the *Australian Constitution* at state level. It would seem, however, that we do not.

---

[143] *Kable v The Director of Public Prosecutions for New South Wales* (1996) 189 CLR 51; 138 ALR 577; [1996] HCA 24, [9].

We have centuries of very good and just law, in the form of case or judge-made law, which has been made in accordance with natural-law principles which protect us from government tyranny. Of course, if a statute is contrary to constitutional or common law then it is bad law and it should be overturned. In most instances, comparing historical common or case law against statutes should be enough to strike out bad law. Doing this, without resorting to judicial activism, should be the correct application of the law to ensure the prevention of tyranny, as was originally intended. This protection from tyranny needs to be at both the state and federal levels, rather than just bypassing our protections and using the states to enact tyrannical legislation. Enshrining rights in the *WA Constitution* would also be an important safeguard to guard against tyrannical legislation which would need to be tested against those rights.

III. THE WESTERN AUSTRALIAN SITUATION

Much has been written and quoted in Government publications under the assumption that the Government of Western Australia has the right of eminent domain. Eminent domain is defined as the inherent right of the government to compulsorily acquire private property for public purposes.[144] This right is assumed without question.[145] However, the Western Australian Government does not stop there. It imposes a number of land taxes upon alienated fee simple property located within Western Australia whereby it assumes ownership, charging a yearly rent. The Government then gives itself the power to confiscate and seize property when these charges are not paid. Examples of these rents include water rates under the *Water Services Act 2012* (WA), council rates under the *Local Government Act 1995*

---

[144] P E Nygh and P Butt (General Editors), *Butterworths Australian Legal Dictionary*, (Butterworths, Sydney, 1997) 412.

[145] For example: William Rupert Johnson, *Private Property Rights and the State A Study of Regard and Increasing Disregard in Western Australia: 1829-2016* (Doctor of Juridical Science Thesis, Faculty of Law, University of Western Australia, 2017) 3.

(WA) and land tax proper under the *Land Tax Assessment Act 2002* (WA).

These charges are not restricted to Western Australia. Other states also impose land tax but this article focuses on Western Australian law. These land taxes are based upon theoretical "valuations" of unrealised gains. These valuations are not independent but come from the Landgate Valuer General, another branch of the State Government. In Western Australia, there is no independence between valuations and the body deriving benefit from those valuations. This tax, whereby the State Government assigns a speculative valuation and then uses this to seize property is contrary to democratic ideals and is an assault on private property rights and ownership.

Current methods of valuation contain subjective components[146] and hence can be used to target specific individuals. The state has assumed ownership of fee simple land, which is supposedly held without benefit to the Crown.[147] A compulsory electronic conveyancing system[148] ensures that these rules create secured debt for fines, court orders, memorials, etc. where none should exist. There are 54 Western Australian statutes which allow memorials to be placed on property. This system is also used to enforce the payment of title transfer fees,[149]

146 Stewart Smith, 'Land Tax: An Update' (Briefing Paper No 5/05, NSW Parliamentary Library Service, 2005).

147 Fee simple is the highest form of ownership with the right to control, use, and transfer the property at will. This may be contrasted with the concept of tenure whereby property is merely held in possession.

148 With the introduction of the *Electronic Conveyancing Act 2014* (WA), from 1 December 2018, it is mandatory for all property transactions in WA to be completed electronically, where possible. In Western Australia these are conducted via the PEXA software platform. Other states use Purcell Partners Pty Ltd. and Sympli Australia Pty Ltd. All 3 are public companies and are known as Electronic Lodgement Network Operators (ELNO's). They have complete databases of who owns property in Australia. They are all registered with the Australian Securities and Investments Commission ('ASIC) and have shareholders who receive dividends on their shares. There is no way of knowing who the share holders are, however the directors details can be obtained by paying a fee and doing a search at ASIC.

149 Emily Piesse, 'The Cost of Buying and Selling WA Homes is About to Rise Thanks to E-Conveyancing', *ABC News*, (Web Article, 30 November 2018).

Stamp duty[150] and Capital Gains Tax. These memorials do not expire, and are not subject to a statute of limitations.[151] They are a first charge upon property[152] and therefore are not subject to the normal common law debt protections.

Land tax is currently assessed according to the formula in Table 3.

Table 3: Figures upon which land tax is currently based

Taxable land value	Land tax rates
$0 - $300,000	Nil
$300,001 - $420,000	Flat rate of $300
$420,001 - $1,000,000	$300 + 0.25 cent for each $1 in excess of $420,000
$1,000,001 - $1,800,000	$1,750 + 0.90 cent for each $1 in excess of $1,000,000
$1,800,001 - $5,000,000	$8,950 + 1.80 cents for each $1 in excess of $1,800,000
$5,000,001 - $11,000,000	$66,550 + 2.00 cents for each $1 in excess of $5,000,000
over $11,000,000	$186,550 + 2.67 cents for each $1 in excess of $11,000,000

Refer to the data in Table 4. It can be seen that the assessment of land tax and MRIT are exponential, effectively preventing any economy of scale from being realised. The formula is also frequently revised, increasing the revenue to the WA State in 2013/2014, 2014/2015 and 2019/2020. However, there is no indexation to account for a rising property market, or declines in "real" value due to inflation. Unlike the ever increasing "valuations" and "quantitative easing", there is, generally, no increase in the base rate before the tax is applied.

---

[150] Under the new system, settlement agents are also involved in stamp duty administration, which was previously done by the Office of State Revenue.

[151] A memorial is a form of "super" caveat whereby the WA State creates an interest in land for itself via a charge against the land, see *Tax Adminstration Act 2003* (WA). Removals of memorials may only occur via a Memorial of Release of Charge under s 81.

[152] *Tax Adminstration Act 2003* (WA) s 76(1).

The base rate was increased from $250,000 in 2007/08 to $300,000 in 2008/09[153] and has remained there since. Similar to income tax, property owners are pushed into higher tax brackets over time. It is bracket creep of an extreme nature on unrealised gains.

Table 4: application of, and changes of the formula, thus increasing WA State revenue over time

Assessed Value	2019/20 rates	MRIT 19/20	Total 2019-20	2014/15 rates	MRIT 14/15	Total 2014/15	2013/14 rates	MRIT 13/14	Total 2013/14
$0	$0	$0	$0	$0	$0	$0	$0	$0	$0
$300,000	$0	$0	$0	$0	$331	$331	$0	$300	$300
$300,001	$300	$0	$300	$0	$331	$331	$0	$300	$300
$360,000	$300	$84	$384	$66	$397	$463	$60	$360	$420
$419,999	$300	$168	$468	$132	$464	$596	$120	$420	$540
$420,000	$300	$168	$468	$132	$464	$596	$120	$420	$540
$420,001	$300	$168	$468	$132	$464	$596	$120	$420	$540
$460,000	$400	$224	$624	$176	$508	$684	$160	$460	$620
$500,000	$500	$280	$780	$220	$552	$772	$200	$500	$700
$999,999	$1,750	$980	$2,730	$770	$1,104	$1,874	$700	$1,000	$1,700
$1,000,000	$1,750	$980	$2,730	$770	$1,104	$1,874	$700	$1,000	$1,700
$1,000,001	$1,750	$980	$2,730	$770	$1,104	$1,874	$700	$1,000	$1,700
$1,100,000	$2,650	$1,120	$3,770	$1,350	$1,214	$2,564	$1,230	$1,100	$2,330
$1,150,000	$3,100	$1,190	$4,290	$1,640	$1,270	$2,910	$1,495	$1,150	$2,645
$1,250,000	$4,000	$1,330	$5,330	$2,220	$1,380	$3,600	$2,025	$1,250	$3,275
$1,420,000	$5,530	$1,568	$7,098	$3,206	$1,568	$4,774	$2,926	$1,420	$4,346
$1,500,000	$6,250	$1,680	$7,930	$3,670	$1,656	$5,326	$3,350	$1,500	$4,850
$1,800,000	$8,950	$2,100	$11,050	$5,410	$1,987	$7,397	$4,940	$1,800	$6,740
$1,800,001	$8,950	$2,100	$11,050	$5,410	$1,987	$7,397	$4,940	$1,800	$6,740
$2,200,000	$16,150	$2,660	$18,810	$7,730	$2,429	$10,159	$7,060	$2,200	$9,260
$2,200,001	$16,150	$2,660	$18,810	$7,730	$2,429	$10,159	$7,060	$2,200	$9,260
$4,999,999	$66,550	$6,580	$73,130	$50,010	$5,520	$55,530	$45,420	$5,000	$50,420
$5,000,000	$66,550	$6,580	$73,130	$50,010	$5,520	$55,530	$45,420	$5,000	$50,420
$5,500,000	$76,550	$7,280	$83,830	$57,560	$6,072	$63,632	$52,270	$5,500	$57,770
$5,500,001	$76,550	$7,280	$83,830	$57,560	$6,072	$63,632	$52,270	$5,500	$57,770
$11,000,000	$186,550	$14,980	$201,530	$156,560	$12,144	$168,704	$142,470	$11,000	$153,470
$11,000,001	$186,550	$14,980	$201,530	$156,560	$12,144	$168,704	$142,470	$11,000	$153,470
$20,000,000	$426,850	$27,580	$454,430	$396,860	$22,080	$418,940	$361,170	$20,000	$381,170

Refer to Table 5 which are based upon the 2019/2020 rates.

---

[153] *Metropolitan Region Improvement Tax Act 1959* (WA) s 10.

Assuming an average valuation of $500,000 and an average gross rental of $20,800,[154] at around 5 properties, the entire gross rental amount of more than one property is consumed by land tax. That is, $500,000 x 5 = $2,500,000 resulting in combined land tax and MRIT of $24,600 versus the gross estimated rental of $20,800 for a single property. Therefore, the entire rent of 1.18 (24,600/20,800) properties are required to fund these taxes. However, gross rental value is not realistically achievable due to other land taxes in the form of water and council rates, owners being held accountable for unpaid tenant water bills,[155] vacancies, money required for ongoing repairs and any mortgage costs.

---

[154] From REIWA data (online).

[155] *Water Services Act* (WA) s 124(b). The Water Corporation holds owners responsible for an ongoing surcharge for sewerage removal etc. in the form of a service charge (formerly rates). Owners are also held responsible for unpaid or late tenant usage bills. In large part this act attempts to override the primacy of property rights and justify trespass. Virtually unconditional entry is allowed under ss 40, 84, 95, 98, 115, 116, 121, 177, 178, 179 and 180. The agents can virtually do anything – s179, take in anyone – s178, take in any equipment – s174(3), give notice after the fact and also invade anyone else's property to do it – s177. Attempts to protect the rights of the owner or occupier in s173(1), s175(2)(e) and s176(1) are effectively overridden in ss 173(2), 175(3)(b) and 175(4). Under s 124(2)(a)(iii) statutory water service charges are based upon the gross rental value, unimproved value or area of the land in respect of which a water service is provided. Charges for use of a service need to be tied to that use and not just be a means to extort money from soft target land owners. Charges are arbitrarily made in respect of land under s124(b), are levied even when not connected under s 124(c), and, even continue when there is no use because the land is vacant. Section 76 refers to certain agreements, binding on successors, being used to justify water service charges in perpetuity. This is a clear violation of fee simple and fundamental freedoms going as far back as the *Magna Carta*. The Water Corporation entitles itself to impose a unilateral agreement overriding the privity of contract of a fee simple property transfer. Silence is not consent and no consideration has been offered or given. When the service is correctly tied to use, there is no longer any reason for involvement with land valuation s 124(2)(e) or a proxy land owner payee under s 124(2)(h). Charges for water supply should have nothing to do with the value of land. Property booms and escalating values should not force owners into a position where they have to sell their property to pay charges for services they do not even receive. Furthermore, lodging of memorials against land under s 128 and any related costs as per s 128(2)(c) should be unlawful unless they are truly, and not just nominally, responsible for the fees or charges. Even then this should not automatically create a charge against land. Prior to the Richard Court Government of 1993-2001 the only charge for water was for excess water use. Much productive time is squandered with these now constant charges.

Therefore, realistically, it is more likely the entire remaining rent available will be consumed by land tax with a much lower number of properties owned. There is no economy of scale achievable thus skewing the market, preventing local accumulation of wealth and capital, and increasing dependence upon foreign capital for investment.

Table 5: Rents required to fund land tax

# Houses	Median Value *	Median Yearly Rent Nov 2020 *	MRIT	Calculator	Total tax amount	Rents required to fund
1	$500,000	$20,800	$280	$500	$780	0.04
2	$1,000,000	$41,600	$980	$1,750	$2,730	0.13
3	$1,500,000	$62,400	$1,680	$6,250	$7,930	0.38
4	$2,000,000	$83,200	$2,380	$12,550	$14,930	0.72
5	$2,500,000	$104,000	$3,080	$21,550	$24,630	1.18
6	$3,000,000	$124,800	$3,780	$30,550	$34,330	1.65
7	$3,500,000	$145,600	$4,480	$39,550	$44,030	2.12
8	$4,000,000	$166,400	$5,180	$48,550	$53,730	2.58
9	$4,500,000	$187,200	$5,880	$57,550	$63,430	3.05
10	$5,000,000	$208,000	$6,580	$66,550	$73,130	3.52
11	$5,500,000	$228,800	$7,280	$76,550	$83,830	4.03
12	$6,000,000	$249,600	$7,980	$86,550	$94,530	4.54
13	$6,500,000	$270,400	$8,680	$96,550	$105,230	5.06
14	$7,000,000	$291,200	$9,380	$106,550	$115,930	5.57
15	$7,500,000	$312,000	$10,080	$116,550	$126,630	6.09
16	$8,000,000	$332,800	$10,780	$126,550	$137,330	6.60
17	$8,500,000	$353,600	$11,480	$136,550	$148,030	7.12
18	$9,000,000	$374,400	$12,180	$146,550	$158,730	7.63
19	$9,500,000	$395,200	$12,880	$156,550	$169,430	8.15
20	$10,000,000	$416,000	$13,580	$166,550	$180,130	8.66
21	$10,500,000	$436,800	$14,280	$176,550	$190,830	9.17

* Source: REIWA.

A one-sided system, favouring tenants, contributes to excessive damage, unlikely to be covered by minimalist bonds. There is no incentive for tenants to care for stoves, air conditioners, hot water systems, plumbing and electrics. If these items are abused, or destroyed, the owners are expected to pay for repair or replacement, often with a new model. Again, contrary to fee simple, the WA State benefits by holding bond money.[156] Replacing bonds with compulsory tenant insurance, which follows tenants, may be a fairer system.

The WA State competes unfairly with owners, in the low income rental category, because it is exempted from rates and duties under ss 17, 20 and 76(8) of the *Land Tax Assessment Act 2002* (WA). Furthermore, it may be the instigator of valuations under s 25 of the *Valuation of Land Act 1978* (WA). Properties on large blocks of land, which might otherwise be rentable, are kept off the market as the land tax is likely to exceed the rent realistically obtainable.

In recent years the imposition of rent moratoriums[157] has removed all incentive to provide rental accommodation. Owners have found themselves without any rent and excessive damage due to being unable to end the tenancies of bad tenants. Rent relief grant programs could only be applied for by these same bad tenants and, although the owners did all the work to provide all the information, there was no disclosure to these owners as to whether these grants were obtained and hence no incentive for these subsidies to be passed on to the owners.[158]

---

[156] *Residential Tenancies Act 1987* (WA) s 29, Schedule 1; *Residential Parks (Long-stay Tenants) Act 2006* (WA) s 22.

[157] *Residential Tenancies (COVID-19 Response) Act 2020* (WA).

[158] Residential Rent Relief Grant Scheme and Residential Tenancy Mandatory Conciliation Service as outlined in the *Residential Tenancies (COVID-19 Response) Act 2020* (WA).

IV Relevant Legislation and "Catch 22" Statute Law "Stitch-up"

The WA laws with relation to land tax are contained in multiple statutes which must be read together. The complex nature of these statutes makes it more difficult for individual taxpayers to fight against these impositions. In addition, it is effectively a "catch 22" situation where the mere serving of a notice is sufficient to give rise to a liability which it then becomes the onus of the taxpayer to disprove.

In clause 1 of the Glossary to the *Taxation Administration Act 2003* (WA) ('TAA') tax is defined to mean tax, duty or another impost, or an instalment of tax, duty or other impost, that is payable under a taxation Act; including penalty tax payable under a taxation Act. Section 60(1) of the TAA provides that unpaid tax is a debt due to the State and pursuant to section 60(2) of the TAA, the Department of State Revenue may recover unpaid tax on behalf of the State.[159]

The TAA, LTAA and *Metropolitan Region Improvement Tax Act* (WA) ('MRITA') are all 'taxation Acts' for the purposes of the TAA.[160] Each taxation Act is to be read with the TAA as if they formed a single Act.[161] 'Assessment' is defined in the Glossary to the TAA as:

> a determination of a kind referred to in section 13(1), whether the determination is made by way of a self-assessment or an official assessment. It is a determination: of the amount of tax payable under a taxation Act; or that no tax is payable; or that a person is liable to pay tax or is exempt from liability to pay tax; or that an instrument, event or transaction is liable to tax or is exempt from tax.

---

[159] Modified by the *Commonwealth Places (Mirror Taxes) Act 1998* (Commonwealth) s 8. Under s 8(2), the Treasurer of a State may use legislation to prescribe modifications of the applied laws of the State, other than modifications for the purpose of overcoming a difficulty that arises from the requirements of the *Constitution*.

[160] *Taxation Administration Act 2003* (WA) s 3(1).

[161] Ibid s 3(2).

The Glossary to the TAA defines an 'assessment notice' as a notice under s 23 of the TAA. Section 23(1) of the TAA provides that when an assessment is made, an assessment notice must be issued.

The imposition of land tax arises under ss 5 and 6 of the LTAA. Under s 5, land tax is payable, for each financial year for all land in the State except land that is exempt under ss 17, 20 and 76(8). Under s 6 land tax is due as payable on an original assessment on the 49th day after the date of the assessment notice and on the date specified in the assessment notice for a reassessment.

Land tax is assessed by reference to the 'taxable value of the land'.[162] Clause 6 of the Glossary to the LTAA defines 'taxable value' by reference to the 'unimproved value of the land'. Clause 2 to the Glossary defines 'unimproved value of land' as 'the unimproved value of the land determined under the *Valuation of Land Act 1978*'.

Part 6 of the TAA s 62, states that a reference to tax is to be read as including: legal costs incurred by the Commissioner in relation to proceedings for the recovery of the tax; costs incurred for lodging a memorial under section 76, 77 or 77A(2), (3), (4A); costs incurred for lodging a withdrawal of memorial under section 81; interest payable under a tax payment arrangement; and, prescribed costs. The imposition of legal costs for instrumentalities representing the Crown is contrary to both historical common law and High Court precedent where there is a well established rule that the Crown neither receives nor pays costs.[163] The principle that the state should not receive costs

---

[162] *Land Tax Assessment Act 2002* (WA) s 10.

[163] William Blackstone, *Commentaries on the Laws of England*, (Sweet Maxwell & Stevens, London, Vol 3, 1st ed, 1768), 400; also see, for example, *Re Powell* (1894) 6 QLJ 36, 38 (Griffith CJ); *Attorney-General (Queensland) v Holland* (1912) 15 CLR 46, 49 (Griffith CJ); *Miller v Baker* (1995) 5 Tas R 322, 324 (Slicer J). See also *Latoudis v Casey* (1990) 170 CLR 534; *Attorney-General of Queensland v Holland* (1912) 15 CLR 46, 49; *Ex parte Hivis*; *Re Michaelis* (1933) 50 WN (NSW) 90, 92. Note that in the *Latoudis v Casey* case the costs were awarded against the Crown following an unsuccessful prosecution. The rule was codified in *The Costs in Crown Suits Act 1856* (NSW), but again with the exemption that a defendant was entitled to costs if successful against the Crown.

has also been confirmed at the High Court level by cases such as *Latoudis v Casey*. This is a very important foundational safeguard to prevent lawfare tyranny by a powerful State which has been overridden by these statutes.

The imposition to pay Late Payment Penalty Tax arises under s 27(1) of the TAA. If tax is not paid by the due date, the taxpayer is charged penalty tax equal to 20% of the amount outstanding on the due date. Accordingly, the Office of State Revenue claim that Land Tax, MRIT, Late Payment Penalty Tax, Memorial Lodgment Fee and Interest are all "tax" for the purposes of s 60 of the TAA.

Any constitutional restrictions on tax being imposed by states is ignored. Section 119 of the TAA provides that an assessment notice is admissible as evidence in proceedings under a taxation Act and, in the absence of proof to the contrary, is proof of the making of the assessment, the amount of tax assessed, the identity of the person liable for the tax, the due date for paying the tax, and any other fact stated in the notice. The Office of the Commissioner of State Revenue claim that the liability to pay the Land Tax, MRIT, Late Payment Penalty Tax, Memorial Lodgment Fee and Interest arises out of the issue of the assessment, or requirement to pay, notice by the Office of the Commissioner of State Revenue.

All power is given to this revenue raising entity. Issuing of an assessment notice is all that is required to establish liability and then the onus is upon the *victim* to prove otherwise Interim assessments are covered in s 16A of the TAA and must be followed by a complete assessment. Reassessments are covered by s 16 of the TAA. Circumstances where the Commissioner **must** make a reassessment are covered by s 16(1) and include if specifically required to do so under a taxation Act; or if specifically required to do so under a direction given in the course of review proceedings; or if a taxation Act provides for a rebate or refund of tax in particular circumstances, and the circumstances were not taken into account when the previous assessment was made.

Circumstances under which the Commissioner **may** make a reassessment include on his or her own initiative, and on the application of the taxpayer but not on the basis of a particular interpretation of the applicable law or on the ground that an interpretation or applied assessment practice was erroneous under s 16(5). A taxpayer is not entitled to apply for a reassessment more than 5 years after the original assessment was made under s 17(1), however the Commissioner may make a reassessment at any time if the Commissioner has been directed, in the course of review proceedings, to make the reassessment; or there are reasonable grounds for suspecting that the previous assessment was made on the basis of false or misleading information under s 17(2). Under s 18(1) a reassessment supersedes the assessment and any earlier reassessment. Any amount to be recovered is to be amended to take account of the reassessment (s 18(4)) and objections may be continued against the reassessments if the reassessment is liable to the same objection or to an objection that is similar, in substance (s 18(5)).

Section 16(2)(b) of the TAA provides that the Commissioner of State Revenue may make a reassessment of tax on the application of the taxpayer. The Commissioner is not required to do so, and is not permitted (by reason of s 16(5) of the TAA) to make a reassessment on the basis that a particular interpretation of the law or a particular practice that was generally applied to assessments of that kind when the assessment was made was erroneous.

Under s 18A(1) the Commissioner may, within 5 years after the issue of a notice of assessment, withdraw the assessment provided no tax has been paid on the assessment (s 18A(2)). There would appear to be room for negotiation under s 20A of the TAA. Under s 20A(1) the Commissioner may make a compromise agreement in relation to the taxpayer's tax liability and make an assessment in accordance with the compromise agreement. Under s 20A(3A)(a), a compromise agreement may include conditions agreed with the taxpayer providing for the payment or remission of interest. However, no action can be brought in any court or tribunal to compel the Commissioner to make a compromise agreement (s 20A(4)) and the decision of the Commissioner to make, or not make, a compromise agreement are final and not subject to objection or review under Part 4 or to any other form of appeal or review (s 20A(3)). It would not seem to be possible for an owner to instigate or force a compromise agreement. There is a Form 39 Offer of Settlement form available from the Magistrate's Court website but this is targeted at cases destined for trial. Compromise agreements are covered by Commissioner's Practice TAA 21.1. Contact with the Department of State Revenue resulted in advice that these agreements were reserved for complex corporate holdings where the costs of litigation were likely to exceed the revenue likely to be obtained. With the ability to lodge memorials, which create a security interest on property, there would appear to be little incentive for the Commissioner to enter a compromise agreement.

Reassessment based upon objection is allowed for in s 39 of the TAA. It is compulsory for the Commissioner to make a reassessment if an objection is allowed wholly or in part (s 39(1)). If an amount is to be refunded, then refunds are also to be paid for any amount paid for the lodging of a memorial under ss 76, 77 or 77A, if the Commissioner has lodged a withdrawal of the memorial as a result of the reassessment; and interest during the reassessment period, on the amount to be refunded.

The imposition to pay MRIT arises under s 200 of the *Planning and Development Act 2005* (WA) and s 10 of the MRIT Act. It is imposed upon those who, at midnight on 30 June in any year, own land in the metropolitan region in accordance with ss 14 and 15 of the LTAA and the TAA. Provisions relating to land tax, in so far as they can be adapted are to apply to the MRIT and land in the metropolitan region.[164] MRIT is assessed in a similar manner to land tax, using the

---

[164] *Planning and Development Act 2005* (WA) s 200.

same base rates and applying a percentage for every dollar of alleged value above that base rate. The base rate and percentages are set out in s 10 of the MRITA. For example, in the year 2007/08 the base rate was $250,000 and 0.18 cents for every dollar in excess of $250,000. In 2008/09 and subsequent years the base rate was $300,000 and 0.14 cents for every dollar in excess of $300,000.

The WA State converts its impositions to secured debt under s 76 of the LTAA.[165] Under s 76(1), from the time it becomes payable, land tax is a charge on the land for which the tax is payable whether or not an assessment notice has been issued for the tax; whether or not the tax is due for payment; whether or not a memorial of the charge has been registered; and whether or not the land is disposed of. Under s 76(2), the Commissioner may lodge a memorial for registration against the land if the land tax is not paid by the due date. Supposedly, under s 76(7) the amount secured by the charge on an individual lot or parcel is the amount that bears to the total amount of the unpaid tax in the same proportion that the taxable value of the lot or parcel bears to the total taxable value of the land. Note that land owned by, or vested in the State, or any agency or instrumentality of the State, or a local government or any other public statutory authority is exempted under s 76(8).

Challenges to assessment must be through administrative review. Part 4 of the TAA provides for the procedure through which the Land Tax, MRIT, Late Payment Penalty Tax, Memorial Lodgment Fee and Interest may be challenged. This would not appear to preclude reassessment or negotiation. Part 4 of the TAA includes sections 31 through 44. Accordingly, s 31 stipulates that the validity or correctness of an assessment, or of any other decision for which rights of objection or review are conferred, may only be challenged in proceedings by way of objection or in review proceedings; or in any other manner

---

[165] Modified by the *Commonwealth Places (Mirror Taxes) Act 1998* (Commonwealth) s 8, s 76.

specifically provided for in a taxation Act. Section 32 provides that the validity or correctness of a valuation under the *Valuation of Land Act 1978* (WA) ('VLA') may only be challenged in proceedings under Part IV of that Act, and not by way of objection against an assessment under the TAA based upon the valuation. Section 33 states that an obligation to pay is not suspended by an objection or review proceedings and that an order cannot be made in review proceedings if it would have the effect of suspending or deferring an obligation to pay tax before those proceedings are finally determined. An obligation to pay tax is not suspended or deferred by an objection or case stated or by review proceedings.[166]

Section 34(1) creates a right to object to an assessment, or another decision under a taxation Act that affects the taxpayer's liability. An objection cannot be made against the determination of an objection; an interim assessment within 3 years after the date on which the assessment notice for the interim assessment is issued;[167] a directly reviewable decision; a decision in respect of which a taxation Act specifically provides other procedures for objection or appeal; or compromise agreements.

Under s 34(3A) an objection against an interim assessment can only be made against the validity or correctness of the interim assessment as at the date on which the assessment notice for the interim assessment was issued. Under s 34(3B) the entitlement to object to an interim assessment ceases if the assessment following the interim assessment is made before an objection against the interim assessment is lodged and, under s 34(3), if a reassessment is made and the time for lodging an objection to the previous assessment has expired, an objection may only be made against an increase in liability. Under s 34(4) within 60 days of being notified of the decision, an application may be made to the State Administrative Tribunal ('SAT') for a review of any directly

---

[166] *Taxation Administration Act 2003* (WA) s 33.

[167] Ibid s 34(2)(ca).

reviewable Commissioner decision. Section 34 also specifies that objections must be in writing and set out fully detailed grounds on which the objection to the assessment or decision is made, and be served on the Commissioner by lodgement at his office, by pre-paid mail or email in accordance with s 115. Contrary to the requirements to only be in writing, Landgate does not consider objections unless they are submitted online or on their Objection to Valuation form.

Section 36 of the TAA provides that an objection must be lodged within 60 days of the assessment notice being issued, although the Claimant may extend the time for lodging an objection on the application of the taxpayer. Under s 36(4), the Commissioner may extend the time for lodging an objection upon application by the taxpayer. Under s 36(5), an application for an extension of time should be made within 12 months after the date on which the objection was to have been lodged and must set out in detail the grounds on which the applicant asks for an extension of time. For interim assessments, under s 36(1)(d), objections may only be lodged after the 3-year period referred to in section 34(2)(ca) ends. Under s 36(1)(c), if a taxpayer has requested a statement of grounds under s 25(2)(a) the objection must be lodged within 30 days of the date upon which the Commissioner serves a statement of the grounds.

The requirement that objections to interim assessments may only be made after 3 years would seem to be incompatible with the rule that the right to object is extinguished by the issue of a subsequent assessment under s 40(2). A person dissatisfied with the Commissioner's decision on an objection or on an application for an extension of time for lodging an objection may apply to SAT for a review of the decision.[168] Under s 37(1) of the TAA the Commissioner must consider and determine an objection, having regard to the grounds set out in the objection. Under s 37(2) the onus of establishing that an assessment or

---

[168] *Taxation Administration Act 2003* (WA) s 40(1).

decision to which an objection relates is invalid or incorrect lies on the taxpayer. On determining an objection, the Commissioner must serve on the taxpayer a notice setting out the decision on the objection; and the reasons for the decision, under s 37(4).

The time limit for determining objections for the Commissioner must determine an objection within the decision period specified in s 38(2). The decision period is 90 days, beginning on the day the objection is lodged with the Commissioner, plus the number of days the Commissioner needs to obtain and consider information required to determine the objection. The Commissioner must notify the taxpayer, before the end of the initial 90-day period, of any periods by which the decision period has been extended, if further delays extending the decision period occur after the initial notification, the Commissioner must keep the taxpayer reasonably informed about the extent and the reasons for the further delays under s 38(3). Under s 38(4), if the Commissioner fails to determine an objection within 120 days of the day that the objection was lodged with the Commissioner, the taxpayer may, by written notice to the Commissioner, require the Commissioner to apply to SAT for directions as to any or all of the matters referred to, including but not limited to the length of the decision period; the time for a taxpayer to comply with a request for information; the information to be provided by the taxpayer; and, the time for the Commissioner to seek advice and assistance from an external agency. On receiving such a request, the Commissioner must apply to SAT for those directions within 14 days of the written notice. However, failure of the Commissioner to comply with these time constraints does not invalidate a determination on an objection. Under s 39(2) if, as a result of the reassessment, an amount is to be refunded or credited to the taxpayer, any amount paid by the taxpayer for the lodging of a memorial under section 76, 77 or 77A; and, any interest on the amount to be refunded or credited, must also be refunded.

Rights of review by SAT on the Commissioner's decision on an objection, or on an application for an extension of time for lodging an objection, are covered in s 40 of the TAA. Under s 40(2) the right to review ceases if the assessment following the interim assessment is made before the person makes an application for a review of the decision. An application to SAT for a review of a decision must be made within 60 days after notice of the decision is served on the taxpayer under s 42(1). Note that under s 43(2ab) the Commissioner may launch an appeal under the *State Administrative Tribunal Act 2004* Part 5, without leave, against any SAT decision on a question of law if the Minister certifies in writing that the question is significant for the protection of the revenue of the State; and agrees to indemnify each other party to the proceeding in respect of any cost involved in the appeal. Until review proceedings (including seeking special leave to appeal to the High Court) have been exhausted or have expired, and no further reassessment can be made a refund or credit of an amount referred need not be made under s 43(4A)(b). Decisions of SAT may be appealed to the Supreme Court, under s 3A, on a question of law, of fact, or mixed law and fact, within 28 days of the Tribunal's decision is made and reasons are given orally or in writing. The Commissioner may state a case on a question of law arising under a taxation Act and forward the case to the Supreme Court to decide the question of law; and to make orders for costs and other incidental matters under s 44 of the TAA.

Under s 17 of the VLA the Valuer-General defines valuation districts for the purpose of determining gross rental values and the whole of the State is constituted into a valuation district for determining unimproved values. Under s 18, the Valuer-General determines the gross rental value or the unimproved value, required by a rating or taxing authority for the purpose of assessing any rate or tax or is, reasonably likely to be so required before the next general valuation of the land is made. Under s 20, the valuations come into force on such day as is determined by the Valuer-General and supersede any previous valuations of gross rental value or unimproved value. Under s 21, the Valuer-General shall, not later than 42 days after a general valuation comes into force, provide public notice of the general valuation in the Government Gazette and in one issue of each of 2 newspapers having general circulation within the valuation district. Under s 22, the Valuer-General determines the frequency of valuations, but so far as practicable, every financial year, and may declare that the previous general valuation accurately sets forth the values of rateable land within that valuation district. The Valuer-General may also make interim valuations under s 23 where land has not previously been valued or separately valued or where in his opinion it is necessary or expedient for any reason that such land be valued such as where in his opinion the value thereof has for any reason significantly increased or decreased in relation to the value of land of the same or a similar character in the same valuation district. Under s 24 the Valuer-General may, in his discretion, aggregate valuations he would have assigned to any parts of which the land is comprised had he been separately valuing each such part; and increase the gross rental value for any improvements made. The valuations may be delegated to rating or taxing authorities who must engage a valuer to make a general valuation of rateable land within a valuation district or to value specified land within a valuation district in respect of which the authority considers that an interim valuation is necessary or expedient under s 25.

Under s 26 of the VLA, the Valuer-General shall, complete and maintain valuation rolls of rateable land for each valuation district. Every valuation roll shall for all purposes and in all proceedings be evidence of every valuation recorded in that roll and of the particulars in respect of rateable land set out in the roll. Copies of entries in valuation rolls are available for a fee and admissible as evidence of the matters and things stated therein in all proceedings and that any valuation to which the entry relates has been made in conformity with this Act under s 29. The Valuer-General makes valuations for the purpose of the *Local Government Act 1995* (WA) under s 31A, and for s 28(7) the LTAA under s 31B. Again, the mere fact that a valuation has been made in accordance with the specified procedures is used to assume accuracy and *victims* must pay to obtain the information required to object to the valuation. Valuations may be made by those who are in direct competition with private rental property owners, for example, the WA State.

Part IV of the VLA provides for an objection procedure similar to that under the TAA. Objections to valuation are covered under s 32(1) of the VLA. Section 32(1)(b) provides that an objection must be lodged within 60 days of the issue of the notice of assessment, although the Valuer-General may extend the time for lodging an objection. The objection must set out in detail the grounds of objection and the reasons in support of those grounds of objection. Grounds may be that the valuation is not fair or is unjust, inequitable or incorrect, whether by itself or in comparison with other valuations in force. A person may not make more than one objection to the one valuation during any 12-month period. Where the Valuer-General decides to allow or disallow an objection, wholly or in part, he shall advise that person of the time within which and the manner in which a review of the valuation may be sought.

Section 33 of the VLA allows for the SAT review of valuation, after objection. Any person who is dissatisfied with the decision of the Valuer-General on an objection may, within 60 days (or such further period as the Valuer-General, before or after the expiry of that time, for reasonable cause shown by the person, allows) after service of notice of the decision of the Valuer-General, serve on the Valuer-General a notice requiring that the Valuer-General refer the valuation to SAT for a review. Upon receipt of such notice the Valuer-General shall promptly refer the valuation to SAT for a review. A similar process is available under s 35 for SAT review of refusal of the Valuer-General to extend the time for service of an objection against a valuation or for service of a notice requiring the Valuer-General to refer the valuation to SAT. Section 34A provides that an amended valuation, including due to a State Administrative review, is not to apply before the year of objection.

General reviews by SAT of valuation are allowed under s 36 of the VLA, but applications are not allowed for questions relating to individual cases. This section is for where there is a question of general interest as to whether proper principles have been applied in the valuation of the whole or a definable part of the land in a valuation district. A rating or taxing authority having an interest in the valuation or any person liable to pay any rate or tax on the basis of the valuation of any part of the land may apply to SAT for a review of the question. Under s 36B(1) if STA considers that an order it makes determining a matter coming before it on a referral under section 33 or 35 is of general interest or significance, it is to prepare written reasons for its order and give a copy of the reasons to each party and publish the written reasons.

Section 28 of the TAA provides for the lodgement of Memorials to charge land to secure the payment of Land Tax and Stamp Duty. Section 76(1) of the TAA states that unpaid Land Tax is a first charge on the land, whether or not the land tax is due for payment and whether or not a memorial of the charge has been registered. Where Stamp Duty, Transfer Duty or Landholder Duty is payable on an instrument under the TAA, but was not paid on the due date, or the payment of the duty is dishonoured, the Commissioner for State Taxation may lodge a memorial against freehold land. The Memorial is lodged under s 77 of the Act. Section 77(4) of the Act states that a charge only arises on land for unpaid stamp duty when a memorial of the charge has been registered under s 83.

The administration of the Act is vested in the Commissioner for State Taxation, and a number of Assistant Commissioners. The Commissioner may delegate his powers to any Assistant

Commissioner or other officer. Any person signing on behalf of the Commissioner should state that he is the holder of a written delegation to do the act achieved by the registration of the document. The effect of lodging the memorial is to prohibit the registration of any subsequent instruments or Judgment without the consent of the Commissioner of State Taxation. Where a Survivorship or Transmission application or a Property (Seizure and Sale) Order is lodged in relation to land over which a memorial under s 76 or s 77 has been lodged by the Commissioner of State Taxation then consent will be required by the Tax Commissioner to allow registration of the Survivorship or Transmission application or Property (Seizure and Sale) Order. The memorial may be removed by the Commissioner for State Taxation by lodging under s 81 of the TAA a document called a Memorial of Release of Charge. Fees are payable on lodgement and withdrawal of these memorials. If Land Tax or Stamp Duty remains unpaid for 18 months after registration of either of the above-mentioned memorials, the Commissioner of State Taxation may apply to the Supreme Court for an order for the sale of the land so that the proceeds of sale may be applied toward satisfaction of the outstanding tax liability (see ss 85 and 86 of the TAA). To complete the sale a transfer of land executed by the court nominated in the order on behalf of the registered proprietor is registered. The transfer will be registered after the procedures set out in s 74 of the *Transfer of Land Act 1893* (WA) have been complied with. A sale by order of the Supreme Court discharges the land from any mortgage or other encumbrance securing a monetary obligation, but the land remains subject to any lease, easement or other encumbrance.

Historical rules of *fieri facias* meant that it used to be difficult to "steal" land in the Supreme Court. However, property may still be "stolen" via an order[169] in a Magistrate's, or any other WA court, using a Property (Seizure and Sale) Order which is then registered

---

[169] Including one based upon a default judgement.

at Landgate. For cases involving unpaid rates court judgement is not required. A local council may sell the land to a third party, transfer the land to the Local Government or the Crown in right of the State of Western Australia, or have the land revested in the Crown in right of the State of Western Australia.

In summary, in a totally tyrannical manner, the Western Australian State (or King) has given itself total power and control over, supposedly, fee simple land via legislation. The WA State values land, imposes taxes on unrealised gains and gives itself the power to steal this land when these taxes are not paid. The "rules" are obfuscated in multiple statutes with the onus always placed upon the *victim,* with the WA State being assumed incapable of any wrong.

V. CONCLUDING REMARKS

All of the feudal taxes upon property need to be removed. This is especially important where taxes are based upon unrealised gains. This is vapourware. The only valid property tax is tax upon any proven income (after expenses) derived from the property and not taxes based upon unrealised gains. Removing these taxes would have the additional benefit of reducing the cost of rental property. The private sector can provide lower cost housing than the WA State without these additional tax burdens, which are not born by the public sector. This would also reduce the building crisis if the state is not competing for these resources. The replacement of rental bonds with compulsory tenant insurance would be essential to ensure that those causing the huge maintenance costs are those that pay for those costs and take responsibility for their actions. Where possible, the provision of social housing should be outsourced to the private sector in the form of individuals, rather than corporations. This would be a legitimate neo-conservative agenda which would both reduce the size and costs of State Government. The Housing Authority is currently competing unfairly with the private sector and they have additional benefits in that they are allowed to take welfare payments directly and have access to full legal support which the competing private sector does not. There will always be tenants who have a history of causing massive damage to properties and will therefore be rejected by private owners. The WA State could underwrite the insurance for these tenants or only provide the most basic of accommodation for these kinds of tenants.

Legislation such as the *Residential Tenancies Act 1987* (WA) and the *Water Services Act 2012* (WA) need to be reviewed to be more favourable to rental property owners rather than guided by tenant lobby groups or in-house Government lawyers. They need to promote and not hinder business. Cases brought by the Crown, or those claiming the authority of the Crown or the State, need to adhere to the ancient law and also the High Court precedent in *Latoudis v Casey*[170] that costs may only be claimed against the Crown and **not** against those defending themselves. This is essential for accountability and good governance and to protect against lawfare by the State with the intention of stealing property. The WA State should not be acting as ravenous wolves in order to raise revenue.

Does voting need to return to only those with *skin in the game*? Although this would probably solve the problem and return the focus of the Government to protecting property, it is unlikely to be achievable due to public outcry and political opposition. However, such a system could include tenants and would not have to have any minimum value of property or rent. The only disenfranchisement would likely be the homeless, couch surfers and young adults still living with their parents. Given that in countries without compulsory voting a large section of the population does not vote, the removal of compulsory voting, at least at state level, should be considered to exclude the apathetic and otherwise obstructive. The link between voting and the protection of

---

[170] *Latoudis v Casey* (1990) 170 CLR 534 per Mason at 2.

property has been lost. Crony socialism[171] has become the norm and is on the ascendancy. Of course, we also need to stop debating the taking of property for fair value. Compulsory taking of property should not exist. If the State wants someone's property then they need to make offers unlikely to be refused and this does not mean merely offering a solatium. Anyone losing their home deserves a windfall gain.

There needs to be an immediate cessation to registration bodies profiting from the sale of what should be private data. With the advent of modern computers the reasons for the implementation of the Torrens system no longer exists. The chain of activity on any given property can easily be stored and accessed. Any central body needs to be independent from the State, or Government intervention, and run as not-for-profit and not charge fees, as the current system has proved to be too big a temptation. There is no reason that properties cannot be returned to deed and any activities on the original grants notarised by JPs, lawyers, etc. No caveats or memorials should be placed on titles before their validity has been verified in the Supreme Court, in front of a jury. In fact, any issue which might result in the forced sale of property should be heard in the Supreme Court, in front of a jury.

As can be seen, the King, in the form of the State of Western Australia, is currently acting in a tyrannical manner and has implemented statutes which imply he can do no wrong and is above foundational law. The State is failing to provide protection for property and has become the main source of attack on property rights. The provision of rental property is not currently viable and hence the record low vacancy rates. These suggested reforms need to be considered as a matter of urgency.

Above all, in Western Australia, there has been a total reversal of the traditional justifications for Government. The Government is meant to uphold and protect property rights, not usurp or steal

---

[171] See (n 73).

them and to punish those entitled to those rights. The basis of "the social contract" is the protection of persons and their property. This is the ultimate reason for the existence of both the legislature and the judiciary. To the extent that this is not occurring is a clear breach of that contract. We have come full circle. The original function of government to protect property has been replaced with government being the fundamental source of attack and exploitation. We are faced with a total "stitch up". The State of Western Australia provides valuations which may be questionable and which may target particular individuals. The onus is on the *victim* to dispute valuations via lengthy and costly procedures rather than on the valuers to justify the validity of valuations, which of course they cannot. It is a process that obfuscates what is going on. There is no buyer, no seller, and hence no agreed value. This is unacceptable. The Government needs to be held to account and, if anything, held to higher standards than the general public.

Although the government was originally established to protect property, a few centuries later the growth, nature and size of the beast has meant that the requirement for this protection seems to have been lost in translation. Successive generations are unaware and have an incomplete understanding of the importance of foundational law.

What can we do about it? Western Australia's Constitution[172] does not ensure the protection of fundamental rights, including those pertaining to property. Changing the *Western Australia Constitution Act 1889* (WA) does not require a referendum; it can be changed by legislation. Hence, legislation could be introduced in Western Australia to enshrine fundamental rights, including those related to property. However, it should go further and enshrine fundamental rights of the citizen such as freedom of speech, freedom of religion, freedom of association and assembly, freedom of movement and privilege against

---

[172] *Western Australia Constitution Act 1889* (WA).

self-incrimination. Such reforms can also include a formal separation of powers between legislative, executive and judicial branches.

We are living with a judicial system operating in accordance with narrow legal positivism, much like the system in Nazi Germany. If the judiciary is only administering statute then it is operating as an arm of Government and not with true separation of powers. There needs to be review of statutes against historical judge and jury made common law precedent and notions of what constitutes justice, rather than the tyranny we currently have. All statutes need to be verified against historical common law rights, established by properly constituted judge and juries, and overturned when they are inconsistent. Before enactment, statutes need to be reviewed for conformity with common law principles and the principles of constitutional and Imperial law. All legislation favouring revenue over rights needs to be re-examined, reversed, amended or repealed. If the judiciary is insisting upon operating according to narrow legal positivism then the implementation of a rights-based constitution for Western Australia, coupled with a proper mechanism of checks and balances, may resolve this issue. The Western Australian State (or King) must **not** do wrong and must **not** be above the law!

7

Against Tyranny of Religious Neutrality:

A Comparative Perspective of the French and American Approaches to Religious Freedom in Public School Systems

WERONIKA KUDŁA[*]

ABSTRACT

Tyranny, in opposition to freedom and democracy, can be strictly linked with oppression, intimidation, discrimination and overt violence exerted on the entire population or a chosen part of it. An interesting correlation between tyranny and legislative power can be discerned in the field of protection and promotion of religious identity in public life, which results to be currently one of the most pressing global concerns. The article analyses the impact of legal provisions concerning religious freedom in the context of public education system of two countries – France and the United States, which despite different legal framework are both based on the separation of Church and State and religious pluralism. The comparative analyses of government's respect for 1) the right to teach religion and about religion, 2) the right to exercise religious practices (individually or collectively) and 3) the right to manifest religious beliefs, eg through symbols, religious clothing and speech, permits to indicate how close to tyranny is the current approach of France authorities toward religious diversity in public schools. The expansion of laws targeting religious practices,

---

[*] Assistant Professor, Pontifical University of John Paul II, Cracow, Poland.

speech, symbols and attire in France subjugates people of faith and results to be incompatible with the spirit of religious liberty that tends to be better protected by American law.

I. INTRODUCTION

Tyranny can exist in many forms and like a chameleon assume different shades according to current circumstances. The most common and classical model of tyranny is associated with oppression, a violent abuse of power and enforcement of demands on an entire group or population, subjected to it in order to control them. For Dante Alighieri in *The Divine Comedy* the concept of *tirannia* refers not only to the figures of tyrants known from antiquity, but is also evoked to assess conditions of life on the Italian peninsula. As in *Canto 12* of *Inferno* Dante proceeds along the shore of Phlegethon, the river of hot blood in the Seventh Circle of Hell, he and his companions learn that among the violent souls submerged in the boiling blood in a graduated fashion, the gravest sinners are indeed tyrants.[1] They both murdered and plundered, and so are the worst offenders in the category of violence against others ('E' son tiranni / che dier nel sangue e ne l'aver di piglio' [*Inferno* 12.104-5]). Dante returns to the question of contemporary *tirannia* in *Canto 27* of *Inferno*, which begins with the image of bronze bull in which the classical tyrant Phalaris of Sicily roasted his victims.[2] This introduction serves to anticipate the first part of dialogue between Dante and Guido da Montefeltro, a great warlord and political strategist who founded the ruling dynasty of Urbino. Dante's reflection on *tirannia* consists of the resume of contemporary tyrants governing throughout the cities of Romagna and all worthy to be immersed in Phlegethon.[3]

---

[1] Teodolinda Barolini, 'Inferno 12: Cupidigia/Tirannia', *Commento Baroliniano*, Digital Dante, Columbia University Libraries, 2018.

[2] Teodolinda Barolini, 'Inferno 27: Disconversion', *Commento Baroliniano*, Digital Dante, Columbia University Libraries, 2018.

[3] Historian John Larner explains that when the medieval communes fell into the hands

Fast forward to the 21st century and tyranny still exists. The list of potential candidates for modern tyrants could be also easily created by commentators of social, economic, cultural, political and legal landscape. Paradoxically, tyranny should have nothing in common with freedom and democracy, but among various fields in which the impact of tyrannic methods can be analysed, I intend to discuss how tyranny, usually understood as oppressive power exerted by autocratic government, can become a looming threat also for the right to religious freedom in the Western liberal democratic states. In this sense an interesting parallel can be discerned between tyranny and the obsessive commitment to "religious neutrality" observed in France, which actually undermines the role and place of religion in public place of this country and takes believers captive rather than setting them free. The legal cage created by legislative power forces both individual believers and religious groups to "negotiate" the limits of religious freedom through court litigation and it is a common threat not only in France, but in other parts of the Western world.[4]

The 2023 Edition of *Religious Freedom in the World Report*,[5] published by the Aid to the Church in Need ('ACN') and containing a global analysis of the status of religious freedom in 196 countries, reveals that 'the retention and consolidation of power in the hands of autocrats and fundamentalist group leaders led to increased violations of all human rights, including religious freedom'.[6] Another key

---

of despots, eventually the rule of the despot (*tiranno*) was legalised, so that the later *signorie* of the Renaissance were in fact legalised *tirannie*. See John Larner, *Italy in the Age of Dante and Petrarch (1216–1380)* (Addison-Wesley Longman Ltd, 1983).

[4] See eg Hans-Martien Ten Napel, *Constitutionalism, Democracy and Religious Freedom: To Be Fully Human* (Routledge, 2017); Grzegorz Blicharz (ed), *Freedom of Religion: A Comparative Law Perspective* (Wydawnictwo IWS, 2019); Grzegorz Blicharz, Maria Alejandra Vanney and Piotr Roszak (eds), *The Battle for Religious Freedom. Jurisprudence and Axiology* (Wydawnictwo IWS, 2020).

[5] Marcela Szymanski (ed), *Religious Freedom in the World Report 2023: Executive Summary* (Aid to the Church in Need, 2023).

[6] Ibid 6.

finding of the report is that the so called "hybrid" cases of "polite" and bloody persecutions became more frequent as governments apply controversial laws restricting the enjoyment of religious freedom or discriminating against religious adherents. Interestingly, while the formula of overt tyranny toward religion is generally associated with autocratic regimes, the application of religiously neutral laws in particular cases may result in the legal, but still unacceptable, tyranny which can be identified also in Europe. In another most recent annual report on the state of religious freedom published in April 2023 the United States Commission on International Religious Freedom ('USCIFR') expresses some concerns over the restrictions on religious practices and discrimination on the basis of religion faced by Muslims, Jews and Christians in Europe.[7]

The main aim of this article is to compare practical application of laws affecting the extent of religious freedom in public schools of two countries – France and the United States. Despite historical differences regarding their attitude towards tolerance, religion and secularism, France and the United States share many similarities concerning the separation of Church and State and religious pluralism. By comparing approaches toward religion in education I hope to gain the necessary perception and analytical clarity of how close to tyranny is the French model of religious neutrality, which is being progressively expanded in the name of preserving republican values. The analysis looks at current challenges to religious freedom in the context of education and by diagnosing (rather than curing) shed some light on current conflicts and controversies over the right to religious expression in public schools. It must be pointed out that problems over the correct accommodation of religious needs and the place of religion in the public square are issue of concern in different national and cross-

---

[7] United States Commission on International Religious Freedom, *2023 Annual Report* (Report, 2023) 71.

national contexts.[8] Even in Poland, regarded as a predominantly Catholic Christian country and still perceived as one of the most religious countries in Europe, the place of religion in public schools is widely contested and tendencies to eliminate religious references from them, even where the majority of students and their parents profess a Christian faith, are becoming more frequent.[9]

II. THE EXCLUSIONARY AND DIVISIVE MODEL OF "RELIGIOUS NEUTRALITY" IN FRANCE

The French Republic is based on the principles of secularism (*laïcité*)[10] and strict separation of Church and State.[11] The Act on the separation of Church and State,[12] adopted in 1905, guarantees freedom of conscience and the free exercise of religious worship, which can be limited in the interest of public order. The French education system is also based on the principle of secularism, which has been developed and improved since the French Revolution of 1791 until now.[13] State education has been secular since Jules Ferry's *Education Act* of 28 March 1882, and the requirement to employ only secular staff in public schools has been

---

[8] See eg Francis-Vincent Anthony, Hans-Georg Ziebertz (eds), *Human Rights and the Separation of State and Religion: International Case Studies* (Springer, 2023).

[9] Piotr Roszak and Weronika Kudła, 'Faith-based education in Polish public schools – From battleground to common ground' (2023) 99 *International Journal of Educational Development* 102773.

[10] More on the implemention of *laïcité* in French public schools, its historical genealogy, practical contradictions and political geographies see eg Christopher Lizotte, 'Laïcité as assimilation, laïcité as negotiation: Political geographies of secularism in the French public school' (2020) 77 *Political Geography* 102121:1-10; Alessandro Bergamaschi and Catherine Blaya, 'Religions and Laïcité in the French Republican School' in *Migrants and Religion: Paths, Issues, and Lenses* (Brill, 2020).

[11] *The Declaration of the Rights of Man and of the Citizen 1789*, art 10: 'No one may be disturbed on account of his opinions, even religious ones, as long as the manifestation of such opinions does not interfere with the established Law and Order.'

[12] 'Loi du 9 décembre 1905 concernant la séparation des Églises et de l'État' [Law of 9 December 1905] (France).

[13] Renata Jankowska, 'Islam w przestrzeni publicznej laickiej Francji' (2018) 25 *Annales Universitatis Mariae Curie-Skłodowska. Sectio K, Politologia* 89.

in force since 30 October 1886. *Laïcité* as a legal and political principle is intended to regulate and protect cultural and religious diversity by rejecting all separatisms. The French education system includes public and private schools, but since the promulgation of the *Debré Act*[14] in 1959, private schools can sign an agreement (*contrat d'association*) with the State in order to receive funds from the state budget. In return, these schools must offer the same standard of education as in public schools and accept all students to enrol regardless of their religious affiliation. In this type of schools religious instruction is allowed, but students can opt out. Since 2015, the number of private Muslim schools in France has been growing rapidly, and many of them have a contract with the state. In these schools, the teaching of the Islamic religion can be organised in various ways. Islamic religious education textbooks have largely integrated citizenship and republican values in an attempt to address public authorities' concerns about Islam in the context of numerous terrorist attacks.[15] However, statistics indicate that 83% of students attend public schools, and 17% private schools, while only a small number of students study in private schools that do not have a contract with the state.[16] It must be clearly stated that the distinction between public and private schools does not necessarily mirror that between nonsectarian and denominational schools. The *Education Act*,[17] in force since 28 July 2019, introduced compulsory education for children aged 3 to 18 (after reaching the age of 16 the law provides for the possibility of undergoing vocational training or civic service as part of a broader formation, and not just instruction).

---

[14] Loi n° 59-1557 du 31 décembre 1959 sur les rapports entre l'Etat et les établissements d'enseignement privés [Law No 59-1557 of 31 December 1959] (France).

[15] Diane-Sophie Girin, 'Islamic Religious Education in France' in Leni Franken and Bill Gent (eds), *Islamic Religious Education in Europe: A Comparative Study* (Routledge, 2021).

[16] Ministry of National Education, 'Key Data On National Education 2021', Direction de l'évaluation, de la prospective et de la performance (Web Page).

[17] Loi n° 2019-791 du 26 juillet 2019 pour une école de la confiance [Law No 2019-791 of 26 July 2019] (France) ('Law 2019-791').

A *Respecting the right to teach religion and about religion*

Till 2015 France was the only European country which lacked religious instruction in public schools,[18] but due to Islamist terrorist attacks and the trauma they caused in society, the "secular teaching of religious facts" was introduced in schools, combined with moral and civic education. In this way elements of religious studies have been included in different subjects, such as history, geography, literature, arts or philosophy in order to enhance the understanding of and respect for cultural heritage of the nation. The current French educational model, which excludes the possibility of receiving religious education, but partially integrates the knowledge about religion in public schools is thus influenced by France's secular political culture, Catholic spiritual heritage, and turbulent relations with Islam. However, the Alsace-Moselle region, where the relationship between the state and the Church is still regulated by the Concordat concluded by Napoleon with Pope Pius VII in 1801, remains an exception. In Alsace-Moselle, religious education in one of the four recognized religions (Catholicism, Lutheranism, the Protestant Reformed Church of Alsace-Lorraine, and Judaism) is compulsory in public primary and secondary schools. Nevertheless, students may, at the written request of their parents, choose a secular equivalent of this subject. Religious classes in this region are taught by laypeople appointed by the relevant religious groups, but paid by the state.

The provisions of the Education Code, in accordance with the principles set out in the *Constitution*, guarantee children and young people enrolled in public educational institutions the opportunity to receive education with equal respect for all beliefs.[19] In order to ensure religious education for students, public primary schools are closed one day a week except Sunday, so that parents can, if they

---

[18] Cf eg Jean-Paul Willaime and Séverine Mathieu, *Des Maîtres et des Dieux: école et religions en Europe* (Belin, 2005).

[19] *Code de l'éducation* [Education Code] (France) art L141-2 ('Education Code').

wish so, send their children to receive religious instruction outside the school premises.[20] This is because the regulations clearly indicate that religious education for children enrolled in public schools may only be conducted outside school hours.[21] Moreover, in public primary schools, teaching is entrusted exclusively to lay staff. The *Education Act*,[22] in force since 28 July 2019, introduced into the Education Code an additional prohibition of behavior constituting an attempt to indoctrinate other students in public schools, their immediate surroundings and during all education-related activities (eg school trips). Failure to comply with this prohibition is punishable by a fine. Such additional provisions in fact undermine students' freedom of conscience leaving no room for manifestations of religious identity.

The emphasis on imparting knowledge about religion rather than faith in public schools is intended to contribute to civic education, living in harmony with one another, respecting religious expression and cultural identity, and promoting dialogue in the spirit of respect and responsibility. Nevertheless, within the model of *laïcité* teaching about religion, unlike moral and civic education, is met with great reluctance on the part of teachers and political representatives. This situation can be explained by anti-religious movements, the fear of speaking on sensitive topics or a sense of insufficient preparation for teaching about religion at school. In fact, almost two-thirds of teachers in France believe they are not sufficiently prepared to teach religious facts in schools, even though an increasing number of French people believe that it should be taught more often in schools.[23] Interestingly, transmitting the principles of secularism remains a priority for public schools, therefore in 2013 the *Charter of Secularism in Schools* (*La Charte de la laïcité à l'École*)[24] ('Charter') was drawn up as an annex

---

[20] Ibid art L141-3.

[21] Ibid art L141-4.

[22] Law 2019-791 art 10; Education Code art L141-5-2.

[23] European Academy on Religion and Society, Education and Religion in Europe (June 2021),

[24] *La Charte de la laïcité à l'École* (online).

to the Law on the Guidance and Planning for the Restructuring of the Republic's Schools.[25] The Charter reminds students that transmitting secular values of the Republic is the mission entrusted to the school by the nation. It presents the secularism of staff, teaching and programs as a guarantee for each student to freely access all intellectual and cultural means necessary for the construction and development of a unique and autonomous personality. The Charter, displayed in a visible place in public schools, is used by teachers in various educational activities, especially on Secularity Day celebrated on 9 December, marking the introduction in 1905 of the Act on the separation of Church and State and is also presented to parents during annual integration meetings. The first five principles of the Charter refer to the secularism of the Republic, stating among other things that: 'the State remains neutral with regard to religious and spiritual convictions', while ten remaining principles serve as a guideline of how to maintain secularism at school, eg '[e]mployees are required to maintain strict neutrality: they must not express their political or religious beliefs while exercising their role' and, in each public school, 'the rules for the life of certain spaces as defined internally are respectful of secularism'. The Charter also states that it is forbidden to wear signs or clothing conspicuously expressing a religious affiliation.[26]

B Respecting the right to exercise religious practices (individually or collectively)

In the French public education system the principle of *laïcité* is regarded as a guarantee to freedom of conscience and it protects the freedom to believe, not to believe and to change one's conviction.[27] Published at the end of 2021 and revised in March of 2024 by French Ministry of National Education and Youth the vademecum of *laïcité*

---

[25] Loi n°2013-595 du 8 juillet 2013 d'orientation et de programmation pour la refondation de l'École de la République [Law No 2013-595 of 8 July 2013].

[26] Point 14 of *La Charte de la laïcité à l'École*.

[27] Education Code art L141-5-2.

in schools offers a complete legal guidance on the limits of religious expression in public schools.[28] Generally, individual prayer of a student on school premises is permitted, but behaviour that violates the freedom of conscience of other students is prohibited, so students' joint prayer is excluded. During school trips combined with an overnight stay, religious practices should also be performed by the student outside the time spent together, which fulfills the requirement to leave religion in the private sphere.[29] Students attending public boarding schools, who cannot freely leave the school premises during the week to attend religious services, should be provided with the opportunity to perform certain religious practices, for example in their room. Nevertheless, the exercise of this right may not include religious practices which, by their ostentatious nature or conditions in which are carried out individually or collectively, would constitute an act of pressure, provocation, proselytism or propaganda and violate dignity or freedom of the student or other members of the educational community, threaten their health or safety, disrupt the course of teaching activities and the educational role of teachers or the normal functioning of public service.[30] If a student's practice of his or her religion results in a violation of the freedom of conscience of other students, in particular those who share a room with him or her, it may be advisable for the head of the educational institution to allocate a separate room open to all students who individually request the opportunity to spend a moment of peace and reflection there. With regard to religious practices, special attention must be taken to ensure that no religion can be considered privileged.[31]

Educational regulations allow students to be excused from school due to the celebration of religious holidays falling on days that are

---

[28] Ministère de l'Éducation nationale et de la Jeunesse 'Vademecum. La Laïcité à l'École' (2024).

[29] Ibid 85.

[30] Opinion of the Council of State No 346.893 of 27 November 1989.

[31] 'Vademecum. La Laïcité à l'École', 86.

not public holidays.[32] However, this right is limited to the list of the most important religious holidays (prepared at the beginning of the school year) and treated as an exception to the general rule of constant attendance at school classes which is prescribed in the Education Code.[33] Students are obliged to attend both compulsory and optional classes for which they are registered, in accordance with the number of hours specified in the institution's lesson plan. Requests for systematic or prolonged absence for religious reasons are rejected. For example, a student's long absence from physical education classes due to fasting related to worship cannot be considered justified. The same applies to repeated absences on Saturday mornings for religious reasons.[34]

In accordance with the principle of neutrality to which all public services, including school catering, are subjected, offering a differentiated menu, whether or not it is related to the religious practices of students, does not constitute an obligation for the authorities to take it into account.[35] Moreover, in a case concerning municipal authorities that introduced meatless meals in school canteens on Fridays, it was stated that 'the provisions on menus, which do not refer to any dietary prohibitions, are not discriminatory on the basis of the religion of children or their parents'.[36] However, while there is no legal obligation to include religious dietary restrictions in the school menu, nothing prevents educational authorities from facilitating students' exercise of freedom of conscience, provided that public order, public health, the proper functioning of services, and the rights and freedoms of other people are protected.[37] In this way, local authorities can

---

[32] Ibid 73, see also *Circulaire du 10 février 2012 relative aux autorisations d'absence pouvant être accordées à l'occasion des principales fêtes religieuses des différentes confessions.*

[33] Education Code art L511-1.

[34] Opinion of the Council of State No 157653 of 14 April 1995.

[35] Opinion of the Council of State No 426483 of 11 December 2020.

[36] Opinion of the Council of State No 251161 of 25 October 2002

[37] Opinion of the Council of State No 426483 of 11 December 2020.

freely determine varied school meals, taking into account all kinds of dietary preferences and medical recommendations. However, this arrangement must not lead students to be grouped together, for example at separate tables in a cafeteria, depending on their eating practices. It is also necessary to ensure that these differences do not create pressure between students.

C *Respecting the right to manifest religious beliefs, eg through symbols, religious clothing and speech*

The Education Code guarantees students of junior high schools (*collèges*) and secondary schools (*lycées*) freedom of expression while respecting the principles of pluralism and neutrality.[38] However, the exercise of this freedom may not interfere with teaching activities. Despite the passage of over 30 years since the so-called "scarf scandal in Creil" (*l'affaire des foulards de Creil*),[39] the presence of Islamic headscarves in French schools is constantly the subject of lively public discussion. In the 1990s, the Council of State tightened the regulations prohibiting religious symbols in classrooms, mainly aimed at limiting the wearing of Islamic headscarves in classrooms. However, until the beginning of the 21st century, the regulations remained unclear. Ultimately, this issue was resolved in a radical way, as "permission

---

[38] Education Code art L511-2.

[39] The scarf scandal in Creil, in the Oise department, broke out on the background of the celebration of the bicentenary of the French Revolution. On 18 September 1989, when *The Satanic Verses* by the British writer Salman Rushdie was published, several newspapers published an article about the college principal's decision to exclude from school three students, Leila, Fatima and Samira, who refused to remove their headscarves during classes. On 9 October, three students were able to return to college thanks to an agreement reached between their parents and the institution, under which they were allowed to put on their headscarves immediately after leaving class and take them off before. The girls were also obliged to refrain from any religious proselytism at the college and to refrain from aggressive behavior, especially towards Muslim students who were less strict than them in the application of Sharia law. See Yohan Blavignat, 'L'affaire des «foulards de Creil» : la République laïque face au voile Islamique', *Le Figaro* (Web Article, 27 July 2018).

in principle" replaced "prohibition in principle".[40] From 1 September 2004, in public schools (and in private schools after this provision was included in their internal regulations) it is prohibited for students to wear visible signs and clothes that openly manifest their religious affiliation.[41] When defining the manner of manifesting religious affiliation with symbols and clothing, the Act uses the adjective *ostensiblement*, which indicates that it is obvious, open and ostentatious behavior. While teachers and public education employees are subject to the obligation to maintain strict neutrality (the *Act on the Separation of Church and State* of 1905 states that they cannot wear any religious symbols), students can therefore wear only "discreet" religious symbols. Despite that, the line between visible and discreet religious symbols seems to be fluid. The law adopted in 2004 does not contain a clear-cut list of prohibited symbols of religious affiliation. It was formulated in such a way with the aim to apply to all religions and emerging new symbols of religious affiliation, and it's common to include in it an Islamic scarf, a skullcap, a Sikh turban, a Hindu bindi, an oversized crucifix or other religious pendant. The French Council of State held that wearing a Sikh turban by a student could also be considered as an overt manifestation of religious affiliation, while the turban itself was not a religious sign (wearing long hair was).[42] A similar case emerged when a student wore a burkini while learning to swim. In addition to the fact that, for health and safety reasons, wearing a burkini is prohibited by most internal regulations of swimming pools where swimming schools offer lessons, this outfit is also a clear sign of religious affiliation. Therefore, a student wearing a burkini should not be allowed in the swimming pool. She must be asked to wear a swimsuit and if she refuses, she will not be allowed to

---

[40] Jacek Falski, 'Wokół zakazu symboli religijnych we francuskiej szkole publicznej' (2011) 12 *Państwo i Prawo* 43.

[41] Loi n° 2004-228 du 15 mars 2004 [Law 2004-228 of 15 March 2004] (France); Education Code art L141-5-1.

[42] Opinion of the Council of State No 285394 of 5 December 2007.

attend swimming lessons. If instead a student fails to comply with the prohibition on wearing signs or clothing indicating religious affiliation, disciplinary proceedings must be preceded by a conversation in which students and their families should be encouraged to understand the functioning and requirements of the school in terms of rights and obligations, which are clearly recalled in the Charter.[43]

The ban on manifesting religious beliefs through symbols and clothing in French public schools has been brought to the attention of the European Court of Human Rights ('ECtHR'). In two cases of *Dogru v France* and *Kervanci v France*, decided on 4 December 2008, the ECtHR unanimously held that France had not violated the applicants' rights to religious freedom and education guaranteed by Article 9 of the *Convention for the Protection of Human Rights and Fundamental Freedoms* ('Convention') and Article 2 of Protocol No. 1, respectively. The case concerned the expulsion of two Muslim girls from school for refusing to remove their Islamic headscarves during physical education classes despite repeated requests from their teachers. The expulsion from school occurred in 1999. As a result, both applicants attended correspondence courses to continue their education. The ECtHR noted that Article 9 'does not protect every act motivated or inspired by a religion or belief and does not always guarantee the right to behave in a way that is dictated by it. [...] in a democratic society in which many religions coexist within the same population, it may be necessary to introduce restrictions on this freedom in order to reconcile the interests of different groups and ensure that everyone's beliefs are respected.' Both cases concerned the facts before the introduction of the official ban in 2004. Later on, in a decision issued on 30 June 2009, the ECtHR unanimously declared inadmissible six complaints[44] which followed

---

[43] 'Vademecum, *La Laïcité à l'École*, 26.

[44] *Aktas v France* [2009], no 43563/08; *Bayrak v France* [2009] no 14308/08; *Gamaleddyn v France* [2009] no 18527/08; *Ghazal v France* [2009], no 29134/08,;*J. Singh v France* [2009] no 25463/08; *R. Singh v France* [2009] no 27561/08.

the ban on conspicuous religious symbols introduced in French public schools. Cases involved six pupils expelled from various schools for wearing religious symbols (an Islamic headscarf and a Sikh turban) during the 2004-2005 school year. After an attempt of dialogue with families, schools finally expelled students for non-compliance with the provisions of the Education Code. Applicants complained the violation of the right to freedom to manifest their religion (Article 9 of the Convention). In its decision of inadmissibility of the complaints, the ECtHR pointed out to the diversity of legal solutions adopted in countries that regulate the presence of religious symbols in schools (within the 'margin of appreciation' of state authorities), and drew attention to the qualified nature of the French ban (it included only symbols considered "conspicuous") and the possibility of receiving education in private institutions or by correspondence.

In a later ruling, *SAS v France* regarding the Law of 11 October 2010 'prohibiting the concealment of one's face in public places' (except places of religious worship), the ECtHR found no violation either of Article 8 or Article 9 of the Convention. The judgment should be considered controversial insofar as it extends the concept of 'rights and freedoms of other persons' as a basis for limiting the scope of rights and freedoms guaranteed by the Convention to the formula of "community life" (*vivre ensemble*). Contrary to ECtHR ruling in this case, the United Nations Human Rights Committee concluded that the ban on face coverings in public implemented in France violated the right to religious freedom.[45]

The battle with religious symbols in public schools continues. Recently, at the end of August 2023, before the official start of the new school year, the French government issued a new national ban on

---

[45] For more on the difference in assessment paradigms used by the European Court of Human Rights and the Human Rights Committee, see e.g. Marcella Ferri, 'How to Strengthen Protection of (Religious) Minorities and Cultural Diversity under EU Law: Some Lessons from Human Rights Protection System' (2021) 12 *Religions* (online).

wearing abayas by female students. In a decision issued on 7 September 2023, the State Council, the highest court for complaints against government authorities, rejected a motion filed by an association representing Muslims for an injunction against the ban, and ruled in favor of maintaining the ban as not discriminatory towards Muslims.[46] On 8 September 2023 the United States Commission on International Religious Freedom ('USCIRF') released a note expressing concern about France's actions which are in direct conflict with Article 18 of both the International Covenant on Civil and Political Rights ('ICCPR') and the Universal Declaration of Human Rights ('UDHR') guaranteeing religious freedom to every person, including the freedom to manifest one's religious beliefs through symbols or clothing. USCIRF Commissioner Nury Turkel noted that:

Muslim girls in France should not have to put aside their religious beliefs and practices when stepping into a classroom, nor should they have to compromise their basic human rights, including their right to an education, in order to uphold their beliefs. The international community should continue to speak out against laws that threaten the religious freedom of all people in France, as well as other countries in Europe.[47]

III. The Inclusive and Unifying Model of "Religious Neutrality" in the United States

In the case of the United States of America, with the introduction of the First Amendment to the *US Constitution* in 1789, religious freedom is often regarded as the 'first freedom'. It is delimited by two religious clauses from the First Amendment to the *US Constitution*, according to the provision that 'Congress shall make no law respecting an establishment of religion, or prohibiting the free exercise thereof'. On

---

[46] Conseil d'Etat, Ordonnance du 7 September 2023, No 487891.

[47] 'USCIRF Concerned by France's Expanding Interpretation of Ban on Religious Outfits in Public Schools', *USCIRF* (Web Page, 8 September 2023).

the one hand, the Establishment Clause prohibits the establishment of an official religion, on the other hand, the Free Exercise Clause guarantees everyone the freedom to disclose and manifest religious beliefs. From a historical perspective, American religious freedom was an inalienable natural right and the desire to unite citizens turned out to be stronger than religious differences which divided them.[48] The Founders of the *US Constitution* and the *Bill of Rights* were strongly convinced that religious morality was an essential factor in the development of the country. However, they were convinced that if religion was supposed to survive, it must receive less rather than more support from state authorities, and besides that God has given man the right to absolute religious freedom, which man cannot limit by his actions. These assumptions determined the fact that it is neither Christianity, nor secularism, but religious freedom understood in terms of "benevolent neutrality" that shapes the nation. In this way, the United States became a testing ground for an attractive and pioneering thought experiment, combining two – seemingly separate, yet close – spheres: secular and religious. This interpenetration of Church and State relations is also visible in the educational model adopted in the public schools of the United States, to which attends approximately 91% of school-age children.[49] Compulsory schooling for children in the USA, depending on the state, begins between the age of 5 and 7 and ends when they reach the age of 16-19.

A *Respecting the right to teach religion and about religion*

Numerous religious conflicts present in the USA since the times of colonialism and formation of independent state structures prompted

---

[48] See Vincent Phillip Muñoz, *Religious Liberty and the American Founding: Natural Rights and the Original Meanings of the First Amendment Religion Clauses* (The University of Chicago Press, 2022).

[49] Institute of Education Sciences National Center for Education Statistics, 'Private School Enrollment. Condition of Education', *US Department of Education* (Web Article, 2022).

the Founders to adopt the model of separation between Church and State. However, they were aware of the fact that it was impossible to separate the spheres of spirit and body, which are by their nature inseparable, or to remove religion from the public sphere. Secular state schools have repeatedly tried to arrange cooperation between secular and religious institutions in a friendly but neutral way so as not to be accused of supporting religion. On the other hand, there was a concern that eliminating religion from the school education program would result in a clear violation of the right of every citizen to religious freedom. The way in which American society developed clearly shows that education in first colonies had its source only in religious teaching based on the Bible. The subsequent removal of religion from schools was the result of society's influence based on the need to regulate matters of religion, which could lead to the breakdown of unity in a democratic state which respects every citizen in terms of his or her origin, race, culture, customs and religion. The main purpose of the ban on teaching religion in public non-denominational schools was to provide students with education in an atmosphere of complete freedom from religious influences. This type of cohesion in the school community, lack of censorship and independence from the pressure exercised by some churches and religious associations was achieved by leaving faith in the private sphere of each citizen. By 1875, the separation of Church and State in public education had become a principle deeply rooted in the nation's consciousness.[50]

In 1925, the Supreme Court of the United States ('the Supreme Court') issued an important ruling in the case of *Pierce v Society of Sisters*,[51] in which it declared as unconstitutional the obligation introduced by the state of Oregon to send children aged 8-16 only to public schools, thus causing the complete collapse of private

---

[50] See Steven K Green, 'Blaming Blaine: Understanding the Blaine Amendment and the No-Funding Principle' (2003) 2 First Amendment Law Review 129.

[51] *Pierce v Society of the Sisters of the Holy names Jesus and Mary*, 268 US 510 (1925).

education, which included religious schools. The Supreme Court found that state authorities cannot in this way prohibit children from attending private religious schools, to which they are sent not only to receive general secular education, but also to develop a proper moral and religious attitudes. From that moment on, public education authorities tried to take into account the religious needs of students also at school, including the right to receive religious education on school premises. For this purpose, buildings and school equipment were lent to religious groups, which organised religious classes in agreement with the school authorities. This type of cooperation ended when, in 1948, the Supreme Court issued ruling in *McCollum v Board of Education,*[52] in which the court, by a vote of 8-1, stated that legal regulations allowing religious lessons in school buildings were unconstitutional. Public schools had to limit or stop supporting the organisation of religion classes on school premises. In return, the released time program was developed and used more often, providing time off from classes, during which students could attend religious classes or spiritual exercises in their own churches or religious associations. In 1952, in *Zorach v Clauson* the Supreme Court upheld the arrangement of the released time program implemented by the state of New York by finding that it did not violate the Establishment Clause. The court stated that:

> We are a religious people whose institutions presuppose a Supreme Being. We guarantee the freedom to worship as one chooses. We make room for as wide a variety of beliefs and creeds as the spiritual needs of man deem necessary. We sponsor an attitude on the part of government that shows no partiality to any one group and that lets each flourish according to the zeal of its adherents and the appeal of its dogma. When

---

[52] *McCollum v Board of Education,* 333 US 203 (1948). See also Weronika Kudła, *Wrogość wobec religii. Ostrzeżenia ze strony Sądu Najwyższego USA* (Księgarnia Akademicka, 2019) 96-103.

the state encourages religious instruction or cooperates with religious authorities by adjusting the schedule of public events to sectarian needs, it follows the best of our traditions. For it then respects the religious nature of our people and accommodates the public service to their spiritual needs. To hold that it may not would be to find in the Constitution a requirement that the government show a callous indifference to religious groups. That would be preferring those who believe in no religion over those who do believe. [...] we find no constitutional requirement which makes it necessary for government to be hostile to religion and to throw its weight against efforts to widen the effective scope of religious influence.[53]

In view of the Supreme Court the government must remain neutral when it comes to competition between religious groups and it may not coerce anyone to take religious instruction, but 'it can close its doors or suspend its operations as to those who want to repair to their religious sanctuary for worship or instruction'.[54] Thus, the released time program for organising religious education outside the school premises is still in force in American public schools, and it shares many similarities with the French model of religious instruction which also takes place out of school.

What makes the American approach different from the French one is the possibility to organise meetings of religious nature by using school's facilities outside school hours, provided that they are open to the public and not sponsored by the school. This solution has been authorised in a 6-3 decision issued by the Supreme Court in *Good News Club v Milford Central School* case in 2001.[55] Within a school's limited public forum, student clubs and associations presenting a religious viewpoint should be treated in the same way as other

---

[53] *Zorach v Clauson*, 343 US 306, 313-314 (1952).

[54] Ibid.

[55] *Good News Club* v. *Milford Central School*, 533 US 98 (2001).

students associations presenting other views.[56] This is possible thanks to the application of equal treatment doctrine which refers to the Free Speech Clause and equalises religious language, including ritual words (liturgy), private prayers, sacred texts (eg the Bible), theological treatises, catechesis, sermons and religious literature, with other types of secular statements, eg political, philosophical, artistic or scientific.[57] The protection of religious expression here seems to have two levels: the principle of equal treatment determines the primary level of protection, while the protection of religious freedom becomes a secondary level. It is thus important to assess whether all entities interested in using school rooms for after school hours meetings have equal access to them. The type of activities they undertake is of no such a great importance as long as it does not threaten common standards of health, life and safety protection of the individual, as well as the entire society. Moreover, the First Amendment to the *US Constitution* prohibits state authorities from regulating freedom of speech in a way that favours certain views and thoughts at the expense of others, which would be the case if religious views were excluded from the remaining set of possible beliefs. There is also the inevitable risk of control and interpretation of the philosophical and religious assumptions presented by students while evaluating the "religious speech". These actions would undoubtedly constitute a violation of the freedom of expression and would potentially strengthen an attitude of prejudice or hostility

---

[56] Ibid 111 (Thomas, J, opinion): 'We disagree that something that is "quintessentially religious" or "decidedly religious in nature" cannot also be characterized properly as the teaching of morals and character development from a particular viewpoint. [...] What matters for purposes of the Free Speech Clause is that we can see no logical difference in kind between the invocation of Christianity by the Club and the invocation of teamwork, loyalty, or patriotism by other associations to provide a foundation for their lessons.'

[57] See also Derek H Davis, 'Editorial: A Commentary on the Supreme Court's 'Equal Treatment' Doctrine as the New Constitutional Paradigm for Protecting Religious Liberty' (2004) 4(46) *Journal of Church and State* 717.

towards religion, which undermines the requirement to respect the principle of neutrality included in the Establishment Clause. Therefore, it seems more beneficial to guarantee everyone a free exchange of views and thoughts, both believers and non-believers. Student religious groups (eg Bible groups), on the same terms as other student clubs and associations, may therefore use school premises.

B *Respecting the right to exercise religious practices (individually or collectively)*

The adopted model of "benevolent neutrality" of the United States towards particular religion or belief professed by citizens allows students to perform religious activities on school premises, provided that they do not put pressure on other pupils or force them to participate in these practices. From the Establishment Clause perspective, these activities cannot be initiated by teachers, however, taking into account the teacher's religious freedom guaranteed by the Free Exercise Clause, in certain situations depending on the actual circumstances, joint prayer between the teacher and students is not excluded. In this respect, we are dealing with a changing judicial paradigm.

When referring to the presence of prayer in schools, one should take into account the *Engel v Vitale*[58] ruling issued in 1962 and regarding the constitutionality of reciting a short prayer in public school initiated by a teacher at the beginning of the day, the content of which was composed by state officials. The Supreme Court held in à 6-1 opinion that the use of school system to facilitate recitation of the official prayer violated the Establishment Clause. Specifically, it imposed on students a specific content of prayer by breaching the symbolic (but eventually misleading) constitutional wall of separation

---

[58] *Engel v Vitale*, 370 US 421 (1962).

between Church and State.[59] In view of the Supreme Court recitation of a prayer composed by state authorities resulted to be an excessive entanglement in the confessional sphere, which could lead to various disputes and divisions among pupils. Unlike prayer recited during public gatherings, in schools there is a risk of peer pressure being exerted on students who, fearing rejection and being considered second-class people, would participate in prayer against their will. This precedent was followed by the Court in *Abington School District v Schempp*[60] decided in 1963, which became one of the most criticised judgments in the history of American judiciary. In this case the Supreme Court analysed the constitutionality of school practices consisting in reading verses from the Bible under teacher's supervision each day before classes. Students not wishing to participate in this activity were advised to be absent from the classroom or, should they elect to remain, not participate in the exercises. The Supreme Court in 8-1 decision held that the Bible may be the subject of literary and historical research as part of the secular curriculum, but it is not permissible to use it as an element of religious worship, towards which the state must remain neutral – it cannot neither advance, nor inhibit it. The day the ruling was issued was called the day when 'God and prayer were thrown out of schools'.[61] This line of jurisprudence unfavorable to the presence of prayer and reading from the Bible in schools was upheld once again in the judgment issued in 1985 in the *Wallace v Jaffree*[62] case. The facts of this case indicated that the one-minute

---

[59] Ibid 425 (Black J, opinion): 'petitioners argue, the State's use of the Regents' prayer in its public school system breaches the constitutional wall of separation between Church and State. We agree with that contention, since we think that the constitutional prohibition against laws respecting an establishment of religion must at least mean that, in this country, it is no part of the business of government to compose official prayers for any group of the American people to recite as a part of a religious program carried on by government'.

[60] *Abington School District v Schempp*, 374 US 203, 225 (1963).

[61] *Encyclopedia of Diversity in Education*, (Seattle. 2012) vol 1 s 1806.

[62] *Wallace* v *Jaffree*, 472 US 38 (1985).

moment of silence at the beginning of the school day, scheduled for Alabama elementary schools, was an attempt to restore common prayer at school, because, taking into account the will of the majority, teachers could use it for the common recital of a short prayer, the content of which was predetermined and written down in the legal act. The majority of the Court found that state authorities had intentionally crossed the line between creating conditions conducive to prayer and imposing it on others. In school circumstances, it is better to leave students with a moment of silence for their own meditation, prayer or contemplation, which may refer equally to religious or secular type of reflection. During the moment of silence, teachers and other school employees may not require, encourage, or discourage students from praying. This solution is adopted and valid in thirty-four American states.[63] Therefore, it should not be assumed that every prayer recited publicly at school is prohibited. The Supreme Court has consistently stated that it is unacceptable under the Establishment Clause for school authorities to promote religion. The prayer recited publicly during the graduation ceremony remains still a controversial issue, but it is acceptable when initiated by students.[64]

The situational context in which collective prayer on school premises is permissible has expanded very recently with the 6-3 decision in *Kennedy v Bremerton School District* issued in 2022.[65] In this ruling the Supreme Court upheld the right of public high school football coach Joe Kennedy to pray at the 50-yard line after games. In 2008 he made a promise to God that after the end of each game he coached, he would recite a short prayer of thanksgiving in the middle of the pitch. Over time, other team members began to join him on

---

[63] The status of state laws with moment of silence or school prayer legislation (current as February 2021) is available on the Gateways to Better Education website.

[64] US Department of Education, *Guidance on Constitutionally Protected Prayer and Religious Expression in Public Elementary and Secondary Schools* (15 May 2023), sec II, G.

[65] *Kennedy v Bremerton School District*, 597 U S ____ (2022).

a completely voluntary basis, which attracted the attention of the public and the school authorities. As a result, the school management fired the coach who did not agree to recite prayers in isolation and far away from the school playground. The Supreme Court held that the coach did not say the prayer as part of his official duties and it did not matter that he was still perceived as a coach for the entire time of his prayer (approximately 30 seconds). As a result, the prayer spoken by the coach was a private statement. For this purpose, the Supreme Court recalled the declaration valid for years that teachers, as well as students, do not 'shed their constitutional rights to freedom of speech or expression at the schoolhouse gate'.[66] In the opinion of the Court seeing a person praying, or even hearing the words of such a prayer, is an element of shaping tolerant civic attitudes in a pluralistic society, and not exerting pressure or indoctrination: 'Respect for religious expressions is indispensable to life in a free and diverse Republic – whether those expressions take place in a sanctuary or on a field, and whether they manifest through the spoken word or a bowed head'.[67]

C *Respecting the right to manifest religious beliefs, eg through symbols, religious clothing and speech*

In the United Sates, in opposition to France, there is no controversial ban for students wearing religious clothing in public schools. Educational institutions have considerable discretion in shaping student dress codes and school uniforms, but they may not target religious attire in general, or the attire of a particular religion. When introducing specific regulation or prohibition of dress codes, schools must apply them equally to religious and non-religious clothing. This is in stark contrast to the French way of intimidating religious groups, particularly Muslims. In addition, students may include religious messages on

---

[66] *Tinker v Des Moines Independent Community School District*, 393 US 503, 506 (1969).

[67] *Kennedy v Bremerton School District*, (n 61) 31 (Gorsuch J).

items of clothing to the same extent that they may include other similar messages of a secular nature. When it comes to religious clothes or symbols worn by teachers, in controversial matters it is suggested to apply the principle of accommodation, not exclusion, eg by taking into account the religious needs of citizens also in labor law.[68] As courts have repeatedly held, religion is an important part of an individual's identity. It is neither realistic nor, in many cases, possible to "cleanse" teachers of all external manifestations of religion. At the same time, schools can and must make sure that a teacher's religious attire does not violate the Establishment Clause and is acceptable, taking into account the requirement of safety and neutrality of teaching. For that reason teachers and other school employees cannot: a) promote a specific religion as superior to others, b) promote religion in general as superior to a secular approach to life, c) have a negative attitude towards religion in general or in particular to a particular religion, d) have a negative attitude towards secularism, e) take actions that would favor or inhibit religion.

In the context of displaying religious symbols, school authorities and teachers may not use religious symbols except for educational purposes. In *Stone v Graham*[69] ruling, the Supreme Court found the unconstitutionality of the requirement introduced by the state of Kentucky to hang a board with the Decalogue in every school room. Despite its clearly secular, universalist message, the purpose of placing the signs in school classrooms was clearly religious, violating the Establishment Clause. Due to this precedent, public schools cannot permanently display religious symbols, as this would mean expressing support for a specific religion by the school. However, religious symbols can be used for educational purposes as teaching aids.

---

[68] See eg *Equal Employment Opportunity Commission v Abercrombie & Fitch Stores*, 575 US ___ (2015) or the most recent *Groff v DeJoy*, 600 US ___ (2023).
[69] *Stone v Graham*, 449 US 39 (1980).

IV. AGAINST TYRANNY OF 'RELIGIOUS NEUTRALITY' – CONCLUSIONS

In light of the above comparative analysis it is clear that the French way of promoting republican values in public schools assumes a tyrannical form of imposing misguided rules suggesting how students and their families should live and interact in society. The all-pervasive influence of *laïcité* threatens primarily religious freedom which gradually becomes subordinated to cultural norms and images that saturate current society. Without any doubt, education in every country constitutes a common good for the entire society, but it can also become a useful tool in the hands of those in authority to help maintain their power. Such a tyrannical way of constructing the new society, which pays insufficient attention to the role of religion for every individual, must be investigated and evaluated. This is especially important when people of different cultural and religious background make up the society and wish for peaceful coexistence in public square.

The reference to the evolving model of 'benevolent neutrality' toward religion adopted in the context of American education system may serve equally as a warning sign against destructive processes resulting in the loss of religious freedom in this area and an instructive lesson toward better accommodation of religious needs based on deeply and sincerely held convictions. School authorities cannot incite to renounce the religious identity in the school setting. For that reason targeting especially Muslim women wearing religiously mandated attire in French public schools results to be a further step toward the perpetuation of divisions, rather than mapping out educational strategies to respect each other and to learn from each other.

Despite significant differences between the axiology of French and American legal framework in each country (and not only there) we are left with a similar problem arising from a similar source: the religious and cultural pluralism of society. We are still far from obtaining a math-like precision in guaranteeing religious liberty for all and by this time we have already got used to the *ad hoc* or case-based solutions to disputes about the proper bounds between religion and government. It is however evident that the misguided and obsessive promotion of secularism which takes place in France can jeopardise the religious integrity of human beings, even if it is motivated by the need to maintain neutrality of the education system and fight against religious fanaticism. As a result, the system of French education oscillates between taking religious diversity into account on the one hand, and attempting to neutralise any differences on the other hand. The troubling threads indicated in my article that run through the relationship between religion and secularism in French public schools need to be addressed through the lens of interdisciplinary and cross-national approach toward protection and promotion of religious freedom. The artificial confinement of religion to private spaces such as the home and the church clearly violates the religious freedom of every individual and can be connected with a tyrannic method of subduing citizens to government's ambitions of making French public schools as sanctuaries of *laïcité* which instead of reconciliation, offer rejection of others.

The religious freedom jurisprudence of the Supreme Court of the United States briefly evoked in my article serves as a counterbalance to current tensions over the place of religion in French schools and up to some point it may help to resolve some issues emerging not only in France, but generally in Europe which becomes a subject of particular concern for the advocates of religious freedom. The American model of accommodations offers much better protection for believers, provided that it serves as a shield, not as a sword, towards other religions and convictions, and it proves that religious freedom, religious equality and religious neutrality are complementary, rather than conflicting notions.

8

C S Lewis, Tyranny, Technology and Transcendence

BILL MUEHLENBERG*

ABSTRACT

Numerous voices over the past century have warned of the damaging and devastating results of a sinister convergence – an unhealthy coming together of things like runaway statism, unchecked scientism, technological tyranny, and moral myopia. It was quickly becoming apparent to these observers that the stuff of dystopian novels was no longer limited to the realm of fiction; those who were alert and aware started to see too many real life cases of this happening – and with horrific results. C S Lewis was one such prophetic writer who warned constantly about where we were heading, be it in his works of fiction or nonfiction. Writing from the 40s through to the 60s, his many important volumes on philosophy, theology and social criticism were very much needed back then – but sadly far too often ignored. We now are paying the price for neglecting this prescient watchman on the wall.

I. FIRST CONSIDERATIONS

Almost everyone reading this collection will have lived through the Great Covid Wars which began in 2020. After what we went through over the past few years with the Covid craziness, government and

---

* BA with honours in Philosophy (Wheaton College, Chicago), MA with highest honours in Theology (Gordon-Conwell Theological Seminary, Boston). The author is currently completing a PhD in Theology. He has his own website called Culture-Watch, which features commentary on the issues of the day: billmuehlenberg.com.

media-led hysteria and panic porn, the lockdown madness, and the health care tyranny fully in place, we now can see clearly just the sorts of things prophetic voices had long been warning about. Most political leaders, media outlets and medical elites decided that fostering a herd mentality was far more important than achieving any sort of herd immunity – and it worked like a charm.

The frightening thing is that all this happened relatively soon after our parents and grandparents lived through the tyrannical rule of both Communism and Nazism – even if from afar. They would have known full well the great evils that out-of-control statism can pose. Noted intellects and authors such as Orwell, Huxley, Tolkien and Lewis – to name but a few – all wrote quite sober works warning about such things, whether in the form of fiction or non-fiction – or both. Yet their warnings largely went unheeded, and tyranny is still with us. As political scientist Waller Newell in his book *Tyrants: Power, Injustice, and Terror* states, 'tyranny is a permanent alternative in human affairs and in explaining political action'.[1] He continues:

> The progress of history, if that has actually taken place, has plainly not gotten rid of tyranny. The genocidal horrors of the last century's totalitarianism are surely proof of that, along with today's aspirants to a worldwide Caliphate, such as ISIS. Believing in the progress of history may actually, as we'll see, contribute to the spread of tyranny itself. Not only because it lulls us into thinking that tyranny is fading away, but because all of the worst totalitarian regimes, after all, have claimed that they were on the side of history, bringing a better world for us all in the future through mass murder and conquest in the present.[2]

The Covid Wars, as I have called them, should certainly have

---

[1] Waller Newell, *Tyrants: Power, Injustice, and Terror* (Cambridge University Press, 2019) viii.

[2] Ibid.

dispelled any notions that the West is progressively moving in the direction of greater freedom and less tyranny. Quite the opposite. And they certainly demonstrated that we were unable or unwilling to learn the lessons of recent history. Moreover, we closed our ears to the many warnings given to us not all that long ago.

Of the four famous authors I mentioned above, I want to focus on the last one: C S Lewis. While widely known as a popular Christian apologist and expert in medieval and renaissance literature, the Oxford and Cambridge professor wrote widely and frequently on political matters and related concerns. Much of this took the form of warnings about the perils of moral relativism, the rise of the omni-state, scientism replacing real science, and the rise of technological tyranny. Two of his works especially can be singled out here: *The Abolition of Man* and *That Hideous Strength.* In addition to these works, I will also briefly mention some of his other writings on these topics.

II. The Abolition of Man

Let me begin with one of his most valuable works in this regard. Some 80 years ago Lewis delivered three seminal lectures that were later put together in the book, *The Abolition of Man.* Regarded as his most pure philosophical work, it may be brief but it contains some of his most important thinking on a number of topics.

Over three evenings in February of 1943 (24, 25 and 26), Lewis gave the Riddell Memorial Lectures at the University of Durham. These talks set out to do several things: examine the philosophical follies of modern education and reductionistic scientism, and make the case for objective values and natural law. They were published in various forms immediately thereafter, including the Macmillan edition of *The Abolition of Man* in 1947. The case he makes against the "Controllers" and other would-be tyrants is tied in with a larger theological and philosophical discussion. Before looking at some specific portions of his book, let me lay out briefly what Lewis sought to argue. He thought the modern notion of objective truth being found only in science, while things like morality are purely subjective concerns, is a key part of why freedom declines as tyranny grows. Raw power then becomes the determination of right from wrong, and the sole question is: Who controls whom? Lewis believed the main controllers to come would wear white labs coats or be from academia. Buttressed by the power of the state, they would decide who should be controlled, and how.

By way of introduction to the book, Michael Aeschliman offers these observations on the case Lewis seeks to make:

> Ideas have consequences, Lewis insisted, and although the problems of modernity have been immensely complicated by technical innovations such as the advent of automation, the factory system, and the massive increases in the speed of communication and transportation, the root of the problem remains philosophical. Lewis's point in *The Abolition of Man* is not simply that the consequences of scientific materialism are bad, but that it is internally inconsistent and false. In his criticism of this heresy he claims no originality beyond that which can be said to derive from remaining faithful to the best that has been thought and said, especially in the tradition of Western philosophy and ethics....
>
> Without a doctrine of objective validity, only individual desire remains a standard to determine action. In the hands of an empowered elite, the capacity to reorder society with the techniques of a vastly powerful and unchecked science is virtually limitless and, of course, open to monstrous abuses – although, Lewis reiterates, the valuation of monstrousness would be irrelevant within an ethical framework based solely on the dictates of personal desire.[3]

---

[3] Michael Aeschliman, *The Restitution of Man: C. S. Lewis and the Case Against Scientism* (Eerdmans, 1998) 75-75.

He continues:

> With the growth of scientism has come a massive increase in the powers of technology and applied science to change and manipulate not only the physical landscape but the mental and human landscape too. As the means and instruments proliferate, the distinction between ends and means seems to grow more obscure in modern culture, so much so that finally man himself can be seen as a means to undetermined ends; he is deluded by what William Barrett calls "the illusion of technique." There is no longer any question of "conforming the soul to reality"; there is only the question of increasing our power over and pleasure in a world of objects.[4]

Here I offer some choice quotes from this brief book and some commentary on it. I break it down into the three chapters that correspond with his three lectures.

III. Chapter 1: Men Without Chests

Early on Lewis explains what he means by a key term used throughout: 'the Tao'. It refers to 'what we can't not know' as J Buziszewski put it in a book by that title.[5] It is about the natural law tradition wherein all people have an innate understanding of a God who is there, and his binding moral law in the universe. Says Lewis:

> This conception in all its forms, Platonic, Aristotelian, Stoic, Christian, and Oriental alike, I shall henceforth refer to for brevity simply as 'the *Tao.*' . . . But what is common to them all is something we cannot neglect. It is the doctrine of objective value, the belief that certain attitudes are really true, and others really false, to the kind of thing the universe is and the kind of things we are ... And because our approvals and disapprovals

---

[4] Ibid 78.

[5] J Buziszewski, *What We Can't Not Know* (Spence Publishing, 2003).

are thus recognitions of objective value or responses to an objective order, therefore emotional states can be in harmony with reason (when we feel liking for what ought to be approved) or out of harmony with reason (when we perceive that liking is due but cannot feel it). No emotion is, in itself, a judgement; in that sense all emotions and sentiments are alogical. But they can be reasonable or unreasonable as they conform to Reason or fail to conform. The heart never takes the place of the head: but it can, and should, obey it.[6]

And on the objectivity of moral values, Lewis says:

Until quite modern times all teachers and even all men believed the universe to be such that certain emotional reactions on our part could be either congruous or incongruous to it—believed, in fact, that objects did not merely receive, but could *merit*, our approval or disapproval, our reverence or our contempt. The reason why Coleridge agreed with the tourist who called the cataract sublime and disagreed with the one who called it pretty was of course that he believed inanimate nature to be such that certain responses could be more 'just' or 'ordinate' or 'appropriate' to it than others. And he believed (correctly) that the tourists thought the same. The man who called the cataract sublime was not intending simply to describe his own emotions about it: he was also claiming that the object was one which *merited* those emotions.[7]

One of the most famous passages from this volume comes at the end of this chapter:

And all the time – such is the tragi-comedy of our situation – we continue to clamour for those very qualities we are rendering impossible. You can hardly open a periodical without coming

---

[6] C S Lewis, *The Abolition of Man* (Macmillan, 1976) 28-30.
[7] Ibid 25.

across the statement that our civilization needs more 'drive', or dynamism, or self-sacrifice, or 'creativity'. In a sort of ghastly simplicity we remove the organ and demand the function. We make men without chests and expect of them virtue and enterprise. We laugh at honour and are shocked to find traitors in our midst. We castrate and bid the geldings be fruitful.[8]

Some summarising words by Donald Williams are apropos here:

We cannot make human beings less than human; but by training them to think of themselves as less than human, we can get them to act as less, with disastrous consequences. In other words, we may not be able to make them unhuman, but we can make them inhuman. Therefore, Lewis speaks with hyperbole perhaps but nevertheless makes a valid point when he says of those who operate on the basis of materialist reductionism that 'it is not that they are bad men. They are not men at all. Stepping outside the *Tao*, they have stepped into the void.' They have tried with mixed success to give up something that is essential to full humanity, at least. The two rival conceptions of humanity stare at each other across a great chasm, and what is at stake is the possibility of a civilization in which man can be whole, develop to his full potential: 'Either we are rational spirit obliged for ever to obey the absolute values of the *Tao*, or else we are mere nature to be kneaded and cut into new shapes for the pleasures of masters who must, by hypothesis, have no motive but their own "natural" impulses. Only the *Tao* provides a common human law of action which can overarch rulers and ruled alike. A dogmatic belief in objective value is necessary to the very idea of a rule which is not tyranny or an obedience which is not slavery.'[9]

---

[8] Ibid 35.
[9] Donald Williams, *Mere Humanity* (B&H, 2006) 33.

IV. Chapter 2: The Way

Just one quote here: Lewis further explains what he means by the Tao, making the case for basic ultimate principles:

> I draw the following conclusions. This thing which I have called for convenience the *Tao,* and which others may call Natural Law or Traditional Morality or the First Principles of Practical Reason or the First Platitudes, is not one among a series of possible systems of value. It is the sole source of all value judgements. If it is rejected, all value is rejected. If any value is retained, it is retained. The effort to refute it and raise a new system of value in its place is self-contradictory. There has never been, and never will be, a radically new judgement of value in the history of the world. What purport to be new systems or (as they now call them) 'ideologies', all consist of fragments from the *Tao* itself, arbitrarily wrenched from their context in the whole and then swollen to madness in their isolation, yet still owing to the *Tao* and to it alone such validity as they possess. If my duty to my parents is a superstition, then so is my duty to posterity. If justice is a superstition, then so is my duty to my country or my race. If the pursuit of scientific knowledge is a real value, then so is conjugal fidelity. The rebellion of new ideologies against the *Tao* is a rebellion of the branches against the tree: if the rebels could succeed they would find that they had destroyed themselves. The human mind has no more power of inventing a new value than of imagining a new primary colour, or, indeed, of creating a new sun and a new sky for it to move in.[10]

Chapter 3: The Abolition of Man

In his final lecture/chapter Lewis drives all this home, showing us just how this plays itself out. And what he envisages does not look very

---

[10] Lewis (n 6) 56-57.

good. He writes: 'What we call Man's power over Nature turns out to be power exercised *by* some men *over* other men with Nature as its instrument'.[11] And again: 'Man's conquest of Nature, if the dreams of some scientific planners are realized, means the rule of a few hundreds of men over billions upon billions of men. There neither is nor can be any simple increase of power on Man's side. Each new power won *by* man is a power *over* man as well. Each advance leaves him weaker as well as stronger. In every victory, besides being the general who triumphs, he is also the prisoner who follows the triumphal car'.[12]

Lewis zeroes in on what is really happening here:

The preservation of the species? But why should the species be preserved? One of the questions before them is whether this feeling for posterity (they know well how it is produced) shall be continued or not. However far they go back, or down, they can find no ground to stand on. Every motive they try to act on becomes at once a *petitio*. It is not that they are bad men. They are not men at all. Stepping outside the *Tao,* they have stepped into the void. Nor are their subjects necessarily unhappy men. They are not men at all: they are artefacts. Man's final conquest has proved to be the abolition of Man. … 'Man's conquest of Nature turns out, in the moment of its consummation, to be Nature's conquest of Man.'[13]

One final quote:

The serious magical endeavour and the serious scientific endeavour are twins: one was sickly and died, the other strong and throve. But they were twins. They were born of the same impulse. I allow that some (certainly not all) of the early scientists were actuated by a pure love of knowledge. But if

---

[11] Ibid 69.

[12] Ibid 71.

[13] Ibid 77, 80.

we consider the temper of that age as a whole we can discern the impulse of which I speak. There is something which unites magic and applied science while separating both from the wisdom of earlier ages. For the wise men of old the cardinal problem had been how to conform the soul to reality, and the solution had been knowledge, self-discipline, and virtue. For magic and applied science alike the problem is how to subdue reality to the wishes of men: the solution is a technique; and both, in the practice of this technique, are ready to do things hitherto regarded as disgusting and impious ... No doubt those who really founded modern science were usually those whose love of truth exceeded their love of power.[14]

His argument is clear enough, but let me add the words of some expert witnesses here. Looking at the power the Controllers will have over the controlled, philosopher Peter Kreeft says this:

The picture is more terrifying than nuclear war to one who values souls more than bodies. Our question here is not that of forecasting whether we will actually create this Brave New World. Nor is that Lewis' question. His question is rather that of the prophets. It is not foretelling so much as forthtelling. It is the publication of the road map and the demand that we ask ourselves: *Quo vadis?* Where does this road lead? It is up to the traveler, both individually and collectively, to choose to turn back or not, to repent or to apostasize, to be regressive or progressive down the mudslide to Hell.

Our question here is neither of these two: neither whether the road is leading to Hell's victory of a Brave New World (I think it is clear that it is) nor whether we will get off the slide before we hit bottom (no one knows that but God); but whether it is possible, whether 'men without chests' can exist, whether

---

[14] Ibid 87-88, 89.

Aquinas is wrong when he says the natural law cannot be abolished from the heart of man.

Lewis pretty clearly thinks it *is* possible: 'It is in Man's power to treat himself as a mere "natural object" and his own judgments of value as raw material for scientific manipulation to alter at will.'

The only dam to this flood is the *Tao*. 'Only the *Tao* provides a common human law of action which can over-arch rulers and ruled alike. A dogmatic belief in objective value is necessary to the very idea of a rule which is not tyranny or an obedience which is not slavery'.[15]

Commenting on this final lecture of Lewis, political philosopher Jean Bethke Elshtain remarks:

What C S Lewis called the "extreme rationality" (not to be confused with reason as such) that consigns to the dustbin of history all claims of intrinsic value – as those embracing such truths cannot, allegedly, meet certain standards of a rationalistic defense of these values – winds up promoting a subjectivism of values it believes is somehow more honest. When this happens, those whose 'values' triumph will be those possessed of the most overwhelming will-to-power.[16]

Lastly, some incisive thoughts on the book as a whole by Michael Ward. He penned an entire volume assessing this work, and his thoughts are well worth sharing:

The Abolition of Man may be understood as a work of prophecy. All great prophets, whether they be ancient religious figures like Isaiah and Jeremiah or more recent political figures such as Martin Luther King Jr and Aleksandr Solzhenitsyn, work

---

[15] Peter Kreeft, *C. S. Lewis for the Third Millennium* (Ignatius, 1994) 116.

[16] Jean Bethke Elshtain, 'The Abolition of Man' in David Baggett, Gary Habermas and Jerry Walls (eds), *C. S. Lewis as Philosopher* (IVP, 2008) 94.

on two fronts at once. They prophesy both to critique their contemporary situation and to indicate likely future states of affairs as and when the logic of the present situation unfolds. The old Sunday School definition can hardly be improved on: prophets tell forth *and* foretell.

If *Abolition* were merely a description of war-time Britain, it would not have become the classic that it has. And if Lewis had merely been prognosticating when he spoke to his original 1943 audience, he would not have gained much of a hearing at the time, for how would they know whether his predictions would come true? What marks out his message as genuinely prophetic is that it resonated with its first hearers and has only attracted further attention as the decades have passed.

His prophecy is largely a jeremiad, largely a negative case. He identifies the subjectivism in his culture and forecasts its probable trajectory. It is chiefly a philosophical forecast, intellectual in intent. He is describing the logical end point of the current situation more than prescribing a remedy to it. There are, to be sure, notes of warning, not to say alarm. There are also some gestures of optimism when he briefly suggests possible mitigating actions that might be taken and considers alternative, more positive, outcomes. But the fact that he ends the final chapter on a hollow note, by depicting moral blindness ('to "see through" all things is the same as not to see'), indicates that his main purpose is less to change our destination than to predict our destiny. He is simply charting the likely course of unchecked subjectivism, saying in effect, 'This philosophical error leads to sub-humanity and if a sub-human fate is what we want, that's the fate we'll get; we shouldn't be surprised by where we end up.' There is something of the same tone in the repeated world-weary words of Hingest, the good scientist, in *That Hideous Strength*: 'It all depends on what a man likes.'

We do not have to adopt subjectivism, but if we decide we like it, and make no course correction, it will usher us inexorably to a bad end. The choice is ours.[17]

VI. That Hideous Strength

That quote by Ward nicely leads us to the second main work to be discussed. In the third volume of his famous space trilogy, *That Hideous Strength* (1945), Lewis turns his non-fiction treatment of these matters into a graphic and powerful work of fiction. In the preface to it he makes the connection: 'This is a 'tall story' about devilry, though it has behind it a serious 'point' which I have tried to make in my Abolition of Man. In the story the outer rim of that devilry had to be shown touching the life of some ordinary and respectable profession'.[18]

This 500-page novel is all about unconstrained tyranny in the form of rogue science, propaganda, and unethical technocrats. It was a clear warning about coming coercive dystopias. Another important Christian thinker and apologist from last century, Francis Schaeffer, once said this about the book: 'I strongly urge Christians to read carefully this prophetic piece of science fiction. What Lewis casts in fantasy and science fiction is with us not tomorrow but today'.[19] Indeed, as Michael Rose put it by way of introduction: 'Sham journalism, fake news, engineered social chaos, the destruction of property rights, incipient totalitarian rule, and the serial misuse of the word 'science' – it sounds a lot like America in the 2020s, but it's also the fictional fabric of C S Lewis's *That Hideous Strength*'.[20]

Just as with today's globalist bully bodies like the World

---

[17] Michael Ward, *After Humanity: A Guide to C. S. Lewis's* The Abolition of Man (Word on Fire Academic, 2021) 187-188.

[18] C S Lewis, *That Hideous Strength* (HarperCollins, 2005) ix.

[19] Francis Schaeffer, *Back to Freedom and Dignity* (InterVarsity Press, 1977) 29.

[20] Michael Rose, *The Art of Being Human* (Angelico Press, 2022) 81.

Economic Forum ('WEF'), the main villain in the novel comes with a euphemistic and sweet-sounding title: NICE. The National Institute for Coordinated Experiments is a government bureaucracy established to help mankind – aren't they all? It of course does nothing of the sort. As David Downing reminds us in his book about the space trilogy:

> The villains in Lewis's fantasies are not hard to find; they do not, as [the Apostle] Paul warned, cloak themselves as angels of light. Lewis's bad characters range from the merely pompous to the outright demonic, but they share a few common traits: they set aside ordinary morality in favor of utility or in favor of some lofty, abstract goals for humanity; they disregard the sanctity of life, whether human or animal; they are "progressive" and find little value in history, tradition, or the classics; they prefer the scientific, artificial, and industrial over the simple and natural; they use language to conceal and distort reality, rather than reveal it.[21]

Many key quotes from *That Hideous Strength* can be offered here, so I will have to be rather selective. On the issue of education, he shows how indoctrination, propaganda and proselytisation are all part of the techno-tyrants toolkit. This includes the use of euphemisms and subterfuge – they are ever the weapons of choice for these technocrats. Consider this bit of dialogue:

> 'You don't mean you want me to write up all this?'
>
> 'No. We want you to write it *down* – to camouflage it. Only for the present, of course. Once the thing gets going we shan't have to bother about the great heart of the British public. We'll make the great heart what we want it to be. But in the meantime it *does* make a difference how things are put. For instance, if it were even whispered that the NICE

---

[21] David Downing, *Planets in Peril: A Critical Study of C. S. Lewis's Ransom Trilogy* (The University of Massachusetts Press, 1992) 84.

wanted powers to experiment on criminals, you'd have all the old women of both sexes up in arms and yapping about humanity. Call it re-education of the mal-adjusted, and you have them all slobbering with delight that the brutal era of retributive punishment has at last come to an end. Odd thing it is – the word "experiment" is unpopular, but not the world "experimental". You musn't experiment on children: but offer the dear little kiddies free education in an experimental school attached to the NICE and it's all correct!'[22]

One of the characters says this about those who are most susceptible to the tyrant's propaganda:

Why you fool, it's the uneducated reader who *can* be gulled. All our difficulty comes with the others. When did you meet a workman who believes the papers? He takes it for granted that they're all propaganda and skips the leading articles. He buys his paper for the football results and the little paragraphs about girls falling out of windows and corpses found in Mayfair flats. He is our problem. We have to recondition him. But the educated public, the people who read the highbrow weeklies, don't need reconditioning. They're all right already. They'll believe anything.[23]

A final quote gives us the bigger picture of this war on humanity:

The physical sciences, good and innocent in themselves, had already ... begun to be warped, had been subtly manoeuvred in a certain direction. Despair of objective truth had been increasingly insinuated into the scientists; indifference to it, and a concentration upon mere power, had been the result ... The very experiences of the dissecting room and the pathological laboratory were breeding a conviction that the

---

[22] Lewis (n 18) 45.

[23] Ibid 126.

stifling of all deep-set repugnances was the first essential for progress.[24]

This important thriller clearly shows the deep concerns Lewis had about where unethical science and unconstrained technocracy can take us. And his premonition of a dark new world has certainly proven to be quite accurate. Eugenics did not die out with the Nazi experiments but is alive and well in the West today. In fact it has only gotten worse. When we combine media-led hysteria and alarmism about things like the climate and corona with these billionaires – be they Klaus Schwab or Geroge Soros or Bill Gates – who believe they know what is best for us mere humans, we are seeing the prophetic novels coming to life in very real and very frightening ways.

Rose offers a fitting summary of the book and its relevance:

In the dystopic vein of Orwell, Huxley, and Bradbury, Lewis's morality tale explores the perennial desire for man to enslave man by means of dehumanization. Unlike the other dystopian classics, however, *That Hideous Strength* is primarily satire, ridiculing academic politics, sham journalism, and the misuse of "science," to name a few of his targets of criticism. And it works not only as satire for Lewis's original 20th-century postwar audience; it's eerily relevant as an indictment of aspects of our own age. Our information technology may have changed, but the propaganda techniques and the political desire to manipulate public opinion have not. And, it is important to note, the desire to apply "science" to social engineering in order to achieve a stated improvement of society or to allegedly protect the well-being of the masses – in the utilitarian sense – resonates all too well...

Given the dubious "follow the science" narrative of 2020's COVID-19 response and recent developments in genetic

---

[24] Ibid 226.

engineering, psychopharmacology, and human cloning, there is, arguably, no greater subject for a cautionary tale in our own time than this.[25]

VII. OTHER WRITINGS

It is worth sharing a few more quotes by Lewis about tyranny, freedom, democracy and politics which are found elsewhere. With his many books, essays, lectures and letters, there are numerous passages scattered throughout the Lewis corpus that can be drawn upon. Here are some of the main ones. The hope is that in sharing them they will entice the reader to peruse in full his many important works that touch on these themes.

As to democracy and the abuse of power, Lewis said this in an essay on equality: 'I am a democrat because I believe in the Fall of Man ... Mankind is so fallen that no man can be trusted with unchecked power over his fellows. Aristotle said that some people were only fit to be slaves. I do not contradict him. But I reject slavery because I see no men fit to be masters'.[26]

More on his views on democracy can be found in another essay:

I believe in political equality. But there are two opposite reasons for being a democrat. You may think all men so good that they deserve a share in the government of the commonwealth, and so wise that the commonwealth needs their advice. That is, in my opinion, the false, romantic doctrine of democracy. On the other hand, you may believe fallen men to be so wicked that not one of them can be trusted with any irresponsible power over his fellows. That I believe to be the true ground of democracy. I do not believe that God created an egalitarian world. ... [S]ince we have sin, we have found, as Lord Acton

---

[25] Rose (n 20) 88-89.

[26] C S Lewis, 'Equality' in Walter Hooper (ed), *Present Concerns* (Harcourt Brace Jovanovich, 1986) 17.

says, that 'all power corrupts, and absolute power corrupts absolutely.' The only remedy has been to take away the powers and substitute a legal fiction of equality. ... Theocracy has been rightly abolished not because it is bad that priests should govern ignorant laymen, but because priests are wicked men like the rest of us.[27]

Scientism, the idea that only that which science can deal with (only the empirical) was a constant bogeyman for Lewis. Morality, truth, love and freedom are all unable to exist in such a narrow worldview. At least there is no proper grounding for them in such a worldview. As he wrote in his 1943 essay, 'The Poison of Subjectivism':

The very idea of freedom presupposes some objective moral law which overarches rulers and ruled alike. Subjectivism about values is eternally incompatible with democracy. We and our rulers are of one kind only so long as we are subject to one law. But if there is no Law of Nature, the ethos of any society is the creation of its rulers, educators and conditioners; and every creator stands above and outside his creation. Unless we return to the crude and nursery-like belief in objective values, we perish.[28]

The connection between science – or rather, scientism – and tyranny gets further treatment in a 1958 essay for *The Observer* called 'Is Progress Possible? Willing Slaves of the Welfare State.' Here are some key portions of it:

I do not like the pretensions of Government – the grounds on which it demands my obedience – to be pitched too high. ... On just the same grounds I dread government in the name of science. That is how tyrannies come in. In every age the men

---

[27] C S Lewis, 'Membership' in *The Weight of Glory* (Eerdmans, 1974) 36-37.

[28] C S Lewis, 'The Poison of Subjectivism', in Walter Hooper (ed), *Christian Reflections* (Eerdmans, 1975) 81.

who want us under their thumb, if they have any sense, will put forward the particular pretension which the hopes and fears of that age render most potent. They 'cash in'. It has been magic, it has been Christianity. Now it will certainly be science. Perhaps the real scientists may not think much of the tyrants' 'science'– they didn't think much of Hitler's racial theories or Stalin's biology. But they can be muzzled...

We have on the one hand a desperate need: hunger, sickness, and the dread of war. We have, on the other, the conception of something that might meet it: omnicompetent global technocracy. Are not these the ideal opportunity for enslavement? This is how it has entered before; a desperate need (real or apparent) in the one party, a power (real or apparent) to relieve it, in the other. ... The question about progress has become the question whether we can discover any way of submitting to the worldwide paternalism of a technocracy without losing all personal privacy and independence. Is there any possibility of getting the super welfare state's honey and avoiding the sting?...

What assurance have we that our masters will or can keep the promise which induced us to sell ourselves? Let us not be deceived by phrases about 'Man taking charge of his own destiny.' All that can really happen is that some men will take charge of the destiny of the others. They will be simply men; none perfect; some greedy, cruel and dishonest. The more completely we are planned the more powerful they will be. Have we discovered some new reason why, this time, power should not corrupt as it has done before?[29]

One last point on this issue. At times Lewis was attacked for supposedly being against science and scientists. For example, one

---

[29] C S Lewis, 'Is Progress Possible?', in Walter Hooper (ed), *God in the Dock* (Eerdmans, 1978) 315-316.

popular science writer at the time that Lewis interacted with was J B S Haldane (1892-1964). He did not care for books like *The Abolition of Man*, and he had so misconstrued what Lewis was trying to argue that he had to write a response to Haldane. In it Lewis had to repeat that it was scientism, and not science as such, that he was so greatly concerned about. Moreover, his main worry was not so much the scientific, but the philosophical.

And similar to what he said above, it was the misuse of science, especially by the state, that was his primary concern. As he wrote in his reply to Haldane: 'I am a democrat because I believe that no man or group of men is good enough to be trusted with uncontrolled power over others. And the higher the pretensions of such power, the more dangerous I think it both to rulers and to the subjects'.[30]

On the matter of law and its relation to tyranny, Lewis wrote at various times about this. While not a legal expert, he was well informed on areas such as the philosophy of law. An incisive article he wrote for the *Australian Quarterly Review* in 1949 titled 'The Humanitarian Theory of Punishment' made some important points. Here is one:

> [M]y argument so far supposes no evil intentions on the part of the Humanitarian and considers only what is involved in the logic of his position. My contention is that good men (not bad men) consistently acting upon that position would act as cruelly and unjustly as the greatest tyrants. They might in some respects act even worse. Of all tyrannies, a tyranny sincerely exercised for the good of its victims may be the most oppressive. It would be better to live under robber barons than under omnipotent moral busybodies. The robber baron's cruelty may sometimes sleep, his cupidity may at some point be satiated; but those who torment us for our own good will

---

[30] C S Lewis, 'A Reply To Professor Haldane' in Walter Hooper (ed), *Of Other Worlds* (Harcourt Brace Jovanovich, 1966) 79.

torment us without end for they do so with the approval of their own conscience.[31]

This article and some replies to it were reprinted in *Res Judicatae* in 1953. Lewis in turn responded, closing with these words:

> We are all at this moment helping to decide whether humanity shall retain all that has hitherto made humanity worth preserving, or whether we must slide down into the sub-humanity imagined by Mr Aldous Huxley and George Orwell and partially realised in Hitler's Germany. For the extermination of the Jews really would have been 'useful' if the racial theories had been correct; there is no foretelling what may come to seem, or even to be, 'useful', and 'necessity' was always 'the tyrant's plea'.[32]

One final quote. Lewis said this in the Preface to the 1961 edition of his famous *The Screwtape Letters*:

> I like bats much better than bureaucrats. I live in the Managerial Age, in a world of 'Admin.' The greatest evil is not now done in those sordid 'dens of crime' that Dickens loved to paint. It is not done even in concentration camps and labour camps. In those we see its final result. But it is conceived and ordered (moved, seconded, carried, and minuted) in clean, carpeted, warmed, and well-lighted offices, by quiet men with white collars and cut fingernails and smooth-shaven cheeks who do not need to raise their voice. Hence, naturally enough, my symbol for Hell is something like the bureaucracy of a police state or the offices of a thoroughly nasty business concern.[33]

---

[31] C S Lewis, 'The Humanitarian Theory of Punishment' in Walter Hooper (ed), *God in the Dock* (Eerdmans, 1978) 292.

[32] C S Lewis, 'On Punishment: A Reply To Criticism' in Walter Hooper (ed), *God in the Dock* (Eerdmans, 1978) 300

[33] C S Lewis, *The Screwtape Letters* (Geoffrey Bles, 1961).

VIII. CONCLUSION

Much more could have been covered here. Consider the whole issue of transhumanism and the rather ominous techno-future which seems so high up on the agenda for the World Economic Forum, Schwab, Yuval Noah Harari and others. Whether or not Lewis uses the term, he certainly had plenty to say on all this, even as far back as three quarters of a century ago.

Taken together, it is clear that Lewis had a very healthy distrust of Statism, scientism, technocracy, and those who in the name of humanity would be so very cavalier about mere humans. He sounded the alarm quite often over the decades on these matters, only to be largely overlooked. As Lewis said in 1955, *The Abolition of Man* 'has been almost totally ignored by the pubic'.[34] Much the same can be said about his other prescient writings and warnings.

Had folks taken heed to what Lewis and the other prophetic voices were saying back then, perhaps we would have coped much better with (that is, resisted much more strenuously) the Covid wars and the Orwellian government overreach that we all had to endure in recent times. We ignore these incisive prophets to our own peril.

---

[34] Quoted in Ward (n 17) 1.

9

The Rise of a Power Class in 'Sheepskins':
A Threat to Humanity

MONIKA NAGEL*

ABSTRACT

This article expresses concern about any early enthusiasm and questions what kind of Covid-19 phase humanity has entered. Under the pandemic strict regulations, politicians, industry leaders and professionals in the medical field obtained privileges and power to make decisions on the world population's health unknown before. Humankind appears to be complacent with the status quo: exhausted from the restrictions with the pandemic and brainwashed by the information about the new drugs against Covid-19. This article is about the rise of power when the world was struck by Covid-19 and people were helpless and sought guidance. In fear of a vicious virus, hasty and unprecedented decisions were made by those in power – the leaders in the political and corporate worlds. Their new orders were meant to combat Covid-19 and be in the best interest of humankind. But in reality, and as time reveals, many were inappropriate; they were wrong and even fatal for far too many people. Still and alarmingly a new class with an enormous power appears to have gained momentum. And that has the potential to be harmful to humanity.

___

* Cert Ed, B Psch, PhD (Org Psych). Former educator.

I. Power: Essential for Order

According to the 17th-century English philosopher, John Locke, by entering from the state of nature into society, people put themselves into the hands of governments, 'to be so far dispossessed of by the Legislative, as the good of the Society shall require'.[1] And, in return and for peace of mind their life, liberty and estates would be preserved.

The role of the legislative power, wrote Locke, '… is the preservation of the Society, and of every person in it. This Legislative is not only the supreme power of the Common-wealth, but sacred and unalterable in the hands where the Community have once placed it'.[2] He explains that:

> Whoever has the Legislative or Supreme Power of any Commonwealth, is bound to govern by established standing Laws, promulgated and known to the People, and not by Extemporary Decrees, by indifferent and upright Judges, who are to decide Controversies by those Laws … to prevent or redress Foreign Injuries and secure the Community from Inroads and invasion. And all this to be directed to no other end, but the Peace, Safety, and public good of the People'.[3]

But how far has society – our political sovereign – distanced itself from that fundamental wisdom? And it was not only Locke who emphasized the value and need for preserving the common good; Aristotle and Socrates and philosophers like Carl Schmitt and FA Hayek in the 20th Century wrote about the important role of the sovereign in doing so. However, they also emphasised and warned that the power of a sovereign can be misused, with catastrophic consequences. To stop that happening, great thinkers like Socrates and

---

[1] John Locke, *The Two Treatises of Government* (Lawbook Exchange edition, 2010) 381.

[2] Ibid 267.

[3] Ibid 265.

Machiavelli considered what it takes to be a good leader, and to avoid bad decisions.

The 21ˢᵗ century is less characterised by those philosophical thoughts; there has been a shift in societies' values and thus how the sovereign rules and how people in power – often – act. Morals have rapidly declined worldwide; and with that blasé attitude and view on values, people pursue what they like and feel is best for them. Respect, avoiding harm to our neighbours, and considering how our personal decisions impact others, our future, and the world, have plummeted.

Man's ambitions today unambiguously resemble what is described by Thomas Hobbes when he said that 'the object of man's desire, is not to enjoy once only ... but assure forever, the way of his future desire'.[4] Man is driven by his power for more. Hobbes sees power as the ultimate desire of all humanity. He salutes the passion for the common good but warns about the downsides of aspirations that disregard morals.[5]

II. John Locke on Rights and Power

Central to Locke's philosophical thought is that people have inalienable rights, such as the right to life, liberty, and property, and that these rights apply generally, independent of the laws of any particular society. Equally important is his debate about the state of nature and his argument that people need order and law. Hence, they become subject to a political power and part of a community by their consent for their comfort, safety and peace – the state of the Common-wealth.[6]

When Locke talks about the legislative power, he stresses that men's actions must be conformable to the law of nature and the will of God, which is fundamental in being the preservation of mankind.

---

[4] Thomas Hobbes, *Leviathan* (Oxford University Press, 2008) 66 8.

[5] Ibid ch 11.

[6] Locke (n 1).

Locke says that it would be impossible for law to foresee 'all accidents and necessities that may concern the public'.[7] Thus, the executive power is left with making decisions that the law does not prescribe, that are meant to benefit and protect the people.[8]

However, those in power, as Hobbes observes, are driven by a desire for more power. This potentially leads to corruption, conflict and decisions harmful to the public, as we have seen with the COVID-19 crisis.[9] People in power have used their privileges to maximise their authority, and then misuse it.

III. The Sovereign and Its Shift in Power under the Pandemic; People in Power in the Past

The power of the sovereign is pivotal. History provides examples of people in power with exceptional vision, abilities and foresight leading nations and societies and influencing humanity because of their wisdom, virtues and achievements. Such leaders, as seen below, shaped in one way or another the world in which we live today. Understandably, one wonders who of our present political leaders may enter the history books because of their outstanding decisions and achievements during the COVID-19 crisis.

Winston Churchill, Britain's Prime Minister during World War II, led the British Empire to its greatest victory, namely defeating the Nazis, while many countries in Europe were overpowered and became part of the Third Reich. Margaret Thatcher became a Conservative Party Member of Parliament in 1959. As the first female British Prime Minister and only British Prime Minister to serve three consecutive terms from 1979 to 1990, she led with a strong belief in doing what was right, regardless of pain and struggles along the way. Likewise,

---

7   Ibid. 202.
8   Ibid.
9   Hobbes (n 4).

Mahatma Gandhi led his population in a non-violent pursuit of independence from Britain and truly set examples by leading peaceful campaigns against foreign domination and poverty, and for civil rights and Indian independence.[10]

Martin Luther King Jr stands out as another great leader, and his dream about equality for black and white people in the future.[11] One of the finest world leaders, Abraham Lincoln, changed the course of history and civilisation when he passed the Emancipation Proclamation that gave respite to millions of African-Americans.[12] Yugoslavia, a federation of over 30 years under Tito's leadership, collapsed after his death.[13] The Dalai Lama has not only left the legacy of his peaceful resistance to Chinese Communist rule in formerly independent Tibet, but he continued to praise how the nature of people's motivation determines their work and the need to think about the purpose behind daily actions. He remarks that life has to be characterised by a sense of universal responsibility between humans but also between humans and other forms of life.[14]

IV. The Transcendence of Power by the Sovereign

The governing of these leaders resembles what great philosophers taught it should be done for their fellow citizens. In Plato's *The Republic*, Socrates compared rulers with guardians to explain what a ruler should be like and said that 'they ought to be wise and efficient, and to have a special care of the State'.[15] And to care, he added, 'the man (ruler) would have to love his country'.[16] He also emphasised

---

[10] 'Mahatma Gandhi quotes', *Good Reads* (Web Page, 25 January 2022).

[11] 'Martin Luther King, 'I have a dream speech', *American Rhetoric.com* (Web Article, 19 June 2015).

[12] 'The Emancipation Proclamation', *National Archives* (Web Page, 4 March 2021).

[13] Djilas, 'Tito's last secret: How did he keep the Yugoslavs together?', *Foreign Affairs* (Web Article, 4 July 2015).

[14] 'The Dalai Lama on Motivation', *Find Center Beta* (Web Page, 18 July 2021).

[15] Plato, *The Republic,* (Capstone Publishing Ltd, 2012) 119.

[16] Ibid.

that 'there is no doubt that the elder must rule the younger'.[17] In *The Prince,* Machiavelli criticised those who became rulers by merely good fortune because men who 'either buy their way into power or are granted it by favour of someone else'[18] lack good personal arms and do not have what it takes to be astute when necessary.

In the 20th century, Dwight D Eisenhower[19] once said that leadership is the art of getting people to do things because they want to. Here, profound wisdom – knowing what is best for people and that they are keen and determined to do things because they realise that those ideas and policies are in their interests – is captured in a few words. From this statement, we feel the assurance that leaders should know best and project their visions to people. It clearly echoes the confidence of leaders in their actions, their devotion to serving their people, their trust in involving people, and making them behave in a way that is beneficial for them.

The vision of what is good for others, for a country, for the environment and for the planet is meant to be the essence of good leadership. When Aristotle talks about the relationship between the dependant and free man or slave and master, he says that 'a ruler must first learn through being ruled, just as one learns to command cavalry by serving under cavalry-commander and to be a general by serving under a general…'.[20]

But what have we seen during the COVID-19 pandemic? Today, political leaders tend to aim for a political career to achieve a personal desire, like power, money and fame. However, leaders would have to acknowledge that they are in their roles to serve the constituents who voted for them and not themselves. They ought to appreciate that their constituents entrusted them to do what is best for the nation and the

---

[17] Ibid.

[18] Niccolò Machiavelli, *The Prince* (Penguin Books, 2003) 22.

[19] 'Dwight Eisenhower Quotes', *Gracious Quote* (Web Page, 2 February 2022).

[20] Aristotle, *The Politics* (Penguin Books, 1992) 182.

welfare of everybody. Leaders have to challenge and debate problems that matter for the long term and make decisions in crises. Accordingly, one wonders what made some leaders coerce their constituents to take experimental vaccinations against COVID-19 when people were desperate worrying about their health and looking for guidance.

V. Decisions by the Sovereign and Implications for Humanity

The world population has been led by their respective governments on how to combat COVID-19 from the time when the news about the emerge of a vicious new virus was announced. In general, but particularly in crises like the COVID-19 pandemic, good leadership is crucial. Politicians must know how to present policies and relevant news that people understand and know are important for them. People have to see that what is said will happen, actually happens and that it benefits them. Otherwise, they lose confidence when promises are broken, or when policies change or remain unfulfilled. Citizens must see how governments work through clearly stated objectives and deliver the outcomes. But with COVID-19, political leaders and leaders in medical fields provided forecasts that proved to be far-off from what unfolded and have the potential to be even harmful.

Who knows why people in power misled their fellow citizens about the effectiveness and safety of vaccines? Originally, the vaccination against COVID-19 was supposed to be a double dose of a vaccine produced by the same pharmaceutical company. The global roll-out of the vaccines began in the UK in December 2020. After, the distribution of the vaccines varied by time, quantity and brand between countries. The then Australian Prime Minister, Scott Morrison, announced the roll-out of the vaccination plan on 7 January 2021. He said that,

> after considerable effort, including with our vaccine suppliers,
> we are now in a position where we believe we'll be able to

commence vaccinations … We are hoping to secure all the final data … We then envisage to be hopeful of an approval subject to all the data.[21]

In the same SBS News webpage there is a comment of Mr Morrison saying, 'It is moving considerably faster than normal vaccine approval processes but without skipping a step, without cutting a corner'. Another comment of Mr Morrison explained that 'The Therapeutic Goods Administration was expected to receive all of the data it needed from vaccine developer Pfizer in mid-January, with approval due by the end of January'.

Similarly, an Aljazeera headline (23 December 2020) said, 'India likely to approve AstraZeneca vaccine by next week'.[22] However, the word "approved" refers to the acceptance of the drug by governments. How many people understood that the drug was not approved by the Food and Drug Administration (US) and that its safety and effectiveness were still being tested while it was used to inoculate the world population?

The data about fast rising numbers of infected and a reluctant response by too many people to get the jabs, was not what the world wanted to see. Subsequently, countries like the US, Bahrain, Haiti, Brunei, China, Thailand and the UK implemented vaccine passports in August 2021.[23] This new policy allowed the vaccinated to get on with their lives while the unvaccinated still faced restrictions. There were no passports in Australia for a while. The country was completely isolated from the rest of the world. But the authorities coerced Australian citizens to get vaccinated. By the end of August only 28%

---

[21] 'Australians to start getting coronavirus vaccinations from next month, Scott Morrison says', *SBS News* (Web Article, July 2023).

[22] 'COVID: India's expert panel approves Oxford-AstraZeneca vaccine', *Aljazeera and News Agencies* (Web Article, 1 January 2021).

[23] Beth Howell, 'Which Countries Are Using COVID-19 Vaccine Passports?', *Movehub.com* (Web Article, 27 Aug 2021).

were fully vaccinated, while the number was more than double (64%) two months later (30 October) and had dramatically increased to 77% by 2 January 2022.[24] The then Tourism Minister, Dan Tehan, vowed that passports would give people 'the right to be able to travel across borders when there are lockdowns', and that 'giving more freedom to people who are vaccinated would encourage more to get the jabs'.[25]

In Austria, the author's native country, where the vaccination passports were already in place, fines were announced to increase the vaccination rates (November 2021). According to a draft of Austria's COVID-19 vaccination law, there were to be fines of up to €7,200 for those who refused vaccination from February 2022.[26] The Austrian chancellor and other counterparts disingenuously described the status quo as the pandemic of the unvaccinated.[27]

Up to 1955, before Rosa Parks defied segregation laws in the US, black people in America were segregated and had diminished access to facilities, housing, education, shops and opportunities by comparison with white people.[28] Seventy-five years later, segregation came to life again. The unvaccinated became marginalised and their access to essential facilities were restricted.

Mandatory vaccinations and vaccine passports created differences in societies: for those who did not agree with the use of the improperly tested drug for inoculation, various opportunities, facilities, services and jobs were on the line. Obviously, the discrimination went far beyond what individuals were and not allowed to do; new regulations

---

[24] 'Statistic and Research – Coronavirus (COVID-19) Vaccinations', *Our World in Data*, (Web Page, 2 January 2022).

[25] 'Covid Passports: How Do They Work Around The World?', *BBC News* (Web Article, 26 July 2021).

[26] Oliver Noyon, 'Austria Considers Euro 7,200 Fine for Unvaccinated', *Euractiv* (Web Article, 30 November 2021).

[27] 'Austrian Chancellor Threatens Lockdown for Unvaccinated', *AP News* (Web Article, 23 October 2021).

[28] 'Rosa Parks', *Wikipedia* (Web Page, 10 January 2022).

gave some arbitrary authority over others in uncommon circumstances. Thus, the regulations inevitably prompted differences in how people perceived themselves and others and created hierarchies and therefore animosity.

The circumstances were avoidable. The rule of law can be described as a 'concept for legal-institutional mechanisms that protect citizens against the arbitrary power of the State'.[29] In other words, the rule of law is designed to minimise political arbitrariness to ensure that the rights and freedom of the citizens are properly acknowledged and legally preserved.[30] Hence, the rule of law is essential to protect individual citizens, but it was ignored during the pandemic.

Dr Peter McCullough warned about vaccine side effects like myocarditis almost from the beginning of the pandemic. Later, in November 2021, he authoritatively explained the risk of myocarditis in children.[31] Still, politicians, their advisors and medical officials have kept convincing people to get vaccinations and boosters. Professor Paul Kelly, for example, the Australian Government Chief Medical Officer, advised Australians to be up to date with their vaccinations one year later, namely, early November 2022.[32]

Brad Hazzard was scrutinized for his decisions as the New South Wales Health Minister. After he resigned, the Sydney Criminal Lawyers' *Weekly Rundown* wrote about his disastrous role in the state's emergency health response, saying that many of his decisions were controversial and his choice to mandate vaccination caused the most upset. Furthermore, a significant number of the COVID-19

---

[29] Augusto Zimmermann and Gabriël Moens, 'Vaccinations, Coercion and the Rule of Law', *Quadrant* (Web Article, 17 August 2021).

[30] Ibid.

[31] Peter Labarbera, 'Peter McCullough, 'The COVID-19 vaccines should have been pulled from the market … for excessive mortality'', *Clark Country Today* (Web Article, 24 January 2023).

[32] 'New COVID-19 variant leads to increase in cases', *Australian Government-Department of Health and Aged Care*, (Web Page, 8 November 2022).

public health decisions made under the *Public Health Act 2010* (NSW) legislation, empowering the health minister to issue public health orders at times of health crises, amounted to massive over-reach. 'Thousands of people were fined heavily for not complying with public health orders, thousands more lost jobs or had their incomes dramatically cut', concluded the *Weekly Rundown*.[33]

But there is a risk with those initiation of new regulations and gain in power by leaders in exceptional circumstances: they can be abused. They can have long-term unfavourable consequences leading to the supremacy of those in power and the dismantling of democracy.

Dr Anthony Fauci, the director of the National Institute of Allergy and Infectious Diseases, who became the chief medical advisor to the President Donald Trump, and later to the Biden administration until he resigned in 2022, was a big influence on COVID-19 issues in America and abroad. A comment by him, for example and according to the *Mint*, saying 'What I would hope is that even though there's a degree of scepticism about vaccines in general, that when the general public sees how effective this vaccine is, we might see a turnaround of the attitude towards vaccination',[34] had an enormous impact on professionals in the medical field, political leaders and the public.

However, almost two years into the vaccination roll-out worldwide, Pfizer admitted at the European Parliament that the vaccines were never tested for stopping the spread of COVID-19.[35]

Now and most tragically, the world knows that the emergency use authorisation for COVID-19 vaccines by the FDA[36] has resulted in

---

[33] Sonja Hickey, 'Covid Dictator's' Days in Politics are Done', *Sydney Criminal Lawyers – Weekly Rundown* (Web Article, 6 November 2022).

[34] 'Pfizer Vaccine's Trial Success May Boost Acceptance: Top US Health Expert Fauci', *Mint* (Web Article, 15 November 2020).

[35] John Campbell, 'Pfizer, blanked out pages' (YouTube, 21 October 2022).

[36] 'Emergency Use Authorization for Vaccines Explained', *US Food and Drug Administration* (Web Page, 20 November 2020).

unprecedented patient harm.[37] Of course, Locke had warned us about the ills of humankind and the danger that faces us. Based on what has been going on around the world, it seems that the sovereign has distanced itself from Locke's key notion, namely 'that being all equal and independent, no one ought to harm another in his Life, Health, Liberty or Possessions'.[38] 'And being furnished with like Faculties', he goes on, 'there cannot be supposed any such Subordination among us, that may Authorize us to destroy one another, as if we were made for one another's uses'.[39]

VI. Man's Perpetual Hunt for New Desires: Potentially Devastating for Humanity

Humanity has accomplished outstanding results in science and technology; innovations seemed to accelerate at the speed of light as the Western world re-established itself in the aftermath of World War II. However, societies fell short on nurturing what makes man human. The morals that typically distinguish man from species in the animal kingdom have been slipping away with no sign of return. They are crucial features of humankind, and their relevance comes even more to the fore when they are missing in crises such as the Covid-19 pandemic.

VII. An Emphasis on Human Rights: Elevating Individual Power

By the 1970s, morals had become negotiable; an almost modern set of morals evolved from our traditional and enduring values. This manipulation and a new conceptualisation of morals brought a unique way of thinking. We saw that new standards in work ethics

---

[37] Stephanie Seneff, Greg Nigh, Anthony M Kyriakopoulos and Peter A McCullough, 'Innate Immune Suppression by SARS-CoV-2 mRNA Vaccinations: The Role of G-quadruplexes, Exosomes, and MicroRNAs' (2022) 164 *Science Direct: Food and Chemical Toxicology* 113008:1-20.

[38] Ibid 169.

[39] Ibid.

caused disasters around the world. At the most fundamental level, these happened because people's values and ambitions to do what is right have been outshone by beliefs in freedom, selfish thinking and pursuing what people think is their right.

Human rights have been established as an alternative to morals. Unfortunately, today's interpretation of our human rights tends to encourage individualism – what is subjectively good for the individual – but it leaves aside obligations, responsibility and what is in the world's best interest. Carl Schmitt was critical about individualism and said about individualism in relation to the state that it 'never produces on its own a positive theory of state, government and politics'.[40] But values guide understanding as to what is right to do, what will benefit societies and the world, and doing what makes common sense. Thus Aristotle warned his fellow citizens that 'there is no such thing as a man's or state's good action without virtue and practical wisdom'.[41]

The COVID-19 crisis is the latest and most horrific disaster resulting from a cumulative waning of morals in societies worldwide. Both individuals and states failed to exercise virtue and practical wisdom.

Fauci was a keen advocate for the vaccination of the world population. *The New York Times* wrote that Fauci 'tended to cite the same 60 to 70% estimate that most experts did'[42] for how much herd immunisation was enough but then 'began saying '70, 75%' in television interviews, and after '75, 80, 85%' and '75 to 80-plus%' in a CNBC News interview'.[43] A telephone interview, to which *The New York Times* referred, revealed Fauci acknowledging that

---

[40] Carl Schmitt, *The Concept of the Political* (The University of Chicago Press, 207) 10.

[41] Aristotle (n 20) 53.

[42] Donald McNeil, 'How much Herd Immunity is Enough?' *The New York Times* (Web Article, 22 September 2021).

[43] Ibid.

'he had slowly but deliberately been moving the goal posts'.[44] One year later, people were asked to take the third and fourth boosters; children as young as five were coerced into vaccination. At the same time countries such as Israel observed a waning immunity from the Pfizer vaccine, which was initially the vaccine that was given to the population in Israel.[45]

Fauci – one single individual – rose to extraordinary power; his decisions had influence on people's health decisions around the world. But when views of one person are taken seriously by many and do harm, then, humanity can be at risk. This sort of behaviour raises concerns about the direction in which humanity is heading. Laws apparently no longer stop wrongdoers from chasing what they want or protect the innocent from harm and loss. And when morals lose their shine, people's thinking changes. And then man is unrestrained in chasing his desires – a tendency with which he is born, as Hobbes, Rousseau and other philosophers pointed out.[46]

Is it power for fame or financial gain what people desire? Surely, the former Australian Prime Minister Scott Morrison stood out with his grasping for more power. He had the audacity to take up five leading ministerial positions between March 2020 and May 2021 even though not all of the five ministers themselves were privy to what went on.[47] He gained additional power by appointing himself as a minister for the health, finance, home affairs, treasury and industry departments.[48]

---

[44] Ibid.

[45] Amy Greenbank, 'Israel shows COVID-19 cases can explode once life returns to 'normal' at 80 percent vaccination', *ABC News* (Web Article, 21 August 2021). See also: 'Covid-19: Vaccines – Israel', *Our World in Data*, (Web Article, 20 January 2022). See also: Rachael Schraer, 'Covid: What Israel Tells Us About the Way Out of the Pandemic', *BBC News* (Web Article, 3 September 2021).

[46] Jean-Jacques Rousseau, *The Social Contract* (JM Dent & Sons Ltd, 1920).

[47] James Massola, Lisa Visentin and David Crowe, 'Morrison's future under a cloud over secret ministries', *The Sydney Morning Herald* (Web Article, 16 August 2022).

[48] Ibid.

The current Prime Minister, Anthony Albanese, expressed his surprise that Morrison's appointments were kept secret by the government from the Australian public and 'accused his predecessor Scott Morrison of orchestrating an 'unprecedented trashing of democracy''.[49] 'Mr Albanese said the former Prime Minister had undermined the checks and balances crucial to the Westminster system of government', as reported by ABC News.[50]

Only months later, the media reported about Morrison's establishment of the Cabinet Office Policy Committee ('COPC') of which the Prime Minister was listed as the only permanent member.[51] It was said that in 2019 Morrison aimed for new policies and ordered his ministers to come up with new ones through consultations with stakeholders including businesspeople. And for that, the COPC was created. But then, he was listed as the only permanent member. Subsequently and not surprisingly, there was an interest in searching for the minutes of the secretive cabinet committee meetings.[52]

Pfizer took the lead in the vaccination against COVID-19. Reports about its innovative technology was in the media and Fauci frequently mentioned Pfizer when he encouraged people to get vaccinated. In the European Union, for example, the Pfizer vaccine was by far the most used vaccine compared to AstraZeneca and Moderna according to Our World in Data.[53]

Despite the strong advocacy for the Pfizer vaccine compared to others, at the end of August 2021, the BBC reported protection waning from double jabs. 'Among more than a million people who received two Pfizer or AstraZeneca doses, the protection of Pfizer jabs decreased

---

[49] Ibid.

[50] Ibid.

[51] Paul Karp, 'Scott Morrison's secretive cabinet committee of one had hundreds of meetings, FOI documents suggest', *The Guardian* (Web Article, 21 September 2022).

[52] Ibid.

[53] 'Covid-19 Vaccine Doses Administered by Manufacturers, European Union', *Our World in Data* (Web Article, June 2023).

from 88% to 74% after five to six months and of AstraZeneca from 77% to 67% after four to five months'.[54]

And as mentioned above, Pfizer said later that the vaccine was not tested for stopping the spread of COVID-19 nor tested for stopping infection.[55] One has to ask how many people took the jab under the assumption that they were protected from getting infected and stopping the spread of the infection to others.

The website of the World Health Organization ('WHO') says that it champions health and a better future for all. It reads that WHO is 'dedicated to the well-being of all people and guided by science' and leads 'global efforts to give everyone, everywhere an equal chance to live a healthy life'.[56] But when COVID-19 broke out, WHO seemed reluctant with its respective responses to COVID-19 matters. By 10 January 2020, for example, when WHO was not recommending restrictions for international traffic and precautions for international travellers, 41 cases were reported by Chinese authorities.[57] But when it announced that there was a Public Health Emergency of International Concern on 30 January 2020, the number of cases in mainland China was almost 9,700, with at least 213 deaths.[58] And when COVID-19 was declared a pandemic on 11 March 2020, there were 118,000 cases in 114 countries and 4,291 fatalities.[59] In early April 2020, over 100 countries (3.9 billion people) were in partial or complete lockdown.[60]

---

[54] Michelle Roberts, 'Covid infection protection waning in double jabbed', *BBC News* (Web Article, 25 August 2021).

[55] John Campbell, 'Pfizer, blanked out pages' (YouTube, 21 October 2022).

[56] 'About Us', *World Health Organization* (Web Page, July 2023).

[57] 'WHO Advice for International Travel and Trade in Relation to the Outbreak of Pneumonia Caused by a New Coronavirus in China', *World Health Organization*, (web Page, 10 January 2020).

[58] Helen Regan et al, 'January 30 coronavirus news', *CNN* (Web Article, 31 January 2020).

[59] 'WHO Director-General's Opening Remarks at the Media Briefing on COVID-19', *World Health Organization* (Web Page, 11 March 2020).

[60] 'Coronavirus: The World in Lockdown in Maps and Charts', *BBC News* (Web Article, 7 April 2020).

Over a year into the pandemic, the investigation by an expert team did not reveal anything more than what had been in the media since WHO made its early report about a cluster of pneumonia cases in Wuhan on 4 January 2020.[61] The WHO investigation into the origins of COVID-19 ended in disagreements about the viability of key data and the initial findings. According to ABC News, Professor Dwyer from Australia, who joined the investigating team, explained that they were not provided with 'raw patient data on the early cases in Wuhan in December 2019' but only received a summary report instead.[62]

After the outbreak and thereafter, those in the public and private sectors looked at the WHO for information and advice about how to protect against the new virus. The WHO's information mattered and its decisions were widely acknowledged. But the controversies about how the WHO handled crucial matters has been of concern. The organisation is paid by people around the world and is supposed to provide accurate advice.

A *Lancet* report in September 2022 was already talking about 'lessons for the future from the COVID-19 pandemic'.[63] The paper is critical about the time that passed before WHO declared the situation with COVID-19 a public health emergency of international concern, endorsed the use of face masks, and clarified the means of transmitting the virus. According to the *Lancet*, in July 2020 the World Health Organisation was asked in a letter by 238 scientists to address the transmission of the virus. But it was end of April 2021 before the WHO updated its information about the transmission of the virus.[64]

Then again, the Working Group on Amendments to the

---

[61] 'Archived: WHO Timeline – COVID-19', *World Health Organization* (Web Page, 27 April 2020).

[62] 'China Refused to Provide WHO with Raw Data on COVID Cases, says Australian Investigator', *ABC News* (Web Article, 13 February 2021).

[63] John Campbell, 'The Lancet Commission on Lesson for the Future from the CO-VID-19 Pandemic' (YouTube, July 2023).

[64] Ibid.

International Health Regulations submitted amendments to the *International Health Regulations* (2005) at its first meeting on 14– 15 November 2022; in general, these have been about an increased power of WHO to regulate such matters as the COVID-19 crisis.[65] The document as forwarded by WHO at the end of July 2023 gives details about the future authority of WHO over the governance of health matters by individual countries.

The amendments by WHO raises questions about where our democracy is heading. F A Hayek seemed to be right when he said that any group behaviour has the potential to rise within any given society and become successful.[66] And it seems even easier for an organisation as WHO to increase its power.

VIII. Carl Schmitt on the 1930s and the COVID-19 Health Crisis

When Carl Schmitt, a philosopher and jurist, wrote *The Concept of the Political* (1932), he was concerned about the weakening position of Weimar Germany and about social and political matters of the time. His views on state affairs were made 90 years ago. However, his observations and critiques about people's values, and their craving to realise their ambitions, remain relevant today.

George Schwab mentions in his introduction to Schmitt's *The Concept of the Political* that the 'traditional European sovereign state was no longer a politically viable entity in a rapidly changing world'.[67] According to Schwab, the infusion of militant ideology into politics undermined the state's foundations; an ideologically committed totalitarian party could set aside the principle on which 'jus publicum Europaeum' was based. Clever tactics made it possible for originally

---

[65] Dr John Campbell, 'WHO New Health Regulations' (YouTube, July 2023).

[66] F A Hayek, *The Constitution of Liberty* (The University of Chicago Press, 2011) pt 1, ch 2.

[67] Schmitt (n 40) 10.

controversial and unfavourable ideologies to become integrated into people's thinking without being noticed. Thus, Schmitt points out how hostile ideas can be turned into acceptable ones; in other words, how enemies become friends.

In the Age of COVID-19, societies went along with accepting experimental vaccines as protection against COVID-19. Though there was some hesitance at first, the intense promotion made more and more people get vaccinated – which encouraged others to do the same. The infusion of medical advice about how to fight against COVID-19 into the population by medical and political authorities undermined the rights of the individual to decide whether they wanted or did not want to take the vaccine. Later, governments of most countries made it mandatory to take the vaccines in order to keep jobs, go to public places and to travel.

In 1929, Schmitt wrote about technology as something refreshingly factual compared to theological, moral and economic questions, which are debatable forever. He believes, nations, generations and people of all religions, races and classes could make use of technical advances and become united. Schmitt refers to a lecture in 1927 by Max Scheler, who said that struggles and arguments about religious, social and national issues were mellowed when it came to technology because on this point there was agreement; technology appeared to be a domain of understanding and peace. On the other hand, Schmitt pointed out that technology is an instrument and a weapon and, because it is for everybody, cannot be neutral. Every people, culture, religion and state could use technology as a weapon and would use it as such much more frequently when they realised its usefulness. Technology would be used beneficially only as long as humanitarian morals remain in force. Schmitt thus perceives the danger of technology, the potential for the misuse of its horrific power, and the importance of morals if technology is to be used wisely.

Schmitt also makes the point that 'no programme … confers a right to dispose of the physical life of other human beings', and says that 'to demand seriously of human beings that they kill others and be prepared to die themselves so that trade and industry may flourish for the survivors … is sinister and crazy'.[68] Further, it is fraudulent to 'condemn war as homicide and then demand of man that they wage war, kill and be killed, so that there will never again be war'.[69]

In 2021, Fauci made headlines in the media because of over 4,000 released emails in relation to the COVID-19 pandemic; these showed his interest in and association with gain-of-function research and the Wuhan Institution of Virology ('WIV') in China.[70] Still, he kept his advisory role to the Biden administration until he stepped down in December 2022. Reports reveal that he appeared determined to make the experiment(s) with deadly pathogens happen despite the high risk to the health and life of humankind. An article in the *New York Post* refers to a paper by Fauci in 2012, in which he 'acknowledged the risky research could lead to serious lab accidents but the chance is rare, and the work is "important" because it helps the scientific community prepare for naturally occurring pandemics'.[71] Doesn't this remind us of the unrestrained chasing of desire that Hobbes and Rousseau warned against? And doesn't it recall Schmitt's condemnation of having men kill and be killed, 'so that there will never again be war?'[72]

The question is how gain-of-function research fits with any moral principles or with human rights. The concept of humanity is founded on key principles, which have endured through the history of mankind. In Plato's *Phaedo*, Socrates names justice, courage and moderation as the core virtues.[73] But in the 21st century, virtues in general, an

---

[68] Ibid 48.

[69] Ibid.

[70] Benedict Brook, 'Dr Anthony Fauci's Thoughts in the Early Days of Pandemic Revealed in 4000 Released Emails', *news.com.au* (Web Article, 4 June 2021).

[71] Gabriel Fonrouge, 'Fauci Once Argued for Risky Viral Experiments — Even if They Can Lead to Pandemic', *The New York Post* (Web Article, 28 May 2021).

[72] Schmitt (n 40) 209.

[73] Plato, *The Last Days of Socrates* (Penguin Books, 2010).

attachment to justice and the human right to life – a significant attribute of humanity – have been lost or has mutated into various new forms.

Man has elevated himself such that he can manipulate nature, create vaccines with the potential to extinguish humanity and keep his ambition away from the public eye. Where have morals gone, particularly responsibility and respect for humanity?

Even though the experiments were known to be a potential hazard for humanity, they were conducted. The central article of the Universal Declarations of Human Rights,[74] namely, Article 3, saying that 'Everyone has the right to life' must have been overlooked or not given enough weight in the pursuit of gain-of-function research.

IX. Concluding Comments: The Power of a New World Order and the Harm to Humanity

During the COVID-19 pandemic, man entered a perilous time. It is unlikely that a new virus like COVID-19 could have emerged and spread like wildfire had there not already been fundamental cracks in our societies. Clearly, values have declined for years and thus, respect for our laws.

Zimmermann points out by referring to Hayek how important the relation between the rule of law and the moral tradition of the community is. And he explains that 'the realisation of the rule of law effectively depends on how widely the ideal of legality is embraced and valued by the general community as an important societal achievement'.[75] But that embracing of legality and values is missing in societies today.

Instead, and as evident with the COVID-19 health crisis, man

---

[74] 'Universal Declaration of Human Rights', *United Nations* (Web Page, 10 December 1948)

[75] Augusto Zimmermann and Gabriël Moens, 'Vaccinations, Coercion and the Rule of Law', *Quadrant* (Web Article, 17 August 2021).

seems obsessed with pursuing his desires irrespective of the harm he does to others. Thus, this article aims to highlight the risk of pursuing desires – including the desire for power – without heeding virtue.

The present world crisis of COVID-19 shows how the misuse of knowledge in science like with gain-of-function research can become a risk to humanity when research is accepted to continue despite its hazard for the man. Moreover, human rights and the needs of the citizens were curbed through emergency policies; constituents who opposed vaccination were discriminated against. Essential information was kept from the public. Some people in power exploited opportunities for personal benefits.

When 'the object of man's desire, is not to enjoy once only … but to assure forever, the way of his future desire',[76] he is driven by a constant urge for more, which can be a restless desire for reasoning in science or the power over other humans for the sake of authority, fame or financial benefits. And because man knows 'how to do something else when he wills',[77] Hobbes warns us about the downsides of man's aspirations when he disregards – and indeed dismantles – morals.[78]

---

[76] Hobbes (n 4) 66.

[77] Hobbes (n 4) 8.

[78] Monika Nagel, *Our Moral Ills: The Origins of COVID-19* (Inspiring Publishers, 2023).

10

Institutional Despotism: A Preliminary Etiology

STEVEN ALAN SAMSON[*]

ABSTRACT

The capture of the administrative state by a Gramsci-style "long march through the institutions" grew out of a cultural/sexual revolution that lifted identity politics from its once precarious position within the rough-and-tumble of interest group competition into an almost unassailable protected status.[1] The question under consideration here is whether pluralistic liberalism as a governing philosophy has the spiritual reserves to revitalize, defend, and preserve its institutional expressions in the American constitutional tradition. This third in a series of articles focuses on the factors which help account for the transition from the institutional liberty depicted in Interposition: Magistrates as Shields Against Tyranny to institutional despotism.[2]

Many of those very attributes of the institution proper, which make it so valuable in the service of liberty, constitute its inconvenience

---

[1] Antonio Gramsci adopted Machiavelli's idea of creating "new modes and orders" for regulating society. Dante Germino, *Antonio Gramsci: Architect of a New Politics* (Louisiana State University Press, 1965) 225-27; Steven Alan Samson, 'A Strategy of Subversion' (2020) (Mar-Apr) *The Market for Ideas* 22.

[2] I have examined this topic from many angles since at least 1970. This article continues a line analysis begun in earlier articles in *The Western Australian Jurist*. It draws liberally from several of my published articles in *The Market for Ideas*. They include such titles as 'Capturing the Commanding Heights', 'Breaking the Long Truce', and 'Edward Rozek: Bearing Witness'. See also 'Interposition: Magistrates as Shields Against Tyranny' (2020) 11 *Western Australian Jurist* 301.

[*] Professor (ret), Helms School of Government, Liberty University.

and danger when the institution is used against it. It is a bulwark, and may protect the enemy of liberty. It is like the press. Modern liberty or civilization cannot dispense with it, yet it may be used as its keenest enemy. – Francis Lieber (1853)[3]

The conscious and intelligent manipulation of the organized habits and opinions of the masses is an important element of democratic society. Those who manipulate this unseen mechanism of society constitute an invisible government which is the ruling power of our country. – Edward Bernays (1928)[4]

A man is not primarily a witness against something. A witness, in the sense that I am using the word, is a man whose life and faith are so completely one that when the challenge comes to step out and testify for his faith, he does so, disregarding all risks, accepting all consequences. – Whittaker Chambers (1952)[5]

I. Voice Lessons

How do we develop the eyes to see and the ears to hear? The best teachers equip us to resist temptation and recognise deception. They enable us to develop the vision to discern truth and the voice to tell it. 'Take everything with a grain of salt' my father advised me more than once. As I went off to college in 1966 to study political science he urged me to get under the wing of Edward J Rozek, a Polish *emigré* who fought first for Poland at the outset of the Second World War, then escaped his imprisoned country to serve as a reconnaissance officer under British command. Blinded in a tank explosion, he underwent several surgeries to remove shrapnel and restore his eyesight.

After the war, Edward Rozek moved to New York City with $50 in his pockets. He worked at a dairy and an auto shop to save up for

---

[3] Francis Lieber, *On Civil Liberty and Self-Government* [1853] (J B Lippincott, 3rd ed, 1877) 315.

[4] Edward Bernays, *Propaganda* (IG, 2005) 37.

[5] Whittaker Chambers, *Witness* (Random House, 1952) 5.

admission to Harvard. He earned scholarships, continued on to a PhD in Soviet studies, and published a pathbreaking study entitled *Allied Wartime Diplomacy: A Pattern in Poland*. A decade after his arrival in Boulder, Colorado, I began my journey – under his guiding eye – from the life of an interested yet detached observer to that of a witness. In a 1998 article I reflected on what his mentorship meant to me:

> Eugen Rosenstock-Huessy's explanation in *Out of Revolution* of 'why teaching is a public trust' is perfectly natural to me, for I have sat under a genuine "public professor" who addressed critical issues and who 'uttered his "All or nothing" from his public *Katheder* (chair).' Dr. Rozek embodies the old ideal of the university as the keeper of the nation's conscience.[6]

What made Edward Rozek a great teacher also made him an inconvenience to the petty tyrants – you find them everywhere – who intend to rule or ruin. Sometimes despots style themselves "Communists," "anarchists," "capitalists," or "civil libertarians." Some become masters of deceit.

Serving on a committee to select speakers for the annual World Affairs Conference, Dr Rozek quickly discovered that the deck was stacked against conservatives. After students petitioned for a more balanced program, he launched an alternative forum, which, unlike the Marxist-oriented World Affairs Conference, was not taxpayer-financed. By 1964, he had made himself *persona non grata* with the university administration. Reflecting on his career and his considerable influence in the wider world, I wrote:

> I am impressed by the men, like Sidney Hook, Edward Teller, [Aleksandr Solzhenitsyn, Vladimir Bukovsky,] and Nikolai Tolstoy, he brought to campus through the W. F. Dyde Forum

---

[6] Steven Alan Samson, 'Edward Rozek: A Teacher's Gift' [1998] (Spring) *Tenth Presbyterian Church* 15; see Eugen Rosenstock-Huessy, *Out of Revolution: Autobiography of Western Man* (William Morrow, 1938) 397-99.

and his Institute for the Study of Comparative Politics and Ideologies, which is held in the summer. My first real lesson in journalistic dissimulation came the morning after a talk by Milovan Drachkovich at the W. F. Dyde Forum in 1967 when the student newspaper carried an account filled with incredible distortions. How could the writer even have been in the audience? I wrote a letter to the editor in protest. My letter was published, but in mangled form.[7]

The hostility toward Dr Rozek by the administration as well as the campus newspaper compelled me to choose sides. Campus – including the Hill district – in the late 1960s was an often-bewildering hodge-podge of New Age spirituality, tie-dyed hippie fashions, "Unisex" couture, the drug culture, and radical anti-war organising on campus. It was nicknamed "Baghdad by the Flatirons" in the student-run daily newspaper. Before I became a commuter student in my junior year, I frequented the bookstores and often the movie theater. When *The Graduate* came to the theater late in 1967, long lines of students wrapped around the block, waiting to gain admission, during the remainder of the school year. During the huge rallies and anti-war marches in the late 1960s, Boulder was also tagged "Berkeley East." Campus organisers were emboldened by success.

In December 1969, I finished my undergraduate studies, then enrolled the following month in my first graduate courses: American Political Thought under Curtis Martin, Soviet Foreign Policy under Edward Rozek, and Research Methods under Dayton McKean. Although I did not specialise in Soviet studies, I took all the courses I could from my mentor, both as an undergraduate and as a graduate student.

Campus turmoil reached a fever pitch near the end of the Spring term, early in June 1970, when four young people were killed at Kent

---

[7] Ibid 16.

State University during an anti-war rally after equally young National Guardsmen opened fire. The incident, designated the Kent State massacre, triggered a massive response around the country and led most professors on our campus to heed a call to cancel final exams. Buildings were surrounded by human barricades as protesters hunched down on elbows and knees to block access.

Some lessons are best learned when students are compelled to decide whether a preference rises to the level of a conviction. Life is full of forced choice questions.

Dr. Rozek confronted us in class with the specter of man's inhumanity to man. Who could fail to hear the force of words that rose from the depth of personal experience, that rebuked the proud halls and mighty towers that could not shroud the [life] that pulsated from this man when he stood in front of his students? [His] was a dignified voice, a cultivated voice. It took much effort for me to hear him, because it was also to my ears a foreign voice. In time and with effort, I learned to attune my ears to the cadences of his speech.

And what a remarkable voice it is! He always spoke with quiet authority, with conviction, about the blight of totalitarian oppression and, closer to home, the petty tyrannies that waylay us. If he was, on the one hand, the lightning rod of conservatism on campus, he was also, first and foremost, my teacher: *our* teacher. Few men have commanded such respect from their students. We crossed picket lines in 1970 to take our final exams. We voted with our feet (one of his favorite phrases in another context). Our contract with him did not contain an escape clause.[8]

Life may be full of forced-choice questions, but Dr Rozek never gave so-called objective tests. We had essay tests in class, which

---

[8] Ibid 15.

forced us to master the art of thinking through what we had read. We also learned the art of writing. I learned to be succinct. I can say in retrospect that, through critical challenges posed by my teachers over many years, I had found my own voice by the time I began graduate studies. I moved back to Oregon – my home state – late in 1975 and returned to the classroom: first to teacher's college, then to adjunct teaching at several colleges, then to a doctoral program at the University of Oregon in 1977.

The all-out assault on Edward Rozek was launched in 1980 following his campaign for a position on the Board of Regents, triggering a smear campaign which led to his defeat in the primary election. Although a Board of Regents investigation exonerated him of any wrongdoing concerning the alleged misuse of funds to bring speakers to campus, a special prosecutor was appointed by a Boulder County judge in November.

The following August, while he was out of town, both his home and his office were raided by university police officers. Despite a failure to find supportive evidence, multiple felony counts were filed against him. Dr. Rozek's defense attorney, knowing the reputation of the special prosecutor, warned him that he might be arrested in class, in front of his students. As Dr Rozek later recalled:

> When my attorney reconfirmed that such a thing was possible and that there was nothing he could do to protect me, my disbelief turned to horror and then to a sense of utter helplessness. Upon reflection, I reconciled myself to such a prospect and accepted it stoically. If such a ghastly thing happened, it would be a reflection not on me but on our legal system which allow a few unscrupulous 'lawmen' to terrorize their victims through abuse of police power.[9]

---

[9] Ann Donnelly, 'The Edward Rozek Case: Profile in Academic Courage' in Les Csorba, III (ed), *Academic License: The War on Academic Freedom* (UCA Books, 1988) 275.

With members of the press to witness, Dr Rozek was arrested on April 15, 1983 and booked on 22 felony counts.[10] The press was conspicuously absent when he was exonerated months later. I can say in retrospect that, through critical challenges posed by my teachers over many years, I found my own voice by the time I began graduate studies. One of the best tributes to Edward Rozek was written during that period. The philosopher Sidney Hook dedicated his book *Academic Freedom and Academic Anarchy* to him as follows:

To

Edward J. Rozek—

Embattled fighter for free men, free society,

And the free university against fascism,

Communism, and totalitarian liberalism.[11]

How ironic that Hook, a student of John Dewey, the original philosopher of American liberalism, should detect something illiberal at the heart of American liberalism. Francis Lieber recognised the same danger a century earlier. The question under consideration here is whether liberalism as a governing philosophy has the spiritual reserves to revitalise, defend, and preserve its institutional expressions. Somewhere along the way both American liberalism and the political science profession took a wrong turn.

II. Dégringolade

Protracted Conflict is the name of one of the books Dr Rozek had me read when I started graduate studies in early 1970. The sixth chapter makes a shocking admission concerning Cold War politics which is difficult to credit but which, upon further consideration, may help

---

[10] Ibid 278: 'The plot against Rozek, as reportedly explained later by one of [the prosecutor's] assistants, was designed to drive the professor to take his own life'.

[11] Sidney Hook, *Academic Freedom and Academic Anarchy* (Delta, 1971).

explain so much of postwar history – including the loss of civil liberty in academia – within a larger strategic context.

> Since 1945, the Communists have marked out the non-Communist territory as the "war zone" and have succeeded in confining the Cold War to this part of the world. World opinion unconsciously accepted the Communist rule of international conduct: under its dispensation the West must condone Communist forays into the non-Communist "war zone" and abstain from launching counterthrusts into the Communist "peace zone." The Communists, in short, have been allowed to inscribe the territorial limits of the protracted conflict.[12]

To understand how the Communists could be so confident requires admitting that something had changed in the West. Nearly a century earlier, the European powers thwarted Russian imperial ambitions and propped up the declining Ottoman Empire via the Crimean War. A decade after Crimea, Otto von Bismarck used a series of wars to maneuver a rising Prussian kingdom onto a collision course with post-revolutionary France under Louis Napoleon. Both states were early experiments in what James Burnham later called "the managerial revolution." One short-lived consequence of Napoleon's defeat in the Franco-Prussian War was the Paris Commune. The birth of a new German Empire was signed and sealed in the Hall of Mirrors at Versailles Palace in 1871. Another decade later, the Berlin Conference represented Bismarck's attempt to redirect imperial ambitions away from Europe and toward Africa. The younger Kaiser Wilhelm II later sacked Bismarck but lacked Bismarck's finesse. In the absence of strong statesmanship, Europe soon began its descent toward war. The phrase *fin de siècle* captures the mood of the time: a lively swirl of artistic innovation, political intrigue, and general optimism.

---

[12] Robert Strausz-Hupé, William R Kintner, James E Dougherty and Alvin J Cottrell, *Protracted Conflict* (Harper Colophon, 1963) 85-6.

Yet by the late nineteenth century cultural and civilizational structures once based on civil liberty and self-government began to be dismantled in favor of an ever more interventionist administrative state which generated impatience with the pace of reform. The historian Perry Miller noted: 'Both America and England absorbed during the nineteenth century two separate "German invasions". The first came in the form of literature.' It gave rise to Transcendentalism in American literature and the public education movement. 'The second invasion came armed with a dialectic, a severe discipline, a rationale of history, and a technique of disputation powerful enough to shatter all opposition.' German Idealism filled niches in the American mind once inhabited by Scottish realism. Although supportive of Christian morality, Idealism proved to be a transitional step to another form of process philosophy which drew on evolutionary biology and then genetics.

America's first political science professor, Francis Lieber, criticised the philosophical implications of both Hegel and Darwin. Lieber was a major cultural figure who had run the first American gymnastics school in Boston, started the first swimming school, launched the *Encyclopaedia Americana* in Philadelphia, met and corresponded with Alexis de Tocqueville, taught in South Carolina and New York, and devised the code of military conduct during the American Civil War which influenced the later Hague and Geneva Conventions.

Following Lieber's death, prominent German-educated political scientists and their students introduced and cultivated a taste for the German administrative efficiency. The legal scholar Philip Hamburger has observed: 'The adoption of European administrative ideas is a direct continuation of the absolutism that persisted in administrative form on the Continent.' Given the sheer size and diversity of the country at the time, the adoption of such ideas as civil service systems and regulatory agencies gradually led to 'a transfer of legislative power to the knowledge class.' The Wisconsin Idea and the Oregon System were also introduced around the turn of the twentieth century to bring a greater measure of direct democracy at the state and local level. Minnesota, Wisconsin, North Dakota, Oregon, and California became Progressive strongholds. Along with Populism, Progressivism had the effect of weakening traditional political structures and redirecting the reform impulse to the national level.

Woodrow Wilson and his rival Henry Cabot Lodge were both charter members of this knowledge class. As a political scientist and college president, Hamburger noted, 'Wilson welcomed administrative governance. The people could still have their republic, but much legislative power would be shifted out of an elected body and into the hands of the right sort of people'.[13]

As President, Woodrow Wilson once notoriously said to a British envoy that 'I am going to teach the South American republics to elect good men'.[14] Similarly, the Great War for him was a "war for righteousness." His Fourteen Points – a manifesto for a new postwar international order – were issued in part due to the Bolshevik takeover of Russia, Lenin's Peace Deal, and Trotsky's publication of secret deals the Allies had made with the Tsar during the war. Wilson's declaration was framed idealistically but had a devastating effect in practice.

Wilson also applied the same humanitarian sentiment to his own people, an attitude that carried over to the rising knowledge class he inspired. As Walter McDougall concluded:

> This class includes all who are more attached to the authority of knowledge than the authority of local political communities. Which is not to say that they have been particularly knowledgeable but that their sense of affinity with cosmopolitan knowledge, rather than their local connectedness, has been the

---

[13] Philip Hamburger, *The Administrative Threat* (Encounter Books, 2007) 55.

[14] Walter A McDougall, *Promised Land, Crusader State* (Houghton Mifflin, 1997) 131.

foundation of their influence and identity. And in appreciating the authority they have attributed to their knowledge, and distrusting the tumultuous politics of a diverse people, they have gradually moved legislative power out of Congress and into administrative agencies – to be exercised, in more genteel ways, by persons like … themselves.[15]

The Great War had a major demoralising effect on all parties. It was also a harrowing whirlpool of treachery and broken promises. Governing cabinets, like revolutionary movements, have been unapologetic for their sudden shifts of policy. A guilty conscience can certainly weaken morale. So might fear of another and even more devastating world war. Postwar Europe was ripe for Revolution.

Vladmir Lenin knew the importance of capturing the "commanding heights" of a political/cultural system, a lesson that seems to be lost on those "conservatives" who simply react to every slow curve-ball that the Left lets drift lazily near the plate. It means 'capturing the robes' of authority, as Gary North put it, who often remarked: 'You can't beat something with nothing.'[16] Any strategy worth its salt requires attention to detail and an eye for "the long game." Divide and rule. Sexual politics and family breakdown became the vehicle of choice. The costs to society of the culture war that followed are too often shrugged off as collateral damages, whether to families, communities, or personal reputations. It is a real war with real casualties.

The interwar period is a blind spot to most Americans. It was a revolutionary period of far greater magnitude than the Revolutions of 1848, liberal revolutions which, though thwarted, smoldered in the background. The German and British welfare states were meant to

---

[15] Ibid 52. As Russell Kirk acidly put it later: 'The humanitarian believes in brother-hood: that is, 'Be my brother,' he says, 'or I'll kill you.' He aspires to assimilate others to his mode and substance'. – Russell Kirk, *The Wise Men Know What Wicked Things Are Written on the Sky* (Regnery Gateway, 1987) 28-29.

[16] Gary North, 'Capturing the Robes', *Gary North's Specific Answers* (Web Article, 4 June 2016). The "robes" here are academic, ministerial, and judicial.

inoculate against outright socialism. But as a result, far from being immunised, the West eventually succumbed to revolutions which were never identified as such. America's Progressivism was intertwined with Fabian socialism, which gave rise to the Intercollegiate Socialist Society in 1905, the League for Industrial Democracy, Minnesota's Farmer-Labor Party, and, later, Students for a Democratic Society. The Fabian Society in Britain gave birth to the Labour Party.

Four empires were dismantled in whole or part after the Great War. After the Second World War, the remaining colonial empires began to unravel – at the insistence of both Roosevelt and Stalin – as a result of the Second World War. It was part of the price for America's assistance in keeping Europe out of German hands and, later, the Russian orbit.

One consequence of the Second World War was to effectively leave the Soviet Union in control of the commanding heights. As for the knowledge class – from Roosevelt's "brains trust" to Kennedy's "best and brightest" – it is important to recognise the effect of years of wartime propaganda in favor of the wartime alliance of the West with the Soviet Union, especially following the German invasion of Russia in June 1941. The standard view of the "McCarthy era"[17] in polite society began to unravel only after Allen Weinstein concluded in *Perjury: The Hiss-Chambers Case*[18] – contrary to his expectation – that Alger Hiss had lied about his role as a Soviet agent. Hiss, the Roosevelt adviser who presided over the initial meeting of the United

---

[17] Two dissenting accounts which generated the usual critical wrath are by two journalists: M Stanton Evans, *Blacklisted by History: The Untold Story of Senator Joe McCarthy and His Fight Against America's Enemies* (Three Rivers Press, 2007); and Diana West, *American Betrayal: The Secret Assault on Our Nation's Character* (St Martin's Press, 2013). Unfortunately, two other books which offered insight into Soviet operations were effectively "consigned to the dustbin of history" by a wall of silence in the American media: Ion Mihai Pacepa and Ronald J Rychlak, *Disinformation: Former Spy Chief Reveals Secret Strategies for Undermining Freedom, Attacking Religion, and Promoting Terrorism* (WND Books, 2013); and Vladimir Bukovsky, tr Alyona Kojevnikov, *Judgment in Moscow: Soviet Crimes and Western Complicity* (Ninth of November Press, 2019).

[18] Allen Weinstein, *The Hiss-Chambers Case* (Alfred A Knopf, 1978).

Nations in April 1945, was convicted only of perjury in January 1950. By contrast, the whistle-blower, Whittaker Chambers, saw his career destroyed. His account of events, including "A Letter to My Children", and his effort to recover his tarnished reputation is detailed in his book *Witness* (1952). Near the conclusion of his account, Chambers wrote:

> No feature of the Hiss Case is more obvious, or more troubling as history, than the jagged fissure, which it did not so much open as reveal, between the plain men and women of the nation, and those who affected to act, think and speak for them. It was, not invariably, but in general, the "best people" who were for Alger Hiss and who were prepared to go to almost any length to protect and defend him. It was the enlightened and the powerful, the clamorous proponents of the open mind and the common man, who snapped their minds shut in a pro-Hiss psychosis, of a kind which, in an individual patient, means the simple failure of the ability to distinguish between reality and unreality, and, in a nation, is a warning of the end.

> It was the great body of the nation, which, not invariably, but in general, kept open its mind in the Hiss Case, waiting for the returns to come in. It was they who suspected what forces disastrous to the nation were at work in the Hiss Case, and had suspected that they were at work long before there was a Hiss Case, while most of the forces of enlightenment were poohpoohing the Communist danger and calling every allusion to it a witch hunt. It was they who, when the battle was over, first caught its real meaning.[19]

III. Effacing the Image of God

In 'How Civilizations Fall', Kenneth Minogue showed how a strategy of subversion – in this instance by radical feminism – can leave the defenders defenseless against what Robert Kennedy called an "enemy

---

[19] Chambers (n 6) 793-94.

within." Marx provided the model [a "proletarian" revolution] for all subsequent movements aiming to take power. His "make your own tribe" kit was found useful by nationalists, anarchists, and many brands of socialist. In socially mobile European states, the workers mostly found better things to do with their time than waste it on revolutionary committees and the baby talk of political demonstrations. Something new was needed.

It was provided by such socialists as Mussolini and Lenin who adopted the principle of the Praetorian Guard: a tightly knit vanguard party, which could use the masses as ventriloquial dummies and seek power on its own terms. This development was part of a wider tendency towards the emergence of oligarchies ruling through democratic slogans.[20]

Cries for "reparations," objections to "cultural appropriation," and demands for "open borders" are simply the latest iterations of a successful formula. These tactics are similarly designed to discredit and discourage the guardians of the existing order, often by threatening to turn family members and neighbors against them.

In this respect, revolutionaries are assisted by larger forces which already have had a long-term disruptive effect. Rapid change, like a forced-march double-time, keeps everything and everyone off balance. Two forces of modernity which have been intertwined virtually from the start are, first, the secularisation and mechanisation of the world picture through philosophical changes which both preceded and accompanied the scientific revolution, and, second, the transformation of traditional social structures, including property laws, which likewise preceded and accompanied the Industrial Revolution.

Joseph Schumpeter described the 'process of industrial mutation' which revolutionises the structure of the economy from within

---

[20] Kenneth Minogue, 'How Civilizations Fall', *The New Criterion* (Web Article, April 2001).

as 'a gale of creative destruction.'[21] From this standpoint, old industries are expendable and, by implication, so is the workforce that sustains them. When the American economy began to "de-industrialise" following the Second World War, the costs to society were incalculable.

Similarly, our imaginative landscape has been radically reshaped within living memory. As Neil Postman once put it:

> Introduce the alphabet to a culture and you change its cognitive habits, its social relations, its notions of community, history and religion. Introduce the printing press with movable type, and you do the same. Introduce speed-of-light transmission of images and you make a cultural revolution. Without a vote. Without polemics. Without guerrilla resistance. Here is ideology, pure if not serene. Here is ideology without words, and all the more powerful for their absence. All that is required to make it stick is a population that devoutly believes in the inevitability of progress. And in this sense, all Americans are devout Marxists, for we believe nothing if not that history is moving us toward some preordained paradise and that technology is the force behind that movement.[22]

Postman describes three revolutions. Vishal Mangalwadi sees the same: 'The 'word' – language, laws, literature – are a nation's software; its soul.' The Carolingian Renaissance of the ninth century renewed western civilization with its educational revolution led by Charlemagne, Alcuin, and Einhard. The print revolution led to the Protestant Reformation and gave rise to the scientific and industrial revolutions. 'Reformed nations developed because they educated the soul – minds, hearts, character – with God's [creatively and

---

[21] Joseph Schumpeter, *Capitalism, Socialism and Democracy* (Harper, 3rd ed, 1950) 82, 83.

[22] Neil Postman, *Amusing Ourselves to Death: Public Discourse in the Age of Show Business* (Penguin, 1985) 158.

innovatively challenging] words.'[23] But in the beginning of the third – the brave new world of cultural revolution – is not the word but the icon, as Postman observes. The culture of the now post-Christian West is being rapidly transformed by ever more invasive ideological pathogens, holdovers of the second revolution. These pathogens are transmitted through a proliferating variety of social media which simultaneously circulate and enforce novel representations of reality – *avant-garde* yet somehow socially-authoritative. At the same time, they neutralise, suppress, or boldly repudiate the customs, traditions, and wisdom literature which – in the manner of Rudyard Kipling's 'The Gods of the Copybook Headings' – once provided civilization's first line of defense. Postman concluded: 'There are two ways by which the spirit of a culture may be shriveled. In the first – the Orwellian – culture becomes a prison. In the second – the Huxleyan – culture becomes a burlesque.'[24] Unfortunately, the sense of reality associated with our cultural revolution tends to be all-inclusive. It is both/and rather than simply either/or.

Today we are discovering many other ways to shrivel a culture. Just follow the money, literally. The corporate world has become a major transmission belt for the ongoing cultural revolution and what Walter Lippmann called 'the manufacture of consent.'[25] One expression is the promotion of novel human rights in documents ranging from the Declaration of the Rights of Man and Citizen, the Humanist Manifestos, and the Universal Declaration of Human Rights, particularly numbers 22-28. As summarized by Philippe Bénéton:

> The rights of man are born in a radical break from Christianity (and the ancient heritage it had assimilated). According to the Christian idea of equality, or to Christian natural law, men

---

[23] Cited in Vincent C Anigbogu, *Manifesting the Kingdom: Essential Leadership and Management Strategies for the End Time Church* (Ayowole Productions, 2021) ix.

[24] Ibid.

[25] See Walter Lippmann, *Public Opinion* (Harcourt, Brace and Company, 1922) ch 15.

share a common vocation, they are governed by the same ends [*i.e.*, 'to glorify God and enjoy Him forever']. In the modern version of equality, what men have in common is the right to pursue different ends, the right to have nothing in common except this right. Ancient natural law appeals to nature in order to remind man of his duties; modern natural law appeals to nature in order to loosen the reins of freedom...

The work of modern political thought, initiated by Machiavelli and then by Hobbes, and further developed by Locke, issues in a liberal or procedural solution: the duties of man give way to his rights, and the rules of life give way to the rules of the game designed to allow men, divided amongst themselves, to pursue each his own way, his own interest.[26]

Pitirim Sorokin regarded the rise of modernity as a shift from an ideational to a sensate era – from a commitment to a common spiritual enterprise to an ever-fragmenting exaltation of will and appetite.

Stripping man of his divine charisma and grace, sensate morality, ethics, and law have reduced him to an electron-proton complex or reflex mechanism devoid of any sanctity or end-value. "Liberating" him from the "superstitions" of the categorical imperatives, they have taken from him an invisible armor that unconditionally protected him, his dignity, his sanctity, and his inviolability. Divested of this armor, he finds himself but a plaything in the hand of the most fortuitous forces. If he is useful for this or that, he may be treated decently and cared for as we care for a useful animal. If he is harmful, he can be "liquidated," as we exterminate harmful snakes. Without any compunction, remorse. No guilt, no crime, no valid reason, is needed for such a liquidation. The

---

[26] Philippe Bénéton, *Equality by Default: An Essay on Modernity as Confinement* , tr Ralph Hancock (ISI Books, 2004) 5-7.

> very existence of a man or group as an unintentional obstacle is enough to eliminate them. … In this tornado of unleashed sensate passions, the whole of sensate culture is being blown to pieces and swept away.
>
> As has happened several times before, in the insanity of a decadent mentality, sensate man again today is destroying the sensate house he has so proudly been building for the past five centuries.[27]

One consequence is reductionism. 'A rat is a pig is a dog is a boy', says Ingrid Newkirk. 'They are all mammals'. The Oregon Health and Science University has become a marketplace for transgender surgeries. When every remnant of wisdom is kicked to the curb, including the Hippocratic Oath, why not? Given the continuing fascination with social and genetic engineering, another dystopia to consider is C S Lewis's *That Hideous Strength*, which dramatises *The Abolition of Man*. As Lewis pointed out during the Second World War, the power to redefine what is human – to deprive people of life, freedom, and dignity – is the power to control the past, present, and future. It seeks to abolish man by effacing the image of God in man.

By contrast, B F Skinner's *Walden Two* was intended as a *eu*-topia. In *Beyond Freedom and Dignity*, Skinner responded directly to Lewis:

> What is being abolished is autonomous man – the inner man, the homunculus, the possessing demon, the man defended by the literatures of freedom and dignity.
>
> His abolition has long been overdue. Autonomous man is a device used to explain what we cannot explain in any other way. He has been constructed from our ignorance, and as our understanding increases, the very stuff of what he is composed vanishes. Science does not dehumanize man, it de-

---

[27] Pitirim A Sorokin, *The Crisis of Our Age: The Social and Cultural Outlook* (E P Dutton, 1941) 164, 165.

homunculizes him, and it must do so if it is to prevent the abolition of the human species.[28]

Perhaps the seeds of this de-homunculisation of man were planted at the outset of what Paul Valéry called 'a conquest by method,' to which he was decidedly ambivalent. The subjects of Valéry's historical and political essays were "Mind" and "Method," symbolised by M Teste (*tête*) and embodied in the figure of René Descartes. If the classic statement of the scientific method was Francis Bacon's *The New Organon* (1620), the confusion of science with positivism – with scientism – may have begun a year earlier with a dream of Descartes on the night of 10-11 November 1619. To Descartes thenceforth space or extension became the fundamental reality in the world, motion the source of all change, and mathematics the only relation between its parts. He had made of nature a machine and nothing but a machine; purposes and spiritual significance had alike been banished. Intoxicated by his vision and his success [in optics], he boasted, 'Give me extension and motion, and I will construct the universe'.[29]

Valéry struggled with the implication nearly three centuries later. However plausible or implausible this mechanistic philosophy may have sounded to his contemporaries, Descartes's dream gave birth to modern philosophy and launched the tradition of French rationalism. It also produced that staple of undergraduate philosophy classes, Descartes's *Discourse on Method*, with its famous line: *Cogito ergo sum*, 'I think, therefore I am.'

But – here is another irony – English empiricism via Thomas Hobbes had much the same starting point: introspection. As Protagoras put it: 'Man is the measure (or measurer) of all things.' Whether or not Descartes fully understood how precarious were the philosophical

---

[28] B F Skinner, *Beyond Freedom and Dignity* (Bantam/Vintage, 1971) 191.

[29] John Herman Randall Jr. *The Making of the Modern* Mind: *A Survey of the Intellectual Background of the Present Age* (Houghton Mifflin, rev ed, 1940) 241-42.

foundations he helped lay, Thomas Hobbes was already prepared to use the new scientific method to reduce man to matter in motion and thereby prop up his own philosophical hedonism. As Floyd Matson put it in *The Broken Image* (1964):

> The original objection soon to be made against Descartes by the philosophers of England and the *philosophes* of France was not that he was too mechanical, but that he was not mechanical enough. The first and the most formidable of these critics was Thomas Hobbes, who had been personally assured by Galileo himself, of the of the correctness of his suspicion that 'the sole and adequate explanation of the universe is to be found in terms of body and motion.' …
>
> With Hobbes … the mechanical philosophy came fully of age; and its major ramifications over the next three centuries are nearly all foreshadowed in his works. His theory of knowledge, in its tough-minded rejection of metaphysics and its influence upon semantic precision, anticipates present-day logical positivism; his psychology contains the mechanistic outlines of behaviorism; and his political philosophy presents a systematic portrait of that totally rationalized new order toward which the vision of modern behavioral scientists has turned no less irresistibly in the unending quest for certainty, predictability, and control over the anarchic realm of politics and human affairs.[30]

Three centuries later, Aldous Huxley was one of many to use these philosophical foundations, including hedonism, to support "sexual liberation."

> For myself as, no doubt, for most of my contemporaries, the philosophy of meaninglessness was essentially an instrument

---

[30] Floyd W Matson, *The Broken Image: Man, Science and Society* (Anchor Books, 1966) 6, 7.

of liberation. The liberation we desired was simultaneously liberation from a certain political and economic system and liberation from a certain system of morality. We objected to the morality because it interfered with our sexual freedom; we objected to the political and economic system because it was unjust. The supporters of these systems claimed that in some way they embodied the meaning (a Christian meaning, they insisted) of the world. There was one admirably simple method of confuting these people and at the same time justifying ourselves in our political and erotic revolt; we could deny that the world had any meaning whatsoever.[31]

IV. IMAGINARY REGIMES

During the Great Depression and after the destruction wrought by the Great War, John Maynard Keynes wrote *The General Theory of Employment, Interest, and Money* (1936). A well-known lesson that he imparted was simply this:

The ideas of economists and political philosophers, both when they are right and when they are wrong, are more powerful than is commonly understood. Indeed the world is ruled by little else. Practical men, who believe themselves to be quite exempt from any intellectual influence, are usually the slaves of some defunct economist. Madmen in authority, who hear voices in the air, are distilling their frenzy from some academic scribbler of a few years back.[32]

As early as Plato, a popular genre of political philosophy has

---

[31] Aldous Huxley, *Ends and Means* (Chatto & Windus, 1946) 273.

[32] John Maynard Keynes, *The General Theory of Employment, Interest, and Money* (Palgrave Macmillan, 1936) 383. A similar observation comes from Henrich Heine: 'Mark this well, you proud men of action: You are nothing but the unwitting agents of the men of thought who often, in quiet self-effacement, mark out most exactly all your doings in advance.' <https://www.goodreads.com/quotes/7375214-mark-this-well-you-proud-men-of-action-you-are>.

concerned itself with founding visions. In the case of Plato's *Republic* the founding is a homeopathic diagnosis of the political ambitions of two of Plato's brothers – Glaucon and Adeimantus – who were presumably among the Athenian youth whom Socrates had been charged with corrupting. Drawing motifs from Homer and the other poets, the Socrates of *The Republic* examines the health of the State – the Soul writ large – in order to dramatically expose the ailments of the civil body politic which he maintained were the true threats to public and personal health. By modeling an ideal city-in-speech – a well-balanced commonwealth – Socrates strives to enable Plato's brothers to free themselves from slavery to changing opinions and passions. The *Republic* addresses a question: What would it take to reconcile the interests of the calling of the Philosopher with the needs of the City?

Plato's dialogue has caused consternation down through the ages. Yet perhaps it was not meant to be the blueprint of what we would call an Ideal City. Perhaps Plato's interest was in defending what Russell Kirk called 'the permanent things.'[33]

Jacob Howland argues that Plato used the storyline of Homer's *Odyssey* as a template: 'the homeward quest of Odysseus is woven into the dialogue as a mythic subtext of its philosophic action.'[34] By symbolically recapitulating the trials of the wily Odysseus through the various scenes of the dialogue, the drama culminates in the Myth of Er. In this concluding myth, Odysseus, having recovered from his love of honor after wrestling – allegorically – with his inner demons, chooses at long last a soul of wisdom.

By way of sharp contrast, Machiavelli, who was called 'a teacher of evil' by Leo Strauss, contributed what he called a 'new science of politics' to this literary genre in *The Prince* and *The Discourses on Livy*. As the first modern political philosopher, Machiavelli drew on

---

[33] Russell Kirk, *Enemies of the Permanent Things: Observations of Abnormality in Literature and Politics* (Arlington House, 1960).

[34] Jacob Howland, *The Republic: The Odyssey of Philosophy* (Twayne, 1993) 32.

his diplomatic and literary experience to imagine himself the author of a unified Italian republic – purged of past imperfection – if only he could inspire a national saviour to rescue Italy from the hands of plundering invaders and foreign rulers. For this purpose he sought out a powerful patron.

Mark Hulliung maintains that other scholars have been 'wary to a fault of spelling out the extent of Machiavelli's paganism' and argues that it was directed 'to destroy part of the pagan tradition (Stoicism) and all of Christianity.'[35] Rather than a reformer, Machiavelli must be regarded as a revolutionary:

> To demythologize Machiavelli, to save him from his saviors, is to engage in an enterprise literally 'radical,' one that takes us to the 'roots' of the Western tradition, to our very origins, upon which Machiavelli commented so memorably. It is to have our heritage usurped or identified as our nemesis. Compared to this, Marx's indictment of liberalism, even when that attack was at its most shrill, was an unthreatening experience – an occurrence that never left the familiar and friendly world of 'humanism.'
>
> Political foundations, [Machiavelli] insisted, are violent, as are all returns to the beginning, all rededications to virtue; they, too, are violent, they take the established symbols of the classical tradition ... and transform them into something explosive. ...[36]

Indeed, Machiavelli – like his later revolutionary disciple Antonio Gramsci – constructs what Roger Scruton has called a 'culture of repudiation.'[37] He proposes a thorough repudiation of "the dead hand of the past." Hulliung adds:

---

[35] Mark Hulliung, *Citizen Machiavelli* (Princeton University Press, 1983) 245, 251.

[36] Ibid 255-56.

[37] See Roger Scruton, *The West and the Rest: Globalization and the Terrorist Threat* (ISI Books, 2002) 68-83.

> As a theorist of subversive methods, Machiavelli advised the politician to preserve the old names and symbols, even as he builds a new world: this is precisely what Machiavelli the political theorist does with our cultural heritage, the foundations. He tries to draw us into a position where every return to our cultural foundations, every conversation with the ancients, is a resurrection of Machiavelli and Machiavellism.[38]

Angelo Codevilla suggests that Machiavelli was even more radical than this. Not only does Machiavelli appropriate and redefine the existing language (or terms of political discourse), he would even substitute an entirely different language if that were possible. 'According to Machiavelli, there is a means of conquering men as final as the drawing of the plow over Carthage, but which leaves both men and material intact. That means consists of changing the terms in which people think.'[39] Four centuries before Gramsci, Machiavelli redefined virtue – reducing it to 'inhuman cruelty and animal cunning' – and introduced 'new modes and orders' designed to replace Classical and Christian political ethics, which meant redefining the language.[40] Angelo Codevilla commented on Machiavelli's strategy:

> Part of Machiavelli's plan of battle was to capture the word *virtue*. First, he disordered the words of which the concept of virtue consisted, then he reorganized them according to his 'new orders' to fight on his side. By doing so, he made it difficult for even the memory of virtue as it once was understood to enter political discourse.[41]

---

[38] Ibid 256.

[39] Niccolò Machiavelli, *The Prince* , tr Angelo M Codevilla (Yale University Press, 1997) xxi-xxii.

[40] Successful revolutions often leave the laws and institutions largely unchanged, as Aristotle observed and Augustus did. See Aristotle, *Politics*, bk IV, v, 3.

[41] Machiavelli (n 39) xxxvii. Every modern revolution changes the terms of political, moral, and cultural discourse. Consider the significance of changes in the calendar, weights and measures, greetings, forms of murder, and tonsorial/sartorial displays pioneered by the French revolutionaries.

Following the Reformation and the Wars of Religion, Thomas Hobbes similarly sought to place his own personal stamp of authority on a new political philosophy. Engaging in his own Cartesian doubt, Hobbes likewise attempted to purge the past of a Christian ethos and its hold on the imagination. Like Machiavelli, Hobbes takes himself as a representative man. Once again political philosophy becomes a specimen of autobiography and a tool of political ruthlessness.

Hobbes imagines his Leviathan state as an artificial man: a personal state which would represent – and embody – the people while reconciling within its corporate self their individual and collective ambitions and actions. Hobbes's influence on Jean-Jacques Rousseau should be evident here. Rousseau sought to purge the soul of social artifice, restore an imagined natural man, and reconcile individual desires with collective needs through a rather utilitarian – hedonistic – general will. Both writers sought to harness human motives, filter out divisive elements, and achieve a working consensus.

To account for human motivation, Hobbes borrowed from Thucydides a list of three principal causes of quarrel: a fierce competition for scarce goods, a fear-driven diffidence or insecurity, and a self-exalting desire for glory. In *The Passions and the Interests* (1977), Albert O Hirschman notes that in Hobbes's view men are motivated by a craving for honor, dignity, respect, and recognition.[42] While these are not virtues, as J Budziszewski points out, they can imitate or supplement virtuous motives much as the addition of Hamburger Helper enlarges the meal and extends the savor of the meat.[43]

Rousseau simplified Hobbes's list of motives into two categories: *amour de soi*, which aims to satisfy 'real needs' (the commodities of

---

[42] Albert O Hirschman, *The Passions and the Interests: Political Arguments for Capitalism Before Its Triumph* (Princeton University Press, 1977) 108.

[43] J Budziszewski, *The Revenge of Conscience: Politics and the Fall of Man* (Spence, 1999) 58.

life) by appropriating a limited amount of goods, and *amour de propre*, 'which is keyed to approval and admiration from our fellow men,' according to Hirschman, 'and which by definition has no limit.'[44] But the reach of human ambition is impeded only with great difficulty. The fertility of Rousseau's thought makes him the intellectual precursor of a wide range of subsequent ideological and political movements.

Adam Smith simplified human motivation even further by reducing the drive for economic advantage into this same desire for consideration on the part of others (ie, *amour propre*). The key here is not mere self-interest: 'It is not from the benevolence of the butcher, the brewer, or the baker that we expect our dinner, but from their regard to their own interest'. Rather, it is 'self-interest rightly understood', as Alexis de Tocqueville put it.[45] This is also the engine which drives market exchanges.

Friedrich Hayek based his theory of market freedom on the idea that market operations, freely conducted under the rule of law, would be homeostatic and produce a spontaneous order. This argues for of a constitutionally-limited government. It corresponds to what Francis Lieber called Anglican liberty, an idea which Hayek cited favorably.[46] Such liberty emerges out of practical experience with diverse and territorially-localized self-governing institutions: families, churches, municipalities, voluntary associations, universities, businesses, and the like, much like Althusius's idea of symbiosis. The best defense against a conquest of the system is to nurture these "little platoons," as Edmund Burke called them. Lieber based his theory of institutional liberty on the vital contribution of independent institutions to a healthy system of 'civil liberty and self-government.'

On the other side is a hierarchical centralisation of initiative that

---

[44] Hirschman (n 43) 109.

[45] Alexis de Tocqueville, *Democracy in America*, vol 2, pt 2, ch 8.

[46] Friedrich A Hayek, *The Constitution of Liberty* (University of Chicago Press, 1960) 55.

Lieber called Gallican liberty, resulting from the centralisation of royal and, later, revolutionary and republican administration in France. The German general theory of the State (*allgemeine Staatslehre*) and its administrative model of scientific management shaped early American political science in the early years, particularly after Lieber's day.[47]

Both Hobbes and Rousseau recognised the drawbacks of the dissociative individualism that Tocqueville and Lieber later identified and named. Both raised the question of how a collective "We" may be derived by transcending the "I." The social contract theorists – led by Hobbes, Locke, and Rousseau – settled the issue in part mythologically by imagining humanity once upon a time living in a state of nature until its dangers and inconveniences compelled them to agree together to – using words from the *United States Constitution* – provide for the common defense and promote the general welfare.

Although some views of Locke are at odds with Hobbes and Rousseau, the social contract ideas they all promoted have helped shape the direction of modern political philosophy. As the memory and influence of Christianity recedes, other cultural institutions and a new secular clerisy have laid hold of Christianity's priestly and prophetic functions. Successive generations of promethean rebels – Robespierre, Marx, Nietzsche, Lenin and more – have stirred up intensifying cultural crosscurrents which often began as heresies within the church but then convey caricatures of the faith into the larger culture and eventually consolidate into transgressive political religions which demand devotion. Today, as Mark Mitchell notes, they are animated by a Nietzschean will to power driven by a secularised Puritan moralism.[48]

The *philosophes*, Jacobins, social sciences, and the Progressive

---

⁴⁷ Dennis J Mahoney, *Politics and Progress: The Emergence of American Political Science* (Lexington, 2004) 19-32.

⁴⁸ Mark T Mitchell, *Power and Purity: The Unholy Marriage That Spawned America's Social Justice Warriors* (Regnery Gateway, 2020).

education movement are among the conduits of this subversive impulse. As the sociologist Philip Rieff observed of Rousseau, Fichte, Pestalozzi, Froebel, and perhaps Dewey: 'All the great educational reformers have died disappointed men.' Citing Emile Durkheim, Rieff characterises education as 'the main institution communicating the modes of authority from one generation to another.' As a vehicle for social change, however, it is less an agent of change than a social disrupter and sower of unrealistic expectations.

> Rousseau set up Émile, a seductive little straw child, who would become a philosopher while all the while he was having fun becoming an artisan. But no education in arts and crafts has ever produced a philosopher. And Rousseau, when he was honest, knew better; his pedagogy was a revenge on philosophy. Nothing pleased him more than to fancy education as a revolutionary instrument, destroying the intellectual and social order by which he had decided to be exquisitely hurt. …

> The great reforming theories of education have been misled by their conception of it as an instrument with which to alter the structure of authority in society. Rousseau and his sort of enthusiasm for education are revolutionary *manqués*, children are their proletariat and the schoolroom is the good society in microcosm. Durkheim had the sense to see that microcosms are never the model of macrocosms; on the contrary, in social life, it is the macrocosm that serves as a model for the microcosm. The school cannot dictate to society; rather, society always dictates to the school. It is a pathetic, and historic, error to treat the school as GHQ for any movement toward the new society.[49]

Here we may consider where Rousseau's general will takes us. In today's Western world, the result may outwardly resemble

---

[49] Philip Rieff, *The Feeling Intellect: Selected Writings*, ed Jonathan B Imber (University of Chicago Press, 1889) 233-34.

what Theodore Lowi called interest-group liberalism but it verges into coercion. The revolutionary *manqués* always fall short of their expectations, and suffer disappointment, but by "pushing the envelope" continuously they succeed in getting at least "half a loaf." As the expression goes, the squeaky wheel gets the grease.

This result encourages even stronger and more radical demands. After all, *amour propre* is unlimited unless it can be deliberately restrained. Society is thus tattooed by the concerted efforts of multiple would-be founders, re-formers, rent-seekers, and swindlers of all sorts. In the resulting crisis of legitimacy, society has succumbed to the logic of what Frederic Bastiat described as 'universal plunder.'[50]

V. Scrutinizing the Long Truce

Ever since the Peace of Westphalia formalised the modern system of states at the end of the Thirty Years War (1618-1648), the idea of sovereignty – the supreme, perpetual, indivisible right to rule – has been attributed to individual states or their rulers. This modern innovation was lifted the from theology during the French Wars of Religion by Jean Bodin (c 1585) and later by Bishop Bossuet (c 1681) to bolster the royal authority. During the Middle Ages the power of kings was more decentralised, effectively shared with and limited by the nobility and the Church. This changed with the rise of powerful monarchs, such the Charles V, Francis I, Henry VIII, Philip II, and Elizabeth I during the High Renaissance and Reformation eras.

Hobbes, who lived through both the Thirty Years War and the English Civil War, elevated the will of the king 'to absolute moral sovereignty,' as Stephen Toulmin put it:

A modern state (specifically, a nation-state) requires, in his view, overwhelming force concentrated at the center, under the authority of a sovereign, whom he likens to an irresistible

---

[50] Frédéric Bastiat, *The Law* (Web Book) <bastiat.org>.

monster, or Leviathan. As willful social atoms, all of his subjects will otherwise go their own ways, and pursue their individual goods independently; so they must be made to understand that their personal activities take place under, and are constrained by, the shadow of this overwhelming social force.[51]

Although Hobbes's and, later, Locke's social contract theories laid the groundwork for classical liberalism, these and subsequent theories were in some respects marred by authoritarianism as well as a utilitarian ethical bent.[52] During the preceding century, a large body of literature and practice regarding resistance to tyranny had circulated, especially among Protestant sects in Germany, France, England, and Scotland during and following the Reformation.[53] Hobbes, like many after him, came to regard Christianity as a potentially seditious force – due to its conscientious adherence to divine authority – unless the

---

[51]　Stephen Toulmin, *Cosmopolis: The Hidden Agenda of Modernity* (Free Press, 1990) 194.

[52]　'All Hobbes' basic theological statements are typical of Humanism. The creed necessary for salvation is limited to a central statement that Jesus is the Christ; the further explication of this, namely, that he is the king announced by the Old Testament prophets, ties this firmly in with the structure of his royalist system. ... His understanding of the Bible is connected with this. ...The legalistic relationship to God was not done away with even by the coming of Jesus Christ, since the forgiveness gained through Christ relates only to past sins, whereas from now on ('for the rest of our time') obedience to the law is once again required of all Christians. Also closely bound up with this legalistic understanding is the typological interpretation of the Old Testament rulers as the model for the role of the sovereign in the present commonwealth which unites state and church. ... Hobbes towers above the circle of his intellectual contemporaries as an original thinker, ...in his intrinsic presuppositions and his religious attitudes, which are also the basis of his entire thoughts, he is completely a child of his time. ... A basic feature of his biblical interpretation, which lies at the center above all of his use of the Old Testament, is the hermeneutical method of royal typology, which hitherto has been left completely out of account; this he uses, extending it, with his characteristic consistency, as far as the figure of Abraham'. – Henning Graf Reventlow, *The Authority of the Bible and the Rise of the Modern World* (Fortress, 1985) 221-22.

[53]　See Steven Alan Samson, 'Interposition: Magistrates as Shields Against Tyranny' (2020) 11 *Western Australian Jurist* 301.

interpretation of Scripture be made to 'depend upon the sovereign authority of the commonwealth'.[54] As Hobbes himself put the issue:

> Having showed, that in all commonwealths whatsoever, the necessity of peace and government requireth, that there be existent some power, either in one man, or in one assembly of men, by the name of the power sovereign, which it is not for any member of the same commonwealth to disobey; there occurreth now a difficulty, which, if it be not removed, maketh it unlawful for a man to put himself under command of such absolute sovereignty as is required thereto. And the difficulty is this; we have amongst us the Word of God for the rule of our actions: now if we shall subject ourselves to men also, obliging ourselves to do such actions as shall be by them commanded, when the commands of God and man shall differ, we are to obey God, rather than man; and consequently, the covenant of general obedience to man is unlawful.[55]

Thus it was very natural that Hobbes sought to bridle political and religious liberty by subordinating the Church to the State. Concerning 'the authority of interpreting the Scripture,' Hobbes earlier wrote in *Leviathan* that 'whoever hath a lawful authority over any writing, to make it law, hath the power also to approve, or disapprove the interpretation of the same.'[56] Thus the sovereign must be regarded as the theologian-in-chief.[57]

---

[54] Thomas Hobbes, *Body, Man, and Citizen* (Collier, 1962) pt 2 ch 6, 346.

[55] Ibid 346.

[56] Thomas Hobbes, *Leviathan: or the Matter, Forme and Power of a Commonwealth Ecclesiasticall and Civil*, ed Michael Oakeshott (Basil Blackwell, 1957) pt 3 ch 34, 355 [Part 3, Chapter 34].

[57] Otto von Gierke wrote the following of the nearly century of controversies over sovereignty: 'at the end of this period [ie about 1650], the political theory based upon natural law received from the radical audacity of Hobbes a form which was at once the culmination of its past and the foundation of its future development. Overreaching itself in the very rigour of its logic, his theory threatened the utter extinction of any genuine public law'. – Otto von Gierke, *Natural Law and the Theory of Society, 1500-1800*, tr Ernest Barker (Beacon Press, 1957) 37.

The effect of the Peace of Westphalia, however, was to marginalise the role of religion in the new international order. Having hewn a civilization out of the ruins of fallen empires and the European wilderness over more than a millennium, Christian churches, monasteries, universities, and leaders were now relegated by the peace settlement into an essentially private supporting role rather than be permitted to remain a collective institutional restraint or counterweight to the ambitions of political bodies and rulers. The diplomats sought to marginalise the international role played by the church, effectively making space for an exclusive system of nation-states which encompassed 'more diverse populations – made the more diverse by divisions in the church. … Toleration was a way of setting aside, as strictly private, the difficult metaphysical and theological dimensions of public life'.[58]

The Swedish Chancellor Axel Oxenstierna's observation to his son about the absence of wisdom in government has largely held true ever since.[59] A red line of inhumanity may be traced from the St Bartholomew's Day Massacre of 1571 through the French, Mexican, Russian, and Chinese revolutions to the present day. The events of the 1640s – at time when it was still possible to speak of Christendom – may continue to shape our situation today as much as the French Revolution of the 1790s and the First World War which finally shattered Christendom.

Just after the Second World War, Bertrand de Jouvenel argued that 'it is impossible to condemn totalitarian regimes without also condemning the destructive metaphysic which made their happening a certainty.'"

---

[58] A J Conyers, *The Long Truce: How Toleration Made the World Safe for Power and Profit* (Spence, 2001) 64.

[59] 'You don't know, my son, with what little wisdom people are being governed'. Attributed to Swedish Count Oxenstierna upon the appointment of his son to the negotiations that resulted in the Westphalian system following the Thirty Years War. See Eric von Kuehnelt-Leddihn, *The Intelligent American's Guide to Europe* (Arlington House, 1979) 70.

This metaphysic refused to see in society anything but the state and the individual. It disregarded the role of the spiritual authorities and of all those intermediate social forces which enframe, protect, and control the life of man, thereby obviating and preventing the intervention of Power. It did not foresee that the overthrow of all these barriers and bulwarks would unleash a disorderly rout of egoistical interests and blind passions leading to the fatal and inauspicious coming of tyranny.[60]

De Jouvenel here summarises a political theory Johannes Althusius worked out two decades before the Thirty Years War. Althusius regarded society as a symbiotic relationship between a multitude of authorities and organisations ranging from kingdoms, principalities, and municipalities to families, churches, guilds, universities, and various community groups. Along with such later ideas as subsidiarity and sphere sovereignty, it supports of a decentralisation and limitation of political power.[61]

The theologian A J Conyers observed how the modern idea of toleration arose in the context of the nation-state system.

In Hobbes we find in precise form the motivation for a modern idea of toleration. ... Theology has been set aside in the interest of the political task of ruling. Therefore, all groups, including the church, but not exclusively the church, are coopted into the general political enterprise. Groups no longer appear distinctly, only the multitude of individuals and the ruler himself.[62]

One consequence is the bipolarisation of society, which may very well account for a tendency to bifurcate political issues, along with

---

[60] Bertrand de Jouvenel, *On Power: The Natural History of Its Growth*, tr J F Huntington (Liberty Fund, 1993) 417.

[61] Johannes Althusius, *Politica* , ed and tr Frederick S Carney (Liberty Fund, 1995). Althusius was largely forgotten prior to Otto von Gierke's reintroduction of his work. See Gierke (n 57) 70-77.

[62] Conyers (n 59) 83.

political parties. Political divisions and conflicts may intensify and lead, incrementally, to the persecution and suppression of dissenters. The general consensus is that competing loyalties, Conyers observes,

> are the most formidable barriers to the spreading efficiency of central administration of authority. The passions must be harnessed to the larger agenda and not be distributed in the untidy natural associations that spring up as freely in a society not well organized, not rational, not subservient to the goals of commerce and power.[63]

Yet the result of such thinking has been to move Hobbes's state of nature into the collective operations of the administrative state itself. As an artificial man or corporation, the Leviathan state faces the problem of how to renew whatever force of attraction holds the people together. In the absence of a natural resilience or renewal which the state by itself cannot engender, it must become progressively more authoritarian and liberty will gradually diminish. Casting political dissenters into the role of enemies of the people leads inexorably to the persecution and economic loss. The Treaty of Nantes gave France a nearly a century of prosperity and growing power. Its Revocation led Huguenots to take what remained of their time, talent, and treasure to distant places in Africa, Europe, and the Americas. France eventually fell into social calcification, fiat money inflation, and Revolution.

Conyers recognises that more is required than a toleration which makes 'the world safe for power and profit.'[64]

> The question raised by the long course of modernity is this: How long can society maintain itself on the residue of a culture's fundamental commitments? Or more precisely: How long can it do so and pretend that the issues once fought out at the theological level no longer matter? How long can it

---

[63] Ibid 224.

[64] Ibid.

pretend that the character and virtue of a people, that which makes social life commodious and predictable, can simply be taken for granted?[65]

This is in part a question of risk management – balancing anticipation with resilience – but it is really about attaining "the good life." As Aaron Wildavsky showed, we must balance a cautious anticipation of danger with a policy of holding resources in reserve to meet unforeseen emergencies.[66]

What remains to be answered is: How does a decaying civilization beset by maladies of affluence hope to replicate the character of the people who laid its foundations once upon a time? Perhaps the question answers itself: How can it?

A self-governing people can anticipate exigencies and make the necessary judgments without the dictates of commissars or bureaucrats. Not so a growing population of dependents. The Leviathan state clears away the undergrowth of perceived rivals to its power and authority, thus becoming a hazard to or an enemy of its own citizens. To do otherwise increases the risk to "business as usual." A J Conyers describes the bitter pill we have chosen to swallow:

> The state that we have learned to expect is a fairly faithful representation of what we might have learned from Hobbes. Yet this Leviathan was always preceded by a shadow. It was preceded by a kind of society in which this state has a chance of coming into being, a society of individuals and dispirited, jejune groups, void of the kind of conviction for which men and women sacrifice and even die. It is the Shadow Leviathan, that loss of power that invites the excess of power. It is tolerant

---

[65] Ibid 64-65.

[66] Aaron Wildavsky, 'If Regulation Is Right, Is It Also Safe?', in Tibor R Machan and M Bruce Johnson (eds) *Rights and Regulation: Ethical, Political, and Economic Issues* (Pacific Institute for Public Policy Research, 1983) xv-xvii.

not in the sense that it expects to learn from others but in the sense there is nothing really to learn of any consequence.[67]

Today the definition of toleration narrows even as the list of thought crimes grow. As J Budziszewski put it three decades ago: 'Things are getting worse very quickly now. The list of things we are required to approve is growing ever longer'.[68] Disapproval often carries legal penalties as well as social ostracism. Herbert Marcuse's "repressive tolerance" holds the field – for now – in the urbane West.[69] Toleration comes to resemble Henry Ford's offer to his Model T purchasers: 'Any customer can have a car in any color that he wants, so long as it is black'.

VI. Reading the Fine Print

Place the lives of children in their formative years, despite the convictions of their parents, under the intimate control of experts appointed by the state, force them to attend schools where the higher aspirations of humanity are crushed out, and where the mind is filled with the materialism of the day, and it is difficult to see how the even remnants of liberty can subsist.
– J Gresham Machen (1923)[70]

What is at stake is the very resilience of a civilization which must draw upon the cultural, moral, spiritual *resources* built up over many generations, often sacrificially, through the stewardship of preceding generations. Among Lord Keynes's 'madmen in authority' are voices that demand the destruction of all obstacles to what many imagine

---

[67] Conyers (n 59) 195.

[68] Budziszewski (n 44) 20.

[69] Robert Paul Wolff, Barrington Moore Jr, and Herbert J Marcuse, *A Critique of Pure Tolerance* (Beacon Press, 1969) 81-123. Some investigative journalists, such as Christopher F Rufo and Andy Ngo, report what the mainstream media either refuses to cover, downplays, or spikes.

[70] J Gresham Machen, *Christianity and Liberalism* (Wm B Eerdmans, 1923) 14.

as a great liberation. Klaus Schwab of the World Economic Forum similarly imagines a Great Reset. This impulse may be characterised, as Eugen Rosenstock-Huessy and J L Talmon did, as a form of political messianism. Far from decentralising or redistributing wealth and power, control is most apt to be held in perpetual trust by those who seize the levers of power.

Roger Scruton has described the western conception of the nation-state as a Personal State in which 'there is a political process generating corporate agency, collective responsibility, and moral personality in the state.'

> It is a moral and legal person, which acts on its own behalf and is liable for what it does. … The very same political process that turns subjects into citizens turns the state into a collective expression of its citizens' way of life. When we speak of the United States as negotiating a treaty, as building up its army, as declaring war on terrorism, we are not speaking metaphorically. These things are the genuine actions of a corporate person, in which all U.S. citizens are to some extent implicated, but which are the actions of no individual.[71]

Herein lies much of the difficulty. When a Personal State adopts an official ideology – such as a religious or ideological establishment – it places immense burdens on those who dissent. The United States was originally settled by religious and political dissenters, some of whom nevertheless were willing to impose similar burdens on others. Massachusetts dissolved its establishment of religion in 1833 only to establish public education in its place four years later. Whether it is tax support of churches or of schools, many families are led to forgo services to which they are otherwise entitled because of the bias of the curriculum or the conditions that are attached. Entitlement is a subtle

---

[71] Roger Scruton, *The West and the Rest: Globalization and the Terrorist Threat* (ISI Books, 2002) 134-35.

trap. When a Personal State subsidises an ideological orthodoxy to the disadvantage of other views, countless individuals and families are conscientiously compelled to pay double for the service. Some vote with their feet, further depleting the common treasury. Controls are tightened rather than relaxed – the logic of despotism. Then the Personal State comes to resemble Rousseau's general will, in which dissenters may be "forced to be free" and made complicit in its actions. Tyrants prefer the invisibility of collective responsibility. Their rule must be regarded as inevitable.

Hobbes, whose discussion of the competition of desire anticipates René Girard's concepts of mimetic desire and mimetic rivalry,[72] may be the first true philosopher of individualism and equality. Much like Plato, Machiavelli, and Rousseau, he sought, in the words of Thucydides, to write an exemplary work for all time.[73] Like them, he also had an agenda in mind. Hobbes wanted no competing loyalty to come between the state and each citizen. All would be equal and all would submit to a sovereign of which each is a part. Hobbes probably would have understood the political uses of what Robert Bellah calls 'expressive individualism.'[74] In this respect, Rousseau – who offered an authoritative appeal to "authenticity" and an authoritarian "general will" as a solution to ruling over individualists – may have been his truest disciple.

VII. METAMORPHOSES

A demoniacal character attaches to everything relative which is transformed into an absolute, to everything finite which is transformed into an infinite, to everything profane which is

---

[72] Girard also recognized the totalitarian aspect of a "passion for equality." See René Girard, *Deceit, Desire, and the Novel: Self and Other in Literary Structure*, tr Yvonne Freccero (Johns Hopkins, 1966) 136-38.

[73] See Sheldon S Wolin, *Hobbes and the Epic Tradition of Political Theory* (University of California, 1970).

[74] See Charles Taylor, *A Secular Age* (Belknap Press, 2007) ch 13.

transformed into the sacred, to everything human which is transformed into the divine. – Nikolai Berdyaev (1939)[75]

Political dreams that began in the minds of philosophers – "fire in the minds of men" – have lately been spilling out of the lecture halls into the streets.

In 1974, the sociologist Edward Shils translated and published the German sociologist Helmut Schelsky's summary of a political strategy developed by left-wing radicals in West Germany and the West more generally.[76] It was and still is directed towards the "conquest of the system" by destroying the most significant features of democratic forms of politics. Underlying the strategy is an intention to root out the fundamental political as well as the social ideals and corresponding patterns of life of the major groups within the system.

Its implementation is to be accomplished by discrediting and replacing the values, historical credibility, and institutional foundations of these groups, their ideals, and their patterns of life. A useful comparison may be drawn with what Thomas Farr calls 'China's Second Cultural Revolution.' Xi Jinping's Communist regime, which controls the commanding heights, is introducing a utilitarian, soft-power "social credit" system to fine-turn its control.[77]

This strategy implicitly acknowledges a reality of civil society that is much neglected today. Society has historically been governed not by a single central authority but rather takes shape through the fluid symbiosis of multiple self-governing institutions. This is easily forgotten since, for generations now, these institutions have been increasingly subjected to centralised command structures. The best

---

[75] Nicolai Berdyaev, *Slavery and Freedom*, tr R M French (Charles Scribner's Son, 1944) 249.

[76] See Helmut Schelsky, 'The New Strategy of Revolution: The "Long March" Through the Institutions' (1972) 16 *Modern Age* (Web Article).

[77] Thomas Farr, 'China's Second Cultural Revolution' *First Things* (Web Article, 16 January 2020).

defense against a conquest of the system is to nurture, as noted above, Burke's "little platoons". The subsuming and coordination of all variables within a centralised authority structure – and the consequent shrinking of the intellectual "gene pool" – makes the system far more susceptible to conquest from within. Such phenomena as "regulatory capture" and "rent-seeking" should serve as a warning to the wise. Yet it is this pluralistic variety and versatility of the classical liberal tradition – institutional liberty – which has provoked the greatest censure by despotic ideologues.

The process is to be carried out by a vague "revolutionary state of mind" – a Nietzschean transvaluation of all values – rather than by direct assault. Its purpose is to transfer the decisive means of exercising power out of the hands of the system's most capable trustees or custodians and into the hands of its opponents. Rudi Dutschke's "long march through the institutions," based upon Antonio Gramsci's writings, is designed to foment a cultural revolution in the West whose purpose is to discredit every aspect of its religious, political, and cultural foundations.

The protracted campaign is directed at three separate targets by way of three sets of revolutionary means. The strategy aims, first, at the conquest of universities and teachers colleges – the cultural sector – in order to staff these institutions and run them. Then, with a prospective fifth column at hand, second, the strategy is directed to disrupting the functions of the state or crippling it through demoralisation. The strategy culminates, third, in the intensification of demands placed on the economy, social security, and entitlements without regard to the functional and productive capacities of the institutional system in order to dominate those who run them.

All three have been so pervasive since the 1970s, a time when the phrase "legitimation crisis" was common among neo-Marxists, that something akin to fatalism or a malaise began to subdue public expectations. Consequently, an attitude of dependency shrank people's entrepreneurial horizons. In this regard, the strategy of the German left bears a strong resemblance to several other movements that have tipped the scales in favor of more authoritarian approaches. But they are nothing new. Consider the words of Alexis de Tocqueville when he addressed the Constituent Assembly in 1848, shortly after the overthrow of the July Monarchy of Louis Philippe:

> Democracy and socialism are not interdependent concepts. They are not only different, but opposing philosophies. Is it consistent with democracy to institute the most meddlesome, all-encompassing and restrictive government, provided that it be publicly chosen and that it act in the name of the people? Would the result not be tyranny, under the guise of legitimate government and, by appropriating this legitimacy, assuring to itself the power and omnipotence which it would otherwise assuredly lack? Democracy extends the sphere of personal independence; socialism confines it. Democracy values each man at his highest; socialism makes of each man an agent, an instrument, a number. Democracy and socialism have but one thing in common—equality. But note well the difference. Democracy aims at equality in liberty. Socialism desires equality in constraint and in servitude.[78]

Tocqueville's discussion of Babeuf's communist strategy during the French Revolution is worth pondering. James Billington described Babeuf's *Plebeian Manifesto* as 'the first in the new genre of social revolutionary manifestos which would culminate in Marx's *Communist Manifesto* in 1848.'[79] It culminated with a call for 'total upheaval:' 'May everything return to chaos, and out of chaos may there emerge a new and regenerated world.'[80]

---

[78] Alexis de Tocqueville, 'Toqcqueville's Critique of Socialism (1848)' *Online Liberty Library* (Web Article).

[79] James H Billington, *Fire in the Minds of Men: Origins of the Revolutionary Faith* (Basic Books, 1980) 74.

[80] Ibid 75.

By the time he wrote, Schelsky contended that this 'strategy of revolution' was successful in West German universities, effectively establishing a new academic order, a Machiavellian template for institutional despotism. In his introductory note to an earlier printing in *Minerva*, the translator Edward Shils observed that the campaign was also directed toward gaining power in the mass media, trade unions, churches, and other institutions. As Schelsky noted in the penultimate paragraph:

> The strategy of 'conquest of the system' is already largely successful as an effort by a group of intellectuals of one generation to take over the positions of power in our society; it is bound up with the aim of establishing a system of social supremacy over the workers under a new working class. I regard the ideological components of this strategy, however brilliantly they are expounded by the supporters and analyzed by the opponents of this development, as only a façade which hides a purposeful and realistic Machiavellian political strategy of the pursuit of power. Because its fundamental principle consists in turning the basic values of the system into a weapon against the system, the inherent defense mechanisms of the system cannot work effectively. Neither can an idealistic value-orientation nor the institutional defenses (*e.g.*, the constitutional courts) be effective since these strategists act "legally" – even though their legality is like that of Hitler before his seizure of power.[81]

Nearly a century has passed since Julien Benda recognised the subordination and politicization of the West's cultural institutions by

---

[81] Schelsky (n 77) 355. Parallels with the rise of the Soviet new class or *Nomenklatura* are evident, See Milovan Djilas, *The New Class: An Analysis of the Communist System* (Frederick A Praeger, 1957) 92. In the Communist system legal theories change according to circumstances and the needs of the oligarchy. See also Michael Voslensky, *Nomenklatura: The Soviet Ruling Class* (Doubleday, 1984).

those who pursue power – favouring either a class interest or a national passion – including 'men of learning, artists and philosophers.' In an earlier age those who wore robes of authority – judges, professors, and clergy – spoke a universal language among themselves and were entrusted with the defense of 'a great universal empire on spiritual foundations.'[82] The new clerisy of intellectuals, administrators, and policy wonks has turned instead to secular power religions. As Roger Scruton expressed it: 'It is not the truth of Marxism that explains the willingness of intellectuals to believe it, but the power that it confers on intellectuals, in their attempts to control the world.'[83] Mao Zedong was more blunt: 'power grows out of the barrel of a gun.' Morality is thus reduced to what serves the revolution.

In conclusion, Schelsky cited the political leader of the Social Democrats of Schleswig-Holstein, Simone Weil (not the philosopher), to the effect that, 'since the freedom of the individual and social justice are the bases of our society, all that has to be done is to idolize them in order to discredit them and the human reality in which they are embodied,' thus clearing space for a new hierocracy – 'the rule of a new priesthood'[84] – similar to Milovan Djilas's *The New Class*.

Similarly, Alan Ryan contends that the Thirty Tyrants of Athens ordered Socrates to arrest an opponent of the regime in order to entrap him:

> [Socrates] was ordered to help seize an innocent man whom
> the oligarchy wanted to murder, but he refused. The point of

---

[82] Benda, *Treason*, 181-82. Gary North characterized what Benda lamented as the political strategy of "Capturing the Robes" of authority: the clergy, the professoriate, and the judiciary. See <https://www.garynorth.com/freebooks/docs/2aca_43e.htm>. Perhaps the treason began much earlier when those spiritual foundations were cast aside. Thomas Sowell detected evident of this in the Enlightenment: 'Class self-interest was, however, seen as the public interest. According to D'Alembert, 'the greatest happiness of a nation is realized when those who govern agree with those of instruct it.' Thomas Sowell, *Knowledge and Decisions* (Basic, 1980) 381.

[83] Roger Scruton, *A Political Philosophy* (Continuum, 2006) 149.

[84] Schelsky (n 77) 356.

sending him on an illegal mission was to implicate him in the oligarchy's misdeeds; his refusal was opposition they could hardly have tolerated. He seems to have been saved by the fall of the oligarchy, only to be executed by the regime that saved him.[85]

The subversive campaigns studied by Schelsky lead to a natural conclusion. The perversion (via entrapment) of our consciences makes accomplices of us and, at the very least, buys our silence if not our consent.

We live among people "who don't know their right hand from their left." Indeed, we live among people who profess to believe you may change your gender but not your race and are untroubled by the contradiction. We have been heedless to the ways subversives have captured authoritative institutions in order to systematically manipulate the public into weakening its moral compass. How do they do so? Through a continuing series of insults to people's ethical sense for which they also are forced to pay.

The principle of the guilty conscience is the intellectual foundation for the endlessly expanding administrative state. Recipients of new privileges believe that "turnabout is fair play." Its driving force is what Frederic Bastiat called 'legal plunder.' The whole charade of Newspeak, doublethink, and thoughtcrime is reminiscent of an observation by Tacitus, who used the words of a captured Scottish chieftain to indict Rome at the end of chapter 30 of *Agricola*: 'To ravage, to slaughter, to usurp under false titles, they call empire; and where they make a desert, they call it peace.'

VIII. THE LIE

And hence it is, that he who attempts to get another Man into his Absolute Power, does thereby *put himself into a State of*

---

[85] Alan Ryan, *On Politics: A History of Political Thought from Herodotus to the Present* (Liveright, 2012) 35.

War with him; it being to be understood as a Declaration of a Design upon his Life: for I have reason to conclude, that he who would get me into his power without my consent, would use me as he pleased when he had got me there, and destroy me too when he had a fancy to it; for no body can desire to *have me in his Absolute Power*, unless it be to compel me by force to that which is against the Right of my Freedom, i.e. make me a slave.– John Locke (1690)[86]

While meditating on the Nazi revolution, the novelist and motivational speaker Andy Andrews asked himself three questions:

Where do we begin to find common ground in regard to what we want (or don't want) for the future of America? Is it possible to write something that doesn't use the words Republican or Democrat, liberal or conservative, yet conveys a message with which everyone could agree? Can it be written in a concise fashion allowing anyone to read it, clearly understand the message, and be empowered in less than fifteen minutes?[87]

Andrews entitled the resulting book *How Do You Kill 11 Million People? Why the Truth Matters More Than You Think*. It tells what happens when deceit is built into the fabric of everyday life.

The answer to the question is quite simple. René Girard drew on the Bible and great literature to identify what he called mimetic desire in order to account for social contagions.[88] Today we see a dramatic rise in such problems as the spread of false stories, the cover-up of real news, manipulation of fear, self-mutilation, drug-taking, scientific chicanery, elective reconstructive surgeries, flash mobs, intrusive

---

[86] John Locke, *Two Treatises of Government*, bk 2 ch 3,[17].

87 Andy Andrews, *How Do You Kill 11 Million People? Why the Truth Matters More Than You Think* (Thomas Nelson, 2011) iv-v.

88 See René Girard, *I See Satan Fall Like Lightning*, tr James G Williams (Orbis Books, 2001) 7-18.

regulations, divisive school curricula, and plummeting test scores.[89] The way governments handled the Covid-19 pandemic – through the lockdown of businesses deemed non-essential, experimental vaccines rushed into production, scare tactics against alternative medicines, masking mandates, and double standards which permitted large urban demonstrations – led many people to make comparisons with the plot of a 1938 play, *Gaslight*, and the subsequent movies. The term "gaslighting" spread very quickly because people began to recognize the lies and irresponsible exercises of power. Some officials resisted illegal or unconstitutional actions. Most did not.[90]

As Andrews himself noted a decade earlier: 'The most dangerous thing any nation faces is a citizenry capable of trusting a liar to lead them.' Echoing a remark made by Max Weber[91] a century earlier, Andrews concluded:

> In the long run, it is much easier to undo the policies of crooked leadership than to restore common sense and wisdom to a deceived population willing to elect such a leader in the first place. Any country can survive having chosen a fool as their leader. But history has shown time and again that a *nation of fools* is certainly doomed.[92]

---

89 See Christopher F Rufo, *America's Cultural Revolution: How the Radical Left Conquered Everything* (Broadside Books, 2023).

90 ee Steven Samson, 'Interposition: Magistrates as Shields Against Tyranny' (2020) 11 *Western Australian Jurist* 301.

91 Weber wrote: 'Everywhere the house is ready-made for a new servitude. It only waits for the tempo of technical economic 'progress' to slow down and for rent to triumph over profit. … (T)he increasing complexity of the economy, the partial governmentalization of economic activities, the territorial expansion of the population – these processes create ever-new work for the clerks, an ever-new specialization of functions, and expert vocational training and administration. All this means caste. Those American workers who were against the 'Civil Service Reform' knew what they were about. They wished to be governed by parvenus of doubtful morals rather than a certified caste of mandarins. But their protest was in vain.' – H H Gerth and C Wright Mills (eds), *From Max Weber: Essays in Sociology* (Oxford, 1958) 71.

92 Ibid 42.

Not to mention a nation of sheep. Another dangerous thing is to whip up a heightened state of fear or let it slip into the fatalism of despair. As the great constitutional historian Edward S Corwin wrote in 1944: 'It was following this war [the Great War] that so sober and conservative a thinker as former Chief Justice Charles Evans Hughes raised the question whether 'in view of the precedents established … constitutional government as heretofore maintained in this Republic would survive another great war even victoriously waged.'[93] Corwin contrasted the wartime Constitution of Powers with the peacetime Constitution of Rights. Emergency powers, which take the place of royal prerogative, have extended the Constitution of Powers into an administrative state. Both war and incompetence have become endemic.[94] Our problem today is not even an insufficiency of rights. Rights, like powers, are now claims upon the public treasury. Having centralised political power, all proportion is lost as people are made dependent upon government. Further, the centralisation of education – 'the institutionalization of indoctrination'[95] – results in a new ideocracy which appears to bubble up to the surface rather precipitate downward.

Chicanery infects all parts of the civil body politic. As Victory Lasky asserted in a book title, *It Didn't Start with Watergate*. In his inaugural lecture at Columbia in 1859, Lieber noted that there are three gusts of passion which taint public affairs: 1) flattery of the people to such a degree that 'philosophic candor is felt by many as a lack of patriotic sympathy,' 2) handling of public business 'with such impunity' that

---

[93] Edward S Corwin, *The Constitution and World Organization* (Princeton University Press, 1944) 58.

[94] The public education system has led to what Peter Turchin calls "elite overproduction," but also to greater illiteracy and innumeracy. See Peter Turchin, *End Times: Elites, Counter-Elites, and the Path of Political Disintegration* (Penguin Press, 2023) 137-58.

[95] See Paul Dragos Aligica and Simona Preda, *The Institutionalization of Indoctrination: An Exploratory Investigation Based on the Romanian Case Study* (Lexington Books, 2022) xiv.

it results in 'a disrepute of politics,' and 3) the politicisation of every conceivable question so that 'fair and frank discussion becomes emasculated.'[96] Lieber anticipated the country's descent into civil war and consequently moved from South Carolina to New York. Too often our institutional watchdogs fail to sound the alarm, often at great cost in human lives. Or else they "cry wolf," as Aesop put it.

In the name of righting past wrongs, ideas and slogans are marshaled in order to rewrite history to justify the shift of power. The idea of reviving Arcadian glory – a past golden age – which had been stolen is the essence of what Lee Harris calls 'fantasy-ideology.'[97] Accusations of "cultural appropriation" are illustrative of the process. The media are the mediators. As James Hitchcock noted decades ago: 'Probably the greatest power which the mass media possess is the ability, in effect, to define reality. What is presented in the media, and the way it is presented, are for many people the equivalent of what is real'.[98]

The rhetoric of justice and fairness – John Rawls's "justice as fairness" – is often designed to discredit existing authority in a bid for hegemony by self-appointed tribunes of the people.[99] This is the common thread which ties various totalitarian movements together, as Hannah Arendt observed:

> The pronounced activism of the totalitarian movements, their preference for terrorism over all other forms of political activity, attracted the intellectual elite and the mob alike, precisely because this terrorism was so utterly different from that of the earlier revolutionary societies. … What proved so attractive was that terrorism had become a kind of philosophy

---

[96] Francis Lieber, *Miscellaneous Writings, vol 1: Reminiscences, Addresses, and Essays* (J B Lippincott, 1881) 383-84.

[97] Lee Harris, 'Al-Qaeda's Fantasy Ideology', *Hoover Institution* (Web Article, 1 August 2002).

[98] James Hitchcock, *What Is Secular Humanism? Why Humanism Became Secular and How It Is Changing Our World* (Servant Books, 1982) 84.

[99] John Rawls made it "justice as fairness."

through which to express frustration, resentment, and blind hatred, a kind of political expressionism which used bombs to express oneself. ...

The members of the elite did not object at all to paying a price, the destruction of civilization, for the fun of seeing how those who had been excluded unjustly in the past forced their way into [society]. They were not particularly outraged at the monstrous forgeries of historiography of which all totalitarian regimes are guilty. ... They had convinced themselves that traditional historiography was a forgery in any case. ...

Not Stalin's and Hitler's skill in the art of lying but the fact that they were able to organize the masses into a collective unit to back up their lies with impressive magnificence, exerted the fascination. Simple forgeries from the viewpoint of scholarship appeared to receive the sanction of history itself when the whole marching reality of the movements stood behind them and pretended to draw from them the necessary inspiration for action.[100]

So we return full circle to Aleksandr Solzhenitsyn's counsel: 'Live Not by Lies.' History, like salt, may be abrasive, but it is also a preservative. For those with eyes to see and ears to hear it may offer insights for restoring integrity and balance, such as making provision for the rule of law, a separation of powers, decentralisation, and a proper set of checks and balances – all irrespective of the outward form of government.

Resistance to abuses of power and privilege requires some form of recognisable constitutional authority, which may take the form of an ombudsman or superior court which is distinct from the government itself. As Otto von Habsburg observed in an interview: 'Theodore

---

[100] Hannah Arendt, *The Origins of Totalitarianism* (Harcourt Brace Jovanovich, 1973) 331-32, 333.

Roosevelt . . . asked the [Austrian] Emperor what a monarch could still do in modern democratic systems, whereupon the old Emperor told him: "Well, my task is to protect my peoples from their governments".'[101]

Kenneth Minogue described the politics of ancient and medieval states as a scrum of masterful characters – 'an association of *independent* disposers of their own resources' – which could not turn into a despotism: 'Having projects of their own, powerful individuals of this kind had no inclination to become the instruments of someone else's project.'[102] Yet today the web of social media, information, and administrative law – along with an alliance of tech Oligarchs with a Clerisy of journalists, teachers, managers, and technicians[103] – makes surveillance, groupthink, and a utilitarian manipulation of everyday life and thought a palpable reality. Jeremy Bentham's Panopticon readily comes to mind.

We now know that any of the safeguards we can imagine – including those offered by James Madison in *Federalist,* nos 10 and 51 – may be derailed or defeated apart from competent and incorruptible public officers along with an independently educated and vigilant citizenry.[104] The real challenge, as always, is how to realistically protect against tyranny.

---

[101] J K Baltzersen interview with Otto von Habsburg, 'If You Can't Fight on Horse-back, Continue on Foot', *Farmann* (Web Article, 24 May 2007).

[102] Kenneth Minogue, *Politics: A Very Short Introduction* (Oxford, 1995) 112.

[103] Joel Kotkin, *The New Class Conflict* (Telos Press, 2014).

[104] As the Irish politician John Philpott Curran put it: 'It is the common fate of the indolent to see their rights become a prey to the active. The condition upon which God has given liberty to man is eternal vigilance; which condition if he break, servitude is at once the consequence of his crime and the punishment of his guilt'. – John Bartlett, *Bartlett's Familiar Quotations* (Little, Brown, 18th ed, 2012).

11

Constitutional Monarchy or Elective Dictatorship?
Why Australia has become an Elective Dictatorship

AUGUSTO ZIMMERMANN* and
GABRIËL A MOENS AM**

ABSTRACT

Over the last few years Australians have become increasingly cynical about Parliament, parliamentarians, and the manner in which the Westminster System operates. The nation's parliamentary system of executive supremacy lies at the very heart of a system that makes government unaccountable and authorises a vast concentration of powers in the hands of a few. The convergence of executive-legislative powers has a number of deleterious consequences for the realisation of the rule of law, each of which may be regarded as being key flaws in our constitutional framework. This article explains how Australia has effectively become an 'elective dictatorship' and why it is now necessary to constitutionally enshrine better mechanisms of checks and balances via the implementation of a more rigid separation of powers.

---

* PhD, LLM *summa cum laude*, LLB, CIArb, DipEd, President, WALTA Legal Theory Association; former Law Reform Commissioner, Law Reform Commission of Western Australia (2012-2017).

** PhD, JD, LLM, GCEd, MBA, MAppL, FCIArb. Emeritus Professor of Law, The University of Queensland; Adjunct Professor of Law; Curtin University.

The authors would like to thank Dr Joshua Esler for his comments and final revision of the article.

The fact that the Constitution gave Australians a system of government on the British model provided a sufficient indication of an intention to reject altogether the principle of the separation of powers, notwithstanding the close resemblance between the relevant provisions of the Australian Constitution and those of the United States Constitution.

– Sir Harry Gibbs (1987)[1]

I. First Considerations

The responses of the Australian governments (federal and state) to the COVID-19 pandemic had an overwhelming impact on the enjoyment of fundamental human rights. These governments exercised coercive powers on a scale never previously attempted, not even in wartime when we were faced with a crisis more serious than that one. The picture we presently see in Australia is of politicians and bureaucrats acquiring a vast concentration of powers. This is a constitutional crisis of enormous significance.

Limited government requires an appropriate separation of powers. However, the Westminster style of government, which our Founders bequeathed to Australia, provides a very weak separation of powers, especially between the legislative and executive branches of government. The Westminster system may have served us well in the past, but it is now sorely in need of a comprehensive overhaul. Under present conditions, few are the laws the Australian governments cannot create and change at pleasure. The effect is that these governments are accountable to no one, except once in a couple of years at general elections. It is no wonder why so many of fundamental rights can be ignored and violated.

---

[1] Sir Harry Gibbs, 'The Separation of Powers – A Comparison' (1987) 17 *Federal Law Review* 151, 154.

II. The Importance of Separation of Powers

The primary characteristic of separation of powers is its assertion of a division of governmental agencies into three different branches: legislature, executive and judiciary. This doctrine is deemed an essential element to ensure that abuse of power is prevented. A stricter application of the doctrine can be formulated as follows:

> It is essential for the establishment and maintenance of political liberty that the government be divided into three branches or departments, the legislature, the executive, and the judiciary. To each of these three branches there is a corresponding identifiable function of government, legislative, executive, or judicial. Each branch of the government must be confined to the exercise of its own function and not allowed to encroach upon the functions of the other branches. Furthermore, the persons who compose these three agencies of government must be kept separate and distinct, no individual being allowed to be at the same time a member of more than one branch. In this way each of the branches will be a check to the others and no single group of people will be able to control de machinery of the State.[2]

This is basically the view that the branches of government should be composed of separate and distinct groups with no overlapping membership. The strict doctrine of separation of powers indicates that the mere separation of agencies is insufficient to secure good government. These functions must be placed in ***distinct hands*** if freedom is to be assured. When each branch of government is placed in distinct hands, there will be a check on the exercise of power by the State. The attempt by one branch to exercise undue power over another will be restrained by those who exercise power via the other

---

[2] MJC Vile, *Constitutionalism and the Separation of Powers* (Liberty Fund, 2nd ed, 1998) 14.

branches of government.[3] Brian Tamanaha explains the rationale for this division of governmental powers:

> Freedom is enhanced when the powers of the government are divided into separate compartments — typically legislative, executive, and judicial (horizontal division), and sometimes municipal, state or regional, and national (vertical division) … This division of powers promotes liberty by preventing the accumulation of total power in any single institution, setting up a form of competitive interdependence within the government.[4]

The idea of constitutional government is traditionally associated with the doctrine of separation of powers. As noted by Article 16 of the French *Declaration of the Rights of Man and the Citizen*: 'A society in which the guarantee of rights is not assured, nor the separation of powers defined, has no constitution at all'. Based on this premise, Professor CL Ten comments:

> The idea of constitutional government refers to specific constitutional devices and procedures, such as the separation of powers between the legislature, the executive and the judiciary, the independence of the judiciary, due process or fair hearings for those charged with criminal offences, and respect for individual rights, which are partly constitutive of a liberal democratic system of government. The requirements of constitutionalism are derived from a political morality which seeks to promote individual rights and freedoms.[5]

Central to constitutional government is the conviction that

---

[3] Ibid 19.

[4] Brian Z Tamanaha, *On The Rule of Law: History, Politics, Theory* (Cambridge University Press, 2004) 35.

[5] Chin Liew Ten, 'Constitutionalism and the "Rule of Law"', in: Robert E Goodwin and Philip Pettit (eds), *A Companion to Contemporary Political Philosophy* (Blackwell, 1993) 113.

separation of powers may combine governmental efficiency and the greatest possible protection of fundamental rights.[6] The idea rests on the premise that whenever power is concentrated in the hands of a few, the risk of arbitrariness increases. As Sir Ivor Jennings pointed out, 'all power is likely to be abused unless it is adequately checked'.[7] This is a problem of unchecked power and here we are reminded of the words of Lord Acton: 'Power tends to corrupt and absolute power corrupts absolutely'.[8]

This idea of separating the powers of the State has a long history. Aristotle, in his *Politics*, advocates for a government which combines royal, democratic and aristocratic elements. The Roman statesman, Marcus Tullius Cicero[9] conceived a relatively democratic type of 'mixed government' that is closely related to the modern doctrine of separation of powers.[10] In the late seventeenth century, John Locke advocated separation of powers primarily for the sake of protecting liberty. In *Second Treatise on Civil Government* (1690), he explained why the executive and legislative branches of government should be rigidly separated:

> Because it may be too great a temptation to human frailty apt
> to grasp at Power, for the same Persons who have the Power
> of making Laws, to have also in their hands the power to
> execute them, whereby they may exempt themselves from
> Obedience to the Laws they make, and suit the Law, both in

---

[6] Vile (n 2) 261.

[7] Sir Ivor Jennings, *The Law and the Constitution* (5th ed., University of London Press, 1959) 31. Sir William Ivor Jennings was a British academic lawyer and a leading authority on constitutional law.

[8] Patrick O'Brien, 'The Real Politics of the West Australian Constitution and the Executive State', in: Patrick O'Brien and Martyn Webb, *The Executive State: WA Inc & The Constitution* (Constitutional Press, 1991) 2.

[9] Cicero, *Republic*, II, 23

[10] Malcolm P Sharp, 'The Classical American Doctrine of The Separation of Powers' (1935) 2(3) *The University of Chicago Law Review* 385, 387.

its making and execution, to their own private advantage, and thereby come to have a distinct interest from the rest of the Community, contrary to the end of Society and Government: Therefore, in well-ordered Commonwealths, where the good of the whole is so considered, as it ought, the *Legislative Power* is put into the hands of divers Persons [from those] who duly Assembled, have by themselves, or jointly with others, a Power to make Laws, which when they have done, being separated again, they are themselves subject to the Laws, they have made; which is a new and near tie upon them, to take care, that they make them for the publick good. But because the Laws, that are at once, and in a short time made, have a constant and lasting force, and need a *perpetual Execution*, or an attendance thereunto: Therefore, it is necessary there should be a Power always in being, which should see to the Execution of the Laws that are made, and remain in force. *And thus the Legislative* and *Executive Power* come often to be separated.[11] [emphasis ours]

Charles-Louis de Secóndat, Baron de La Brède et de Montesquieu, was inspired by these teachings. In *The Spirit of the Laws* (1748), he proposes a rigid separation of powers as a necessary protection against tyranny. According to him, the executive branch, being more rigidly separated from the legislative one, can check arbitrary impulses of the latter by refusing legislative enactments that violate the rule of law. Montesquieu commented:

When the legislative and executive powers are united in the same person, or in the same body of magistracy, there can be then no liberty, because apprehensions may arise, lest the same monarch or senate should enact tyrannical laws, to execute them in a tyrannical manner.

---

[11] John Locke, *Second Treatise on Civil Government* [1690], ch 10, [143]–[144].

Again, there is no liberty, if the power of judging be not separated from the legislative and executive powers. Were it jointed with the legislative, the life and liberty of the subject would be exposed to arbitrary control; for the judge would be then the legislator. Were it joined to the executive power, the judge might behave with all the violence of an oppressor.

Miserable indeed would be the case, were the same person, or the same body whether of the nobles or of the people, to exercise those three powers, that of enacting laws, that of executing the public resolutions, and that of judging the crimes or differences of individuals.[12]

Montesquieu also explains that 'constant experience shows us that every man invested with power is apt to abuse it, and to carry his authority as far as it will go.'[13] This made him argue that the protection of liberty is better afforded if the executive and legislative branches do not repose in the same person or group of persons. With these branches of government more rigidly separated, if one becomes corrupt the other should be able to check the wayward influence.[14] Relying on an understanding of human corruptibility, Montesquieu contended that it is 'necessary from the disposition of things that power should be check of power.' As noted by Nick Spencer, Montesquieu's separation of powers,

lies in that fundamental Christian conviction of inherent human fallibility. Perfect freedom and perfect order are unrealisable because our very nature makes them unrealisable. Put another way, because humans are sinful, we are apt to abuse our freedom in a way that harms others. Although we

---

[12] Charles Louis de Secóndat, Baron de Montesquieu, *The Spirit of the Laws* [1748] (Prometheus Books, 2002) 151-152

[13] Ibid, Bk XI, Ch V.

[14] David Barton, *Original Intent: The Courts, the Constitution & Religion* (Wallbuilders, 2005) 215.

should use our freedom for the common good, we tend not to, preferring instead, even if unconsciously, to deploy it for our own ends, even when those ends damage others. We need political order to keep us in check.[15]

Sir William Blackstone (1723–1780) was profoundly influenced by Montesquieu's writings. In *Commentaries on the Laws of England* (1765), Blackstone described the British monarchy as a limited government whereby the King, the Lords spiritual and temporal, and the Commons, comprised a mutual check upon each other. He stated: 'Like three distinct powers in mechanics, they jointly impel the machine of government in a direction different from what either acting by itself would have done but at the same time in a direction partaking of each and formed out of all'.[16] In the England of those days, Blackstone continued, 'power is divided into two branches; the one legislative, to wit, the Parliament, consisting of kings, lords, and commons; the other executive, consisting of the king alone'.[17]

Blackstone's view of the British monarchy as a limited government inspired the American Founders to develop their own model of separation of powers. Thomas Jefferson, the main drafter of the American *Declaration of Independence*, considered *Commentaries* 'lucid in arrangement, correct in its manner, classical in style, and rightfully taking its place by the side of Justinian's Institutes'.[18] He also referred to *Commentaries* 'the last perfect digest of both branches of law, common law and chancery'.[19] As stated by Professor Albert Alschuler, *Commentaries* 'instructed the children, grandchildren, and

---

[15] Nick Spencer, *Freedom & Order: History, Politics & the English Bible* (Hodder & Stoughton, 2011) 11.

[16] Sir William Blackstone, *Commentaries on the Laws of England* [1765] (21st ed, London) 146.

[17] Ibid 147.

[18] Paul Leicester Ford (ed), *The Writings of Thomas Jefferson* (Paul Leicister Ford) 335.

[19] Thomas Jefferson, *The Works of Thomas Jefferson: Correspondence and Papers, 1808–1816* (Cosimo Classics, 2009) 23.

great-great grandchildren of his initial American readers on the virtues of the English common law'.[20] One of the most remarkable statements to be found in this book reads as follows:

> In all tyrannical governments the supreme magistracy, or the right both of making and of enforcing the laws, is vested in one and the same man, or one of the same body of men; and wherever these powers are united together there can be no public liberty. The magistrate may enact tyrannical laws, and execute them in a tyrannical manner, since he is possessed, in quality of dispenser of justice, with all the power which he, as legislator, thinks proper to give himself. But where the legislative and executive authority are in distinct hands, the former will take care not to intrust the latter with so large a power as many tend to the subversion of its own independence, and therewith of the liberty of the subject.[21]

III. Problems Inherited from the English Constitution

The classical view of the rule of law that historically guided England has been overturned by novel ideas that take no account the principles upon which the nation was founded. As a consequence, appreciation for the importance of separating the branches of government has diminished. As Russell Kirk correctly pointed out, 'since the closing decades of the nineteenth century the English Constitution has lost many of the features that Montesquieu had praised at the middle of the eighteenth century'.[22]

The seventeenth century was an age where monarchs turned to the

[20] Albert W Alschuler, 'Rediscovering Blackstone' (1996) 145 *University of Pennsylvania Law Review* 1, 2.

[21] Blackstone (n 16) 146–7.

[22] Russell Kirk, *Rights and Duties: Reflections on Our Conservative Revolution* (Spence Publishing Co, 1997) 8.

doctrine of divine right of kings.[23] The idea of 'divine right' received its fatal blow when the English Parliament went to war with Charles I, the second Stuart King of Great Britain, in 1625. From 1629 to 1640, Charles ruled without Parliament but a war eventually broke out, which forced him to summon the Short Parliament, in 1640, followed by the Long Parliament (1640–60). When the King tried to impeach five members of the Commons, members of that House vigorously defended their peers' right to dissent, and the King also ordered their arrest. From this date (1642) the *English Civil War* became inevitable.

The forces of Parliament prevailed and Charles was executed. The execution of a monarch led to the temporary abolition of monarchy, in 1649. England, for its first and only time, became a republic. After Charles's execution, new forms of government were tested and a document entitled the *Instrument of Government* enacted, in 1553. Drafted by Major-General John Lambert, the *Instrument* established a Protectorate under which the Executive would be vested in the 'Lord Protector of the Commonwealth' and assisted by a Council of State comprised of up to 21 members.

The Lord Protector was given a limited power of dissolution of Parliament and the latter had no power to alter the fundamental structure of the *Instrument of Government*. The *Instrument* became the nation's written constitution, from December 1653 to May 1657. Since it required a special majority in Parliament to be amended, the *Instrument* can be regarded as the world's first modern written constitution. However, the *Instrument* clashed with the doctrine of the separation of powers in that it entrusted the Council of State solely to the members of Parliament. The document did not prevent members of the Council from being drawn from among the parliamentarians.[24]

The eleven years of Republican rule came to an end with the restoration of monarchy, in 1660. The new King, Charles II, was the

---

[23] Malcolm N Shaw, *International Law* (Cambridge University Press, 4th ed, 1997) 25.
[24] Vile (n 2) 53.

eldest surviving child of Charles I. His reign saw the re-establishment of Anglicanism. However, when Charles II died, in 1685, his younger brother, *James, a Roman Catholic, inherited the throne*. On 10 June 1688, James' son James Edward was born, thus threatening to create a Catholic dynasty that excluded his Anglican daughter, Mary, and her Protestant husband, William of Orange, from the throne. Hence, the political class staged a *coup* by inviting William and Mary to assume the throne. The last Stuart monarch in the direct line was deposed via the *Glorious Revolution* of 1688, which consolidated the House of Commons as the dominant ruling class. Such 'revolution' was accomplished by means of a new settlement embodied in two legal documents — the *Bill of Rights* of 1689 and the *Act of Settlement* of 1701.

In 1714, the Hanoverian succession to the throne brought about the union between Great Britain and the German electorate of Hanover. Thanks to the *Act of Settlement*, George, the prince of Hanover, became the nearest Protestant eligible to take the Crown. George found it good to be the King of Great Britain but a bore to attend cabinet meetings, which, as a German, he couldn't understand. Sir Robert Walpole then volunteered to act on his behalf, or, in effect, to become his 'Prime Minister'.[25]

Throughout the 18th century, the Cabinet, now exclusively comprised of members of Parliament, became the principal feature of the U.K. system of government. In a country with no written constitution but only a collection of statutes, this meant that any statute could now be easily created and repealed by Parliament, even this were done at the cost of violating fundamental legal rights and freedoms. The King would remain as the Head of State but his executive functions would become either ceremonial or indirectly exercised by the Ministers of the Crown, who also are members of Parliament.

---

[25] *See* Sir Ivor Jennings, *The Queen's Government* (Penguin Books, 1954) 98.

It is in this context that 'Parliamentary sovereignty' acquires paramount importance. Parliamentary sovereignty means that legislation incompatible with fundamental human rights must be enforced by the courts, even if retrospective.[26] Parliamentary sovereignty is defined as follows: 'Parliament is competent to make any law on any matter of its choosing and no court may question the validity of any Act that it passes.'[27]

According to Lord Beatson, 'under the classical model of the UK's constitution there are no legal limits on what Parliament may do by primary legislation, including altering the period between general elections and amending or repealing legislation protecting individual rights'.[28] In other words, 'there are under the constitution of the United Kingdom no rights strictly fundamental, in the sense of entrenched (basic, inalienable), because of the supremacy of Parliament and the absence of a written constitution with entrenched provisions and judicial review of Acts of Parliament'.[29]

Due to Parliamentary sovereignty, therefore, under no circumstance can the judiciary hold an Act of Parliament to be invalid. Sir Edward Coke did, of course, famously commented in the *Dr Bonham's Case*, in 1610, that 'a statute contrary to common right and reason would be void'.[30] However, this comment has never been entirely accepted, and not even at the time it was proclaimed. In fact, this statement was one of the reasons for Coke's dismissal as Chief Justice of the Court of Common Pleas.[31]

The Court of Queen's Bench declared, in 1872: 'There is no judicial

---

[26] Jack Beatson, *The Rule of Law and Separation of Powers* (Hart Publishing, 2021) 26.

[27] United Kingdom, 'Rights Brought Home: The Human Rights Bill' (Cm 3782, 1997) [2.13]. Quoted from Tom Bingham, *The Rule of Law* (Penguin Books, 2010) 165.

[28] Beatson (n 26) 6-7.

[29] O. Hood Phillips and Paul Jackson, *O Hood Phillips' Constitutional and Administrative Law* (Sweet & Maxwell, 7th ed, 1987) 423.

[30] (1610) 8 Co Rep 113 b, 118a; 77 ER 646, 652.

[31] Bingham (n 27) 163.

body in the country by which the validity of an act of parliament could be questioned. An act of the legislature superior in authority to any court of law … and no court could pronounce a judgment as to the validity of an act of parliament'.[32] This implies that there is no fundamental legal right that government cannot abrogate. The same view is confirmed by Sir Thomas Bingham KG, PC, FBA, a judge who was the Master of the Rolls, Lord Chief Justice and Senior Law Lord in England. Lord Bingham commented:

> The courts have no inherent powers to strike down, supersede or disregard the provisions of an unambiguous statute duly enacted by the Queen in Parliament, and indeed, an extremely limited power to enquire whether a statute has been duly enacted. For Parliament may under our constitution enact any legislation it chooses, and no court has any power to annul or modify such enactment, it necessarily follows that Parliament can legislate so as to abrogate or infringe any human right, no matter how fundamental it may be thought to be.[33]

Lord Bingham was one the greatest lawyers of his generation. His statement confirms the absence of legal-institutional mechanisms for holding Parliament to account, the effect being that the government that controls Parliament is accountable to no one, except once in a couple of years at general elections.[34] Presently, the 'subjects' of the Crown live under a legal-institutional framework that makes government entirely 'sovereign'. In his 2006 Hamlyn Lectures, Sir Francis Jacobs QC stated:

> Legally, it is difficult, if not impossible, to identify today a State which 'sovereign' legislature is not subject to legal limitations on the exercise of its powers. Moreover, Parliamentary

---

[32] *Ex parte Canon Seluryn* (1872) 36 JP 54 (Cockburn CJ and Blackburn J).

[33] Bingham (n 27) 162.

[34] Jonathan Sumption, *Law in a Time of Crisis* (Profile Books, 2021) 220.

sovereignty is incompatible with another concept which also has a lengthy history, but which today is widely regarded as a paramount value: the rule of law.[35]

Due to the enormous power accumulated by the Commons, the present constitutional framework facilitates arbitrariness, or as Lord Hailsham put it, 'elective dictatorship'.[36] And even if Hailsham's warning appeared to be an overstatement in the 1990s, now many commentators undoubtedly agree with him. During the alleged pandemic, writes Jonathan Sumption, the celebrated legal historian who served the UK Supreme Court,

> [T]he British state has exercised coercive powers over its citizens on a scale never previously attempted. It has taken effective control, enforced by the police, over the personal lives of the entire population: where they could go, whom they could meet, what they could do even within their own homes. For three months it placed everybody under a form of house arrest, qualified only by their right to do a limited number of things approved by ministers. All of this has been authorised by ministerial decree with minimal parliamentary involvement. It has been the most significant interference with personal freedom in the history of our country.[37]

Sir Jack Beatson served at the English High Court between 2003 and 2013, and then as Lord Justice of Appeal between 2013 and 2018.[38] He is now convinced that separation of powers, indeed, is

---

[35] Francis Jacobs. *The Sovereignty of Law: The European Way* (Cambridge University Press, 2007) 5.

[36] Q Hogg, *A Sparrow's Flight* (HarperCollins, 1990) 318.

[37] Sumption (n 34) 218.

[38] The Rt. Hon Sir Jack Beatson was a High Court Judge between 2003 and 2013 and a Lord Justice of Appeal between 2013 and 2018. He was previously a Law Commissioner and Rouse Ball Professor of English Law at the University of Cambridge, and is now Visiting Professor at Oxford University.

not recognised as a constitutional principle in the United Kingdom, because the functions of the legislative and executive branches are now intimately related. Lord Justice Beatson comments:

> Ministers are also members of Parliament and, save in the rare case of a 'hung' Parliament, a coalition or a minority government, or acute internal divisions within the majority party, the executive controls the House of Commons. And, since the Parliament Act 1911 the House of Lords has no veto over legislation, only a delaying power shortened by the Parliament Act 1949 to one year or, in the case of money bills, one month, the executive generally controls the legislative process. Our institutions and the principle of Parliamentary sovereignty have therefore created what Hailsham described as a 'elective dictatorship'.[39]

The overall effect of the Parliamentary Acts of 1911 and 1949 was to aggravate the problem by further eroding checks and balances. When the Crown, Lords and Commons were independent, checks and balances still existed but the abolition of the Lords' veto on legislation, in 1949, while justified by its unelected nature, left the Commons as the unconstrained power of the State. This erosion of checks and balances strengthens the case for constitutional change, although, perhaps not surprisingly, reforms initiated by the Commons have never occurred.[40]

IV. Separation of Powers According to the U.S. Presidential Model

The model of separation of powers designed by the drafters of the *United States Constitution* is commonly traced to *Montesquieu's The Spirit of the Laws*. The first English translation of this book, in 1750,

---

[39] Beatson (n 26) 6.
[40] Ibid 9.

became quite popular in America. During ratification debates for the US Constitution, those who supported the new Constitution and those who advocated against it equally relied on Montesquieu's teachings. It was from him that the Founders got the idea of rigid separation of powers. At constitutional convention, nobody was quoted more often than Montesquieu.

Thomas Jefferson, the main drafter of the *Declaration of Independence*, in a 4 August 1787 letter to Edward Carrington, stated: 'I think it very material to separate the Executive and Legislative powers, as the Judiciary already are in some degree. This I hope will be done.'[41] In *Notes on Virginia* (1782), Jefferson contended that the British system of government gives a few parliamentarians 'overwhelming executive power'. Thus he advised that 'the Legislative, Executive and Judiciary Departments [should] be separated and distinct so that neither exercise the powers properly belonging to the other; nor shall any person exercise the powers of more than one of them at the same time.'[42] As Jefferson also pointed out,

> Concentrating these powers in the same hands is precisely the definition of despotic government. An elected despotism was not the government we fought for, but one which should not only be founded on free principles, but in which the powers of government should be so divided and balanced among several bodies of magistracy, as that no one could transcend their legal limits, without being effectively checked and restrained by the others.[43]

In a letter written in 1776, John Adams, the second U.S. President (1797–1801) and leader of the *American War of Independence*, advocated that 'the sovereign power of the people' should be divided

---

[41] *Jefferson's Works* (Ford ed, 1892) 424.

[42] Ibid 13.

[43] Ibid 223–4.

into rigidly separated departments. 'People cannot be long free, nor ever happy, whose government is concentrated in one assembly', he said. The reason for keeping a rigid separation of powers, he added, 'is because a single assembly, possessed of all the powers of government, would make arbitrary laws for their own interest, execute all laws arbitrarily for their interest, and adjudge all controversies in their own favour'.[44] John Adams strongly believed that,

> The people are the fountain and original of the power of kings and lords, governors and senates, as well as the house of commons, or assembly of representatives. And if the people are sufficiently enlightened to see all the dangers that surround them, they will always be represented by a distinct personage to manage the whole executive power; a distinct senate, to be guardians of property against levellers for the purposes of plunder, to be a repository of the national tradition of public maxims, customs, and manners, and to be controllers, in turn, both of kings and their ministers on one side, and the representatives of the people on the other, when either discover a disposition to do wrong; and a distinct house of representatives, to be the guardians of the public purse, and to protect the people, in their turn, against both kings and nobles.[45]

James Madison, too, believed that the executive branch should have its own 'sphere of independence'. Hailed the 'Father of the Constitution' for his leading role in the draft of the *American Constitution*, Madison often spoke of 'legislative tyranny' and the need of this threat to be avoided through a Head of the Executive who is not a member of the legislative branch, and whose power should include the ability to veto parliamentary bills. According to Madison, to secure a more effective separation each branch of government must

---

[44] *Works of John Adams* (C F Adams, 1851) 185–206.
[45] Ibid 397.

have its own capacity to act independently and resist encroachments by another branch.

Above all, the American Founders were in common agreement about the need of separating the arms of government more rigidly, thus making them truly independent of each other.[46] Edmund Randolph, the famous Virginia lawyer who served as Attorney-General under George Washington's presidential term, defended a rigid separation of powers in the following terms:

> Are we not taught by reason, experience, and governmental history, that tyranny is the nature and certain consequence of uniting these two powers [that is, legislative and executive] in the same body? If anyone denies it, I shall pass by him as an infidel not to be reclaimed. Whenever any of these powers are vested in on single body, they must, at one time or other, terminate in the destruction of liberty.[47]

V. Separation of Powers in Australia?

The Westminster System is a model of parliamentary government whereby the executive ministers are invariably members of Parliament (as required under s 64 of the *Australian Constitution*). This system envisages a Head of Government and a Ministry comprised of members exclusively drawn from the legislative. For a period of time, executive ministers were appointed by the Crown and responsibility was enforced through impeaching by Parliament. These days, however, by convention the King (or his representative) appoints executive ministers on the strict recommendation of the Prime Minister, a leading member of the Lower House. Under 'responsible government', ministers who lose the confidence of Parliament will

---

[46] Suri Ratnapala, 'Separation of Powers: The Cornerstone of Liberty under Law', in: Suri Ratnapala and Gabriël A Moens, *Jurisprudence of Liberty* (LexisNexis, 2nd ed, 2011) 54.

[47] *Elliot's Debates* (1863) 83.

have to resign. And yet, as properly noted by Emeritus Professor Suri Ratnapala,

> The logic of this view is seriously weakened by the fact that in parliamentary systems, the legislature obeys the executive which is in office precisely because it commands the loyalty of a majority in parliament. In unicameral parliamentary systems the will of parliament is mostly the will of the executive. In bicameral parliamentary systems, upper houses may check executive ambitions from time to time but they have little time or capacity to police the vast amounts of discretionary power accumulated by the executive under permissive legislation. Therefore, parliamentary democracies rely heavily on judicial oversight of executive action. Courts and administrative review tribunals remedy individual grievances but cannot address the general problem of the systematic arbitrariness of government.[48]

Australia was originally under 'the Crown of the United Kingdom of Great Britain and Ireland'.[49] Legally, the government is comprised of the Governor-General in Council. In reality, collective decisions are made by the Cabinet and not the constitutionally designed Executive Council, which serves only as a rubber stamp for decisions taken elsewhere. The vast majority of the Governor-General's powers are either ceremonial duties or exercised on the advice of the government of the day, instead of personal discretion. This encompasses the functions of the 'Governor-General in Council' to call an election of the House of Representatives,[50] to create government departments,[51] to appoint public servants[52] and to appoint federal judges.[53] And even where

---

[48] Ratnapala (n 46) 55.

[49] Preamble to the *Commonwealth of Australia Constitution Act 1900* (UK)

[50] *Commonwealth Constitution* s 32.

[51] Ibid s 64.

[52] Ibid s 67.

[53] Ibid s 72.

the *Australian Constitution* does not refer to the 'Governor-General in Council', but rather only to the 'Governor-General', conventions, developed over the last few decades, require the incumbent to exercise his/her power strictly on the advice of the Prime Minister. This is understood to apply wherever the Governor-General exercises a vast range of powers, including:

- to summon, prorogue and dissolve Parliament;[54]
- to recommend money Bills to Parliament;[55]
- to order a double dissolution and convene a joint sitting;[56]
- to assent to legislation;[57] to appoint members of Executive Council[58] – a power exercised on the advice of the Prime Minister;
- to serve as Commander-in-Chief of the armed forces;[59] and
- to submit constitutional amendments to a referendum.[60]

Section 5 of the *Australian Constitution* states that '[t]he Governor General may appoint such times for holding the sessions of the Parliament as he thinks fit, and may also from time to time, by Proclamation or otherwise, prorogue the Parliament, and may in like manner dissolve the House of Representatives.' However, the High Court has decided that such discretion vested in the Governor-General concerning her decision to dissolve Parliament must be exercised at the behest of the Prime Minister, the leader of the majority in the Lower House.[61] Although the Governor-General may ask the Prime Minister

---

[54] Ibid ss 5, 6, 28.

[55] Ibid s 56.

[56] Ibid s 57.

[57] Ibid s 58.

[58] Ibid s 64.

[59] Ibid s 68.

[60] Ibid s 128.

[61] *Western Australia v Commonwealth* (1975) 134 CLR 201 ('*First Territorial Senators Case*') and *Victoria v Commonwealth* (1975) 134 CLR 81 ('*PMA Case*').

to reconsider the advice the latter is tendering, ultimately, effect must be given to such advice.

One of the powers the Governor-General theoretically exercises under s 59 of the *Constitution* is that of disallowing legislation. This power has been made redundant at least since 1926, when the *Dominion Conference* established that the power to disallow legislation must never be used by the Head of State. The power of disallowance is among the inoperative sections of the *Constitution*.[62]

Of course, s 60 still allows the Head of State to reserve a bill passed in Parliament for a decision on assent directly by the King. This would be a possibility only with respect to abolishing appeals to the Privy Council under s 74. Subsequent to the enactment of the *Privy Council (Appeals from the High Court) Act 1975* (Cth), which was assented to by the Queen following reservation, these appeals are only possible through a certificate issued by the High Court, which the Court has made clear it will never issue.[63]

What is more, the Governor-General apparently can dismiss a Prime Minister if he no longer has the confidence of the Lower House, but refuses to resign and persists in the action. The chances of this happening are extremely low because the Governor-General is appointed by the King on the advice of the Prime Minister.

It is also important to consider that 'Parliamentary sovereignty' ensures that legislation always prevails over case law. The power to make law in Australia is limited only by the division of legislative power between the Commonwealth and the States. When acting within the federal-constitutional limits, each Parliament (federal and state) is sovereign within its own sphere of power. To the extent that it can vary or repeal any law or a rule of equity, an Act of Parliament is the superior source of law and it prevails over the common law.

---

[62] Gabriël A Moens and John Trone, *The Constitution of the Commonwealth of Australia Annotated* (LexisNexis, 8th ed, 2012) 252.

[63] *Kirmani v Captain Cook Cruises Pty Ltd (No 2)* (1985) 159 CLR 461.

The imperfect implementation of separation of powers in Australia enables a powerful executive to rule with very minimal parliamentary oversight. Of course, this has the potential to undermine the realisation of the ideal of legality known as the rule of law.[64] The rule of law values legal certainty and predictability. Accordingly, '[t]he public must not be vulnerable to interference by public officials acting on any personal whim, caprice, malice, predilection or purpose other than that for which the power was conferred'.[65] This also means that any legal discretion granted to the executive cannot be expressed in terms of unfettered power.[66] Unfortunately, however, Lord Justice Beatson comments:

> Discretionary power became much more pervasive during the twentieth century as the modern state (to a greater or lesser extent) regulated the economy and provided social services. These involved the delegation to ministers and officials of side powers including the ability to make policy choices limited only by an increasingly skeletal legislative framework.[67]

VI. The Role of the Executive as a Lawmaker in Australia

Under the usual type of delegation of legislative power to the executive, a regulation must be consistent with the empowering Act. A Henry VIII clause, however, authorises legislative amendment by means of executive regulation. The High Court of England and Wales has defined a Henry VIII clause as 'a power granted by Parliament to the Executive to make subordinate legislation which itself counts as if it were primary legislation'.[68] By enacting a Henry VIII clause,

---

[64] See: Augusto Zimmermann and Gabriël Moens, *Foundations of the Australian Legal System: History, Theory and Practice* (LexisNexis, 2024) ch 5.

[65] *R (Gillan) v Metropolitan Police Commissioner* [2006] UKHL 12, [34].

[66] *Malone v UK* (1984) 7 EHRRR 14, [67]-[68].

[67] Beatson (n 26) 25.

[68] *Oakley Inc v Animal Ltd* [2005] RPC 3o, 713) [79]: [2005] EWHC 210 (Ch)

Parliament delegates its own legislative power to the executive.[69] These clauses give executive ministers the power to amend or repeal any Act of Parliament with little or no parliamentary scrutiny. Of course, 'broad framework provisions coupled with power to repeal or amend primary legislation for a wide range of purposes does not foster certainty'[70].

These clauses were named after Henry VIII due to his autocratic reputation as an absolute monarch whose arbitrary will acquired the force of law via proclamations. Henry VIII was 'the impersonation of executive autocracy and his preference was to legislate by proclamations made under the Statute of Proclamations 1539 rather than through Parliament'.[71] Henry VIII clauses are a constant 'temptation to seize authority which properly belongs to Parliament'.[72] They push the boundaries of the principle that only the legislative may amend or repeal primary legislation.[73]

The Australian Parliaments have enacted numerous Henry VIII provisions authorising the amendment of an Act via executive regulation.[74] Unfortunately, the High Court has not questioned the constitutionality of Henry VIII clauses.[75] In the *Dignan case*, in 1931, the Court held that 'the Executive, through a Henry VIII clause, can override Acts of Parliament itself.[76] As a consequence, broader delegations of legislative power to the executive in the form of power

---

[69] *Thoburn v Sunderland City Council* [2003] QB 151, [13]; [2002] EWHC 195.

[70] Beatson (n 26) 25.

[71] Ibid 69.

[72] Ibid 25.

[73] Ibid.

[74] Ibid 133.

[75] Gabriël A Moens and John Trone, 'The Validity of Henry VIII Clauses in Australian Federal Legislation' (2012) 24 *Giornale di Storia Costituzionale* 133, 135.

[76] P.H. Lane, 'Lane's Commentary on the Australian Constitution (LBC Information Services, 2nd ed, 1987) 429.

to make regulations were upheld.[77] More recently, pressures of putting in place legal structures for dealing with a pandemic led to a significant increase in the use of Henry VIII clauses, with very real dangers for the operation of the rule of law.[78]

VII. An Elected Australian Head of State?

When the Australian Framers began to write the *Constitution of the Commonwealth of Australia*, they were faced with decisions regarding the institutions and practices to be adopted.[79] Although they agreed that the Constitution should be under the Crown, this did not necessarily commit themselves to having a Governor-General appointed by the reigning monarch.[80] According to law professor Helen Irving, the original debate over the election or appointment of the Head of State (that is, the Governor-General) did not occur in the context of republicanism but instead of representative government. 'That Australia would hold allegiance to the British monarchy was never in doubt, but that did not mean that the Governor-General could not be elected', she says.[81]

The idea of electing the Governor-General as the King's representative was first raised at the *National Australasian Convention* in Sydney in 1891. There, 45 representatives from 7 colonies (including New Zealand) came together to embed into the Constitution the principles

---

[77] *Victorian Stevedoring & General Contracting Co Ltd v Dignan* (1931) 46 CLR 73, 83-86; *Attorney-General (Cth) v R: Ex parte Boilermakers' Society of Australia* (1957) 95 CLR 529, 545; *Radio Corporation Pty Ltd v Commonwealth* (1938) 59 CLR 170, 179, 186, 193; *Plaintiff S157/2022 v Commonwealth* (2003) 211 CLR 476, [102].

[78] Ibid. 25.

[79] Helen Irving, '"They Will Choose Well, They Will Choose Wisely": The Idea of Direct Election of the Governor-General in Australia in the 1890s' in Andrew Murray (ed), *Trusting the People: An Elected President for An Australian Republic* (Optima Press, 2001) 35.

[80] Ibid 36.

[81] Andrew Murray, 'Introduction' in Andrew Murray (ed), *Trusting the People: An Elected President for An Australian Republic* (Optima Press, 2001) 11.

of federation they had agreed upon at the Federation Conference, in Melbourne, one year earlier.[82] One of the representatives at that *Convention* was Sir George Grey of New Zealand. At the age of 79, he was the oldest delegate attending the Convention. Previously, he had been appointed as the Governor of South Australia, and then the Governor of New Zealand, in 1845. Then he entered the House of Representatives in New Zealand, becoming that nation's Prime Minister in 1877.

Lord Grey proposed that the section about the selection of the Governor-General should read as follows: 'There shall be a governor-general who shall be her Majesty's representative in the Commonwealth.'[83] This proposal left open the means of selecting the Governor-General. Moving this amendment, Grey contended that this would allow for the possibility of the Governor-General being democratically elected. It was essential, in his view, 'that every officer should be elected by the people of Australia. The electors should be free to choose their governor-general'.[84] Above all, Grey regarded as unfair that Australians should support the office of Governor-General without having the opportunity to choose the incumbent.

The first response to this proposal came from James Munro, then Victoria's Premier. Since the Governor-General was 'the representative of the Queen', Munro argued that 'the only way in which we can have Her Majesty's present is through her representative, and if her representative is to be elected by us, and not by herself, he will not be her representative, but ours'.[85] Grey was not convinced and argued that the Queen would not, in fact, appoint the Governor-General. Instead, Cabinet ministers would make the decision by 'advising' the Queen as to who she would appoint for the position. 'To my mind', Gray

---

[82] Irving (n 79).

[83] Ibid 38.

[84] Ibid.

[85] *Official Report of the National Australasian Convention Debates* (Legal Books, 1986) 565. Quoted from Irving (n 79) 40.

argued, 'to subject the people of this new federation to a rule of this kind is to degrade, and not to ennoble; is to lower them in their own estimation'.[86] Grey thus concluded by asking rhetorically:

> I say that you should rather allow the people to give the advice. Why cannot the united people of Australia be capable of choosing a man, and advising the Queen as beneficially as a person who knows nothing about us?[87]

George Grey believed that the choice by the electors of the highest Commonwealth officer should be essentially democratic.[88] Charles Kingston, soon to be the Premier of South Australia, was sympathetic to the idea and believed that all the Governors of the colonies should be elected by the Australian electorate.[89] Sir Samuel Griffith, the Premier of Queensland, who later became the new Federation's first Chief Justice, to a great extent was sympathetic to the idea of an elected Governor-General. Eventually, he concluded that 'the government of England would ascertain and exercise proper care to deliver what was acceptable to the Australian people; and when the people of Australia were of the opinion that an Australian should be elected, this course would be followed'.[90]

The issue re-emerged at the *Second Australasian Federal Convention*, in 1897. At that time Grey was 85 years and no longer able to attend the convention. Edmund Barton, who later served as the nation's first Prime Minister, reminded his colleagues that 'there are some who are in favour of the election of the Governor-General by our people'.[91] 'I am aware', Barton added, 'that it is said that the election

---

[86] Ibid 40.

[87] *National Australasian Convention Debates*, 566. Quoted from Irving (n 81) 41.

[88] Irving (n 79) 40.

[89] Ibid 42.

[90] Ibid.

[91] *Official Report of the National Australasian Convention Debates*, Adelaide 1897 (Legal Books, 1986) 23.

of the Governor-General by the people is quite compatible with the relations which exist between us and the mother country'.[92]

Ultimately, Barton decided to not support the proposal on grounds that 'it would mean the sundering of the strong, and perhaps almost the last bond that exists between us and the mother-country'.[93] Frederick Holder, South Australian delegate, disagreed because he thought that framing the constitution 'under the Crown' did not bind it as to the manner in which the Governor-General should be chosen. 'The mere appointment by the Crown of the Governor-General is not a real bond', Holder said.[94] Although the final decision was to have the Governor-General 'appointed by the Queen', the debate remains of interest in itself. It reveals that the appointment of the Australian Head of State was not treated as a forgone conclusion. As noted by Professor Irving,

> While supporters of direct election might now regret that Grey's original motion was not taken more seriously, they cannot fail to recognise the logic in the argument that, as 'the Queen's representative', the Governor-General could not at the same time be the Australian people's representative. This argument — as some of the dictum in the Conventions, debate indirectly acknowledged — only held so long as the Governor-General *was* the Queen's representative and even more so, so long as this meant, in practice, that the Governor-General was the representative of the Crown or more precisely, of the British government.[95]

Until 1926, the Governor-General had to report directly to the British Colonial Secretary. After that year, following the *Balfour Declaration* and its determination that UK legislation no longer applies in the self-governing British colonies, the Governor-General will not have to

---

[92] Ibid.

[93] Ibid.

[94] Irving (n 79) 48.

[95] Ibid 50.

report directly to the King. At the present, while nothing prevents the Governor-General from reporting informally to the King, she does not truly represent the King. So, who does the Governor-General actually represent? According to Professor Irving,

> If it is the people, or the nation as a whole, the original opposition no longer stands. Indeed, the logic of the opposition to direct election in the 1890s suggests that he should now be chosen by the people. It might be replied that the Governor-General is no longer a representative at all. If so, his historical role as a representative (indeed his job-description as one, in section 2 of the *Constitution*) has been changed. If he is no longer a representative of any description, what then is he? Opponents of direct election today are perfectly entitled to answer that he should be nothing more than a ribbon-cutter or medal-giver. But we know that this is not an accurate description of either his duties or his constitutional powers, let alone his 'reserved powers'.[96]

Australia has all the powers bequeathed to it by the British monarchical tradition. And yet, according to political science professor Campbell Sharman, the Head of State has low political legitimacy and such a low legitimacy 'is in part a result of the lack of popular involvement in the choice of the Governor-General'.[97] Arguably, one possible solution for this is to have the Governor-General elected by the people. Naturally, any change in the way by which the Head of State is chosen requires a constitutional reform. Under s 128, the people have no right to initiate constitutional amendments of their own choosing. As noted by the late Martin Webb, who was emeritus professor of geography at the University of Western Australia, 'this

---

[96] Ibid 51.

[97] Campbell Sharman, 'Over Powered and Under Legitimized: Redesigning the Australian Head of State' in Andrew Murray (ed), *Trusting the People: An Elected President For An Australian Republic* (Optima Press, 2001) 176.

means that any further hope of peaceful change rests entirely with Parliament and the willingness of the government of the day to put forward a proposal which takes into account the already well-known preference of the people for a directly elected head of state'[98]

Therefore, any constitutional reform leading to a better constitutional framework and more democratic outcome is extremely difficult. Nothing will be achieved unless Australians start to press for genuine democratic government. The durability of our system of government has made many Australians unconcerned about the dangers of the concentration of excessive power. Andrew Murray, former Senator for Western Australia (1996 to 2008) once observed that 'the worship of authoritarian leadership ... is strong in Australia' and 'it accounts for those who knowingly vote for measures that increase the power of government and its leaders'.[99] One plausible explanation for such an authoritarian culture, Professor Webb commented,

> is that the continuance of Australia's colonial past, rooted as it was in the foundations laid by its London-appointed autocratic governors helped create an authoritarian constitutional culture in which democracy is merely the means to secure and to exercise in the same autocratic way the powers of long-dead governors. There can be little doubt that having exchanged one governing class for another, the new class is holding on to its powers, patronage and privileges with just as much tenacity as did the old moneyed class.[100]

Curiously, during Anglo-Saxon times, there was an elective element in succession to the English throne, and 'there are still traces of this

---

[98] Martyn Webb, 'When No Means No: The Failure of the Australian November 1999 Republican Referendum and Its Roots in the Constitutional Convention of 1998', in: Andrew Murray (ed.), *Trusting the People: An Elected President For An Australian Republic* (Optima Press, 2001) 154.

[99] Andrew Murray, 'Introduction' in Andrew Murray (ed), *Trusting the People: An Elected President For An Australian Republic* (Optima Press, 2001) 22.

[100] Webb (n 98) 152.

in the coronation ceremony'.[101] As a matter of fact, a similar model of 'royal succession' via popular legitimacy is actually provided by the *United States Constitution*. As stated by Henry Sumner Maine in *Popular Government* (1885), the drafters of the *U.S. Constitution* were heavily inspired by political theories that were a revisited version of the *Old English Constitution*. On the face of this, Maine concluded: 'The resemblance of the President of United States to the king of Great Britain is too obvious for mistake.'[102]

VIII. WHAT ABOUT JUDICIAL INDEPENDENCE?

Judicial independence is one of the essential principles of constitutional government. An independent judiciary may ensure that no one disrespects laws with impunity, not even the government itself. As noted by Sir Gerard Brennan, 'judicial independence does not exist to serve the judiciary; nor to serve the interests of the other branches of government. It exists to serve and protect not the governors, but the governed'.[103] However, judicial independence in itself is not enough to deliver impartial law enforcement. Without strict impartiality, independence can make judges a law unto themselves. According to political theorist Pasquale Pasquino,

The person who judges exercises, in a sense, the most worrying power of all. In daily life it is not the legislator who renders judgment or passes sentence, but the judge … The judge protects the citizen from the caprices and arbitrary will of the legislator, just as the existence of the law protects the accused from the caprices and arbitrary will of the judge.[104]

---

[101] AA Preece, 'The British Influence on the Australian Constitution' in MA Stepheson and Clive Turner (eds), *Republic or Monarchy? Legal and Constitutional Issues* (University of Queensland, Press, 1994) 135.

[102] Sir Henry Sumner Maine, *Popular Government* (John Murray Publisher, 1885) 212.

[103] Sir Gerard Brennan, 'Judicial Independence'. Speech at the Australian Judicial Conference, Canberra/ACT, 2 November 1996.

[104] Pasquale Pasquino, 'One and Three: Separation of Powers and the Independence of the Judiciary in the Italian Constitution' in J Ferejohn, JN Rakove and J Riley (eds), *Constitutional Culture and Democratic Rule* (Cambridge University Press, 2001) 211.

Australian judges are chosen from the ranks of legal practitioners. Under s 72 of the *Australian Constitution*, federal judges are appointed by the Governor-General in Council, although the choice is actually made by the Cabinet. Likewise, state judges are appointed by the Governor in Council on the "advice" of the state Cabinet. Given the notorious incapacity of the judiciary to limit executive discretion, it should not come as a surprise that, in *Kassam v Hazzard; Henry v Hazzard*,[105] Chief Justice Beech-Jones of the NSW Supreme Court summarily dismissed the plaintiffs' challenge that executive (public health) orders had violated the *Australian Constitution*.[106]

In *Victorian Stevedoring and General Contracting Co Pty Ltd and Meakes v Dignan*, the Court held that, within the limits of delegated legislation, the power of the executive to legislate is "unregulated" and its discretion is "unguided". This makes accountability difficult to achieve. Despite having full judicial power to do so, 'the High Court has declined to impose on Parliament any significant constraint on its competence to delegate its legislative power to the executive'.[107] As noted by Sir Harry Gibbs, 'the Court has paid no more than lip service to that principle when it has come to consider the separation between legislative and executive power'.[108] The courts have accorded to Parliament 'a virtually unfettered power to delegate to the executive the power to make laws'.[109] These courts, Gibbs writes, 'have held that such a delegation will be valid even though the Parliament does not prescribe any principles or standards to govern the exercise of the powers'.[110] Insofar as separation of powers is concerned, Gibbs concluded:

---

[105] *Kassam v Hazzard; Henry v Hazzard* [2021] NSWSC 1320.

[106] Ibid [275].

[107] Suri Ratnapala, 'Sri Lanka at the Constitutional Crossroads: Gaullist Presidentialism, Westminster Democracy or Tripartite Separation of Powers' (2003/2004) *LAWASIA Journal* 33, 55.

[108] Gibbs (n 1) 154.

[109] Ibid 155.

[110] Ibid.

> There is no constitutional impediment to the exercise by one branch of government of the powers of another. No statute can be held invalid because it confers powers of one kind on an instrumentality of another kind ... The executive and the legislature are closely connected; one the one hand, ministers retain office only so long as they have the confidence of a majority of the House ..., while on the other hand the cabinet will normally control the workings of the legislature by means of the majority which it commands.[111]

Suri Ratnapala argues that 'the rule against the delegation of wide law-making power to the executive is a major component of the classical doctrine of 'separation of powers'. Of course, 'when officials can both legislate and execute their legislation, they have the potential to place themselves above the law, for the 'law' is what they command'.[112] Ratnapala thus laments the fact that the Australian courts have chosen not to draw any clear line in the sand against excessive delegation of legislative power to the executive, despite parliamentary democracies relying on judicial oversight of executive action.[113] And yet, the Australian courts have accepted that a legislative power of the executive to be 'exercised in disregard of other existing statutes, the provisions of which concerning the same subject matter may be overridden'.[114] This indicates that, in Australia, the executive branch is endowed with a function that is essentially legislative in nature.[115]

---

[111] Ibid, 152.

[112] Ratnapala (n 107) 49.

[113] Ibid.

[114] *The Victorian Stevedoring and General Contracting Company Proprietary Limited v Dignan* (1931) 46 CLR 73.

[115] Gibbs (n 1) 155.

IX. Should Australia Have a National Bill of Rights?

The delegation of uncontrolled legislative power to the executive – and its potential for violating human rights – may lead to arguments in favour of a bill of rights.[116] This concern about the lack of protection to fundamental rights is understandable. As law academics we are appalled to see how the Australian political class endeavours to so often abuse their powers.

However, the tendency of governments to acquire ever increasing power is better curtailed not by a bill of rights but through a well-designed system of checks and balances. According to Sir Harry Gibbs,

> The most effective way to curb political power is to divide it. A Federal Constitution, which brings about a division of power in actual practice, is a more secure protection for basic political freedoms than a bill of rights ... Anyone who has seen the film 'The Killing Fields' will know that the fact that Khmer Republic had adopted a bill of rights did not assist the inhabitants of that unhappy country. We are all familiar with the abuses that have occurred in Uganda: that country had a bill of rights on the European model, and had judges that bravely tried to enforce it, but were unable to resist the forces of lawlessness.[117]

The delicate balance of power between the judiciary and the legislature that is basic to a functioning democracy can be compromised by a bill of rights.[118] Since these vague, deeply aspirational documents,

---

[116] Michelle Elias, 'Craig Kelly is out: From the fringes of the Liberal Party to the UAP captain's pick', *SBS News* (Web Article, 21 May 2022).

[117] Sir Harry Gibbs, 'A Constitutional Bill of Rights', in: K. Baker (ed), *An Australian Bill of Rights: Pro and Contra* (Institute of Public Affairs, 1986) 325-340.

[118] John Gava, 'We Can't Trust Judges Not To Impose Their Own Ideology', *The Australian* (Web Article, 29 December 2008).

no real guidance is provided on what interests rank the highest. There is an obvious potential for the partisan administration of justice. As previously noted by one of the authors of this article,

> The possibility of attributing different meanings to provisions of bills of rights creates the potential for judges to read their own biases and philosophies into such a document, especially if the relevant precedents are themselves mutually inconsistent. Indeed, in most rights issues, the relevant decisions overseas are contradictory. For example, rulings on affirmative action, pornography, hate speech, homosexual sodomy, abortion, and withdrawal of life support treatment vary remarkably. These rulings indicate that the judges, when interpreting a paramount bill of rights, are able to select quite arbitrarily their preferred authorities. Since a bill of rights will often consist of ambiguous provisions, judges can deliberately and cynically attribute meanings to it which are different to the intentions of those who approved the bill, in Australia's case the electorate.[119]

The decision-making rule in the top courts is that 5 votes beat 4. This process reduces the size of the franchise by giving judges the power to decide on moral-political issues by invalidating legislation. Arguably, 'those who favour a bill of rights may delight in the vagueness of these documents, for they sometimes assume that its very ambiguity will enable them to achieve through judicial decision, what they have been unable to achieve though Parliament.'[120] According to law professor Jeffrey Goldsworthy,

> in countries such as Britain, Canada, Australia and New Zealand, a substantial proportion of the tertiary-educated,

---

[119] Gabriël A Moens, 'The Wrongs of a Constitutionally Entrenched Bill of Rights' in MA Stephenson and Clive Turner (eds), *Australia: Republic or Monarchy?: Legal and Constitutional Issues* (The University of Queensland Press, 1994) 236.
[120] Ibid 238.

professional class has lost faith in the ability of their fellow citizens to form opinions about public policy in a sufficiently intelligent, well-informed, dispassionate and carefully reasoned manner. They may be attracted to the judicial enforcement of rights partly because it shifts power to people (judges) who are representative members of their own class, and whose educational attainments, intelligence, habits of thought and professional ethos are thought more likely to produce 'enlightened' decisions.[121]

There is also a real possibility that, despite their superficial attraction, a federal bill of rights would become a factor in further depriving Australian of their democratic rights.[122] By providing a small legal elite such a powerful interpretative tool by which they can force their own moral biases upon the reluctant majority, Professor Goldsworthy comments:

> The traditional function of the judiciary does not sit altogether comfortably with the enforcement of a bill of rights. In effect, it confers on judges a power to veto legislation retrospectively on the basis of judgements of political morality. ... This involves adding to the judicial function, a kind of power traditionally associated with the legislative function, except that the unpredictability inherent in its exercise is exacerbated by its retrospective nature. That is why, on balance, it may diminish rather than enhance the rule of law.[123]

Jeremy Waldron contends that judicial enforcement of a bill of rights is entirely inconsistent with the ability of citizens to influence

---

[121] Jeffrey Goldsworthy, 'Losing Faith in Democracy', *Quadrant Magazine* (Web Article, 25 May 2015).

[122] *Dred Scott v Sandford*, 60 US (19 How) 393, 407 (1957),

[123] Jeffrey Goldsworthy, 'Legislative Sovereignty and the Rule of Law', in T. Campbell, KD Ewing and A Tomkins (eds), *Sceptical Essays on Human Rights* (Oxford University Press, 2001) 75.

decisions via the democratic process.[124] As Professor Waldron explains, the enactment of a bill of rights basically amounts to 'voting democracy out of existence, at least so far as a wide range of issues of political principles is concerned.' [125] This is especially so in the context of controversial social issues where there is no moral-political consensus across the general public. As noted by law professor James Allan,

> What a bill of rights does is to take contentious political issues – ... issues over which there is reasonable disagreement between reasonable people – and it turns them into pseudo-legal issues which have to be treated as though there were eternal, timeless right answers. Even where the top judges break 5-4 or 4-3 on these issues, the judges' majority view is treated as the view that is in accord with fundamental rights. The effect, as can easily be observed from glancing at the United States, Canada and now New Zealand and the United Kingdom, is to diminish the politics (over time) to politicize the judiciary.[126]

X. CONCLUDING REMARKS

Accountability, a central element of representative government, is not achievable when too much power is concentrated in the hands of a few. In Australia, however, 'there is a tendency for both executive and legislative power to be concentrated effectively in a very small group

---

[124] 'If we are going to defend the idea of an entrenched Bill of Rights put effectively beyond revision by anyone other than the judges, we should ... think [that] ... even if you ... orchestrate the support of a large number of like-minded men and women and manage to prevail in the legislature, your measure may be challenged and struck down because your view of what rights we have does not accord with the judges' views'. – Jeremy Waldron, 'A Rights-Based Critique of Constitutional Rights' (1993) 13 *Oxford Journal of Legal Studies* 18, 50-51.

[125] Ibid 46.

[126] James Allan, 'Why Australia Does Not Have, and Does Not Need, a National Bill of Rights' (2012) 24 *Journal of Constitutional History* 35, 40.

of senior ministers, dominated by the prime minister or premier.'[127] This allows, for example, the executive branch of government to create policy outside the legislative branch by means of delegated legislation, which clearly violates separation of powers.[128]

The American Founders regarded the doctrine of separation of powers as one of the most important principles of constitutional government. However, as Sir Harry Gibbs properly reminded us, there is no real separation of powers in Australia. For example, s 64 of the *Australian Constitution* requires executive ministers to be members of Parliament. This provision is in sharp contrast to Art 1, § 6, cl 2 of the *United States Constitution*.

The rise to dominance in Australia of the executive ruler confirms the massive shift of power away from the legislative to the executive branch of government. This process allows executive ministers (who are also MPs) to intervene on every single aspect of our lives without accountability. This concentration of powers is aggravated via delegated legislation which confers to the executive a power to legislate that can set aside any right of the citizen. In Australia, Professor Ratnapala writes,

> The executive has become the master of the legislative agenda, gaining a degree of power over the legislature not enjoyed even by the Tudor monarchs ... In one of the great ironies of political history, the growth of Parliament's legal power to remove a government from office actually reduced its political power to hold a government to account.[129]

Australians would do well with a constitutional reform providing a more rigid separation of powers. This could be done by vesting

---

[127] Nicholas Aroney, 'Bicameralism and Representations of Democracy' in Nicholas Aroney, Scott Presser, and JR Nethercote (eds), *Restraining Elective Dictatorship* (University of Western Australia Press, 2008) 29.

[128] Ibid.

129 Ratnapala (n 107) 79.

an elected Head of State with a real power to veto parliamentary legislation. Crown Ministers, of course, should never be MPs but always appointed by merit, although impeachable on the grounds of serious misconduct. The idea of a bill of rights is undesirable because such abstract documents eventually give unelected judges the power to act as legislators, thus equally undermining separation of powers.

Above all, 'since power corrupts and absolutely power tends to corrupt absolutely' any constitutional reform in Australia should provide for a more rigid separation of powers between the executive and legislative branches of government, and have as its foundation stone the democratic ideal manifested in the Charter of Bakery Hill, proclaimed at Ballarat in 1854: 'The people are the only legitimate source of all political power'.[130]

---

[130] John Molony, 'Eureka and the Prerogative of the People', *Parliament of Australia* (Web Article).

12

Legal Note

Review of *Dobbs v Jackson Women's Health Organization* 597 US (2022)

CHRISTOPHER BROHIER*

I. Introduction

Dobbs v Jackson Women's Health Organization 597 US (2022), the case which overruled *Roe v Wade* 410 US 113 (1973), has been hailed as a great win for the cause of life or a disaster for women. I will attempt in this paper to summarise the judgments and provide my view as to why it was a correct decision. One thing is clear: *Dobbs* has had an immediate and massive effect on the abortion rates. *Dobbs* was handed down on 24 June 2022. These are the statistics for Texas abortions in 2022 to up to August:[1]

January	February	March	April	May	June	July	August
0	0	0	0	0	0	0	0
1	1	0	1	0	0	0	0
11	6	6	9	9	8	2	0
31	25	43	45	48	21	3	0
133	132	187	172	176	155	5	1
705	741	972	937	932	768	16	0
742	742	973	924	833	760	21	0
514	489	662	682	598	538	14	2
280	294	345	316	293	270	5	0

---

[1] 'Induced Terminations of Pregnancy', ITOP Statistics, *Texas Health and Human Services* (online, accessed 27 January 2023).

* LLB (Hons) GDLP, Barrister-at-Law South Australian Bar, Counsel Assisting the Human Rights Law Alliance.

116	84	111	105	104	76	2	0
0	0	0	0	0	0	0	0
2,533	2,514	3,299	3,191	2,993	2,596	68	3

Law can lead culture. The Society of Family Planning, a pro-abortion group reported in October 2022:

> Nationally there has been a decline in abortions since *Dobbs*. The estimated number of abortions provided by a clinician decreased from 85,020 abortions in April 2022, before the decision, to 79,620 abortions in August 2022. This change represents a decrease of 6% in the number of abortions nationally, comparing April and August 2022 (Table 1).
>
> - Since the *Dobbs* decision, there were 5,270 fewer abortions in July and 5,400 fewer in August, for a cumulative total of 10,670 fewer people who had abortions in those months (Table 1).
>
> - The national abortion rate decreased from 14 per 1,000 women of reproductive age in April to 13 per 1,000 in August.[2]

II. The majority decision (Alito J, Thomas, Gorsuch, Kavanagh and Barrett concurring and Roberts CJ also concurring with judgment)

The majority stated the critical question as follows: *Does the Constitution confer a right to obtain an abortion?* The question is whether the *United States Constitution* ('*US Constitution*'), as part of its provisions, created an inalienable right to abortion? The answer was 'No'.[3]

While *Roe* had been upheld in a later decision of *Planned*

---

[2] 'We#Court Report', *Society of Family Planning* (Web Article, 28 October 2022).

[3] *Dobbs v Jackson* 597 US (2022) 5.

Parenthood v Casey 505 US 833 (1992). *Casey* did not consider whether there was any such right in the *US Constitution*, but merely whether according to the principle of *stare decisis* (that is generally speaking a court will stand by something previously decided) the decision should stand. However, as the final court in the United States, as in Australia, the US Supreme Court may overrule one of its prior decisions, if it is wrong. The majority therefore considered whether *Roe* was correct.[4]

Roe had based the abortion right on a combination of the First (freedom of religion, speech etc), Fourth (protection against unreasonable search and seizure), Fifth (right to not self-incriminate), Ninth (enumeration of rights not to deny other rights retained by the people) and Fourteenth (no state to deprive a person of life, liberty or property without due process) Amendments to the *US Constitution*.[5]

Casey reduced the reliance to only the Fourteenth Amendment.[6] Prominent in this consideration was the concept of liberty. The majority held that to understand what the Fourteenth Amendment protects one must draw a distinction between the liberties judges think Americans should enjoy and what may be derived from the *US Constitution*. To find what liberties are protected, the Court held that they had to be 'deeply rooted in history and tradition' and were 'essential to the Nation's scheme of ordered liberty'.[7] So guided, the *US Constitution* via the Fourteenth Amendment did not provide a right to an abortion. No State Constitution recognised that right. At common law abortion was criminal at least after quickening (when a woman first felt her baby move). By the time of the Fourteenth Amendment (19th century) three quarters of states had criminalised abortion at any stage. This was much the same up to the time of *Roe*.[8]

---

[4] Ibid 6.

[5] Ibid 9.

[6] Ibid 10.

[7] Ibid 12.

[8] Ibid 11-25

Abortion was not also part of a broader right such as a right to make 'intimate and personal choices' that are central to 'personal dignity and autonomy'.[9] However, ordered liberty sets limits between competing rights and the historical understanding of liberty does not stop the people's representatives from deciding differently how abortion should be regulated.[10]

While other decisions had supported autonomy-based rights like the right to contraception, same-sex marriage etc, abortion is in a unique position as it destroys what some term a potential life and that which the Mississippi law under challenge in *Dobbs* called an 'unborn human being'.[11] Therefore, the Fourteenth amendment did not provide a basis for an abortion right.

Other factors to be considered in relation to *stare decisis* were:

a. The nature of the Court's error: Whether like *Plessy v Ferguson* 163 US 537 (1896) (upholding a constitutional right to segregation), *Roe* was egregiously wrong. The majority held the decision cut across the democratic process by making it impossible for Americans who disagreed with *Roe* to change the law;[12]

b. The quality of the reasoning: Without reference to the constitutional text, history or precedent, *Roe* created a set of rules for terminations of pregnancies, as it were created by a legislative committee. *Roe* chose viability as the time when a state could legislate against abortion, but this was an arbitrary line which has found little support. *Casey* changed the *Roe* criteria from its trimester scheme to a preclusion of 'undue burden' on the abortion right. It therefore did not support *Roe* and created a new test which

---

[9] Ibid 30-31.

[10] Ibid 30-32.

[11] Ibid.

[12] Ibid 40.

was itself not grounded in the text of the constitution, history or precedent;[13]

c. Workability: The experience of Courts of Appeal shows that the *Casey* test is unable to be applied with precision;[14]

d. Effect on other areas of law: *Roe* and *Casey* have distorted other areas of law such as standing, res judicata principles, etc;[15]

e. Reliance interests: Reliance interests traditionally are where advance planning is needed such as contractual and property rights. The argument that people had organised intimate relations based on the right of abortion, and that the full participation by women in the life of the nation depends on the right to have an abortion, was hard to assess as distinct from assert, and the Court is ill equipped to resolve these issues. The Court should not substitute its own social and economic judgments for that of the legislatures. There are women on both sides of the abortion debate and returning the issue of abortion to the legislatures allows all women to have their say. In Mississippi 51.5 per cent of the population are women and 55.5 per cent of people who cast ballots are women.[16]

f. Therefore, there was no bar to overruling *Roe* on the basis of stare decisis.[17]

Finally, the majority dealt with the minority's argument that overturning *Roe* would be seen as surrendering to political pressure. However, the Court could not consider such arguments. It had to apply the law as it saw it.[18]

Justice Thomas went further than the plurality. He held that the

---

[13] Ibid 45-56.

[14] Ibid 56-62.

[15] Ibid 62-63.

[16] Ibid 63-66.

[17] Ibid.

[18] Ibid 66-69.

Fourteenth Amendment did not protect "substantive due process rights", arguing that substantial due process was an oxymoron. The due process rights protected by the Fourteenth Amendment were procedural rights, not substantive rights. While the Court did not disturb the other substantive due process cases because of the unique nature of abortion, Thomas J considered that the Court in future cases should revisit the other substantive due process cases which found rights to obtain contraception, to engage in private consensual sexual acts and the right to same-sex marriage.[19]

Justice Kavanagh stated that many Americans had widely divergent views about abortion. However, the issue before the Court was not the policy or morality of abortion. Rather it was what 'the Constitution says about abortion'.[20] He reasoned that the *US Constitution* was neither pro-choice or pro-life; the 'Constitution is neutral'[21]

Chief Justice Roberts delivered a concurring judgment in which he held that the majority was right is saying that the Mississippi law which restricted abortion after 15 weeks was not unconstitutional. Hence, *Roe v Wade* was wrong insofar as it used viability as the point from which abortions may be restricted. However, Roberts J declined to overrule *Roe*, saying the Court should follow the fundamental principle of judicial restraint and not decide more than was needed to be decided.[22]

III. THE MINORITY OPINION (BREYER, SOTOMAYOR AND KAGAN JJ)

The minority held that *Roe* and *Casey* affirmed that the *US Constitution* safeguards a woman's right to decide for herself whether to bear a child. The government could not control a woman's body or the

---

[19] Ibid (Thomas J) 3.

[20] Ibid (Kavanagh J) 2.

[21] Ibid.

[22] Ibid (Roberts CJ) 7.

course of her life: 'Respect for a woman as an autonomous being, and granting her full equality meant giving her substantial choice over this most personal and consequential of all life decisions'.[23]

Roe and *Casey* held that, until viability, a State could not impose a substantial burden on a woman's right to elect to have an abortion.[24] This allegedly struck a balance between the right of the woman and the legitimate interest of the State to protect 'the life of the fetus that may become a child'.[25] The decision of the majority would reject the balance by stating that from the moment of conception a woman has no rights and a State can force her to bring her pregnancy to term at whatever cost.[26] This is a core constitutional concept that some issues are beyond majority rule: 'The rights of individuals to make their own choices and chart their own futures'.[27] Accordingly, both *Roe* and *Casey* had grounded this right in the Fourteenth Amendments guarantee of liberty, a 'full throated restatement of a woman's right to choose'.[28] The ratifiers of the Fourteenth Amendment were men and so they would not be properly attuned to the importance of reproductive rights to a woman's liberty or right to participate equally in society.[29]

The majority decision, so they argued, mean that women's rights to participate as free and equal citizens in the nation's economic and social life is curtailed.[30] The decision would mean that other rights such as the right to use contraception, the rights to same sex intimacy and marriage are also under threat.[31] The effect of the Fourteenth Amendment is that the practices of the States at the time of the

---

[23] Ibid (Minority Opinion) 1.

[24] Ibid 2.

[25] Ibid 2, quoting *Casey* at 846.

[26] Ibid 2.

[27] Ibid 7.

[28] Ibid 9.

[29] Ibid 14.

[30] Ibid 4.

[31] Ibid 5-6.

amendment do not mark its limits but it was the basis of striking down bars to interracial marriage and like matters.[32]

Accordingly, it would be 'flat wrong' to separate abortion from other rights: all are interwoven in decisions in relation to bodily autonomy, sexual and family relations.[33] As Scalia J said in relation to the same-sex intimacy decision in *Lawrence v Texas* 539 *US* 558 (2003), the assurances that this did not mean same sex marriage could only be correct if there was not principle and logic in the Court's decisions. He was correct and the same may apply in relation to this decision.[34]

The minority also considered that the majority ignored the principle of *stare decisis*. For no good reason it sets off an upheaval in law and society. The views of individuals rule and the law is not applied 'faithfully and impartially'.[35] The decision is not neutral as it takes away rights women have had for 50 years.[36] *Roe* and *Casey* were workable, as general standards are common in law.[37] Women have relied on *Roe* and *Casey* in organising their intimate relationships.[38]

IV. ANALYSIS OF THE OPINIONS

The opinions reveal the irreconcilable split in judicial reasoning in the US Supreme Court, which is reflective of American society. The majority says *Roe* and *Casey* were an exercise of 'raw judicial power'.[39] The minority say the same thing of the majority's decision.[40]

What is clear is that the majority have made a significant effort to

---

[32] Ibid 19.

[33] Ibid 21.

[34] Ibid 28.

[35] Ibid 5-6.

[36] Ibid 21.

[37] Ibid 33.

[38] Ibid 48.

[39] Ibid (Majority Opinion) 53.

[40] Ibid (Minority Opinion) 53. The location of these conclusions, while coincidental, is symbolic of the divide.

analyse the history of Supreme Court decisions and have demonstrated that *Roe* and *Casey* had little basis to read into the Fourteenth Amendment the right to abortion. The minority do not so do, but rather attack the majority on the basis that for equal participation in the nation's life, women had to have a right to reproductive choice as part of their bodily autonomy. The problem with that argument is that if that were the case the *US Constitution* provides a means to effect it; by another amendment.[41] That leaves the issue of abortion rights to the American people and the fundamental principle of the *US Constitution* is that the power comes from the people.[42]

It is also clear that the Fourteenth Amendment is facially a guarantee of due process not substantive rights. It provides:

Section 1.

All persons born or naturalized in the United States, and subject to the jurisdiction thereof, are citizens of the United States and of the State wherein they reside. No State shall make or enforce any law which shall abridge the privileges or immunities of citizens of the United States; *nor shall any State deprive any person of life, liberty, or property, without due process of law; nor deny to any person within its jurisdiction the equal protection of the laws* [emphasis mine].

It is therefore a stretch to hold that this provision could support a right to abortion. Most importantly, the majority found that the issue of abortion rights must be left to the people in each State or, if there is Federal Power, to the US Congress. Characterising that as meaning women have "no rights to speak of" must be necessarily wrong.

---

[41] *US Constitution* art V.

[42] *US Constitution*, Preamble: '**We the People** of the United States, in Order to form a more perfect Union, establish Justice, insure domestic Tranquillity, provide for the common defence, promote the general Welfare, and secure the Blessings of Liberty to ourselves and our Posterity, do ordain and establish this Constitution for the United States of America'.

Women can (as they have in many states) campaign for the right to abortion to be provided by legislation.

The minority's argument that the decision will affect the ability of women to participate in the life of the nation fails to grapple with the fact that a 'highly disproportionate percentage of aborted foetuses are Black.'[43] According to the Pew Research Organisation the Centre for Disease Control ('CDC') figures show that 'Among those ages 15 to 44, there were 24.4 abortions per 1,000 non-Hispanic Black women; 11.4 abortions per 1,000 Hispanic women; 6.2 abortions per 1,000 non-Hispanic White women; and 12.7 abortions per 1,000 women of other races or ethnicities in that age range, the CDC reported from those same 29 states and the District of Columbia.'[44]

The CDC also communicates that:

> Among the 30 areas that reported race by ethnicity data for 2020, non-Hispanic White women (White) and non-Hispanic Black women (Black) accounted for the highest percentages of all abortions (32.7% and 39.2%, respectively), and Hispanic women and non-Hispanic women in the other race category accounted for lower percentages (21.1% and 7.0%, respectively) … White women had the lowest abortion rate (6.2 abortions per 1,000 women aged 15–44 years) and ratio (118 abortions per 1,000 live births), and Black women had the highest abortion rate (24.4 abortions per 1,000 women aged 15–44 years) and ratio (426 abortions per 1,000 live births).[45]

Those women who have least abortions (white women) are those most represented in U.S. political and national life.[46] Therefore,

---

[43] *Dobbs v Jackson* 597 US (2022) (Majority Opinion) 30, n 41.

[44] Jeff Diamant and Besheer Mohamed, 'What the Date Says About Abortion in the U.S.', *Pew Research Center* (Web Article, 11 January 2023).

[45] 'Abortion Surveillance, United States 2020', *Centers for Disease Control and Prevention*,(Online, 25 November 2022).

[46] 'Numbers Matter: Black Women in American Politics', *CAWP – Center for American Women and Politics* (Web Article, 7 November 2023).

the argument that untrammelled access to abortion is necessary for participation in national life must be questioned. Further, it must be a significant cause for concern that those women who have the least privilege in US life (black women and Hispanic women)[47] have the most abortions. This may accord with the views of one of the pioneers of the pro-choice movement, Marie Stopes, who 'advocated for eugenic birth control, wherein inferior women of the lower classes would be prevented from having children.'[48]

The minority argue that the *Roe* doctrine flowed from that which is fundamental in the *US Constitution* – namely 'the rights of individuals to make their own choices and chart their own futures'. The same concept was also expressed in arguing that abortion was not different from rights such as interracial marriage 'as all are interwoven in the decisions in relation to bodily autonomy, sexual and family relations'. However, as Os Guiness has persuasively shown in his book *The Magna Charta of Humanity*, the *US Constitution* is grounded in ideas from the Hebrew and Christian scriptures which called for an ordered liberty.[49] The concepts of bodily autonomy and the rights of individuals to make their own choices in the sense espoused by the minority are more akin to the ideas of the French Revolution and its successors, the Russian and Chinese Revolutions. Therefore, it could not be claimed that these rights are grounded in the *US Constitution*.

The minority's understanding of bodily autonomy leads to one of the central planks of their argument (though not expressed as such) namely their views of the personhood of the unborn child. At page 2 of their opinion they said 'the life of the fetus [sic] that may become a child'.[50] The concept that the foetus was not a child but may become

---

[47] Irene Browne (ed), *Latinas and African American Women at Work: Race, Gender, and Economic Inequality* (Russell Sage Foundation, 1999).

[48] 'Marie Stopes', Encyclopaedia Britannica (Online: Accessed 30 January 2023).

[49] Os Guiness, *The Magna Charta of Humanity* (IVP, 2021) 4-11.

[50] *Dobbs v Jackson* 597 US (2022) (Majority Opinion) n 22.

one, leads to their view that the bodily autonomy of the woman must have precedence over the foetus' life, as that life was not yet a child's life and so not yet a human life. And yet what science has enabled us to see since *Roe* was handed down, is that from conception and later implantation, the development of the embryo and foetus is the development of something living. What kind life is it if not human life? If that is for the moment conceded, the logic of the majority's view that the *Roe* viability demarcation was not grounded in logic or law, is established.

As to the issue of *stare decisis* little needs to be said. The US Supreme Court, as the final court of appeal, has always had the right to reverse one of its decisions. The US jurisprudence is full of such cases.[51]

V. CONCLUSION

Therefore, it must be said that in terms of legal reasoning and fact, the view of the majority is to be preferred.

---

[51] Ibid (Majority Opinion) 40.